D1570449

The Life and Thought of
Chang Hsüeh-ch'eng
(1738–1801)

David S. Nivison

The Life and Thought of
Chang Hsüeh-ch'eng
(1738-1801)

Stanford University Press, Stanford, California *1966*

Stanford University Press
Stanford, California
© 1966 by the Board of Trustees of the
Leland Stanford Junior University
Printed in the United States of America
L.C. 65-13112

In Memory of
Queen Lois Shepherd Green
1884–1930
Formerly Instructor in Philosophy
at the University of Illinois

Preface

Not many years ago, the study of China was divided between two quite separate camps. There were the historians and observers of China's interaction with the West, and there were the scholars who preferred to study China's ancient past. The effect of this division was a China seen through bifocals, with no unifying intelligence to bring the two fields of view into relation. Two decades of world-wide scholarship have done much to correct this double vision. But, in all things, the present and the past will always make competing claims on our attention, requiring effort if we are to see a single picture.

My interest in Chang Hsüeh-ch'eng began when this was an acute problem in Chinese studies. I wanted to examine something searchingly, something so situated in history that I could neither ignore its present relevance nor hope to understand it other than as an integral part of China's great tradition. My need could best be satisfied, I found, by recording and interpreting the intellectual odyssey of a single man. Biography, if successful, makes the past plausible and relevant by bringing it to life. But it can do more than this. For China, the eighteenth century was both the climax of the last of the imperial dynasties and the beginning of the agony of modern times; it shows us both the last brilliant flowering of Chinese tradition and the shape of that tradition on the "eve of the great encounter." In his thought, Chang Hsüeh-ch'eng drew together and reworked his cultural past, and revealed it as a developing configuration of values and problems. And in so doing he wrestled with the most fundamental problems he could recognize. These problems are important ones by any standard—the nature of history, the value of learning and writing, the importance of individual insight. Sometimes, too, Chang labored over absurdities and was caught up in pettiness. He is both intellectually great and unmistakably human.

My work leading to this book did not begin recently, and I owe thanks to many for advice and instruction. Professor William Hung first introduced me to Chang Hsüeh-ch'eng at Harvard in 1948, and has honored me by inscribing the text on the title page. (The text is from the *Chin T'ang Shu*. See p. 42 of this book.) Professor Francis Cleaves, in 1942, started me in the study of Chang's language. Professors Lien-sheng Yang and James Robert Hightower guided my dissertation on Chang at Harvard in 1953, insisting that I should make it a serious piece of interpretation and not merely a philological exercise. Chang himself would have been especially quick to commend their wisdom in this. I am indebted, also, to the Harvard-Yenching Institute, to the Ford Foundation, to the Fulbright Commission, and to the Committee on East Asian Research at Stanford University, for generous support at important stages of my work.

I am deeply indebted to other friends. Mr. Chao-ying Fang read my completed dissertation, gave me invaluable criticism, and directed me to much important material. To Professor Arthur F. Wright of Yale I owe a large debt for encouragement, guidance, and continued education. The series of conferences of the Committee on Chinese Thought, for which Professor Wright was primarily responsible, have been an especially important testing ground for my interpretations of Chang Hsüeh-ch'eng and his intellectual background. From all of the participants in those conferences I have learned much. Friends who have called my attention to a useful book or article or an important fact include Robert H. Brower, Jerome Cavanaugh, Shau Wing Chan, David Y. Ch'en, Patrick Hanan, Kai-yu Hsü, Conrad Schirokauer, Hellmut Wilhelm, and many others. My friend Curtis Bennett, recently visiting lecturer in Classics at Stanford, generously read and criticized my manuscript. Sara H. Boyd, assistant editor at the Stanford Press, performed the same office over many months. This book owes much to their patience. To my wife Cornelia and to my children I owe a debt of another kind, and one impossible to measure.

I must make a final acknowledgment to Chang Hsüeh-ch'eng himself. My study of him has led me repeatedly to insights I have developed in other publications. I have spent more than a decade exploiting the mind and exposing the private life of a man whose only protection has been the passage of a century and a half since his death. Chang has become a friend as real as any other. I have laughed at him, and sometimes become impatient with him; but I have also admired him and learned from him, more than he could have imagined. I am aware that he was a man, and that my profit at his expense requires at least a repayment in gratitude.

The plan of this account of his life and thought is a simple one. This book is first a biography. As Chang's life unfolds, I present his ideas as they develop. Where the richness of Chang's thought at some period in his life requires it, I have departed from biography and have devoted one or more chapters entirely to philosophical exposition. Chang's interests at any one time tended to gather around one problem; and it has therefore been possible to center these chapters on certain topics. But this has been only partly satisfactory, and in stating Chang's thought I have reached forward and backward in time when logic demanded it, attempting always to make these moves clear. Finally I have occasionally said frankly what I think of Chang's ideas. Some may think this a mistake. They may hold that Chang's problems were his and not mine, and that his conceptions must therefore be outside the range of my criticism, good or ill. I differ with this view. For it seems to me that if it were right I could not have understood Chang at all.

D. S. N.

September 1965

Contents

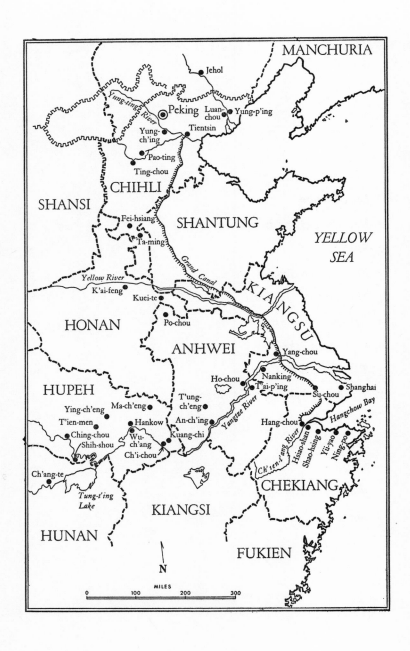

MANCHURIA

Jehol

Yung-p'ing River
Peking
Luan-chou
Yung-p'ing
Tientsin
Yung-ch'ing
Pao-ting
Ting-chou

CHIHLI

SHANSI

SHANTUNG

Fei-hsiang

Ta-ming

YELLOW
SEA

Yellow River
K'ai-feng
Kuei-te
Grand Canal

KIANGSU

HONAN

Po-chou

ANHWEI

Yang-chou

Ho-chou
Nanking
Shanghai

HUPEH

Ma-ch'eng
T'ung-ch'eng
Tai-p'ing
Su-chou

Ying-ch'eng

T'ien-men
Hankow
An-ch'ing
Hang-chou

Ching-chou
Wu-ch'ang
Kuang-chi
Hsiao-shan
Yü-yao

Shih-shou
Ch'i-chou
Shao-hsing
Ning-po

Ch'ang-te

CHEKIANG

Tung-t'ing
Lake

KIANGSI

HUNAN

N

FUKIEN

MILES
0   100   200   300

The Life and Thought of
Chang Hsüeh-ch'eng
(1738–1801)

Introduction

> If you examine systematically a man's writings, and then set
> down the things that occurred during his life, and show
> how he himself was involved in them, you will understand
> why he wrote what he did; in this way . . . you can know a
> man by appraising his world.
>
> —*Postscript to the Chronological
> Biographies of Han Yü and Liu Tsung-yüan,
> in "Drafts of 1790–91."*

Chang Hsüeh-ch'eng, a native of Chekiang, was an essayist, literary critic, bibliographer, and historian who lived and wrote during the second half of the eighteenth century. His essays are the most important part of his writing, although he compiled or assisted in the compiling of a dozen local histories, many of which are lost. He fancied himself a serious writer of classical Chinese prose; and although his countrymen have not thought him a great literary artist, the infrequent western reader will find his style often both moving and powerful. Like many Chinese literary men, Chang was also seriously interested in philosophy. He developed an organic view of history and the state that approaches Hegelian thought, and then built this view upon and into a theory of culture that sometimes suggests Vico. In a few essays he shows a power of concentrated and careful thought seldom equaled in Chinese writing, and in the construction of his ideas he exhibits great originality and imagination.

Chang was not, in his own time, a highly influential person. On the contrary, he persistently criticized the philological scholarship that was in vogue, and exhibited in his own work a fondness for general statement and a speculative temper that was not only uncommon but suspect and unfashionable. Although he had a small circle of important friends—and a few distinguished and carefully chosen enemies—he was relatively unknown until a century after his death. Toward the end of the nineteenth century, however, he began to have a noticeable and as yet unmeasured influence among the more daring political thinkers, who, if they did not accept his views, were at least stimulated to contradict them.

And Chang has excited a growing interest among Chinese and Japanese scholars since Naito Torajiro (1866–1934) first read, in 1902, his two most widely circulated books of essays, the *Wen-shih T'ung-i* (*General Principles of Literature and History*) and the *Chiao-ch'ou T'ung-i* (*General Principles of Bibliography*). Naito called these works to the attention of his friends in Japan and later obtained a manuscript of a larger part of Chang's writings, from which he prepared a brief chronological biography of the author.[1] This appeared in 1920. After this, Chang began to attract increasing attention in his native land. In 1922 a much fuller chronological biography in book form was published by Hu Shih, and in the same year the first nearly complete edition of Chang's surviving writings was also published. Since that time, writers in both China and Japan have published articles on various aspects of his work and thought or have treated him at length in books on Chinese history and scholarship. In Europe and America, however, he is much less well known. The most extensive discussion of him in English (and there is scarcely anything else in a Western language) is an excellent sensitive biographical article by Professor Paul Demiéville of the Collège de France. Those who have read it will not need to be persuaded that Chang Hsüeh-ch'eng is one of the most fascinating thinkers that China has produced.

But scholars dealing with Chang have been, for the most part, professional historians who have been concerned with his theories of historical writing, especially those on local historiography. Chang has come to be known, therefore, as a critic of historical method; relatively little interest has been shown in his ideas on bibliography or literary criticism. And he does not have, even in China, a generally recognized position in the history of philosophy. But Chang does, I am convinced, merit an important place as a Chinese philosopher, and it is time that this is recognized.

Chang has enjoyed this very late flurry of interest because in many ways he is "modern." One continually finds in him—in strange context—ideas that seem more characteristic of our time than his. In keeping perspective, therefore, we must remember that his world was very different from ours. The China of a century and a half ago had not really been touched by the world outside. Chang wrote his most important philosophical essays in 1789, and lived for another twelve years in complete ignorance of the "Great Revolution" in France, perhaps of the very existence of that country. But if Chang was unaware of other peoples' worlds, he had an intimate acquaintance with his own. Its traditions were rich and beautiful, and they filled his life. The Classics, the great historians, Han Yü and the great essayists Chang knew line by line, felt them as contemporary in a way we never can. He knew the history and literature of his world probably far more intimately than we know ours, and was able to look back to its most ancient beginnings and see it as an unbroken cultural, political, and linguistic continuity. We see this sense of continuity constantly in his philosophy of history.

But Chang's world was subject to time and change, and in examining his life and thought, we must know the land forms, storms, and currents that shaped his attitudes and fashioned the problems he faced. This background is political and social as well as intellectual.

The Manchu conquest of China had taken place in 1644, slightly less than a century before Chang's birth. In his lifetime the bitterness it had caused among the defeated Chinese gentry had subsided. But in the middle seventeenth century this bitterness had been intense. Many of the literati had been driven in despair to suicide. Repeated attempts were made to continue a hopeless military resistance. The writings of scholars driven into retirement show their reaction to events: political protest in Huang Tsung-hsi's (1610–95) *Ming-i Tai-fang Lu*; injured national feeling in the historical thought of Wang Fu-chih (1619–92).[a] It is generally

---

[a] The *Ming-i Tai-fang Lu* has been translated as part of a doctoral thesis by Professor Theodore de Bary of Columbia University. Chang Hsüeh-ch'eng would have been fascinated by Wang Fu-chih's ideas. But it is probable that Wang's writings escaped proscription only by remaining unpublished until the nineteenth century.

agreed that the frustration of the Chinese literati, who at this time
were suffering pangs of conscience for having allowed the barbarians to conquer China, had a profound effect on the development of Neo-Confucian thought in the seventeenth century. The
Manchus gradually mollified the literati, but not the more submerged classes, who continued to express their anti-Manchu feeling in the secret societies. Chinese, though always kept subordinate to Manchus, were given more and more important government positions; and the rulers, as patrons of Chinese culture, succeeded in shedding their identity as a barbarian group. By the
eighteenth century it was possible for the government to grant
posthumous honors to leaders of the resistance. Although he came
from an area where the loyalist resistance had been especially
strong, Chang appears to have accepted the reigning dynasty without reserve.

How had the Manchus managed this? For a half-dozen centuries
before the Manchus seized power in the Chinese state, the authority
and majesty of the throne had been gradually increasing, and the
position of the officials gradually weakening. Many elements had
contributed to this development. During the Ming (1368–1644),
the imperial court had grown apart from the official class. To
carry out its commands, it had a staff of eunuchs, a class of beings
traditionally despised by the Confucian bureaucrat. Officials exercising the age-honored prerogative of remonstrance could be sum-
marily executed, consigned to special prisons, or flogged, perhaps
fatally, in court. Sometimes such treatment was earned by a hundred or more at once; for in the Ming, the official class retained
its spirit. As the end of the dynasty neared, factional strife within
the bureaucracy increased, especially between those who accommo-
dated themselves to the power of the eunuchs and those who did
not. Peasant rebellions completed the picture of a Chinese political
order sick with dissension.

And so when the Manchus came, although they came in fact as
conquerors, they were able to assume the role of reformers, within
the Chinese world order, of Chinese ills. They did not submit to

Chinese culture; they championed it. Within that culture they stressed the themes that supported harmonious submission to authority, painting a picture of late-Ming factionalism as totally depraved and urging the good official to make no common cause with others, to tend to his business, and to trust his prince in the decisions of government. At the same time, the fact of conquest remained. In a sense the Manchus succeeded to the role, in relation to the Chinese bureaucracy, of the late Ming eunuchs. They were a separate group, and their strength depended on their separateness and upon the imperial power that supported them. And so the Manchus combined their acceptance of Chinese culture with an insistence on their own separateness on the one hand and with a constant suspicion of Chinese loyalty and subservience on the other. A galling symbol of this subservience, the wearing of the Manchu queue, was imposed on all Chinese; and the military establishment remained a virtual Manchu monopoly until the T'ai-p'ing Rebellion in the mid-nineteenth century.

As time went on the Manchus ceased, inevitably, to be conquerors, ceased even to be warriors. They forgot their own language, and their prince came to be simply the legitimate Chinese sovereign. As this development progressed, the separateness of what was after all a tiny minority became dangerous. It would be fatal for the Manchus, whose power was coming increasingly to be rooted in their position in the political structure, to be isolated and identified as an alien group. In the eighteenth century, Manchu policy responded to this danger in various ways. The majesty, authority, and power of the emperor was built up as never before and guarded, by the Yung-cheng and Ch'ien-lung Emperors, with new jealousy. The court's patronage of Chinese arts and letters, begun in the seventeenth century, continued with greater flourish. A series of grandiose imperial projects of compilation involved the interest and participation of scholars, and thereby encouraged the scholar to think of official position as an opportunity for scholarly achievement rather than one for political action.

At the same time, official ideology urged submissiveness and re-

6 *Introduction*

spect for the throne upon the scholar-official class. Over and over again, the last years of the Ming were cited to show what could happen to the state if factionalism were to spread. The Yung-cheng Emperor's essay "On Factions," was ordered to be read regularly in government schools. This official ideology was first of all intended to reinforce imperial authority, but it had another aspect, as the edicts of the Ch'ien-lung Emperor show clearly. At times, the Emperor feared, there was a tendency for Chinese and Manchus to group around different court officials, or for the Chinese officials, who tended to be those who gained their positions by passing the examinations, to cover up for one another while being too ready to criticize their Manchu colleagues.[b]

The Emperor's anxieties seem in fact a bit overblown. The Manchus were perhaps a separate group; throughout his life, Chang Hsüeh-ch'eng seems to have had none among his acquaintances. But the problem of Manchu-Chinese relations was not on his mind at all, and I suspect this was true of the great majority of the scholar-official class. Nonetheless the ideological and cultural climate encouraged by the court influenced him profoundly. Both in attitude and in philosophical theory he shows great respect for the state (after all, Emperor Kao-tsung, who reigned until almost the end of Chang's life, had ascended the throne before Chang was born). Imperial patronage of letters was an important factor in Chang's life, and he himself said that these imperial projects set the direction of intellectual interest for all of China.[c] The imperial

[b] For an analysis of the Ch'ing condemnation of factionalism and the Yung-cheng Emperor's essay, see D. S. Nivison, "Ho-shen and His Accusers," in D. S. Nivison and A. F. Wright, eds., *Confucianism in Action* (Stanford, 1959), pp. 218–32, especially p. 229, on Kao-tsung's anxieties about Chinese-Manchu rivalry. Another document that reveals this anxiety is found in *Kao-tsung Shih-lu,* 1173.17a–18b, dated 1783. Prince Chao-lien (*Hsiao-t'ing Tsa-lu,* Shanghai, Chin-pu Shu-chü edition, 1.10a–b) wrote that Kao-tsung frequently lectured his officials using his father's essay "On Factions" ("P'eng-tang Lun").

[c] Chang speaks specifically of the special *po-hsüeh hung-tz'u* examinations at the beginning of the dynasty and the long labor on the *History of the Ming* as "drawing learned scholars and eminent men together in great numbers." For two decades or more after the K'ang-hsi Emperor's death there was no activity of this kind at court; everyone's interest turned to the writing of examination essays; other kinds

malediction on factions has a more than curious parallel, as we shall see, in Chang's own philosophy of history and learning.

The Manchu regime undoubtedly had some cause for anxiety. Popular resistance to the Manchus was part of a latent anti-foreign sentiment that has been part of Chinese culture since before the Yüan. The Manchu house was extremely sensitive to seditious remarks about its national origin, and up to the middle of the eighteenth century there had been a series of cases in which the government attempted to extirpate the writings of men who were considered to have offended this way. After 1774, a literary "inquisition" became general. But if the Manchus could not eradicate anti-foreignism, they seem to have diverted it and then to have ridden with it, by allying themselves with Confucian orthodoxy and against any influence—non-Chinese or other—which might challenge that orthodoxy. Thus, inquisition was combined with the grandest of the great imperial projects, the compilation of the Imperial Manuscript Library, *Ssu-k'u Ch'üan-shu* and its catalogs, a thoroughly Confucian summation of Chinese civilization. Chang Hsüeh-ch'eng himself seems to have accepted the inquisition as a proper safeguard against disrespect for legitimate authority. Concurrently, external influence was minimized. European trade was restricted to Canton. Christianity was suppressed. The risings of the secret societies, the Mohammedans, and other non-Chinese ethnic groups constituted a challenge to a Chinese, Confucian state by elements outside and alien to it. And although the state in the eighteenth

---

of writing and scholarship were scorned. "But our present sovereign has assisted letters and promoted inquiry into the past. He has opened, one after another, offices for compiling the supplements to the *T'ung Tien,* the *T'ung Chih,* and the *Wen-hsien T'ung-k'ao* and for assembling the Imperial Manuscript Library (*Ssu-k'u Ch'üan-shu*). Many literary officials were rapidly promoted as compilers, and poor scholars, offering proposals through others, could quite easily get excellent secretarial jobs if they were good at bibliographical research; in this way they might even start careers of their own. Indeed there was a harvest of real talent." But with this development, Chang adds, people have become ashamed to talk of preparing for the examinations, and the fad of philology has gotten out of hand. *I-shu,* 9.36b–37a, "Reply to Shen Tsai-t'ing on Study," 1790. Chang makes similar comments in *I-shu,* 21.15a–b, "Preface to the Literary Collection of Yeh Ho-t'u," 1782. (See Bibliographical Note for explanation of abbreviated citations.)

century engaged in a broad campaign of expansion in Central Asia and the south, the attitude of the Chinese was defensive and more and more introspective. In the seventeenth century, some writers were at least aware of Western civilization. But in the eighteenth, people such as Chang seem to have been completely oblivious to the non-Chinese world.

The most important problems of the time were social and economic. With the growth of urban areas in Neo-Confucian China, the social base of the literate class had gradually expanded. A new popular literature of fiction and drama grew in importance; there was a new demand for the polite literature of occasional poetry, epitaphs, and biography, in which convention dictated not only modes of expression but content as well. Though popular literature was not respectable, it was nonetheless written—normally anonymously—by scholars for money; scholars received money, too, for much of their polite writing. This development was significant: it illustrated the fact that the literati were frequently hard pressed and were becoming far too numerous to be absorbed into the civil service.

For most, the avenue to appointment in the civil service was the Chinese examination system. During the entire last millennium of imperial China, the examinations played a very large part in a literary man's life, molding his education from early youth. But in the Ming and increasingly in the Ch'ing Dynasty, there was intense social and economic pressure placed upon the educated man to pass and qualify, if not for official position then at least for some intellectual means of support—such as teaching the sons of other literati how to write examination essays. One had the opportunity to take the examinations every three years. The provincial examination, the first really important test, was in the autumn. A successful examinee became a *chü-jen,* a "person sent up" to take the metropolitan examination in Peking early the following spring; success in this higher test made one a *chin-shih,* a "scholar admitted" to the Emperor's presence, where a final testing and grading took place. Only a tiny percentage reached the top, and many spent most of their lives either preparing for the examinations or repeatedly taking them. Chang himself succeeded only in middle age. The examinations did not require a detailed knowledge of administration and law, as one might have expected, but skill in writing on classical subjects in precise literary forms, the most important of these being the *pa-ku*—the eight-legged essay. Some young men, unable to be sensible, rebelled inwardly at this grotesque institution, though most—as did Chang—in the end resigned themselves to it.[2] In the eighteenth century, however, even if one passed, one was not assured of a career. Appointment, except for those at the top of the list, was seldom immediate, and one might easily wait a decade, as did Chang's father.

As competition for appointments increased, public morality declined. Bribery became an inevitable part of the routine business of acquiring, exercising, and retaining office. And the difficulty was compounded by a dangerous ambiguity. What is a bribe? Confucian harmony calls for smooth relations among officials and between officials and people. Is the giving and receiving of presents wrong? The Emperor himself set the example, by expecting his officials to send him regular gifts (*kung,* "tribute") as an expression of their gratitude for the handsome additional stipend he granted them to enable them, ironically enough, to resist bribes.[3]

Official corruption became more and more serious in the last half of the century. It may have been that the dominant Manchus, who as officials were in a position to apply great pressure to their Chinese subordinates, were becoming more luxury-loving; in any event in the last quarter of the century a Manchu, Ho-shen (1750–99), dominated both the civil service and the aged Emperor Kaotsung. He created a network of political alliances throughout the empire and used his position to amass wealth rivaling that of the imperial house. During this time there were a number of celebrated prosecutions for large-scale embezzlement brought against officials who were said to be Ho's henchmen; one of the most dramatic of these was the arrest and execution of the governor and lieutenant governor of Shantung in 1782.[4] Ho-shen's execution in

1799 did not repair the damage done. Corruption, together with the great cost of military campaigns at home and abroad, left the state at the end of the century with enormous deficits; the increasingly avaricious behavior of the officials, together with the increase of the population against the limits of subsistence, made recurrent rebellions more frequent and more serious.

This was the situation in which Chang's later years were spent. The confusion resulting from internal rebellion at the end of the century affected him personally, for it was directly or indirectly the reason why his most ambitious writings were left unfinished or unpublished and were subsequently lost. Moreover, the economic plight of the petty scholar describes Chang's own situation. Chang's family belonged to the poorer stratum of the gentry, and lived in one of the areas—Chekiang—where the population increase seems to have been most intense. Chekiang had in recent centuries been one of the richest and most populous provinces, supplying revenue and food for the rest of the country and showing a corresponding fecundity in arts and letters. It had been hard hit by the military turmoil of the conquest in the seventeenth century, and before it could completely regain its former position, it had to cope with the eighteenth-century population explosion.[5] The deterioration of the civil service had important effects upon Chang's life: his father's career, hardly started, ended in a disgrace that reduced the family to virtual poverty; Chang himself never held more than a nominal appointment; and his bitter reaction to Ho-shen's activities is recorded in his own writings.

The poorer members of the official-scholar class, as we have seen, were extremely insecure. As a petty official, the scholar was in constant danger of being unseated by less honest or more successfully unscrupulous competitors; outside the official ranks he might pay for his status as a gentleman by living virtually from hand to mouth. His surest prospects were as secretary in a yamen. This, in fact, seems to have been the way Chang's immediate ancestors lived. A scholar might also be employed as "secretary" or tutor in the household of some well-to-do official, always dependent upon the continued favor and affluence of his benefactor. As a "secretary," he might be asked by his patron to take part in some project of writing and research. The circles of literary men that formed first around one and then around another wealthy benefactor and the cooperative scholarship that resulted from situations of this sort were two distinctive features of learning in the eighteenth century. The scholar-patron was, perhaps, simply aping the greatest patron of all, the imperial court. A third means of livelihood for the poor man of letters was to produce for a consideration or for temporary support some specific piece of writing, such as a biography of a dead relative of his employer, an epitaph, a genealogy, or the editing of a book.[d] A borderline case that might easily become a cooperative project was the compilation of a local history—which would be sponsored by a local official and bear his name. This was a type of work Chang engaged in frequently, and in which he considered himself an expert.

And, of course, the petty scholar could teach. As a teacher, he could do well if he became master of a local academy or *shu-yüan,* but for this, too, he was dependent on patronage. The *shu-yüan* was a distinctively Neo-Confucian institution. During the Sung, the teachers and students of the local academies had been instrumental in formulating the theoretical part of Neo-Confucian thought. In the Sung and Ming the *shu-yüan,* which were then usually private schools, were also a potential source of criticism of established political and philosophical assumptions. The autocratic Ming court regarded these institutions as fostering dangerously independent philosophical ideas. In the mid-sixteenth century many were suppressed. And in the early seventeenth century the defeat of an anti-eunuch faction that had formed around one of these academies led to a political suppression of them on a wider scale.

In dealing with the academies, as in other matters, the Manchus were more efficient than their predecessors. The method used by

---

[d] It is said that the poet Yüan Mei, who was wealthy and very successful as a writer of this kind, was once paid 1000 taels silver for a single funerary inscription (*ECCP,* p. 955).

the Ch'ing was the simple one of patronizing the academies to death. Beginning in 1657, the Ch'ing government established *shu-yüan* in various provinces. In 1731, government subsidies were made available to academy students, and many more *shu-yüan* were established to permit promising men in any locality to study for the examinations. The academies in the Ch'ing were thus virtually incorporated into the state education system and the main business pursued in them was learning to write *pa-ku*. In many of them, routine examinations were administered not by the headmaster but by the local commissioner of education; this practice became regular in 1785. At least as early as the 1730's, it was the regular practice for schoolmasters to be selected by local officials.[6]

An important part of Chang's career was spent as master of one or another of these schools. But although the academies were virtually government institutions, a mastership was not an official post. One obtained it by having some claim on a local official who might be a friend or indebted to a friend; and one could lose it quickly. For these positions and for his other means of livelihood, Chang was wholly dependent on personal connections. His predicament was typical. The economic insecurity of the scholar's existence caused him to place a high value on associations based upon kinship, membership in the same class or examination group, and community of native place (often made obvious by dialect or accent). Men bound together by such natural ties had a claim upon one another's friendship and assistance in trouble. It is not surprising, then, that many of Chang Hsüeh-ch'eng's close friends or benefactors come from the eastern Chekiang area.

In the Sung Neo-Confucianism had been shaped by a meeting of minds between the masters and students of the local academies and certain important statesmen. Since it espoused a political viewpoint that advocated a return to certain ancient ways, it seemed, on the surface, a conservative philosophy; but at the same time it was radical in its wish for a complete departure from contemporary mores. The ancient past, as an ideal, was interpreted with utopian daring. From its beginnings, Neo-Confucianism was characterized by an intense desire for a moral regeneration of men that would end the need for self-assertion and reintegrate and perfect the social order. It stressed the importance to the state of sound moral instruction; its intellectual leaders were therefore much concerned with the proper ends and methods of education, particularly of moral self-education.[7] It was in this area, the question of the nature of moral "knowledge," that significant developments in later Neo-Confucian thought were to occur. The Neo-Confucians were primarily interested in morals and self-knowledge, but the assumptions they made were extended, especially in the Ch'ing, to knowledge of other kinds.

In the late Ming, two main schools of thought existed within Neo-Confucianism. One, the school of the Sung philosopher Chu Hsi (1130–1200), had the support of the state. It divided all reality, including human personality and human action, into two metaphysical parts: *ch'i,* matter or perceived reality, and *li,* intelligible principle or moral law. Although the object of learning was the attainment of an essentially mystical moral enlightenment, the learning process itself involved the study of actual perceptible "things"—including books. Classical learning and careful scholarship consequently had an important place in the intellectual life of this school. The leading rival school of thought owed its popularity to the teaching of Wang Shou-jen (1472–1529), better known as Wang Yang-ming. Wang, like Chang, was a native of the Shao-hsing area of eastern Chekiang. His school, which was not considered orthodox, criticized its opponents for holding the view that moral law or principle is isolatable from the action of one's own mind in given situations, a view subtly tempting the individual to delay moral action while engaging in the study of an objective and external *li*. According to this school *li* and *ch'i,* moral truth and moral existence, were identical. Moral truth could only be grasped intuitively; it could not be stated, for to state is to abstract; to form a concept of it is to separate it from reality. Wang was thus led to a theory of intuition that identified moral *knowledge* with moral *action,* and consequently he did not value highly learning from books. The influence of Ch'an Buddhism can be plainly detected in this point of view.

In the Ch'ing a certain synthesis of these viewpoints took place. Although it became almost improper to mention Wang, except disparagingly (Chang characteristically took pleasure in praising him while insisting that he preferred the orthodox school), the basic assumptions of his thought remained quite influential, but with a new application. The effect of Wang's thought was to throw doubt upon the validity of general statements in metaphysics or moral philosophy; hence any kind of theoretical discussion (*k'ung-yen,* "empty words") came to have a bad odor, to seem dangerously distant from "actual facts." As a result, the school of Chu Hsi remained orthodox, for the answering of questions on the examinations at least, but it became unfashionable to show much interest in its speculative side. Chu had spirited partisans in certain literary circles, notably the T'ung-ch'eng group in the eighteenth century. And a number of moralists, neglecting most of his metaphysical theory, morbidly overdeveloped his discipline of personal self-perfection.[8] Nevertheless, the Sung school's real influence was the value it placed on classical scholarship.

The intellectual temper of the Ch'ing was consequently one of extreme nominalism. Chang, echoing Chuang Tzu, expresses it in a platitude that drops from his writing brush naturally and almost accidentally: "Names are the 'guests' of things; classes arise out of examples."[9] But the assumptions of this nominalist temper were seldom stated and never systematized. The Ch'ing criticism of earlier philosophical concepts was not analytic; it expressed itself rather in its disregard for earlier thought—whether Buddhist, Taoist, or Neo-Confucian (commonly referred to as *chiang-hsüeh,* "discussion about learning")—and in a preference for a "solid learning" that ferreted out historical and philological facts with a minimum of interpretative integration. Interest in the study of the Classics was confined to solving textual puzzles or to unraveling historical and institutional detail. Epigraphy and ancient phonetics received much attention. The "search for evidence" as a definition of scholarship extended also to history, where the most important new work was in the careful treatment of isolated topics gathered in collected notes. But while Chang Hsüeh-ch'eng exhibited a preference for "solid learning" in certain ways, he did not share the general fondness for minute detail; and although he was willing to recognize the worth of the great philologists, he objected to the philological concept of historical scholarship.

The philology of the Ch'ing was probably well suited to the needs of its greatly enlarged learned class, most of whom could scarcely hope to achieve fame in scholarship or become proficient in more than a very small area of human learning. The scholar could still achieve a measure of individual justification by polishing and bringing to light some unique fact or facts of ancient history, or by clearing up uncertainties in the meaning of a classical text. Perhaps in the intensity of the discipline involved in the "search for truth in actual facts" and in the renunciation of the vapidity of "empty words," Ch'ing philology had become what Neo-Confucian "study" had always been: a means of self-realization. To the eighteenth-century educated man, all philosophical speculation had come to seem more or less alike; differences in the broader reaches of understanding seemed meaningless or at best artificial. But not so achievement in some specialty within the scope of one's own limitations.

The Ch'ing intellectual temper was probably influenced by the impact of the conquest. Literary men who had been politically active or who had helplessly watched the old regime fall were in need of an intellectual activity that did not seem ineffective. Ku Yen-wu (1613–82), whose work was the first important application of the methods of the "search for evidence," assumed that the justification of knowledge must be in its usefulness to society or to a future ruler; the loyalty to a Chinese nation that he had been unable to save he transferred to the "world" of Chinese civilization.[10] Yen Yüan (1635–1704) was suspicious of books altogether, and argued that education should consist of learning how to do things. One must not imagine that a great revolution in thought took place: most of Ku's useful knowledge is derived from the Classics and ancient history; and Yen Yüan turns out to be interested in such practical subjects as archery and playing the lute. But both Ku and Yen in their ways reflect a widespread persuasion: the Ming Dynasty had died of philosophical indigestion; its most intelligent men had wasted themselves in meaningless bickering while their world fell to pieces. There was, however, one important scholar and devoted Ming partisan who did not share this aversion for ideas. Huang Tsung-hsi was an admirer of both Wang Yang-ming and the Sung philosophers. In youth he had been in the thick of Ming political struggles. In later life he worked on the history of the dynasty he had served and wrote invaluable histories of the Sung, Yüan, and Ming intellectual traditions he honored. The life of learning, he held, must include both solid scholarship and reflective thought. "Unless you read history extensively," he wrote, "you will be unable to ascertain the development of *li*; and even if you do, but do not seek [for truth] within your mind, you will be a crude pedant."[11]

Ku Yen-wu was far the most influential of the early Ch'ing scholar-philosophers. He was regarded in the next two centuries almost as the founding father of Ch'ing philological scholarship. His work on phonology was intensely admired and imitated; his collected notes were widely read and supplied with commentaries. But his readers probably overlooked the aspect of Ku's notes that makes them of interest today—the rich admixture of opinion on the nature of literary value and on the ills of political administration. Ku seemed influential because his name was attached to a trend; neither Yen nor Huang ever had this kind of influence. Yen was almost unknown, in any case, and is best seen, I think, as an exaggerated indication of the direction of winds of doctrine. Huang was known and respected, at least in his own part of China, even though much of his work remained unknown and unpublished until late in the dynasty. And he has an especial importance for the study of Chang Hsüeh-ch'eng because Chang held views like Huang's and consciously identified himself with a local "Eastern Chekiang" tradition of learning in which he saw Huang as a giant.*

Chang made this acknowledgment only at the end of his life. But he must have owed much to the intellectual temper of his native region. The eastern Chekiang area had produced a number of distinguished historians in the first century of the Ch'ing. Wan Ssu-t'ung (1638–1702) of Ning-po, who worked on the *History of the Ming,* was Huang's student. Ch'üan Tsu-wang (1705–55), also of Ning-po and Huang's editor, was Chang's older contemporary. And Huang himself, like Chang a native of the Shao-hsing area, was (again like Chang) both a historian and a philosopher.

There is another resemblance between Huang and Chang: neither took office in the Manchu state. But in this case the resemblance is misleading. Huang was a Ming patriot. He had given heroic service to the Southern Ming cause, and his avoidance of office under the Ch'ing was dictated by the Confucian code of loyalty. He was the author, furthermore, of perhaps the most eloquent criticism of imperial power before the twentieth century. His was a posture of political protest by a man of great eminence who could have had high office without asking. Chang was in no such position. At one time he could probably have had a minor magistracy if he had actively sought it, and he did not do so. But he accepted the Manchu regime wholeheartedly. As a good Confucian, to be sure, he should accept it, having been born under it. But Chang was not in any case a critic of power. More than most Confucians he favored a strong state authority.

And this is not surprising, for the political climate of the eighteenth century was not that of the first half-century of the Manchu dynasty. The regime's ideological self-justification, difficult to accept at first, was by the eighteenth century a real intellectual fact, solidly founded in Confucian doctrine. The Manchus came as reformers of a Chinese polity sickened by dissension and appealed

* The "Eastern Chekiang" scholars are more precisely those who were native to Shao-hsing, Ning-po, and other localities "east of the Che," i.e., east of the Ch'ien-t'ang River. See Demiéville, "Chang Hsüeh-ch'eng and His Historiography," p. 170.

to the strong Neo-Confucian ideal of a harmonious social and political order. When there is good order in the world the *tao* is not
a matter of argument; it is left (as the seventeenth-century writer
Fei Mi said it should be) to the rulers.[12] Such an order is in every
way unified. It is not split into political factions or into bickering
schools of thought. In it there is "unity between high and low," as
the Yung-cheng Emperor wished.

In such an order, ruling men and guarding truth are not two
separate roles. Li Kuang-ti (1642–1718), a high official close to the
Kang-hsi Emperor, had said just this to his imperial master. In antiquity, Li argued, the *tao* and government had been united in the
persons of sage-rulers; later, with Confucius and Chu Hsi, Heav-
en entrusted the *tao* to sages outside the state; but now, the present
sovereign has indeed shown himself to be a sage. "Surely, Heaven
is about to recommence the succession of Yao and Shun, and the
authoritative line of the *tao* and government will again be united."[13] This was not mere flattery; in effect Li was making a philosophical point: in the present imperial power the principles of
knowledge and action, government and learning, were again one.
Even the "search for truth in actual facts" had its political twist in
support of authority. We find the Ch'ien-lung Emperor lecturing
his censors instead of being lectured by them, as he would have
been in an age in which men of learning restrained the throne.
The Emperor cautioned them not to make charges of a general
nature, but to keep their criticisms of conditions as specific as possible and to support them with evidence. For to do otherwise is to
behave like Ming officials, who attacked each other with "empty
words" and criticized the court merely to seek fame.[f] The ideo-

---

[f] *Kao-tsung Shih-lu,* 1173.17a–18b. By the end of the eighteenth century it was
possible to question this official evaluation of the Ming demise. Chao-lien (*Hsiao-
t'ing Tsa-lu,* 10.9b) maintains that people are greatly mistaken when they argue
that the Ming perished from too much "discussion about learning" and ignorance
of basic values—which is, he says, the common opinion of those who criticize Neo-
Confucian speculative philosophy. The real cause he thinks was the misrule of the
last Ming emperors; the fall would have come even sooner if it had not been for the
efforts of good men such as the Tung-lin partisans to protect the throne.

logical atmosphere built up by the Manchu establishment must surely have had as pervasive an effect intellectually as any single thinker or school of thought.

This was the world in which Chang lived and breathed. How then did Chang Hsüeh-ch'eng fit into this eighteenth-century Chinese world? We will see that in important ways he was a misfit. Surely he thought of himself as such. He was a man who constantly felt—not without excellent reason—that others regarded him as odd. And he reacted by neglecting no opportunity to press his differences with others in argument. Such men are always interesting—to their biographers; to his acquaintances Chang must often have been a trial. But men like Chang are interesting not because they are oddities. Their interest often lies in the fact that they grapple with the same problems everyone faces, think the same ideas everyone thinks, and push forward to conclusions others are too unimaginative—or too sensible—to settle on. In this way, if history is kind, they may lead men on to something new and valuable. But whatever history grants, they show us in sharp relief, by the refraction of their thought, the basic commitments of an age.

1. Background and Education

My teacher admonished me vehemently: "Literary art
knows neither past nor present," said he. "Your one
object should be to grasp it thoroughly. If you have no
understanding of modern prose, how can you have any
grasp of poetry or ancient prose?" But my head was
turned. I heard him not.

—*Biography of K'o Shao-keng* ... 1778

Chang Hsüeh-ch'eng was born in 1738 in K'uai-chi district, Shao-
hsing prefecture, near the shores of Hangchow Bay in northeast-
ern Chekiang. He belonged to a clan of indeterminate status
among the lesser gentry. The Changs had lived in the vicinity of
Shao-hsing for over six centuries, and they traced their ancestry
back to the Five Dynasties Period (907–60), when one Chang Tzu-
chün established himself in the city of P'u-ch'eng in Fukien. Chang
Tzu-chün held high office in the kingdom of Min; the Chang family histories proudly relate how his wife once saved the people of
her city from being massacred by interceding with the commanders
of an invading army of Southern T'ang.[1]

At the end of Northern Sung, a descendant of Chang Tzu-
Chün, one Chang Liang, moved from Fukien to Shan-yin, adjoin-
ing K'uai-chi. Sometime in the late twelfth or early thirteenth century, a later ancestor, Chang Yen-wu, moved to the village of
Tao-hsü (then called Ch'eng-shan) in K'uai-chi. This was to remain the clan's ancestral home up to Chang's own day. By the
Ch'ien-lung period, the Changs of Tao-hsü had become very numerous and widespread; a colony of a hundred or more lived in
Peking. The soil in K'uai-chi was too poor to grow rice well, so
the clan supported themselves variously by raising tree-cotton,
brewing wine ("the finest in K'uai-chi"), and serving as yamen
secretaries. Chang's immediate ancestors appear to have had a perceptible rise in estate. Thirty or forty years before his birth, his own

family had moved into the city proper. His grandfather, Chang
Ju-chang, was a certified yamen secretary, and his father, Chang
Piao (d. 1768), was married to a daughter of a certain Shih I-tsun,
who had obtained a posthumous honorary title as prefect. Chang
Piao attained the *chin-shih* degree in 1742, and in 1751 he became
a district magistrate. His son ultimately attained the same degree,
but their immediate branch of the family seems to have risen no
further.[2]

The literary tastes and attainments of Chang's father and grandfather are significant. Chang wrote of his grandfather that he devoted the last years of his life to a study of the connection between
"the way of Heaven and the doings of man" as revealed in the
monumental history of China, *Tzu-chih T'ung-chien* (*A Comprehensive Mirror for Aid in Government*), by the Sung historian
Ssu-ma Kuang (1019–86). Both grandfather and father were deeply
interested in the popular Taoist moral tract, *T'ai-shang Kan-ying
P'ien* (*The Treatise of the Exalted One on Reward and Retribution*), and its thesis that events in history and in life are guided by
moral justice. Chang says that his father was an avid reader; he
would borrow books, copy from them extensively, and become
quite distressed if he had to return a book before he had finished
his note-taking. Chang's father was something of a poet, and a few
of his poems, with an introductory sketch by Chang, still exist.
"My late father did not read books in order to gain a reputation,"
Chang says in this preface. "When he wrote in classical style his
language was carefully chiseled and terse. He believed that the
popular histories and novels of the T'ang and Sung were useful
to supplement standard history; but he felt they were too wordy
and involved, so he took ten or more titles, . . . paragraphed them,
and copied out readings from them. In poetry he preferred the
T'ang forms to the older styles. His last instruction was that I
should be careful about showing these verses to others."[3]

We cannot, of course, completely extract the characters of the
father and grandfather from Chang's pious representation of them.
But it would seem that some of Chang's most characteristic atti-

tudes toward literature and history—his insistence on the importance to the historian of the significance of his material and the
art employed in presenting it, his catholic definition of the historical, and his self-conscious disdain for popular esteem—were theirs
as well. Chang always acknowledged his father's profound influence on him. Later in life, he wrote to his own sons of a revealing
incident that occurred in his twentieth year. He had bought a copy
of the collected writings of the poet Yü Hsin (513–81), with commentary by Wu Chao-i (fl. 1672). In it he found the line, "Amid
the spring waters I looked at the peach blossoms," with Wu's note
citing, in philologue's fashion, a similar passage from an ancient
text on the seasons. Chang's father took the book, struck out the
note, and wrote in, "Looking at peach blossoms in the midst of
spring waters—what a beautiful and profound conception!" After
that Chang found Wu's commentary tasteless and was no longer
captivated by textual analysis. Thereafter, when he read books he
was able to form his own ideas and understand the inner meaning
of the writers of old.[4]

Of Chang's early years, we know very little. Much of that comes
from Chang's own writings of forty or fifty years later, when the
distant world of memory and the writer's world of literary fancy
may have become blurred. He was an only son. There was one
"big" sister, six years older, and several younger sisters. He had
no uncles on his father's side and only one aunt, who had married
into a family of the Tu surname in K'uai-chi. The aunt died when
he was eleven, but before that time she had occasionally returned
to the household to help his mother with the family accounts. In
his second or third year, he recalls, when he was learning to talk,
his elder sister would carry him around in her arms all day and
would amuse him by inducing him to speak. Another relative frequently took young Chang to a neighboring wine-shop, with the
result that he grew up with a fondness for drink.[5]

In 1742, Chang's fifth year, his father passed the metropolitan
examination, thus becoming eligible for official appointment. For

the next ten years, however, the elder Chang supported himself by teaching. Chang eventually became one of his father's pupils, but his first teacher was his mother.[a] Later, probably, he attended a school for young children. Of this early period Chang wrote, "In my childhood, I was sick a great deal, and in the course of a whole year...I would be able to work hardly two months. By nature I was stupid, and would cover but a hundred or so words a day in my reading, and then was apt to fall sick again and have to stop."[6]

In 1751 we find him studying at the Cool Breeze School, which was maintained by his relatives, the Tu family. There were three Tu cousins in the school. The youngest, Tu Ping-ho, was only a little older than Chang, and the two became firm friends. Chang may have been a little slow, but poor Ping-ho was a complete dull-wit and by far the poorest of the seven or eight students. In very hot weather, Ping-ho would wake before daylight, light a lamp, and read to supplement the day's assignment. He was afraid of ghosts in the dark and would make Chang (who seems to have been in residence at the school) get up with him. Chang did this, even though it meant exposing himself to a nightly attack of gnats. Another source of irritation was the schoolteacher, a bigoted, old-fashioned pedant who used the rod freely as a remedy for lapses of memory. Ping-ho was his usual victim, though Chang attempted to intercede. What Chang himself went through can only be imagined.[7]

In his fourteenth year, Chang was married to a girl surnamed Yü. In this same year Chang Piao was appointed magistrate of Ying-ch'eng in the lake district of Hupeh, and he moved his family there.[8]

At fourteen, Chang had not finished reading the Four Books. Two years later, he was still a trial to his teachers (he was so imma-

---

[a] HY, pp. 4–5. Chu Yün, *Ssu-ho Wen-chi* (Peking, 1815), 16.20a–b. Chu Yün says that Chang's mother first taught him from the widely used primer *Po-chia Hsing,* a versified list of common surnames composed in the Sung Dynasty, which Chang was made to memorize.

ture, he says, that he giggled while attending his father's lectures), and visitors expressed pity for the father of this backward student. Chang was only exhibiting, however, that combination of immaturity and precocity common to unusually gifted adolescents. In spite of evidence to the contrary, his understanding was developing. He liked to read widely, but his father, who wanted to prepare him for the examinations, thought his education should be "pure." He restricted his access to unassigned books and hired a tutor to teach him how to write examination essays. Chang had the usual student reaction to *pa-ku*. At first he rebelled by trying to write poetry, but found that he had no talent for it. The prohibition on outside reading he evaded, so he tells us, by picking up a copy of Han Yü, and reading it lovingly in secret. Revered as a master of "ancient prose," Han Yü was looked at with suspicion by connoisseurs of *pa-ku*. With his idealistic disdain for pursuing the noble art of writing for so unworthy a motive as gaining a living, he had always spoken sympathetically to students in Chang's plight; and there is no doubt that Chang found the great T'ang writer's spirit of lofty disaffection a heady draught.[b]

But his interests were now turning rapidly to history, for which, he later recognized, he had a natural aptitude. He relates that he set about to write a condensed version of the *Tso Commentary*. But his father, seeing his efforts, pointed out to him that the result

[b] HY, pp. 6–7. *I-shu*, 22.37a, "Letter to Chang Ju-nan"; 17.13a–b, "Postscript to Chu Hsi's *Han Wen K'ao-i*," 1790–91. It is not clear just what Chang was remembering when he wrote (in 1790 or 1791) of this first encounter with Han Yü; the Sung writer Ou-yang Hsiu has recorded a suspiciously similar experience and assigns it, as does Chang, to his seventeenth year. See my "Protest against Conventions" in Arthur F. Wright, ed., *The Confucian Persuasion* (Stanford, 1960), p. 181.

Ancient prose (*ku-wen*) is a style that avoids tight parallelism between phrases and sentences, and avoids also the constant grouping of words into phrases of four or six characters. The term "ancient prose" was used by Han Yü who, rebelling against "modern" fashion, consciously turned back to ancient classical models. Its antithesis, "modern prose" (*shih-wen*) refers to the "four-six" style or to any style, such as the examination-essay form with its eight parts ("eight legs," *pa-ku*), which is governed by rigid rules of parallelism. When Chang Hsüeh-ch'eng uses the term *shih-wen*, he means the examination-essay form. In translating him I shall always use the more familiar word, *pa-ku*.

of his work would still be, like the *Tso,* a history in chronological (*pien-nien*) form. It would be more useful, the elder Chang urged, to rearrange the material in standard-history fashion. Chang then made an intensive study of annal-biography (*chi-chuan*) form. He pawned his wife's jewelry to buy paper and employed yamen clerks to copy Eastern Chou writings, which he arranged into a *History of Eastern Chou* (*Tung Chou Shu*) of over one hundred chapters. He worked on this for three years without finishing it. His tutor discovered these efforts, chided him, and counseled him first to learn to write, all to no avail. His writing, Chang admits, was not even always grammatically correct (writing the Chinese literary language, we should remember, presented the same kind of difficulty to Chang as did Ciceronian Latin to his Western counterpart). But he was now very confident about his historical abilities and would not listen to advice.[9]

But even though young Chang seemed a bit wild, he was at least intellectually alive, and even though his interest in history was one-sided, it was still genuine. He writes that there was a marked change in himself after his twentieth year; for one thing, he became an avid reader. He still had no understanding of the Classics, but history came to him naturally. "No sooner did I look at historical writings than they seemed to be things I had been studying for a long time. I was able to discuss freely their good and bad points, and my criticisms were always apt."[10]

By this time the family fortunes had suffered an abrupt change. We are told that Chang Piao's conduct in office earned him the lasting affection of the townspeople of Ying-ch'eng. Neverthless, in 1756 he was charged with "excessive leniency" in the handling of a criminal case and dismissed from his magistracy. His successor accused him of other irregularities. As a consequence he was obliged to pay a large sum of money, which left him too poor to return to K'uai-chi. From this time until his death in 1768 he remained in Hupeh, supporting himself as best he could by teaching in local academies and compiling local history. In 1760–61 he was

master of the local academy in Ying-ch'eng; in 1764 he had a similar position in nearby T'ien-men. During this and the following
year, he was employed by the magistrate to compile, with his son's
collaboration, a history of that locality.[11]

His father's difficulties did not prevent Chang from continuing
his studies; Chang Piao's teaching and writing provided at least
some family income. In 1760, in his 23rd year, Chang made his first
journey away from his family and his first attempt at the *chü-jen*
examination. For this purpose he went to Peking, where the quota
was more advantageous than in Chekiang, but he was still unsuccessful. In Peking he stayed with Chang Yüan-yeh, a cousin his
father, too, had visited when taking his metropolitan examination.
Among the sizable Chang colony in Peking, Chang found congenial friends in Chang Shou-i and Chang Ju-nan, with whom he
discussed intellectual matters and later corresponded. His critical
approach to history was developing in originality; later, he wrote
that at this time he was already thinking new and bold ideas. Standard history, he was convinced, should contain a section of maps
and diagrams in addition to the four conventional divisions (annals, tables, monographs, and biographies), and furthermore the
biographical section should contain a sub-category for official historians.[12]

In 1762, after a brief return to his native K'uai-chi, Chang returned to Peking to try the *chü-jen* examination again. He did not
pass, but this time did well enough to qualify for the Imperial
Academy (Kuo Tzu Chien). That winter he enrolled as a resi-
dent student, a position he held, with some interruptions, for the
next ten years. In eighteenth-century China, the life of a *chien-
sheng* (student in the academy) was similar in some ways to the
life of a Western university student. The Chinese student might, as
did Chang at first, live in residence at the Academy, or he might
live elsewhere in the city. The important thing was to be in Peking,
the center of Chinese intellectual and political life and the place for
making personal connections essential to one's education, advancement, and future employment. An instructor in the Academy de-

voted only a part of his time to teaching. He seldom lectured, but tutored his students individually, assuming some direction of a student's reading, and, from time to time, assigning literary compositions, which he then edited and corrected. The object of the training, here as everywhere, was to prepare the student to pass the provincial or metropolitan examinations.[13]

At the Academy, Chang received a small stipend; anything not needed for personal expenses, he spent on books. He wanted especially to have the Standard Histories, but the price was too high for him to buy all of them at once, so he picked them up one by one, in different editions, over a period of three years. For the time being he had no family responsibilities, for his dependents remained in Hupeh in his father's household. (He had two sons, Chang I-hsüan [b. 1760] and Chang Hua-fu [b. 1765], and in 1768 we read of a son by a concubine née Ts'ai; this third son, Chang Hua-shou, was adopted by Chang's cousin Chang Yüan-yeh.)[14] In the Academy he was in low spirits, for he regularly stood among the lowest in his class. The others considered him without talent; even the attendants would smile in amusement when Chang would hopefully scan the top of the list of posted examination grades. However, he made a number of new friends at the Academy; among them were Tseng Shen, who was quartered near him, and Chen Sung-nien. The next year he corresponded with Chen several times, discussing the compilation of local histories, in which he was now becoming interested.[15]

This correspondence apparently took place during a prolonged absence from the Academy beginning in the summer of 1763, when Chang returned to Hupeh. Early the next year his father was teaching in T'ien-men, where the magistrate had engaged him to compile a local history. Chang Piao asked his son to collaborate in this undertaking. This prompted Chang to write his first important theoretical essay, "Ten Proposals for the Compilation of Local Histories."[16] In this essay and in his letters to Chen, we find a number of interesting ideas that Chang continued to develop in later years. For example, Chang urges the advantages of maintaining a depart-

ment of archives in local governments to keep materials in readiness for the local historian. One can guess that Chang and his father
sometimes found it difficult to obtain the documents they needed.

Chang brings up a more interesting problem, which must concern every thoughtful historian, the problem of objectivity. Chang
urges his friend Chen to resist pressures to include in his histories
flattering biographies of local inhabitants; historical biography and
"social" biography (such as epitaphs) have different standards in
this respect. Criticism is to be avoided; the historian's narrative
should be impartial and factual, "letting good and evil appear of
itself." Nevertheless, the good is to be given an edge. Filial sons,
virtuous wives, and loyal officials not only merit mention in a history, but should be given enough biographical space to provide
moral inspiration for the reader.[17]

But impartiality does not require that one discard the customary
practice of including appraisals (*lun*) in various parts of the history (e.g., after the close of a biography). Chang would allow these
appraisals, but says that they must be "restrained." He concedes
that over the centuries practice has varied. The Emperor Ming
T'ai-tsu instructed Sung Lien, who was in charge of compiling the
History of the Yüan Dynasty, to avoid such comments altogether
and "to write straightforwardly according to the facts." This,
Chang objects, "preserves the idea of restraint but misses the principle of justice. I would say that if, in praise and blame (*pao-pien*),
you seek only to be fair, there is no harm in including appraisals
and encomiums. But one may not exalt or make light of someone
according to one's fancy, nor may one arbitrarily pity or slander a
person."[18] This matter of the historian's judgment, too, was to be
an important problem in Chang's later thinking.

In the "Ten Proposals," we also learn that it is not good historical practice to give space in biography or literature sections of the
local history to living persons; for historical treatment of a person,
even if there be no explicit praise or criticism, is a sort of final evaluation. This principle has certain exceptions, however: biographies
are allowed for distinguished officials who have retired and for virtuous women whose work in this world is done, provided they are

so old that future events are not likely to upset the judgment of the historian. Another matter Chang deals with is curious: often the historian, following Chinese practice, will want to include large blocks of text from existing documents, historical narratives, and biographies. Cutting and arranging this material to work it in smoothly involves special problems, and Chang advises the historian to make proper acknowledgment of sources in such cases.[19]

The letters to Chen Sung-nien (who was compiling a local history of his own) contain a number of commendable formal recommendations for local historiography. These recommendations are the first formulation of what was to become one of Chang's most important ideas. Local histories normally contain chapters on literature (*i-wen*); these may have no historical interest at all. Often the historian uses such a chapter as a pocket in which to tuck a selection of poems and other ornamental pieces by local writers. Chang makes the following recommendations: (1) The *i-wen* section ought to be a critical bibliography of local writing, similar to the bibliographies in the three *T'ung* (T'ang and Sung political encyclopedias) and the *Seven Summaries* (a bibliography by the Han imperial librarian Liu Hsin, which was revised by Pan Ku and included in his *History of the Han Dynasty*). Then the local history will later serve an important use for official bibliographical research of broader scope. (2) Literary pieces that are directly pertinent to local political and historical problems should be quoted in the appropriate parts of the history, e.g., in the sections on taxes, geography, and local customs; epitaphs, if accurate, and individual writings, if important, could be included in the biographies. (3) Other literary matter that is interesting but not precisely relevant should be collected into an anthology, which would serve as an appendix to the local history. Chang calls this anthology a *wen-hsüan* and asks Chen to use the famous Liang Dynasty anthology of Hsiao T'ung (Prince Chao-ming, 501–31) as a model for it.[20]

Chen accepted Chang's anthology idea, but not without some argument. Chang felt obliged to write back appealing to stronger precedents than Hsiao T'ung's *Wen Hsüan*. His argument turned to the Classics, particularly the *Odes*:

The Four Categories classification system is not ancient. When the Six Arts began, there was no "Classics" category. The *Changes* was not revered as the work of the sages; it was just a book of philosophy. The *History* and the *Spring and Autumn* were just history books. The *Odes* was just a literary collection [*wen-chi*]. The *Decorum Ritual* and the *Offices of Chou* were just books of law and descriptions of government [*hui-tien*]. Except for the *Changes,* which was kept by the grand diviner, the other four were all books entrusted to the palace historian; people later used them to examine and verify the many incidents of past and present time. One never hears that the ancients were so fussy as to take just those books that are in historical form and make a special category of history out of them. . . . "The *Odes* passed away and the *Spring and Autumn* was made" [says Mencius]; the *Odes* were like the modern *Wen Hsüan,* and still they were able to dovetail with history. What are we to say to this?[21]

One thing to say to this is that modes of argument seem to belong uniquely to the culture in which they are used. But for Chang's thinking the importance of this argument was his assumption that the sharp conceptual distinction between Classics and histories was a mistake, and that in a sense (as he was to notice excitedly later) the Classics were originally documents kept by ancient officials.

It is significant that these questions concerning local historiography should rest on such weighty matters as the nature of the Classics and the policies of the first Ming emperor. For Chang was insisting that the local history is a genre of historical writing equal to any in dignity and importance. A remark at the end of the first of the letters to Chen clearly reveals his thoughts at this time: "If a man of spirit," he writes, "is unable to become an official historian, he may still become a secretary in the retinue of a person of note or a high official, and in this way be able to discuss critically his age and gain significant employment for his literary skill. One possible activity in such a capacity is the compilation of local histories."[22] At this time in Chinese history, with an increasing population, and a foreign elite claiming the lucrative posts, competition among the literati was so keen that humbler activities, such as the writing of the often scorned "gazetteer," had to be raised to a level of respect. Chang could not have failed to notice these conditions; no doubt they had a bearing on the interest he soon developed in the writing of family histories.

In 1765 Chang returned to the Academy, bewildered and without friends; he attempted the *chü-jen* examination once more. This time Shen Yeh-fu (1732–1807), a sub-examiner and a native of Yang-chou, recommended his essays to the chief examiner, but without result. Disappointed, Shen took Chang into his home and kept him at his studies.

At this time Chang made an acquaintance that was to advance his estate considerably. Shen introduced him to Chu Yün (1729–81) who was nine years Chang's senior, of wealthy family, and a native of Peking, though his ancestors had come from Hsiao-shan in Chekiang. Chu had attained the *chin-shih* degree in 1754, in a distinguished class that included his friend Shen Yeh-fu and the historians Wang Ming-sheng and Chi Yün. Since 1757 he had been a compiler in the Imperial Press and Bindery (Wu-ying-tien), and had served as associate examiner in the metropolitan examinations. He was an accomplished writer and numbered among his friends the famous men of letters of his day. He was highly thought of by the Emperor, and his brother, Chu Kuei (1731–1807), was the teacher of the succeeding Emperor, Jen-tsung.[23]

Chang now began the study of writing under Chu Yün, who presently took him into his house. Here Chang met several congenial young men studying with Chu, among them Wu Lan-t'ing and Feng T'ing-cheng, the latter exactly his own age. Chu was in mourning (his father had died the year before) and was consequently enjoying a period of obligatory inactivity. He was a complete gentleman, a man of mild temper who took keen pleasure in having intellectual friends about him. When an acquaintance—such as Feng T'ing-ch'eng (1728–84), a cousin of Chang's fellow student and at this time secretary of the Grand Court of Revision—called at Chu's studio, an evening of wine and conversation would often follow. Chang cherished for a long time the memory of such gatherings.[24]

In Chu, Chang had found a valuable teacher, patron, and friend.

Chu discussed with him the art of writing *pa-ku* (the essay style
required in the examinations), told him he had no talent for it,
and that it was not worth his attention. When Chang objected that
his family was poor, and that he should therefore try to pass the
examinations, Chu reassured him: "Why should passing the examinations be difficult? And why should this require you to study
pa-ku? Follow your own way, trust to your own nature, and a degree will not necessarily be unobtainable."[25]

Chu held the critical view that mastery of style does not come
through formal imitation but is instead a spontaneous achievement, a "hearing of the *tao*" that results from a total cultivation
of the intellect; in short, that style cannot be achieved if it is an
end in itself. Chang was very sympathetic to this point of view
and soon made it his own. Thirteen years later (1778) in an essay
in honor of Chu's fiftieth birthday, Chang made the observation
that some people admire the style of the great prose writers of the
Tang and Sung periods without really understanding their principles of writing, and that others become completely absorbed in
the cult of *pa-ku*. In both cases, these are interests in style:

Master Chu, however, holds that no writer who makes a fine style his
goal ever achieves it. One shouldn't be concerned with how difficult it
is to write, but only with what one has to say. If one does this, one will
come close to the ancient ideal that writing should merely be sufficient
to convey one's meaning. It's a matter of secondary importance to edit
one's writing dispassionately, smoothing out the language and considering whether it fits the subject. The essential thing is to grasp the *tao*.
Master Chu maintains that if a writer's concern be with style rather
than with the *tao,* one will not be able to find a single genuine line in
what he writes.[26]

This, at the time it was written, was a clear statement of Chang's
own ideas about writing. For the present, however, in spite of Chu's
assurances, Chang continued to be obsessed by a feeling of failure.
He was also having financial difficulties; but through Chu's good
offices, his name was becoming known among persons of importance.[27]

One older scholar to whom Chu may have introduced his pupil

was Tai Chen (1724–77), a leading philologist and a man who, unlike most advocates of "solid learning," was seriously interested in philosophy. It is likely that Chang first met Tai Chen in 1766, when Tai was in the capital to lecture and to attempt the *chin-shih* examination.[28] In a letter of that year to his friend and kinsman Chang Ju-nan, Chang gives an indication of how strongly Tai impressed him:

Formerly in reading books I set out to get the general meaning, and being young and enthusiastic I applied myself merely to wide reading in all branches of literature, without having any end in view. I was fond of advancing theories that were lofty rather than acute, and attacked textual scholarship, soaring about in emptiness. I was always pleasantly satisfied, supposing that I understood things. But I was astonished when I heard Tai Tung-yüan of Hsiu-ning shake his fist and shout, "Present-day scholars, no matter what they deal with, are primarily guilty of never having learned to read correctly!" Startled, I asked him what he meant; he said, "If I were unable to comprehend the ideas of 'before heaven' and 'after heaven' or the subtle wealth of meaning in the books from the Ho and the Lo, I would not pretend to have read the *Classic of Changes*; if I were unable to understand the courses of the stars, the variations in the heavens from year to year, the constellations, and the patterns of earth, I would not pretend to have read the astronomy sections of the *History*."

Chang then recalled the conversations that he, Chang Ju-nan, and others had had in earlier years, and added, "We were indeed perfect examples of what he was saying, for we actually never opened a volume of a single Classic of the Four Books. How shameful! How frightful!" But this powerful impression of Tai's philological point of view did not remain fixed. When Chu Yün expressed himself in a similar vein, decrying shallow scholars who talk ignorantly of philosophy and advising his own students first to investigate facts and then to try to see what they mean, this advice produced in Chang a somewhat different chain of reflection. Chang felt that philological strictness should not be thought of as just the mastery of more and more facts and should not prevent one from developing deep insights in the areas of one's special interests: "It seems to me that the scholar will surely devote himself to some special subject; extensive study of detail is really not incompatible with economy in learning.... The more you concentrate on something you value, the more you will achieve in understanding." One should not desire shallow reputation or be concerned with popular praise; then "even if you spend a decade or so doing something that ordinary people do not deem worth doing, there will suddenly come a day when you are close to perfection."

Where Tai would have his students avoid "soaring about in emptiness" by carefully attending to matters of fact, for Chang the important thing seemed to be not the facts, but the degree of concentration their study requires and the genuineness with which the student can devote himself to his work. Chang's reflections addressed to his cousin contain other hints of his developing philosophy of scholarship, points of view that would eventually lead him to criticize Tai sharply. For example, Chang sees three broad areas within which men of learning do their work—the study of facts, literary art, and philosophy. These are complementary: facts support ideas, and writing is the means of expressing conclusions about both facts and ideas. But men do not realize this; each pushes the special thing he values, and the resulting discord opens the way for much mischief.

This conception shows that Tai Chen and Chu Yün were not the only influences on Chang as a young Peking student. His fact-art-philosophy synthesis was an idea with a very wide currency in middle-Ch'ing China. It was particularly stressed by Yao Nai (1732–1815), literary critic of the school of "ancient prose" writers of T'ung-ch'eng, Anhwei. Much of Chang's thinking from this time on was close to T'ung-ch'eng persuasions. It is not hard to see why these persuasions were appealing. Yao talked grandly of "the unity of the *tao* and art," and "the unity of Heaven and Man." He restored philosophical speculation, which had become almost a contraband quantity, to the cult of literary skill, an obligatory concern for everyone.[c]

---

[c] As Hellmut Wilhelm has written, "Rising into prominence when the political sphere tolerated nothing but the compliant, the [T'ung-ch'eng] school provided the medium of escape for all individualisms and creative urges." See "Chinese Con-

But it is as a personal document that Chang's remarkable early letter is most revealing; it brings out vividly the anxieties and aspirations of the young writer: "My . . . family is poor and my parents are old, so I have endeavored to study shallow and worthless *pa-ku*, dreaming vainly of official employment. This is called 'doing what others most despise, thereby to seek what they most prize.' " Yet he can do nothing else, even though he realizes that in so taxing his strength he cannot hope to attain the perfection of understanding of which he dreams:

Since I was young, I have been by nature inclined to the study of history. But because historical books are so very numerous, I had to pawn my clothing to buy the sixteen or seventeen histories from Ssu-ma Ch'ien to Ou-yang Hsiu and Sung Ch'i. My power of comprehension was limited, and I would often absent-mindedly lose the thread of thought; with red ink I would go over and over the text four or five times before I began to get the idea, and still I wasn't able to comprehend all the phrasing or the technical details. I thought that the twenty-one histories had impurities of form and exhibited many faults in content, and so I wanted to make a general scrutiny of their merits and defects, formulate some general rules, and write a book of a few chapters discussing critically the great principles of historical writing. But my knowledge was so scanty that I hadn't the least hope of completing such a work, and now that I am burdened with *pa-ku* and oppressed with schoolwork, I don't know whether I shall ultimately realize my object at all.[29]

A desire to achieve something "immortal," to do something of lasting value that others had never done before, was characteristic of Chang Hsüeh-ch'eng from the beginning. Chang had read the

---

fucianism on the Eve of the Great Encounter," in Marius Jansen, ed., *Changing Japanese Attitudes toward Modernization* (Princeton, 1965), p. 303. But it would surely be a mistake to place Chang himself in this school. Later on, he knew Yao Nai at least slightly, and he may have known him at this time (when Yao was in Peking). But in writings where one would expect it he makes no acknowledgment of any debt to Yao's ideas, and he appears to have been only slightly familiar with the work of Fang Pao (1668–1749), the most important of the T'ung-ch'eng theorists. See also Suzuki Torao, "Dōjō Bumpai no shuchō to Bun ni taisuru Sho-Isetsu" ("The Main Tenets of the T'ung-ch'eng Literary School and Various Divergent Theories of Literature"), *Shinagaku*, VI (1932), 55; and Kuo Shao-yü, *Chung-kuo Wen-hsüeh P'i-p'ing Shih* (*A History of Chinese Literary Criticism*), Vol. II (Shanghai, 1947), pp. 375, 478.

Shih T'ung (General Principles of Historiography) by Liu Chih-chi (661–721) for the first time only the year before, and his thought shows that he had read and reread with care this famous eighth-century treatise.[30] Before his own writing began to take distinctive shape, however, he had partially freed himself from Liu's influence.

Chang's status at the Academy now improved slightly. In 1766 the new libationer at the Academy gave Chang a high rating among the students, and when this caused amusement, he defended Chang as an out-of-the-ordinary sort of person. In the fall of 1767, he asked Chang to work exclusively on the *Academy Monograph (Kuo Tzu Chien Chih)*, then being compiled; Chang's position in this work seems to have been a minor one. During the next summer (now lodged in a studio rented from his cousin Chang Yüan-yeh) he was largely occupied with reading in preparation for the autumn *chü-jen* examination. In the examination he made the supplementary list (tantamount to failure with distinction). This was an improvement, though not a pass; and one of his essays, discussing the *Academy Monograph,* drew the enthusiastic attention of the associate examiner Chu Fen-yüan (1727–82). The following year Chu Fen-yüan was appointed tutor in the Academy and gave Chang some welcome support. In his work on the *Monograph* Chang frequently found his original ideas in conflict with the preconceptions of his superiors; his examination essay, with which Chu had been so pleased, may have been an outlet for pent-up frustration.[31]

Late in 1768 Chang's father died, leaving him responsible for the entire family. He found himself too poor to go to Hupeh until early the next year. He decided to move his family to the capital; taking his household belongings and his father's coffin, he joined a north-bound grain barge in Hupeh in order to travel as cheaply as possible. On the journey, a third of his father's library of three-thousand-odd volumes was water-soaked and lost. In the sixth month of 1769 the family reached Peking, where Chang had already rented lodgings from Chu Yün's friend Feng T'ing-ch'eng. The quarters were expensive, and the move had been costly; to help him out, Chu got Chang a job editing part of the *Hsü T'ung Tien* (an imperially sponsored continuation of the political encyclopedia *T'ung Tien* by the T'ang scholar-official Tu Yu). Even so, Chang's situation at this time must have been difficult.[32]

He remained in Peking for over two years. He made many new acquaintances, notably Wang Hui-tsu (1731–1807), who remained a close friend to the end of Chang's life; this fellow provincial had a methodical temperament and a keen interest in history, which Chang found admirable. Chang worked with his cousin, Chang Yüan-yeh, on a genealogy and continued his work on the *Academy Monograph,* becoming more and more dissatisfied with the latter. When Chu Fen-yüan asked him to prepare an appendix for it, he refused. It was thus probably with some relief that toward the end of 1771 he accepted an invitation from his teacher Chu Yün, who had just been appointed educational commissioner of Anhwei, to accompany him to his place of office at T'ai-p'ing.[d]

[d] HY, pp. 22–24. Chang did not take the *chü-jen* examination regularly scheduled in the fall of 1771. He was still in mourning for his father at this time and therefore ineligible.

2. Success

Heaven and earth being as vast as they are, what a man
knows and is capable of doing is bound to be less than
what he does not know and cannot do. So if it is your
ambition to achieve something lasting, you should measure
your own strengths and turn them to account, and it is
even more important to assess your own shortcomings
and acknowledge them frankly.

> —*Letter to the Son of Chou Chen-jung,*
> *Discussing the Printing of the*
> *Latter's Works ... 1792*

In his thirty-fourth year, Chang's extended connection with the
Imperial Academy came to an end, and with it, for the time being,
his life in the capital. His departure from the Academy and from
Peking was the beginning of a long period of moving about the
country, first in Anhwei and later in the north; during this time
he wrote and talked with other scholars and thinkers, accepted
patronage or secretarial employment wherever he could find it,
took commissions to compile local histories, and taught in local
academies. Most of this time he was discontented, and for a number
of years he was harassed by money worries. His main interests
seem to have been bibliography, local historiography, and (later)
teaching the art of writing. This period embraced two major developments of literary importance in the eighteenth century: the
compilation of the Imperial Manuscript Library, the *Ssu-k'u
Ch'uan-shu* and its famous catalog, and the infamous Ch'ien-lung
literary inquisition. Chang was concerned with both of these developments. He did not officially take part in the compilation, but
many of his friends did; his *Chiao-ch'ou T'ung-i,* finished in 1779
(see Chapter 3), is evidence of his interest in the project. This same
work also contains arguments that suggest that Chang approved of
the inquisition, even though at least one of his friends was a victim of it.

From 1771 through 1776, except for one compiling commission,

Chang seems to have been supported directly by Chu, who employed him as a secretary and reader of examination papers in his T'ai-p'ing office, and by Feng T'ing-ch'eng, now circuit intendant at Ning-po. In spite of this occupational insecurity, Chang was intellectually active and confident. And he was writing more and more.

Joining Chu Yün at his post in the winter of 1771–72 were several other protégés, among them the poet, essayist, and geographical scholar Hung Liang-chi (1746–1809), the poet Huang Ching-jen (1749–83), and the historian Shao Chin-han (1743–96). Chu's Peking student Wu Lan-t'ing was also one of the party. Wang Chung (1745–94), a young man who gave a quick impression of originality and brilliance, joined the group in 1772. During that year Tai Chen, who now taught in Chekiang, and Wang Nien-sun (1744–1832), who was to distinguish himself as a philologist, were frequent visitors. When Chu and his little court arrived in T'ai-p'ing, they found another friend; the local prefect was Shen Yeh-fu, the sub-examiner who had befriended Chang after his third examination failure. Chang was welcomed at the prefect's residence, where he met his friend's son, a young man named Shen Tsai-t'ing. His friendship with the younger Shen was to be warm and lasting.[1]

At T'ai-p'ing Chang continued his student relationship to Chu. To refine Chang's literary style, both master and pupil would write essays on the same topic. When they ran out of subjects, Shao Chin-han would draw upon his amazingly detailed knowledge of Ming history to suggest others. Chang was impressed, and thereafter he and Shao found a strong common interest in history.[2]

Shao Chin-han was a native of Yü-yao, Chekiang, very near Chang's own home. Chang may have known Shao for several years; in any case, they had been acquainted earlier that year in the capital, when Shao, an expert in *pa-ku*, had passed first in the metropolitan examination. Their friendship, which was to last until Shao's death in 1796, was further reinforced by Chang's enthusiasm for the writings of Shao's great-uncle, Shao T'ing-ts'ai (1648–1711). Chang's admiration for Shao T'ing-ts'ai was of long standing. He has told us that Shao's works were highly esteemed by his father, Chang Piao, and in Peking he had endorsed the seventeenth-century writer's ideas about the writing of family history. Shao had been a friend of the great Huang Tsung-hsi. Chang's preoccupation with the elder Shao not only constitutes a link with earlier Eastern Chekiang traditions but also suggests the focus of his interests. Shao was a historian of the Southern Ming regimes. His literary collection, *Ssu-fu-t'ang Wen-chi,* consists in large part of biographies of Sung and Ming loyalists and of Ming and early Ch'ing philosophers; there are also several essays on economics, government, theory of historical succession, and types of historical writing. Shao was a third or fourth generation disciple of Wang Yang-ming, whose philosophy of moral intuition he firmly defended throughout his life. Chang's reverence for the elder Shao was not, however, for his ideas on any one subject but for the comprehensive range of his knowledge and understanding and for his literary skill. At this time Shao T'ing-ts'ai was little known, and Shao Chin-han reacted to Chang's praise with modesty. Chang persuaded his friend to take his great-uncle's worth more seriously. Apparently he did, for, later, Shao Chin-han persuaded Chu Yün to write a biography to be inscribed on his great-uncle's tombstone.[3]

It is difficult to estimate how greatly this friendship influenced the development of Chang's thinking; Chang insists that his and Shao's attitudes largely coincided, and in Chang's collected works one does find a fair number of supportive comments by Shao at the end of essays or letters. Both were dissatisfied with the excessively philological tendency of the scholarship of their time; both, in an age when it was not fashionable, defended Sung philosophy, and both saw in history the means to express and develop the central ideas of the Sung school.

Yet in many ways the two men differed strangely. Shao was enough of a philologue to complete (in 1785) a commentary to the ancient classical glossary *Erh Ya.* He was taciturn, cautious, perhaps even dull compared with Chang, who (as he admits) always spilled out whatever strange speculations came into his mind. Evidently the two needed each other.[4]

In the summer of 1772, Chang visited Feng T'ing-ch'eng at Ning-po. Like Chu, Feng was supporting men of letters and gradually gathered around him a number of the men who had been in Chu's company. In the autumn, however, Chang was back again at T'ai-p'ing.[5] At this time he wrote to his former master at the Academy, Chu Fen-yüan, to justify his leaving work on the *Academy Monograph* and added, "Since leaving the capital, I have busied myself much with writing: I have worked over the entire field of letters and have written a *Wen-shih T'ung-i [General Principles of Literature and History]*; and although the work is not complete, I have shown the general drift in three essays from the first part of it, which I copied into a letter to Ch'ien Ta-hsin [1728–1804]. I enclose them here for you also."

Ch'ien Ta-hsin, well known for his monumental *Critical Notes on the Twenty-two Histories (Erh-shih-erh Shih K'ao-i),* was ten years Chang's senior and at this time a reader in the Hanlin Academy. It is strange that Chang should have written to Ch'ien at this time, for although they were both interested in history, they must have had little in common in scholarly method or temperament. Chang had made Ch'ien's acquaintance a year or so earlier in Peking and obviously respected him highly.[6]

In these letters Chang mentions for the first time the name of the volume of essays which is now his best-known piece of writing. But we can only guess what this early *Wen-shih T'ung-i* must have been. Most of the work now in existence was written later. Moreover, there is an indication that Chang at one time intended to use this title as a collective title for all his writings, or at least for all that he proposed to save. What, exactly, does Chang's title mean? "Literature and history" is at best a mechanical rendering of *wen-shih.* A more specific meaning of the term, and the one used by bibliographers for many centuries, is "literary and historical criticism"; in this category we find such books as Liu Chih-chi's *Shih T'ung* and Liu Hsieh's sixth-century classic of literary criticism, *Wen-hsin Tiao-lung*. It is certain that Chang had this meaning in mind, as well as the literal meanings of the words *wen* and *shih*, "literary art" and "historical writing." But Chang sometimes seems to treat these as inclusive categories involving the entire world of writing. We will later find him trying to grasp the development of "literary art" as essentially personal and emotive writing, and contrasting it with writing (best exemplified by the work of the historian) that is objective, factual, and severe. It is likely that he had read and remembered the biographies, in the *Old Tang History* (*Chiu T'ang Shu*), of Liu Chih-chi and his fellow historians; their biographer praised them as men "whose learning joined together the realms of Heaven and of Man, whose literary talent embraced both *wen* and *shih*," whose talent was, in other words, all-encompassing. Perhaps Chang, in applying a name to his life's work, was influenced at least subconsciously by this encomium of Liu. If this is so, was Chang's attitude toward Liu one of identification or rivalry? Or was it both?[7]

Another letter Chang wrote early in 1773 to a friend in Peking will show something of the nature of the problems he was wrestling with:

As time flies on, I am daily getting through more and more in my reading. As I go through it carefully, my understanding grows apace and my preoccupation with data subsides more and more. I thought I would cull out the essence of my reflections and make up a study of bibliography [*chiao-ch'ou*]; so I studied the writings of Pan Ku, Liu Hsiang, and Liu Hsin, reasoning back from them to Chou institutions, and I examined the *Wen-hsin Tiao-lung* and the *Shih T'ung*; I have analyzed and distinguished between assertions and facts, and have classified and evaluated divergent traditions, and have written a *Wen-shih T'ung-i*."[a]

Chang's mention of his *Wen-shih T'ung-i* in this report is probably less significant than his mention of work in the field of bibli-

[a] HY, p. 29. Chang's intention to develop these ideas in a book can be traced back at least to 1770, when he was in Peking with Chu Yün. In the fall of that year

ography (for Chang, *chiao-ch'ou* will turn out to have much more meaning than bibliography in the pedestrian sense). At this time Chang was undoubtedly working on his *Chiao-ch'ou T'ung-i,* which he finished in 1779. What Chang was attempting, we shall see, was a free-ranging historical study of books and the traditions of writing and learning to which they belong, a study that was to be somehow at the same time both explanatory and critical.

That Chang, even at this early date, should have groped for almost indefinable concepts in order to describe his work and interests shows something important about his image of himself. In 1790 or 1791, Chang wrote to his sons in a self-appraising mood. His own intellectual interests and talents, he said, were quite different from those of other educated men of his time. The others were all absorbed in the study of minute details—the meaning of terms, phonetics, orthography, etc.—and they were good at it. He was not good at it, and he knew it; and although he gave his fellow scholars their due, he really couldn't be interested. "The things I do," he says, "are things no one else in the world does." Genuine literary art has indeed some devotees; but "as for the true prin-

---

Chu served as provincial examiner in Fukien and while en route sent Chang a poem from Shantung:

> I have wanted to forget my affection for you a little [by finding
> other friends to talk with], but I have had no time yet for this;
> Truly, I still have countless attachments in the capital.
> You were much vexed with Feng's prejudices about *wen-shih;*
> He never would accept any of the insights of the Lius.
> Since setting out from the city of Yen [Peking] I have had few
> friends to drink with me;
> On my journey to Min [Fukien] I am separated from home
> and think fondly of my library.
> I have trusted you to watch over it and shake out any stray
> bookworms;
> Do you perhaps have in mind writing an immortal work?

"Feng" I assume to be Chang's fellow-student, Feng T'ing-cheng (Chang was actually very fond of him) and "the Lius" are clearly the Han court bibliographers, Liu Hsiang and Liu Hsin, whose ideas are the basis of many of Chang's speculations in his *Chiao-ch'ou T'ung-i.* It would appear that these "insights of the Lius" were persistently defended by Chang in Chu's circle of students in Peking (WTJ, p. 254).

ciples of historical study and the essential method of *chiao-ch'ou,*
these are all things men have never dealt with before, and there
have not even been terms to denote them." A friend was once
asked, Chang relates, "What field my work really belongs to," and
the friend had to answer that he didn't know—not because he actually didn't, but "because he genuinely understood that the essential flavor of these things is hard to discuss with others." Even to
his fellow scholars, then, Chang's ideas were not simple. His mind
was indeed the mind of no ordinary man; he was different, even
odd, and he knew it.[8]

Chang's interest in the theory of bibliography at this time has a
larger significance. In the winter of 1772 the court had first issued
its appeal for rare books; in response, Chu Yün had made his his-
toric proposals for the collecting and cataloging of books and the
copying of lost texts from the huge unprinted Ming encyclopedia,
Yung-lo Ta-tien. It is quite likely that the ideas expressed in these
proposals grew out of discussions with Chang, Shao, and others in
Chu's circle. Indeed, one biographer gives Chang himself entire
credit for these ideas. Chu's proposals led in the spring of 1773 to
the formation of a board of scholars charged by the throne with
the task of compiling a large manuscript library for the Emperor's
use, the *Ssu-k'u Ch'uan-shu* (Complete Library in Four Branches
of Literature, i.e., Classics, history, philosophy, and literary collections, the general classification scheme used by most Chinese bibliographers). To this board, Shao, Tai Chen, and another friend of
Chang's, the bibliophile and Confucian Buddhist Chou Yung-nien
(1730–91), were appointed. Chang, not yet having attained even
the *chü-jen* degree, was passed over; but Shao Chin-han shortly
became associate editor for history, and in the course of his work
turned to the Ming encyclopedia, resurrecting from it the lost *Old
History of the Five Dynasties* (*Chiu Wu Tai Shih*). It seems likely
that Chang continued to have at least an indirect influence on the
project. Chu Yün was a connoisseur of books (fourteen works were
copied into the collection from his own private library), and he saw
the compilation as a valuable and necessary task, not realizing that

the throne would soon use the project as a pretext for a vast literary inquisition. It may have been that one of Chu's motives for initiating the *Ssu-k'u* project was the hope of providing employment for some of his promising protégés. A man like Chu, with the inclination and means to play the patron on a small scale, would probably attract more scholars than he could support. At any rate, we find Chang spending more and more time with Feng T'ing-ch'eng in Ning-po, and in the spring of 1773, writing to a friend that he was in difficult circumstances and looking into the possibility of a clerkship at the capital.[9]

At about this time, Chu secured for Chang a commission to write a local history for the magistrate of Ho-chou, across the Yangtze from T'ai-p'ing. Chang finished it in 1774. It was the first local history he had done on his own, and he approached it in a consciously theoretical fashion, starting with a statement of rules of compilation. One distinctive device was an appended *wen-cheng* in eight chapters, an innovation in form that he was later to defend theoretically. This was a collection of texts and documents (*wen*) that throw light on (*cheng,* "attest") the history of the locality or are notable as fine writing.

Another unusual feature was an extensive analysis of earlier histories of Ho-chou, with biographies of the compilers. Indeed the entire work must have struck its commissioners as disturbingly odd. For one thing, it was liberally sprinkled with philosophical essays on the history of civilization, in the form of "prefaces" to its various parts. One group of essays (running to some forty pages) stood at the beginning of the section entitled "A Monograph on the Literature of Ho-chou." These essays are particularly interesting because they are an early expression of Chang's philosophy of history and his theory of the history of literature and quite similar to the speculation in his *Chiao-ch'ou T'ung-i.* The work was printed but not distributed. Chu had been removed from his post by the time it was finished, and his successor (narrow-minded man!) objected to the fact that Chang had included little or nothing about an entire subordinate district within Ho-chou.[10]

Chang, having failed to achieve for his work the status of an official local record, set about to preserve those parts that really mattered to him. He cut it down by about one-half and called it *A Synopsis of the History of Ho-chou* (*Ho-chou Chih-yü*). The preface (dated the third month of 1774) is an invaluable statement of Chang's appraisal of himself and his work:

> Cheng Ch'iao [1104–60] had historical understanding but not histori-
> cal learning; Tseng Kung [1019–83] possessed historical learning but
> not historical method; Liu Chih-chi grasped the historical method but
> not the "idea" of history [*shih-i*]; and this was my object in writing
> my *Wen-shih T'ung-i*.[b] Yet I have shown my *T'ung-i* to others, and
> they still have hesitated to read it with confidence, presumably think-
> ing it is mere theory [*k'ung yen,* "empty words"] without any demon-
> stration in reality [*shih-shih,* "actual facts"]. My *Synopsis* in twenty
> sections will give a hint as to how it may be applied, and by inference
> one may see that the *Wen-shih T'ung-i* is not vague and impractical
> theory.[11]

There are repeated indications that Chang was inwardly troubled by his penchant for "empty words" or "mere theory," as his specu-lative generalizations about history and writing would be con-ceived in his day. Here was one way out: a writer could reflect and express his thought, if he had some work of substance and practi-cal value to illustrate and attest to the applicability of his ideas. In Neo-Confucian metaphysical language, if the essential character (*t'i*) of his thought was to be theoretical criticism, he must have a function (*yung*). Chang's *yung* was to be historical writing.

---

[b] Chang's conception of his difference with Liu Chih-chi is restated in just these terms in one of his "family letters" in 1790. Perhaps he had in mind a mot ascribed to Chieh Hsi-ssu, the Yüan historian who directed compilation of the histories of Liao, Chin, and Sung. Chieh counseled his staff: "If you wish to grasp the method of writing history, you must first seek the idea of writing history." For this inci-dent, see *Yüan Shih,** 181.17b. (An asterisk after any title indicates *Ssu-pu Ts'ung-k'an* edition, or, for histories, *Po-na* edition.) But for Chieh, as he makes clear, the "idea" is the just appraisal of the moral worth of historical acts. For Chang, I believe, the "idea" of historical writing is an indefinable intuitive notion the historian has of the significance of his material, a significance that cannot be represented by applying a set of formal rules of method. This intuitive "idea" guides the historian in using or modifying the rules as his material demands. See Chapter 8.

In 1773 Chang had two important meetings with Tai Chen. The first of these took place in the summer at Feng T'ing-ch'eng's headquarters in Ning-po, where Chang and Tai were both guests. Tai Chen, who was just past fifty at the time, was then head of the local academy at Chin-hua, Chekiang. He had the distinction of having been one of the five persons selected recently by the Emperor for participation in the *Ssu-k'u* project. He had an impressive list of writings to his credit: two local histories, *Fen-chou Fu-chih* and *Fen-yang Hsien-chih,* 1769 and 1771 respectively; two philosophical works, *Yüan Shan* (*Analysis of Goodness*), 1763 and *Hsü-yen* (*Prolegomena,* criticizing Sung thought), 1773; and a number of works in the field of classical scholarship. Moreover, Tai had been working for many years on a critical study of the famous ancient work on waterways, *Shui-ching Chu,* and was at this time preparing to print it. His work on this text was undoubtedly well known in the circle in which Chang moved, and one may assume that Tai had a reputation as an expert in historical geography.[12]

Chang, as we have seen, had known Tai earlier in Peking and had been much impressed with his insistence on the need for careful study as a prerequisite to genuine understanding. Chang appears to have thought highly of Tai's *Yüan Shan,* perhaps less for its philosophy (which differs significantly from Chang's later abstract thought) than for the fact that it was a piece of philosophy by a philologist, and because it represented a side of Tai that, Chang could tell himself, only he could appreciate.[13]

Now, however, Chang's first attempts at writing had begun to crystallize his own distinctive point of view toward history and letters. Tai dazzled the Feng household with his verbal brilliance and display of learning, but Chang was not impressed. The differences between them ranged from the relatively trivial to the most fundamental. Tai made light of the cult of literary expression (which Chang, who had labored long at it, regarded as equal in importance to philological scholarship) and claimed that he had taught himself to write in a few days; Chang upheld Sung orthodoxy in philosophy and saw Tai as the representative par excellence of modern "fashions" in learning. Tai, for his part, flatly declared Chu Hsi to be out of date.[14]

But it was chiefly on the subject of local historiography that they first disagreed. In a conversation that took place at Ning-po, Chang showed his just-written "Rules of Compilation" for his projected Ho-chou history to Tai, who scoffed at the idea that a "gazetteer" was important enough to merit any special attention to form and said that in his own local histories he had simply followed the usual way of writing without trying to be different. He objected, too, to Chang's emphasis on literary matters, arguing that a local history need merely concern itself with the details of historical geography. Chang, however, vigorously defended his concept of the local history as a true historical work and a document of contemporary significance and usefulness. It is to be compared, he said, with the ancient *kuo-shih,* the histories of feudal states in the Chou era, and should not be considered merely a specialized work in geography.[15]

Furthermore, Chang argued, the details of the earlier history of a locality can always be checked from other books; they are less important to the compiler than primary historical evidence, such as the recollections of living persons and unprinted documents that are bound to disappear with time. "Historical writings in general," he said, "treat the recent past in detail and the remote past briefly; this is not true only of local histories"; and he supported his contention with examples. Indeed, if earlier local histories had been done properly, each new one could be a continuation of the preceding one. As it is, however, the scope of such a work usually must include the past three or four centuries. But mere delving into antiquities is not its function. "The aim of the compiler of a local history," Chang maintained, "should not be to produce something pleasing to look at, but something actually useful; since times differ and situations change, old histories of a locality cannot include everything one may look for, and so there should be a new one compiled every thirty to one hundred years."[16] Chang, it would seem, conceived a local history to be not merely a description or explanation of historical changes but a description of the present institutional and social situation viewed with a certain historical depth.

This argument was a relatively early expression of Chang's belief in the importance of the present to the student of history. But the argument exhibits an obvious failure of sophistication. It provides us with no reason why history should be rewritten rather than merely extended. Chang is not yet prepared to admit that among the changes that occur with time are changes in the interests, insights, and values of historians and their readers. True, "times differ and situations change." But the new situations, Chang thinks, simply lead us to want information about these new situations. They do not seem to produce a new understanding of the importance and significance of what has already happened.

The second meeting of the two occurred later in Hang-chou, when Chang sat in on a conversation between Tai, a certain Wu Ying-fang (1701–81), and others.[c] Here, the subject of discussion was the *T'ung Chih* (*General History*) by Cheng Ch'iao (1104–60). Tai criticized it as unscholarly, and was supported by most of those present, the consensus being that it was distinctly inferior to Ma Tuan-lin's thirteenth-century political encyclopedia, *Wen-hsien T'ung-k'ao*. Chang took sanguine exception to the course of the argument. In his reading and thinking on bibliography, out of which the *Chiao-ch'ou T'ung-i* was growing, he was coming to regard Cheng as very significant. He expressed these thoughts, directed at Tai though not mentioning him by name, in an essay entitled "In Defense of Cheng Ch'iao" ("Shen Cheng").[d] The question of the relative merits of Cheng and Ma, the first standing in Chang's mind for true history concerned essentially with "mean-

---

[c] Wu Ying-fang was a well-to-do gentleman who had shunned the examinations and official preferment to devote himself to poetry, music, and archaeology. See Arthur Waley, *Yuan Mei: Eighteenth Century Chinese Poet* (London, 1956), p. 173.

[d] *I-shu*, 4.42b, "Answers to Objections, I," 1790; the essay "In Defense of Cheng Ch'iao" (*I-shu*, 4.40a–42b, of uncertain date) was apparently first conceived as a comment on Tai's preface to his "Hsü T'ien-wen Lüeh" ("Monograph on Astronomy"), which was prepared as part of the imperially sponsored *Hsü T'ung Chih* but not accepted for inclusion in that work; see Tai's *nien-p'u*, p. 36a–b, in *Tai Tung-yüan Chi.** In this preface Tai is quite critical of Cheng.

ing," and the second for mere encyclopedism concerned with dead facts, became almost an obsession with Chang and was later to provoke some of his most interesting philosophical and historical thinking. These encounters with Tai must have greatly stimulated Chang. A number of important essays, written over the next twenty years, deal with points of difference with Tai, some of which were first introduced in the conversations at Ning-po and Hang-chou.

In the ninth month Chu Yün was demoted from his Anhwei post and transferred to the *Ssu-k'u* board. The *Ho-chou Chih* was finished the next year (1774), and Chang found himself without support. In the autumn he went to Hang-chou to attempt and fail once more the provincial examination, and then on to Ning-po to spend the winter with Feng T'ing-ch'eng. In the spring, Feng was transferred to Formosa and his literary circle dispersed. Chang stayed for a while in his native K'uai-chi, but turned up again in Peking in the fall of 1775. He was no longer in the quarters rented from Feng; he had (apparently in absentia) moved his family twice since those days, and he now moved them again to an even humbler location, for his household was poorer.[17]

One can only guess how he was able to maintain his family during his long absence (which was not to be the last) in the provinces. Presumably he forwarded to his dependents much of the income he received in Anhwei. For the present, there were means of support in the capital that he may have depended upon: recompense for an occasional biography or epitaph, or pay for an informal bit of editorial piecework, perhaps from imperially sponsored projects of compilation and scholarship.

In 1777, after the family's circumstances had improved a little, a writer named Lo Yu-kao (d. 1779), to whom Shao Chin-han had shown some of Chang's essays, called at his house, eager to make his acquaintance. Chang was out of town, but his mother sent her seventeen-year-old grandson I-hsüan to acknowledge Lo's courtesy. Lo, noticing the boy's frayed clothing, gave him a hundred coppers. When Chang came back, he returned Lo's call at once, and

the two spent a long cold winter's evening talking around a bra-
zier. For some things, indigence made no difference. Chang even
managed occasionally (incurable scholar's addiction!) to buy just
one more book.[18]

The capital was now thronging with talented persons, for the
Ssu-k'u board was in the midst of its collecting and editorial activities. Chang's connections with it were close; Chu Yün, Chou
Yung-nien, and Shao Chin-han were all members. Shih Ch'ao
(1729–77), who had been a proctor in the Imperial Academy when
Chang worked on the *Academy Monograph,* was also one of this
distinguished group. Shih Ch'ao's office was, until his death, a favorite retreat for Chang and some of his close friends.[19]

Later Chang rather acidly described the capital milieu at this
time in his biography of Chou Yung-nien:

I came to Peking in 1775, . . . and at this time talented men from all
around were coming to the capital with notebooks in hand and with
extravagant notions of making discoveries and doing research in the
imperial libraries. Those who submitted writings to high officials [in
hopes of patronage] usually no longer claimed skill in poetry and examination-essay writing, but claimed instead to be expert in philology,
text-criticism, "phonetics," or "ideography," trotting along with changing popular fashion.[20]

In a later biography (of Shao Chin-han) Chang wrote of the
intellectual activity in the capital at this time and of the current
trends in historiography, which he found deplorable. The admiration for Ma Tuan-lin, who confused "completeness in every detail"
with "meaning," and for Wang Ying-lin (1223–96), who confused
the search for lost texts and mere industriousness with true learning, represented to Chang different aspects of the sin against understanding. Chang and Shao agreed that the later Standard Histories were the most deplorable examples of these intellectual errors;
they were inferior in literary quality, conveyed nothing of the
meaning of historical events, and exhibited no sense of selection
in the presentation of data. Shao, judging the *Sung Shih (The History of the Sung Dynasty)* to be the most flagrant example of un-

warranted length and complexity, resolved to write a history of the Sung according to proper principles.[21]

In 1776 Chang had been appointed sub-archivist in the Imperial Academy. This "appointment," however, was purely a formality (though he was still using the title in his signature as late as 1794). It did not solve Chang's economic problems. Chang needed a new patron, and so, with this in mind and with introductions from Chu Yün and others in hand, he approached a certain Chou Chen-jung (1730–92). Chou was from Chekiang, and although he was at this time only a minor official in Chihli, he would become magistrate of Yung-ch'ing district later in the year.[22]

Chang had some reason to hope that his name was already known to this man. In Anhwei Chang (or more likely Chu Yün) had sent the manuscript of Chang's *Ho-chou Chih* to Chou. But it had failed to engage Chou's attention; he had lost it, and Chang had been unable to resurrect all of it from other copies. Chang was now introduced to him in person, and Chou arranged a banquet to which some of the intermediaries in the proceedings were invited. Some of Chang's other manuscripts were produced and passed around at the banquet, but Chou didn't look at them until they were specifically called to his attention. In spite of this awkward beginning, the two somehow became close friends. In the spring of 1777 Chang obtained, through Chou, the headship of Ting-wu Academy in Ting-chou and a commission to compile a history of Yung-ch'ing. This was the beginning of more than a decade of teaching positions for Chang. Most of them were in Chihli and within easy reach of Peking, which he frequently visited.[23]

In the fall of 1777 Chang went to Peking to take the provincial examination and won at last the elusive *chü-jen* degree. The chief examiner was Liang Kuo-chih (1723–87), a native of Shan-yin, Chekiang, and at this time one of the highest and busiest officials in the capital; he held concurrently the positions of Grand Councillor, president of the Board of Revenue, and personal secretary to the Emperor. Liang disliked the conservative, unreflective quality of prevailing classical scholarship, and had therefore assigned in the examination some questions of general scope and historical import. He was delighted with Chang's paper, and congratulated him personally when he discovered that Chang was a native of his own town. That meeting was the beginning of a friendship that would prove to be very profitable for Chang, but for the moment he saw only the triumph of the hour. Chang and some of his fellow examinees had met and compared their essays after the exams were over, and he writes with evident relish that few of them had been willing to concede him a chance of passing.[24]

After struggling so long for the provincial degree, Chang passed the *chin-shih* (metropolitan) examination on his first attempt in the spring of 1778. He made a call at the Imperial Academy to pay his respects to his teachers there, and an old clerk congratulated him warmly. Chang must have recalled with grim satisfaction those bitter years when as a mere *chien-sheng* he had stood perennially at the bottom of the lists.[e] Chang was forty-one the year he passed the metropolitan examination. His mother died that year; she had lived just long enough to share her son's triumphs.

By now Chang had acquired a certain reputation, as much for his opinionated and argumentative nature as for his literary talent. The impression Chang made upon others in Chu Yün's circle may be guessed at from a recollection of a fellow *chin-shih* of 1778, Li Wei. Li wrote that "master Chu's student Chang Hsüeh-ch'eng ... would talk like a bubbling fountain, and master Chu enjoyed conversing with him. Chang would joke in a manner quite out of place for a *ti-tzu*, and when onlookers were surprised, Chu smiled and did not think it strange." (The term *ti-tzu* is usually rendered "disciple," which is accurate enough except for its Galilean flavor.)

---

[e] HY, pp. 36–42. WHL, p. 260. In 1796 (*I-shu*, 29.66b), Chang wrote to Wang Hui-tsu, reflecting, "It was my fate that I did not obtain the degree until after forty. In all, I sat for examinations seven times." The seven occasions (including both provincial and metropolitan examinations) were 1760, 1762, 1765, 1768, 1774, 1777, and 1778. In the *chin-shih* examination of 1778, Chang ranked fifty-first in the second class. This made him fifty-fourth in a total passing list of 157. Others passing in the same examination were Li Wei (see below), who ranked above Chang, and two friends important in Chang's later life, Chang Wei-ch'i and Ch'en Shih, both of whom ranked below him.

Chu, apparently, so loved the company of interesting people that he would put up with anything to keep them coming to his home. Li Wei says that he himself could become quarrelsome and maudlin with drink without angering his host. Chu's friends came, in fact, in such numbers that the doorkeeper could not keep up with them, and it was understood that anyone could enter unannounced. Even late at night, after the guests were gone, Chu would call in his students and his two sons and settle down for more wine, refreshments, and talk.[25]

An incident on Chu's fiftieth birthday illustrates further the informal atmosphere of his establishment. Chang had written a literary piece in honor of the occasion. Chu looked it over and nodded approval. Chang said boldly, "With your permission, sir, if I live to a ripe old age I could also write an epitaph for you!" Chu laughed. "All right. But the human lot is unpredictable. You might die before I do, and then I could write a fine epitaph for you!" The conversation is recorded in the epitaph that Chang ultimately did write for his teacher.[26]

Other friends of Chang's were often treated to this irreverent side of his character. In Peking in the spring of 1788 to take the metropolitan examination, he frequently went to see his former supporter Feng T'ing-ch'eng.[f] At Feng's, Chang occasionally met his new friend Lo Yu-kao, who like Chou Yung-nien was both a Confucian scholar and an ardent Buddhist, given to fasting and learned conversation with monks in mountain temples. Chang made mischievous fun of Lo's religious vegetarianism: "Buddhists say that when a man dies he may become a sheep, and that when a sheep dies it may become a man. Do you believe that in your next life you'll be punished by becoming what you eat?" Lo admitted he did. Chang pursued, "Then if a poor man wants to get rich, all he has to do is kill and rob a wealthy merchant, or if a person of low status wants honors, all he has to do is to assassinate

---

[f] Feng T'ing-ch'eng had been incriminated for failure to investigate a case of alleged sedition in the literary inquisition in Kiangsi and had been imprisoned in Peking. At this time he had just been pardoned (HY, p. 42).

a high official, and through karma he'll become a rich or high-ranking person in his next life." And whenever Lo and his friends were involved in a serious discussion of religion, Chang would interrupt with a jest and turn the talk into laughter. In his reflective writing, to be sure, he offers more tolerant and reasonable criticisms of Buddhism.[27]

At this point in his life, Chang had reason to feel self-assured. "My friends," he writes, "were all persons of importance, and within a year's time my name was twice presented to the Emperor; I was generally regarded as fortunate."[28] The picture we have of Chang at this time is that of a man in early middle age, transformed from a discouraged and uncertain student into a writer with a strong faith in his own ideas and a certainty that he would produce something of lasting value. Looking back into his writings of this time, we can see that the central ideas in all of his later thinking were rapidly taking shape.

3. Books about Books

The Six Canons perished and became the *Seven Summaries*; this was because officials failed to preserve what was in their charge. The *Seven Summaries* perished and became the Four Categories; this was because teachers failed to preserve their traditions.

—*The History of Ho-chou* ... 1774

In the decade through which we have just followed Chang Hsüeh-ch'eng, we have seen him striking out more and more boldly in his thinking. We have seen him forming an image of himself as a person with profound ideas; ideas that others would be sure to misunderstand and reject as shocking. And we have seen him reinforcing this image by becoming more and more argumentative, more and more ready to question accepted views, willing, perhaps needing, to be outrageous.

This was a productive time for Chang, for in spite of the demands of the examinations, he was writing. He mentions a book of essays. There was the Ho-chou history in 1774. And in 1779, in spite of a serious illness, he completed the *Chiao-ch'ou T'ung-i*. This book works out, in technical detail, ideas that Chang had written on at length (and rather inappropriately) in his history of Ho-chou. It is a theoretical work, ostensibly on the unpromising subject of bibliography; in other words, it is a book about books—how to analyze and catalog them, after comparing texts to determine questions of authenticity, authorship, and completeness. Certainly it is this, but it is also in tight and systematic form a presentation of Chang's most fundamental theses on the philosophy of history and the criticism of literature and scholarship. It is a basic statement of his philosophical position as far as it had developed at this time. As we examine this statement, we may begin to feel that Chang's image of himself was not unrealistic.

The *Chiao-ch'ou T'ung-i* has an unusual history. It is likely from indications in Chang's correspondence that the book had been developing in his mind and in his notes for half a dozen years. Many of its central ideas appear, even to the exact words, in his Ho-chou history, in the long series of prefaces to the chapter on bibliography. Originally it had four chapters rather than the present three and was entitled "Chiao-ch'ou Lüeh" ("Summary on the Study of Books") after a chapter in Cheng Ch'iao's *T'ung Chih,* which Chang much admired. The book, in its original form, was stolen, then partially reconstructed from other copies, and in 1788 completely revised. In that year Chang asked his friends to return all existing partial copies—apparently he had given little thought to the book for almost a decade—and set about to restore a continuous text, only to find that his friends' copies often contradicted one another. Unable to reconcile these contradictions, he proceeded to edit freely, so that the final result was "quite different" from the varied originals.[1]

Nevertheless, Chang's aim in 1788 seems to have been to make the book say, whenever possible, what it had said in 1779, and the ideas and attitudes it expresses do fit reasonably well into the context of that phase of his life. His work was consciously modeled on Cheng Ch'iao's monograph, which in turn had been a critical reaction to the compilation of the Sung imperial catalog, *Ch'ung-wen Tsung-mu.* Chang's own work was surely stimulated in much the same way by the *Ssu-k'u Ch'üan-shu* and its catalog, compiled between 1772 and 1780.

The *Chiao-ch'ou T'ung-i,* as I have said, was a development of what were for Chang the most important parts of the *Ho-chou Chih.* In this chapter, I shall first describe briefly the contents of the *Chiao-ch'ou T'ung-i* and the relevant parts of the *Ho-chou Chih.* I shall then discuss the concepts of cultural history central to these two works, as much as possible in Chang's own words. I shall also explain the origins of these concepts and show their philosophical possibilities. Then I shall consider Chang's method of bibliographical analysis and his central concept of *chia* (fam-

ily), i.e., a school or genre of writing and learning. This will lead
to an examination of certain philosophical difficulties in this concept that have important consequences as Chang's thought develops later. Finally, I shall take up two important organizational
recommendations Chang makes in his *Chiao-ch'ou T'ung-i* and
discuss their significance.

The Ho-chou Chih and the Chiao-ch'ou T'ung-i

The structure of Chang's Ho-chou history was a modification of
the standard-history form.[2] It included a number of "monographs,"
which in the Standard Histories are normally called *chih*, but
which Chang called *shu*, following the *Shih-chi* (*Record of a Historian*) by Ssu-ma Ch'ien (c. 145–86 B.C.). One of these, probably
the longest, was a "Monograph on Literature" ("I-wen Shu"). The
precedent for this section was the "I-wen Chih" in Pan Ku's *History of the Former Han Dynasty* (*Ch'ien Han Shu*), an abridg-
ment of the now lost catalog of the Han Imperial Library by the
court bibliographer Liu Hsin. The original work was called the
Seven Summaries (*Ch'i Lüeh*). These seven summaries were (1)
a "Collective Summary" discussing the remaining six, which was
not preserved by Pan Ku (another opinion, not accepted by Chang,
was that it was broken up by Pan and distributed among the other
six);[3] (2) a "Summary of the Classics" and the books about them;
(3) a "Summary of the Schools of Philosophy"; (4) a "Summary
of *Fu* and Poetry"; (5) a "Summary of the Books on Military Art";
(6) a "Summary of the Calculating Arts" (astrology, divination,
geomancy, etc.); and (7) a "Summary of Techniques" (medicine,
the art of sex, etc.). Chang Hsüeh-ch'eng's "Monograph on Literature" followed this scheme within the limits imposed by the works
of the writers of Ho-chou. The monograph was introduced by a
preface; only the preface, "Collective Summary," and fragments
of the "Summary of the Classics" remain today.

Chang's preface is a collection of five short essays: (1) "On the
Tao" ("Yüan Tao") explains how writing began and evolved in
antiquity and the implications of this for the bibliographer today.
(2) "Understanding [What] Time [Determines]" ("Ming Shih")

discusses changes in bibliographic conventions since antiquity, their causes in the history of learning and their evil effects on literature. (3) "Restoring Antiquity" ("Fu Ku") argues that bibliographers should scrap the Four Categories (Classics, histories, philosophers, and collections) and return to Liu Hsin's system of six. (4) "The Disciplines of Schools" ("Chia Fa") exhorts bibliographers to sort writings and authors into the "schools" to which they belong and to trace these schools back to antiquity. (5) "A Standard for Local Histories" ("Li Chih") gives reasons why local histories and local government should be concerned with bibliography. The *Ho-chou Chih* contains another innovation that was important to its author: a section in the "Biographies" devoted to earlier Ho-chou histories and historians. This section has a preface of three brief essays, in which Chang argues that historians should be treated in the pages of a history as belonging to a distinct school of learning, and should not be placed in the same category with other literary men; this, he says, will revitalize the tradition of historiography.

The *Chiao-ch'ou T'ung-i* is, of course, much longer than the Ho-chou prefaces and very systematically presented; each of the three chapters is divided into named and numbered sections, which are in turn subdivided into numbered paragraphs. The first chapter presents Chang's very general principles for the science of "bibliography." It starts with a brief essay "On the Tao," which contains a bare set of historical theses on the origin of writing and learning, and continues with a longer essay, "In Honor of Liu." The remainder of the chapter presents more technical matter. Some of it, such as the desirability of cross-referencing, had already been proposed in the *Ho-chou Chih*; but some of it is quite new and startling.

In the first part of the second chapter Chang criticizes the organization and coverage of Liu Hsin's bibliography; in spite of his great reverence for Liu, he is quite ready to take him to task. Then, in the next two sections, he turns around and refutes the criticisms of Liu made by Cheng Ch'iao (who, as Chang notes, had a blindness to the value of much of Liu's work because of his well-known hostility to Pan Ku) and by the Ming bibliographer, Chiao Hung.[a]

The final chapter contains a section on each of Liu Hsin's substantive six summaries. Here Chang refines Liu's system by proposing an occasional reclassification, double entry, or cross-reference; but he also often anticipates ideas about the Classics and the history of literature that he will deal with in later essays.

Concepts of Cultural History

The essay "On the Tao" in the *Chiao-ch'ou T'ung-i* continues an argument that was first advanced in "On the Tao" in the *Ho-chou Chih*. Chang begins at the beginning; in his mind is the sketch of the history of civilization in the *Classic of Changes*:[4]

In the most ancient times there was no writing. Government records were at first kept by knotting cords, and only later were written symbols used. The sages, explaining the use of these devices, said, "In this way all the officials were kept in order and all the people were kept under observation." Of course, keeping order and keeping informed, so as to bring to light anything hidden and to communicate rules and standards, were things that had to be done. If writing was adequate for this that was enough. But as government became more complex and problems more numerous ... the sages established different offices and divided responsibilities among them, and written language came to be organized accordingly.[b] With offices came laws, and so the laws were embodied in the offices. With laws came books, and so each office preserved its own books. With books came learning, and so teachers perpetuated this learning. With learning came professional traditions, and so disciples practiced these professions. The offices, their special functions, the learning, and the professions all had a single source, and government in the empire consisted in a unity of letters. Since there were no writings of private parties, it followed that the divisions of administrative responsibility corresponded to the divisions within bibliography, and there was never any system of bibliography apart from this.

Writings of later times must be traced back to the Six Arts. The Six Arts are not the books of Confucius, but are actually the old statutes of

---

[a] Author of *Kuo-shih Ching-chi-chih*, an important bibliography covering the Ming Dynasty.
[b] I have translated "principles got bigger" as "government became more complex." That this was Chang's meaning is made clear in the fourth paragraph of "On the Tao" (1789).

the offices of Chou. The *Changes* was kept by the grand diviner, the *History* by the annalist of the exterior, the *Rites* by the master of ceremonies, the *Music* by the minister of music, the *Odes* by the grand music-master, and the *Spring and Autumn Annals* by the recorders of the states. Confucius himself said that he was merely transmitting and not creating, for he understood that government offices had failed to preserve the learning that was their charge, and that the traditional professions of teachers and disciples had decayed. The Ch'in empire forbade idle discussion of the *Odes* and the *History,* and announced that those who wished to study the laws should take the officials as their teachers. It was wrong for Ch'in to cast aside the *Odes* and the *History,* but its rule that officials should be teachers recalled the old unity of official function with learned professions. From this position of Ch'in, let us visualize then the age when the Three Dynasties were flourishing: for the *Rites,* the master of ceremonies was teacher; for the *Music,* the minister of music was teacher; for the *Odes,* the grand music-master was teacher; for the *History,* the annalist of the exterior was teacher, and the *Three Changes* and the *Spring and Autumn* were simply handled in like fashion. How could there then be any writings of private parties?[5]

We can identify three steps in Chang's thinking in these sections. Each step allows certain inferences about literary value. First, he assumes that writing had not always existed, and that its origin was official and functional: it came into existence in response to needs, which were, significantly, governmental ones. With this notion is an implicit conception of the historical process as an evolutionary development (also in response to needs) of political and cultural institutions. Writings, Chang thinks, are good when they are produced in response to needs; he will have much more to say about this in later years.

Second, Chang sketches a distinctive conception of the classical past. And for him, as for almost all Confucians, classical antiquity embodies values that make it a reproach to the present, if not actually a model for it. Chang's classical world was an undivided whole, completely state-centered. Since everything evolved out of one beginning, Chang feels that the functional, governmental, *active* aspect of the human order must have been at one time institutionally indistinguishable from its traditional, cultural, *know-*

ing aspect: "Officials were teachers." *Knowledge* was specialized
in an office, and it and its propagation were inseparable from the
activities of the official who was master of that office. It would seem
to follow that it is of the nature of knowledge to be specialized,
and that knowledge is only valid when it is connected with
or authenticated by the state. In a phrase he does not yet use,
but will use later, "government (*chih*) and teaching (*chiao*) were
identical." Chang's ancient unity, though he himself does not describe it explicitly in these terms, we can see to be, in effect, a
"unity of knowledge and action" given historical expression.
Chang states in his Ho-chou history that this unity of the ancient
order brought with it both esthetic and moral perfection: "The
tao and the arts were kept in balance; virtue and conduct were
kept in accord." Chang therefore smiles on the authority of the
state. His curious left-handed praise of the authoritarian Ch'in
Dynasty appears again and again in later essays. "Government
through a uniformity of letters" is not only beautiful and good but
proper: learning that was not preserved by the "official-teachers"
was not lawful, he says in his Ho-chou history. Even Confucius,
when studying the rituals, had to consult the proper official at the
Chou court (i.e., Lao Tzu).[e]

Consequently there were no private writings, no private schools
of doctrine. The Classics, therefore, have to be thought of not as
books of the ordinary sort, written by an author to expound his
knowledge and his ideas, but as documentary remnants of the ancient state. To maintain this characterization of them, Chang distinguishes severely, in the third chapter of his *Chiao-ch'ou T'ung-i,*
between the basic Six Classics, i.e., the remains of the Six Arts, and
other writings in the Confucian canon, such as the *Li Chi* and the
Lun Yü, that are only "traditional" Confucian teachings (*chuan*).
From this conception of the Classics, Chang will draw conclusions
of the greatest importance.[e]

The writer, when he tries simply to be an author, produces that
which is unlike the Classics; because he does what is unnecessary,

---

[e] *I-shu,* 12.1a–b. The same distinction between *ching* and *chuan* is expounded in
Chang's later "Explanation of the Classics" ("Ching Chieh"), 1789; *I-shu,* 1.36a.

he separates himself from the whole of things, from what is real and valuable. This is the third direction Chang's thought takes in "On the Tao." Somehow—and Chang never explains this discontinuity—after the Classical Age the entire knowing side of human life was separated from its active side: officials ceased to be teachers. The ancient state fell to pieces, "offices ceased to preserve their traditions," and learning, now alienated from government, became private property: "the regulations in government offices came to be distinct from the professions of teachers and scholars, and eventually each man wrote his own writings and each school had its own theories." Consequently, writing and learning entered a long decline. But, Chang suggests, we can at least see what has happened, and perhaps do something about it, if we can distinguish the origin of each kind of writing and learning. This, then, is the job of the bibliographer, and it is clear at once that bibliography performs far more than a mere technical service for the world of letters.

Once writing was no longer connected with the state, Chang says in the Ho-chou history, it became scattered and disorganized. Therefore, some scheme of bibliographical classification had to be devised. But only the Han court bibliographers, Liu Hsiang and his son Liu Hsin, had the insight to approach bibliography by tracing traditions back to the age when "government was a unity of letters," seeing in each genre a corruption of some official tradition; these insights, Chang's *Chiao-ch'ou T'ung-i* tells us, must be largely inferred from the bare suggestions that remain:

When Pan Ku adapted Liu Hsin's *Seven Summaries,* he took out the "Collective Summary" and preserved the other six. Yen Shih-ku says the "Collective Summary" discussed the general principles of all books, and we may therefore assume that in it Liu analyzed the essentials of bibliography. This would have been of the greatest philosophical interest, but, unhappily, the text was not preserved. All that can now be seen are the few words, at the end of the summary of each section, which analyze the course of development of that particular branch of writing. From what we can see in these few words, it is apparent that Liu Hsin had a profound understanding of the ancient principle of the identity of official and teacher, and was able to see why at first there were no writings of private parties. How so? Because when he finishes with the Six Arts and then discusses the schools of philosophy, he always says such-and-such a school probably originated in the learning kept by such-and-such an ancient office, which evolved into the learning of such-and-such a person, and declined, becoming the corrupt doctrine of such-and-such a person.[7]

If the Lius' procedure were generally followed, then the connections between even trivial and base writings and the "great *tao*" could be brought out. People could then determine just what these writings are worth, and ancient learning could be restored. Indeed, only in this way can one, with Han Yü, "distinguish between the valid and the false in writings of old," or with Mencius, "understand words" (i.e., diagnose the moral illness behind bad writing), or with Confucius, "choose and attend to the good among the many things one hears."[8]

In short, the work of the bibliographer is the basis of all criticism. His procedure, Chang thinks, must be to assign correctly each piece of writing to the school (*chia*, "family") to which it belongs, tracing each school back to its beginnings in the Chou political order and identifying the "method" or discipline (*chia-fa*) to which each type of writing should adhere:

The fact that *chia-fa* is not clear is the reason for the continual decline of writing; the fact that classification is not refined is the reason why scholarship daily becomes more disorganized. If we could take the existing system of the Four Categories and analyze the evolution of types of writing in it, in order to make perfectly clear their origins in the ancients' identification of officials and teachers, then the ills of literature could be somewhat remedied.[9]

This is the real task before the student of books. Yet all we have, Chang complains, are men who display wide but shallow learning, or men who pride themselves on making this or that little philological point.[d]

The Origins of Chang's Ideas

There is serious philosophical mischief in this method of Chang's. To uncover this mischief, one must look more carefully

---

[d] Chang presses this criticism of Ch'ing philology by insisting that scholars no longer understand what *chiao-ch'ou* really is. Liu Hsiang explained it as a meta-

at Chang's concept of a school and see how he uses it. We will be better able to do this when we see more exactly what his central ideas are. To do this and to grasp the dynamics of his thought, we must ask where Chang got his ideas, and what he does with them ultimately.

Chang had not always thought what he thought in 1774 and 1779. Writing to Chen Sung-nien in 1764, he expressed a somewhat different conception of the Classics. He assigned the *Changes* to the grand diviner, but at this time it was "simply a book of philosophy." The other Classics were books official historians kept and used; Chang did not assign them to the different Chou offices as he does now. They were not the documents in Chang's present theory of the "identity of officials and teachers" in a completely holistic ancient world. In Chang's correspondence with Chen this conception of antiquity is quite absent.

Now, the assignment of the Classics to Chou offices is the same sort of contrivance we find in Liu Hsin and Pan Ku. In the Han "monograph," however, it is not the Classics but the several schools of "philosophy" that are traced back to offices of the Chou state. Chang plainly thought of his own view of the Classics as an extension of Liu's idea about schools of philosophy and as an improvement on him. In the second chapter of his *Chiao-ch'ou T'ung-i* he chides Liu gently, saying that Liu should have also applied his ideas to the Classics, and should have listed each of the various

---

phorical "battle of enemies": when two scholars are comparing two texts of a book word by word, one will read from one text and the other will break in when he notices a discrepancy in the other (WHL, p. 262b). But, Chang maintained, the Lius understood that the "comparing and correcting of words and phrases" is only an incidental part of *chiao-ch'ou*; it is primarily concerned with using these methods to establish the history of texts, as part of the task of tracing traditions of learning back to their classical sources. This concept died with them; Cheng Ch'iao began to grasp it again; but now only Chang understands. Scholars are now only interested in digging into the meaning of words and phrases. Thus, "If there are old books with chapters out of place or discrepancies in structure that need examination [so that the history of the texts can be gone into] then people will say that in antiquity, bibliography [*mu-lu hsüeh* or text history] was a separate discipline." They will argue "all you need to do with this book is study its meaning. Bibliography has nothing to do with meaning. Why do you need to go into it? Chang ridicules this attitude. "Random Notes" ("Hsin Chih"), *I-shu*, "wai-pien," 1.8b–9a; and WHL, p. 263a.

categories of writing under the Classic from which it derived; Liu
does do this for history, placing it under the *Spring and Autumn
Annals,* but poetry, for example, should have been placed under
the *Odes,* and *yin-yang* philosophy under the *Changes.* The relation between a Classic and its derivatives is essentially that between
the *tao* and *ch'i* (matter).[10] We will see Chang attempting to carry
out this program in his later writings. It is tempting to see Liu
Hsin as the source of Chang's philosophical position, to see Chang
expanding imaginatively on what was implicit in Liu. Chang himself thought this to be the case.

But it was not the case. It is normal to find a Chinese philosopher
"deriving" his thought from some ancient writer, book, or phrase;
this is, however, a cultural compulsion, not a truly derivative process. What actually happens is something much more like reading
ink-blots—or interpreting the hexagrams. For example, Chang, in
his *Ho-chou Chih,* uses a classical Chinese term—*kuan-shih,* "official"—in a perfectly straightforward manner. Then, in "On the
Tao" in that same work, he seems suddenly to notice that if the
word is split in two and each half read separately and literally, one
gets both "official" and "teacher."[11] So ancient officials must really
have been "official-teachers!" But it would surely be absurd to suppose that Chang derived his philosophy from an analysis of the
term for "official."

Actually, Chang's entire vision of antiquity seems to be an affirmation of Chu Yün's ideals of writing. This vision had probably
taken form by 1770, when Chu Yün referred in a poem to Chang's
interest in Liu.[12] It is clear from Chang's correspondence of 1772
that, while in Chu Yün's circle in Anhwei, he was already working out, in his early essays, this idea and related ideas about the
history of literature.[e] It is not necessary to ask why Chang sought
validation for his ideas in antiquity, for this quest was common to

[e] Essays that have probably been lost (see Chapter 4). It is worth noting that one
of the group in T'ai-p'ing in 1772, Wang Chung, defended some unusual theories
on the relationship between government offices and learning in antiquity which are
very similar to Chang's. It is possible that one of the two influenced the other.
Chang later came to dislike Wang Chung intensely. See Chapter 9.

all Chinese philosophers. Why then did Chang seek an ancient society that was so strikingly undivided and state-centered? To understand this we must examine the broader utopian vision that had its roots in the Sung Confucian revival.

This utopian vision saw human society as the perfect family, where each member would play his part without enticements and pressures to advancement, where "men's minds would be composed" in their quest for virtue, where there would be "no corruption of empty words," where none would be subject to "extravagance of speech and composition," and none would "strive for honor and advantage." This ideal envisioned society as a harmonious organic unit (Wang Yang-ming likened it to the "body of a single person"). The ideal was implicitly authoritarian, indeed totalitarian, for in it each one must accept his role completely, and any kind of tension-engendering division, even between the state and society, must be inimical to it.[13]

Confucian utopians believed that such a perfect order existed once, in the ancient, pre-bureaucratic, feudal past, and they wished, in spirit at least, to bring it back. They disagreed on the details of this perfect state, and they were interested in different aspects of it. Some, such as Ou-yang Hsiu in the eleventh century, had wanted most to revitalize ancient rituals and Confucian social values among the people, to bring society back to a state of health and cure it of the "illness" of Buddhism. Some were concerned with refashioning central political institutions, such as the examination system, and some were interested in a personal moral cultivation that would make the individual the sort of person one would find in such a perfect world—Chu Hsi had both of these interests. The court, especially in the last two dynasties, dwelt understandably enough on the authoritarian aspects of the vision: each subject should accept his place without rancor or partisan quarreling (eschewing "private schools" in the political sense). Chang Hsüeh-ch'eng apprehended and reflected this cultural vision in terms of his own interests. He was only indirectly interested in moral self-cultivation and only in rather special ways in institutional reform;

he accepted the state's ideological adaptation of Confucian utopia completely, but only half consciously. He was chiefly concerned with the vision's implications for the life of learning and writing, and it was from this concern that his theory of history and his conception of ancient society would develop. It should be clear that even though his immediate concerns were bibliography and literary value, his thought was always ranging far beyond these interests.

The "unity of knowledge and action" in Wang Yang-ming's moral philosophy in the sixteenth century was a further manifestation of this Neo-Confucian utopian vision. Wang feared that if a man's moral acts do not spring directly from the response of his character to the needs of the situation, he will act for calculated, ulterior, and morally corrupting motives; or he will be morally paralyzed (like King Hsüan of Ch'i in *Mencius*) and not act at all; or still worse he will take pride in this knowledge unrealized in action as a thing in itself. Chang Hsüeh-ch'eng, in identifying institutionally the pursuit of knowledge with the use of knowledge, sees Wang's individual moral problem as a problem for the whole social-political organism.[14] In the Confucian utopia, self-assertion and striving for "gain and fame" are evils. Chang's picture of antiquity already contains this dimension. But he also has an entrenched attitude that could conflict with it. This attitude is revealed not so much in the content of Chang's vision as in the way he reached and defended it. The attitude is the value Chang placed on vision itself. He felt himself to be one who saw things others couldn't see. And as he saw himself, so he saw those with whom he identified. The historian's work, he felt, required unusual qualities, qualities that were intellectual rather than merely literary (this is why historians should have special biographical treatment). Liu Hsin and Cheng Ch'iao he admired as men who had in essence seen what he himself passionately believed to be true. Chang thought that they were men of great insight who had given the world much because they understood things ordinary men could not grasp. Therefore, in Chang's scheme of things there must be room for two apparently contradictory concepts—affirmation of individual genius as a unique and valuable quantity, and denial of the individual ego as a quantity that must be, in the Confucian utopia, submerged in the whole.

Chang's concept of a school responds to both these needs, but it contains another complexity of equal importance. Chang has said that writings should be traced back to their beginnings. The task is to ascertain the essence of a kind of writing, its real nature and value, by grasping its origins. Assigning a book to a *chia,* therefore, is going to have to be both an analytical inquiry and a historical one.

Chang's Method: The School Concept

Chang's method is embedded in still more historical theory. Although the *Chiao-ch'ou T'ung-i* and the Ho-chou preface are close in thought, there is one striking difference. When he wrote the Ho-chou history Chang argued that Liu Hsin's system of classification should be brought back into general use. In the *Chiao-ch'ou T'ung-i* he argues vigorously against his own former position (without identifying it as his own): the Four Categories system has to be retained, he says, for it is the outgrowth of a historical evolution in literature itself.[15] Chang had noticed the pattern of this evolution in the earlier book. In the age of the Classics, the natural system of classifying writings was according to the Six Canons (*liu tien*), i.e., the six-fold organization of the state as described in the *Rituals of Chou.* Then, all learning was official and every text or specialty belonged to some one office. Although the ancient state fell apart and "books were scattered," specialized traditions of learning continued to exist apart from the state; Liu Hsin, when he identified these specialized schools in his *Seven Summaries,* was describing a situation that still existed as late as the middle of the Han Dynasty. But "in the Wei and Tsin Dynasties specialized schools gradually disappeared, and a writer produced writings just as something showy and beautiful," various ornamental literary pieces governed merely by his whim of the moment, without any underlying principle tying them together; "these were collected and sorted out, and called 'literary collections.'"[16]

This change led to the Four Categories system (which in fact started to be used at this time). This system regroups Liu's classes under "Classics" and "philosophers" and adds to these two more categories—"history," into which Chang thinks too much has been indiscriminately crammed, and "collections," for which there is no criterion of content at all. By 1779 Chang was willing to keep the Four Categories system, but he felt that the bibliographer had much to straighten out if he were to remedy the "ills of literature."

A few examples from the *Chiao-ch'ou T'ung-i* will indicate just what sort of straightening out Chang had in mind. Sometimes he would simply shift the conventional listing of a book to a different sub-category. It was ridiculous, he felt, to classify Kuei Yu-kuang's editing of the *Shih-chi* and Su Hsün's editing of *Mencius* under "history" and "Classics," for both are supplied with critical punctuation to serve as models of style. They are degenerate forms of literary criticism, and should be so listed. Sometimes a sub-category should be eliminated and its contents distributed under others. Encyclopedias (*lei-shu*) are not really "philosophy"; some are primarily historical and should be listed in an appropriate part of "history" (an example is the *Wen-hsien T'ung-k'ao*); others are more general and belong in the "general collections" (*tsung-chi*) section of the fourth category.[17]

Frequently, Chang thinks, one should list a book under two different headings when logically it belongs to each, with cross-references noted. (In his Ho-chou history he had argued that no bibliographic system can any longer be a perfect map of literature; cross-listing was therefore desirable because it made bibliography less rigid.) And sometimes, he says, a book is composite in origin, one chapter having been incorporated from a now lost work. When this happens, the book and the single chapter should be given separate listings. Indeed sometimes a "lost" book can be at least partly recovered by assembling the pieces of it embedded in existing works.[18] Since Chang gives the bibliographer the task of keeping the entire body of literature in good condition, it is natural for him to think that this kind of research is part of his job. It is likely that he had in mind the recovery (proposed by Chu Yün) of lost books from the enormous Ming encyclopedia *Yung-lo Ta-tien*.

Perhaps the most revealing suggestion Chang makes is that the bibliographer add notes under titles that are neither to be moved nor cross-listed. This suggestion applies chiefly to "collections," the category that Chang, in his Ho-chou history, wanted to eliminate altogether because it was not in Liu Hsin's scheme. The thing to do, he said in the Ho-chou preface, is to determine the essential intellectual direction and temper of a writer, and then list his literary works, not under "collections," but under the appropriate "Liu Hsin" category. In the *Chiao-ch'ou T'ung-i,* Chang rejects this idea and suggests instead that the essential nature of the writer be established in footnotes: thus, among the "eight great masters" of T'ang and Sung, Han Yü belongs to the *ju chia* (Confucian scholar) category of philosophy; Wang An-shih belongs to the legalists (*fa chia*), and Liu Tsung-yüan belongs to the "school of names" (*ming chia*).[19] Chang is not just making arbitrary and doubtful assignments to schools. He is trying to rescue these writers from characterlessness, to identify each as an individual with his own special quality; this is one of the things Chang wants to establish when he identifies a man's *chia*.

The historian who herds all writers of a dynasty indiscriminately into a collection of biographies of "literary men" shows the same lack of sensitivity to individuality as does the bibliographer who shovels their works into a category of "literary collections." Some historians are correspondingly virtuous, as was Ssu-ma Ch'ien, in putting together in their biographies writers and philosophers who really do resemble each other (e.g., Chia I and Chü Yüan) and are different from others.[20]

Chang is clearer about what he means by a school when he recommends, as he does in the Ho-chou history, that in the biographical part of a history past historians be distinguished from the mass of literary men, and presented as specialists with their own interests and principles of learning. Classical scholars were distinguished in just such a way in the early Standard Histories: scholars who had specialized in one Classic were grouped together to form the school of that Classic. In the treatment of a man such as Ssu-ma Ch'ien, one should first discuss the sources of the *Shih-chi,* then its authors, the persons who preserved the text, and its commentators. The "biographical" chapter doing this would have the book as its subject, bringing in men as they were involved; this is the way all histories should be treated. "If this were done," Chang adds, "then it could be said that the essential tradition of the *Spring and Autumn Annals* lives even today." Unfortunately it is now common practice for the historian to treat all writers more or less as literary artists with the result that people give little attention to historians and the special features of their tradition of writing. "So easy does the world find it to talk about literary art and so difficult to talk about history!" As an illustration of what he is advocating, Chang offers his own Ho-chou history, which had a chapter on earlier histories of the district and their authors—an innovation he took pride in. If his lead were followed by other local historians, he thought, the result would be to revitalize "the *chia-fa* of the historian."[21]

The school involves the scholar in something larger than his own ego, just as the ancient "official-teacher," from whom Chang's school-specialist is derived, was part of something larger—his office and tradition, the world-whole. This dimension of Chang's concept became important to him later. But here, in placing a writer or scholar within a school, Chang means to give him individuality, a "discipline" distinguishing him from others, making of him (like the ancient "official-teacher") a specialist with a special ideal. And by distinguishing writings and the schools they belong to, the bibliographer and the historian not only improve writing and learning but also preserve traditions by giving them identity. Chang was to argue later that it is only when a school dies out as a historical tradition that its writings are lost.

But what, really, is this identity, which the bibliographer must put his finger on and which enables a tradition to preserve itself? When Chang talks about a school, he seems to be talking about two quite different concepts. On one hand, he sees the tradition of learning that produced the *Shih-chi* as a "school," a tradition that involved traceable historical steps and causal connections—sources, authors, commentators. On the other hand, he places Wang An-shih in the "legalist school" because he senses that this label catches his general intellectual direction—because he thinks his thought is similar to that of the writers in the ancient "legalist" group. In the first instance a school is a historical entity; in this case the bibliographer must be an intellectual historian. In the second instance, it is a logical category; here he need merely be a librarian (or perhaps an analytic philosopher). Does Chang see what he is doing when he makes it the job of "bibliography" to sort writings into historical traditions as well as subject categories? And does he see that these are two distinct jobs?

It is possible to begin to make out a case that they are not two distinct jobs—that recognizing and characterizing a thing adequately necessarily involves explaining it; and that the explanation must guide the characterization and enter into it. In a sense, I have not really seen the hole in that pane of glass for what it is until I have it pegged as a bullet hole. Moreover, things can be sorted out by qualities in different ways. The botanist does not group all pink flowers into the same genus. But he does assign to one genus flowers that have *some* common qualities—qualities that for him are significant because he has a theory about how these plants came to have them. Might not the bibliographer do the same with books, so that his subject categories are always genetically meaningful, chosen and filled for historical reasons?

If this were all Chang were doing we might hesitate to object (though such a method would surely be difficult to employ). But this is not all. In another revealing passage in the *Chiao-ch'ou T'ung-i,* Chang says, "if one is to explore the basic principles" of writings, original and otherwise, "one must understand their derivations." The ancient school of names and the school of Mo Tzu have not been "transmitted" since Han times. But "we can find the idea of analyzing terms and being precise about things" in the *Chien-ming Shu* by the Five Dynasties scholar Ch'iu Kuang-t'ing; thus the school of names is seen to survive in Confucian philology. And "we can find the ideas of praising economy and of universal love in both the Taoists, who value frugality, and the Buddhists, who preach universal salvation; thus the school of Mo Tzu exists within the Two Religions."[22]

Apparently Chang has to think that the essential quality and value in a book must have some source in the very beginning of things. It is inconceivable to him that there might be more than one possible source for such a quality, wherever or whenever it may occur. If so, then to identify a classifying characteristic in an author's work is to say that it "derives" from whatever is the source of that characteristic. But how does the bibliographer fix upon the essential classifying characteristic? How does he know that "the ideas of praising economy and of universal love" are the essential ideas of the Mohists? Apparently, he just knows.

What Chang is talking about here can be perhaps better understood if we see what we might do with a word like "Platonist." Bertrand Russell in his early years was a "Platonist" (he believed as did Plato that there are ideal mathematical objects); John C. Calhoun was a "Platonist" (he read and admired the *Republic*); a student in Plato's Academy was a "Platonist" (Plato taught him, or at least taught the man who did). Suppose now we bring together these quite different senses of "Platonist" and speak of a "Platonic school" as made up of all who could be called "Platonist" in any of these senses. This is very much the sort of thing Chang does. When he uses classification in a school or line of derivation in order to throw light on the worth or significance of a writer, the result is much the same as if we were to think of some Platonic intellectual essence reaching down through time and expressing itself in the mind of the young Russell.

This is just the direction in which Chang's thought is heading. Consider what he has to say in an essay written in 1792. Chang wants to persuade us (for reasons that need not now concern us) that certain writings, all of which he considers essentially historical, are derivations (*liu-pieh*) from one or another of the Classics. For example, history in annal-biographical form has derived from the *Spring and Autumn,* and legal and administrative compendia (*hui tien*) have derived from the *Rites*. But the process of derivation is mysterious indeed. It cannot be traced continuously, step by step, in history. On the contrary, "After Confucius recorded the taking of the unicorn and stopped writing [i.e., the *Spring and Autumn Annals*], few men of learning were able later to understand completely the real character [*ta t'i*, "great essence"] of the ancients. It had to build up for a long time, and only then did it gradually come forward and manifest itself." And in fact, Chang thinks it was not until the *Shih-chi* that the "thread" of the *Spring and Autumn* tradition was "continued," and not until Tu Yu's *T'ung Tien* in the T'ang Dynasty that the Ritual Classics were "continued"—some fifteen hundred years after the Western Chou period to which Chang assigns those Classics.[23] In such cases, Chang explicitly says, the return to the ancient idea is not deliberate. It just happens.

We could try to make naturalistic sense of this. There are ways, detectable by a sufficiently subtle historian, in which configurations of habits, values, political and social forms and needs persist to produce strikingly similar results at widely different times in a civilization.*f* But a final example will show that what Chang was involved with was not naturalism but historical metaphysics. Over the years, Chang wrote a series of essays in which he attempted to show, discipline by discipline, how later literature was derived from the Classics. We see that Chang was committed to account in this way for everything of importance and value in the history of Chinese thought and letters. The philosophers and the historians

---

f Thus Collingwood's notion of a thought persisting through time and reinstating itself in the mind of a later writer (*The Idea of History,* Oxford, 1946, pp. 282ff) is perhaps partly naturalized in his much less alarming notion of encapsulation, explained in his *Autobiography* (Oxford, 1939, p. 141).

were easy prey; to one with Chang's imagination, even poets and essayists presented no great difficulty. But what of the writings of Buddhism, that one great pre-modern intrusion into the Chinese world? It is to Chang's credit that he at least faced the difficulty this presented to his system. He was too sensible to trot out the threadbare story of the "conversion of the barbarians," and too broad-minded to ignore Buddhism or dismiss it as nonsense. So Chang was true to his method and grappled for its essence. Buddhism, like philosophical Taoism, makes much use of mythology, allegory, and imagery of all kinds; so does the *Classic of Changes*. Therefore, in what is probably one of the first of the essays on classical traditions, "The Teaching of the *Changes*," Chang concludes that Buddhism (and indeed also Taoism) "must have come originally from the teaching of the *Changes*," even though the Buddha did not know Chinese and never came to China.*ᵍ*

Chang's historical and cultural world is so incredibly *one* (and therefore so totally Chinese) that in it there can be only diffusion from a common source, from one *tao* in the beginning of history; there is never genuine intellectual convergence. If two or more pieces of writing are alike in some important respect, the principle of resemblance between them must be, for Chang, a metaphysical essence, a "surviving idea" (*i-i*), causally efficacious, which has somehow persisted through time to realize itself in each. We will deal with this kind of thinking in all that Chang writes.*ʰ*

ᵍ I-shu, 1.7b. Chang's analysis of Buddhism is dealt with more fully in Chapter 5, pp. 126-27. By a similar argument, Lao Tzu and Chuang Tzu are assigned to the tradition of the *Changes*; see Chapter 5, p. 118.

ʰ As we have seen, Chang wants to trace types of writing back to the Classical Age primarily in order to evaluate them. In examining his idea of derivation, moreover, we see that it is not just tendencies, subject-interests, and formal properties that are traceable in this way but also values. It may then be asked whether Chang commits what is sometimes called the genetic fallacy. This is a defect in reasoning that is supposed to occur when we accept (a) that person or thing A has a certain value (or disvalue) v; and (b) that A has "caused" or "produced" B; and therefore conclude (c) that B has value v. A performance of a Bach concerto, for example, is really only the result of scratchings of horsehair on catgut.

But I do not think Chang does this. Sometimes he reasons like the Chinese art critic who finds a painting good esthetically and explains its excellence by sup-

Two Important Proposals

The concepts of classification and derivation Chang uses in his bibliography (and in his intellectual history) may seem arbitrary, guided wholly by intuition. But when Chang talks about anything as concrete as classifying books, he makes a fetish of method and organization. Chang thought this method and organization neces- sary in order to recognize and encourage specialization, which would in turn tend to preserve traditions of learning. Chang was indebted to Cheng Ch'iao, the Sung historian, for this idea. In the *Chiao-ch'ou T'ung-i* Chang castigates Cheng for being so hostile to Pan Ku that he failed to see that the bibliographer, like Liu Hsin, must trace traditions of writing back to Chou beginnings.[i] Nonetheless Chang, in the very act of writing his book, accords Cheng the ultimate flattery of imitation.

Cheng, too, saw the relationship of good bibliography to special- ization and the preservation of books. From watching the compila- tion of the Sung imperial catalog, *Ch'ung-wen Tsung-mu,* and from studying ancient bibliography Cheng saw that many books known to have existed could no longer be found. Chang Hsüeh- ch'eng must surely have been familiar with Cheng's analysis of the reasons for this:

The reason why learning is not specialized is that authors have no clear conception of what their books should cover. And this is not clear be- cause categories are not distinct. When specialized books exist, there is

---

posing some (perhaps otherwise undetectable) excellence in the character of the painter; he reasons from (c) and (b) to (a), as did Confucius when he said "The man who wrote this poem must have understood the *tao!*" (*Mencius* 12.2A4.) And this reasoning is at least not absurd. Often he reasons from (a) and (c) to (b), i.e., he notes that an author and a Classic have a value (or quality) in common and infers a causal connection. This is the reasoning about which I have been complain- ing. Finally, he uses a counterfeit form of the genetic fallacy, reasoning from (a) and (b) to (c') that B *ought* to have value v—i.e., having decided that a type of writing derives from a classical source, he concludes that it *ought* to have the values present in the source, values that it lacks or has "lost."
[i] Cheng Ch'iao's famous diatribe against Pan Ku is found in the preface to his *T'ung Chih.* Cheng charges that Pan plagiarized Ssu-ma Ch'ien without due acknowledg- ment and created a pernicious precedent in writing the first history of a single dy- nasty instead of simply continuing Ssu-ma Ch'ien's "general" history.

specialized learning; when there is specialized learning, it is possible for it to be preserved by a tradition from generation to generation. Men maintain their learning and the tradition of learning preserves the books, and the books in turn preserve the categories. The learning will not be broken off even though individual men may die, and though there be changes in fortune from one generation to another, the books will not be lost.

In a clever analogy, Cheng suggests that just as good military discipline improves the troops' chances of surviving in battle, so good bibliography enables books better to face the onslaught of time. He gave Buddhism and Taoism as examples of traditions that have preserved their literature by consciousness of their own identity, and the ancient legalist school and the Han traditions of the *Classic of Changes* as examples of those that have failed.[24]

Chang wonders if perhaps the Buddhists and Taoists have a lesson to teach on this subject. He observes that they have their *Fo Tsang* and *Tao Tsang,* libraries of all the major and minor texts of their traditions, reproduced in vast printed compendia and preserved in various places. But Chang cites history to show that the maintaining of libraries is an even older practice in the Confucian state.[25] The court and provincial governments in Chang's day did, of course, have their libraries for official use. But Chang suggests some interesting refinements to enable the state to preserve books more systematically.[j]

Chang first suggested these refinements in his Ho-chou history in 1774. In ancient times, he tells us, documents and popular literature were collected and preserved by officials. Later, individuals and schools produced their own books, and literature became scattered, so that even on those rare occasions when the state did take a strong interest in cultivating letters and collecting texts, its offi-

---

[j] Chang's friend Chou Yung-nien's ideas about libraries were surely known to Chang: Chou had a "lending library" in Peking called the Chieh-shu Yüan; Chang visited him there in 1775, and wrote a preface for Chou's library catalog; and this preface is very similar in thought to the *Chiao-ch'ou T'ung-i*. Chou advocated that public libraries should be maintained in safe places and should exchange catalogs, and argued that Confucian writings should be preserved in great collections like the *Tao Tsang* and the *Ta Tsang* (*Fo Tsang*). See HY, p. 34 and *ECCP*, p. 175.

cials could not gather and place in the imperial libraries more than seventy or eighty per cent of what once existed. Furthermore, unless rewards were offered for books, none could be obtained, and if rewards were offered, there was danger that books would be forged. Evidently Chang had in mind the Ch'ing government's efforts to collect rare books for the Imperial Manuscript Library, the *Ssu-k'u Ch'üan-shu.* These difficulties could be overcome, Chang thought, if the ancient spirit of "government through a unity of letters" could be recaptured. The solution, Chang thought, was to have the state in the book-collecting business not just occasionally, when some project is underway, but all the time. It should be the routine duty of local teachers and historians to preserve writings of all kinds in their localities, in readiness for collection, preservation, and criticism by the central government. Specifically, the local historian should as a regular practice prepare and keep up to date a bibliography of local writing. These bibliographies, he says, are to be literally a census of books. They will be to writing what local records, supplying population statistics and data on local production, are to the local economy.[26] Chang was extending here the view he had long held, that the compiling of local history should be a regular function of local government.[k]

These were Chang's views in 1774. In 1779, in the *Chiao-ch'ou T'ung-i,* he assigns the foregoing functions to the local teacher rather than the historian, and in so doing makes him the local instrument for a pervasive and continuous state censorship and surveillance of the written word:

In the case of records made from secondhand sources and miscellaneous essays on the Classics, truth and error are mixed together and hard to distinguish; books that tell popular tales sometimes show great understanding and sometimes little; songs that perpetuate popular customs are sometimes proper and sometimes not. . . . It should be the responsi-

[k] Chang presented this view in an essay entitled "A Proposal that Bureaus of Historiography be Created in Local Governments" ("Chou Hsien Ch'ing Li Chih K'o I"); the essay was printed in 1796 (Ch'ien Mu, p. 426). The proposal for local bureaus of historiography appears as early as 1763, in the first of his letters to Chen Sung-nien. See Chapter 1.

bility of the teachers in the prefectural and district schools to search out, study, and correct writings of this sort, and to prepare bibliographical lists of them, much after the fashion of census registers for population. ... If this procedure were followed, then books would be in the care of the officials and would not be scattered and lost. This would be the first advantage. And if there were constant investigation and checking, then queer and false sayings and wicked and heretical statements could not be concealed in violation of prohibitions. This would be the second advantage. The search for books could be carried out by means of the register, and there would be no difficulty in collecting them. This would be the third advantage. Books that were not in the Imperial Library could be found in the provincial libraries, and when books in the provincial libraries prove to be falsified or in error, they could be corrected by books in the Imperial Library; the benefit would be mutual, and the unification of writing would attain perfection. This would be the fourth advantage.[27]

Chang adds in a note, "To have books in the charge of the officials and to forbid private parties to conceal writings is very much in accord with ancient practice." The methods Chang proposed were not specifically those of the Ch'ien-lung literary inquisition, but the rooting out of "wicked and heretical statements" that are "concealed in violation of prohibitions" is what any inquisition tries to do.

This proposal that the government should examine, catalog, and censor books is but one of two striking organizational recommendations that Chang makes in his *Chiao-ch'ou T'ung-i*. A second recommendation proposes a method for official bibliographers to use in handling the many books they must examine. Chang observed that in ancient times the critical study of texts was the duty of a special official who, like the other officials, held his position for life and then bequeathed it to his son (he is thinking here of Liu Hsiang and Liu Hsin). This made possible great attainment. But the specialist's method of apprehending and transmitting his knowledge was purely intuitive and incommunicable outside of his family; therefore such a system cannot work now. Now many persons must take part in the work, for it is too much for a man of even the greatest attainments to do alone. This makes a standard procedure imperative, and Chang prescribes the following: all books to be examined should be brought together, and "the names of men, places, official ranks, and book titles in them—in fact any name that could be dealt with or any number that could be investigated—should be completely organized by rhyme, roughly after the fashion of the *P'ei-wen Yün-fu* [the great poet's thesaurus published by the K'ang-hsi Emperor]. And under each entry should be noted its locations in the book from which it came ... from the first and second occurrence to whatever number." With such a master file as a tool, labors that were formerly beyond the strength of the wisest of scholars could be performed easily by persons of ordinary ability.[28] This proposal is interesting not only because it illustrates Chang's love of organization and method but also because it anticipates modern concepts of indexing.[1]

---

[1] Professor William Hung, for example, pays tribute to Chang's idea in his essay "Yin-te shuo" ("On Indexing"), *Harvard-Yenching Institute Sinological Index Series,* Supplement No. 4, p. 12. Chang's interest in indexes and reference works of a proto-index type was evident in 1773–74, when while working on the *Ho-chou Chih* he had assistants index for him the biographical section of the *Ming Shih* (HY, p. 31), and later in 1796–98, when he wrote two prefaces to books by Wang Hui-tsu, one for Wang's *Shih Hsing Yün-pien* and *Erh-shih-ssu Shih T'ung Hsing-ming Lu* (1796), the other for his *San Shih T'ung Ming Lu* (1798) (HY, pp. 120, 131–32). But Chang did not have any adequate conception of the mechanical difficulties of his proposal. Only today with our recently developed electronic computers are we able seriously to consider indexing an entire library.

4. Master of Academies

People say that an official must fear being ruined by
frequent changes of assignment. But how much worse
it is for the poor man dependent on officials for his
means to live!

— An Expression of My Feelings ... 1797

Chang had attained the metropolitan degree in 1778. He probably
took it for granted at first that the degree would eventually lead
to an official appointment and, probably without thinking much
about it, wanted one simply to support himself. But this was still
in the future. Chang knew that he might have to wait, as his father
had, about a decade for his appointment, and, as his father had, he
supported himself in the meantime by teaching and by occasional
writing assignments. This mode of life meant constant insecurity,
for one's tenure in a teaching position lasted only as long as one
had some sort of personal claim on the official who controlled it.

From 1777 through 1788, Chang held five academic posts, four
in Chihli and the fifth and last in Honan. At first he did well.
He had the friendship of Chou Chen-jung, who turned out to have
more influence, both among local officials and among people of
much greater consequence, than one would have expected in a
person of his rank. And Chou quickly came to admire Chang
warmly. While in Ting-chou and Yung-ch'ing, Chang was reasonably close to Peking and was able to maintain and extend his con-
tacts there. Frequently he and Chou went to the city together, and
we read of an occasional dinner party of persons Chang was to come
to think of as his "group"—Shao Chin-han, Chu Yün's son Chu
Hsi-keng, and others such as Chou Yung-nien, Liu T'ai-kung, and
a young man named Shih Chih-kuang, who was destined to have
a brilliant official career and seemed to have special respect for

Chang.[a] Being so close to Peking, Chang was able to avoid the expense of moving his family out of the capital.

In 1779 Chang finished a history of Yung-ch'ing for Chou. This local history was more or less similar in form to the *Ho-chou Chih*. The treatment of the section of monographs (*shu,* corresponding to the monographs in the Standard Histories), however, was slightly different; they were now subdivided into six parts, named for the six departments of local and central government (personnel, revenue, ceremonies, military affairs, justice, public works)— an illustration of how seriously Chang regarded his institutional approach to local history. Oddly enough, Chang did not include in his Yung-ch'ing history a monograph on literature. In compiling the work, he had been given every assistance by Chou and had traveled about the district incognito, gathering old documents and biographical data. He paid special attention to biographies of living women; those who were selected for the honor of inclusion in his history he interviewed personally, often sending carriages to bring them to the yamen to tell their life stories. In this way he sought— he felt successfully—to introduce variety and human interest into these more or less obligatory accounts of feminine virtue. Chang's monographs were equally unconventional. The monograph dealing with economics and revenue ("Hu Shu") listed the current prices of various commodities and discussed market conditions; it is especially rich in detail, running to about one hundred pages or almost three-fourths of the entire monograph section. The monograph on ceremonies ("Li Shu") included a description of local customs. If all local histories contained material of this sort, this vast category of Chinese historical writing would be far more valuable to the modern social and economic historian.[1]

---

[a] Shih was a native of Shan-yin and may have been a kinsman of Chang's mother (née Shih), who had many relatives living in Peking (*I-shu,* 16.54a). He rose in the Chia-ch'ing reign through a series of provincial posts, eventually becoming governor-general of Yunnan and Kweichow, and then returned to the capital as senior president of the Censorate; he died in 1828 (*Kuo-ch'ao Chi-hsien Lei-cheng Ch'u-pien,* 106.1a–9a). Many of Chang's manuscripts were preserved in his family. (HY, pp. 44, 50, 61, 65, 126.)

The *Yung-ch'ing Hsien-chih* is the one local history most clearly Chang's own among those that have survived intact. It has great virtues, but it also contains material that, in retrospect, probably caused its compiler considerable anguish. Among the prominent families of Yung-ch'ing district was one surnamed Chia. No less than nine members of this house receive short biographical sketches in Chang's history. The last of these was an old licentiate named Chia P'eng (1702–78), who qualified himself for the biographical section by managing to die just before Chang stopped work. (We remember that ordinarily a living man could not be given a biography.) In 1777 Chia P'eng had brought the collected manuscripts of his essays and occasional writings to Chang for criticism. Chang responded to this flattery with the most incautious enthusiasm, not hesitating to mark up and "correct" each composition, appending to each a critical comment of his own. When Chia P'eng died, Chang selected the composition he judged the best and included it in Chia's biography (a common practice of the great Han historians). This essay, which does indeed have literary merit, was entitled "O-hsiang Chi" ("An Account of the Land of Hunger"); it belongs to a well-established genre in Chinese literature—a witty description of a visit to a land of fantasy that is, in various ways, a parody of the real world.

But Chang's literary discovery was too good to be true. Old Chia (to make the most charitable judgment) was utterly befuddled: the "O-hsiang Chi" was in fact a well-known piece written in 1710 by an early Ch'ing writer named Lan Ting-yüan (1680–1733). It is amazing that Chang, a *chin-shih* and over 40 by this time, had apparently not even heard of it. Worse than this, the manuscripts that Chang so carefully "edited" contained other pieces that were not by their pretended author. One other is partly copied from Lan Ting-yüan, and half a dozen essays are the work of the well-known writer of the T'ung-ch'eng School in Anhwei, Fang Pao (1668–1749). It is strange that Chang was not more familiar with Fang Pao's work, but at any rate he had the literary sensitivity to find Fang's style worthy of praise.[2]

One can only guess how long it took Chang to discover that he had been deceived. In an essay written several years later ("Yen Kung," which I shall discuss later on), he writes bitterly about the practice of literary plagiarism. In judging this accident, we should of course remember that in the China of Chang's time public libraries did not exist, and that a man's formal education did not include a survey of contemporary literature.

This defect in Chang's history was not noticed. Chou was delighted with the work and displayed it to his friends, several of whom sought to retain Chang to compile local histories for them. But Chang declined all offers, and during the remainder of this and the following year was employed by Liang Kuo-chih as a tutor for his son.[a]

Chang's fortunes now took a disastrous turn. Chang and Liang Kuo-chih did not get on together, and at the end of 1780 Chang had to give up his position.[b] Early in 1781 he made a journey from the capital to Honan, presumably in search of new employment. On his way back in the summer, he was attacked by brigands and was robbed of everything, including the clothes he was wearing and the drafts of all his personal writings. Many of these writings were lost permanently. From friends' copies of his local histories and occasional literary pieces, Chang was able to reconstruct less than half of his earlier work. All drafts of his *Wen-shih T'ung-i* were gone; gone too was the fourth and final chapter of the *Chiao-ch'ou T'ung-i*. Chang soon began work on a new *Wen-shih T'ung-i,* and after this always made several copies of his writings.[4]

After the robbery, Chang took refuge in the house of a fellow *chin-shih,* Chang Wei-ch'i, then magistrate of Fei-hsiang district in Chihli. Chang Wei-ch'i obtained for him the directorship of the local Ch'ing-chang Academy. This assistance, however, did not repair Chang's fortunes, and he found the company of his pro-

---

[b] HY, p. 48. Hung Liang-chi, in a poem to Chang in 1794, says that Chang while in Liang's employ was "not willing to defer to his wishes in anything." In a note, Hung adds, "you were obdurate and blunt in temper, and . . . his excellency was very much afraid of you." (WTJ, p. 259.)

vincial students no substitute for Peking intellectual life. Hoping for deliverance, he wrote repeatedly to influential friends for help, including Liang Kuo-chih, who apparently did not respond. To add to his depression, word arrived that his patron and teacher Chu Yün had died in Peking. Chang wept when he received the news.[5]

In the winter of 1781 Chang Wei-ch'i was transferred to Ta-ming district and Chang followed, assisting for a short time in the compiling of a history of Ta-ming. Soon he left for Peking. The following year, after more unsuccessful efforts to find employment, he received (possibly through Chou Chen-jung's influence) the directorship of Ching-sheng Academy in Yung-p'ing prefecture in Chihli; here he moved his family, uprooting them from Peking, where his son I-hsüan had been studying with Shao Chin-han.[6] This trip was the beginning of a long odyssey for the Chang household, an odyssey that would eventually lead them back to their ancestral Chekiang. The travelers included both the living and the dead, for Chang's father and mother would someday have to be interred with proper ceremony in the family gravesite in K'uai-chi—an office quite out of the question for Chang in his present state of life.

Yung-p'ing, near the Manchurian border, seemed to promise little intellectual excitement; but Chang soon found congenial friends, especially among the officials of the local administration. One turned out to be a *chin-shih* in Chang's class. Another was Ts'ai Hsün (1729–88), who had had a career of ups and downs and was now department magistrate of nearby Luan-chou. Ts'ai had a relative who had received his *chin-shih* with Chang's father—an important past relationship.[7]

Ts'ai, as Chang describes him, was good-hearted and honest, but proud, incautious, and strong-tempered; these qualities were enough to recommend him to Chang. They became friends, and several of Chang's literary pieces were written for him or about him. One of these is curious—a preface, written by Chang in Ts'ai's name for a collection of poems by Ts'ai's wife, revealing in Chang a rather conservative view of the place of women in a man's world.

Chang carefully points out that the lady's qualities are by no means only literary, for she has always been filial, respectful, and virtuous; he closes by half suggesting that the printing of her poems is an act of uxorious indulgence.[8]

One of these pieces is utterly charming. Magistrate Ts'ai had been given a citation for honesty and ability during his past three years of service; to mark the occasion—and Chang will suggest, to keep himself in a properly modest frame of mind—he had a painter do a portrait showing him holding a *yao-tsao* (a plant symbolic of long life) while gazing upon a wooded mountain scene. Chang was invited to write an essay to accompany the picture.

In his little comment—which is both serious and frivolous—Chang plays with the idea that paintings are like dreams and mirrors: all are "illusions" (*huan*), like the real world but not really what they seem. But dreams are partly incomprehensible; and mirror images change from moment to moment. Paintings lack both of these shortcomings, being both intelligible and permanent, "using illusion to preserve the real." Exact representation is not the special virtue of a painting, however, for there is a limit to what can be captured in the form of a thing; but the spirit "lodged" in a painting is infinite, ineffable. "When the moment of inspired feeling of a man of old is preserved in a painting, a thousand years later it is as if you can see him smiling," and we, who look upon such art, are freed in thought from the petty preoccupations of the humdrum world. Then how much greater the effect when you yourself are the subject: as night and day you face your likeness "you forget the distinction between form and spirit, and the very springs of nature are revealed to you."

Life is impermanent, evanescent, itself in a sense an illusion, Chang continues ("and here you are in your picture, imprisoned within an illusion-within-an-illusion! A hard lot!"). Ts'ai himself, first honored, then disgraced and exiled, then restored to position, has "undergone all the vicissitudes of this uncertain web of life." Yet somehow the painting has caught his essential self in the midst of change—"his noble spirit, his refined yet bold character revealed like tempered steel in his eyes." It has been foretold that someday he will become a censor. Will this come to pass, Chang asks, or will he, as the picture suggests, become an immortal in the mountains?[9]

So Chang closes. This piece of half-serious fancy was indeed one of those patches of sunlight that only accentuate the sadness of "this uncertain web of life." For Magistrate Ts'ai's story was to end not in the censorate or in mountain solitude, but in black tragedy.

The esthetic ideas in this bit of polite writing are not unusual taken singly, but they are combined by Chang in an odd way. It was a commonly held view (and one of the earliest values looked for in art) that a portrait should inspire and improve its beholder by capturing and presenting for his edification the virtue of its subject. But the notion of a "spirit" being "lodged" in a painting, of the moment of inspiration being captured as the brush is wielded, belongs to a later and more sophisticated esthetic, which applies not just to portrait painting but to painting of any kind, and sees not the subject but the painter himself as the one whose "virtue" enters into the painting and gives it value. It is *his* spirit, *his* moment of inspiration that is "lodged" there.[10]

Chang scrambles these ideas; and in so doing he makes of a portrait an instrument of self-cultivation and heightened self-knowledge for the man portrayed, who is both subject and beholder. Even the background elements of landscape, Chang hints, contribute to this function of catching the subject's personality and holding before him his better self, since as objects of his meditation and admiration, they suggest those values that he should always hold first. Here the actual quality of the art involved seems curiously irrelevant. It would be rash to make Chang out as a serious art critic, although this was not his only essay of this kind; in others we find him expressing a very similar point of view.[c] The

---

[c] See Chang's "Comment on a Painting of the Li Brothers of Ta-hsing Enjoying Themselves During the Four Seasons," *I-shu*, 28.27a–29a. Here, in an essay of 1786, he states explicitly the idea that background landscape suggests the virtue and personality of the subject of the portrait.

view, it should be noticed, completely loses sight of the usual ideal in "literary man's painting" that great painting is the work of a cultivated temper in the artist—strange, since this ideal is exactly similar to Chang's and Chu Yün's ideal in literary art. It would be unfair, however, to suppose he was ignorant of this ideal or rejected it; perhaps Ts'ai's portrait was just too mediocre for its artistic quality to be worth noticing. This may well have been the case, for Chang does not even give us the painter's name.

Chang's real concern, of course, was not with pictures. It was with literary art, and his immediate problem was the business of teaching students to write. His academy positions and his students' dull wits had apparently stimulated him to an interest in the theory and practice of teaching, and now, distressed at his students' lack of application, he prepared for them a textbook (now lost) of literary selections illustrating good style and sound learning. His Yung-p'ing students vexed him, but his former students at Fei-hsiang had been even more discouraging. There his pupils had been timid and unimaginative in the extreme, and the first time Chang had examined them (on the ideas in the Four Books) they all had handed in blank papers. So he had tried to stir them up a bit by preparing instructions for their guidance, including a sample set of questions. In these he tried to elicit from his students their objectives in the pursuit of learning, attempting to direct their attention beyond the immediate goal of passing the examinations, which, he had always felt, was not an adequate motive for study. Specific questions were provocative, with no ready answer. But it was labor lost, and Chang had been greatly relieved to move on.[11]

Chang's new role as master of Ching-sheng Academy was not without its difficulties, thanks to the prefect of Yung-p'ing, one Chu Ying-yü. On one occasion Chu assigned a theme to Chang's students and, when the papers came in, criticized a student severely (much to the amusement of the class) for an essay Chang had judged quite good, an act that did not endear him to Chang. Chu further undermined Chang before his students by saying openly to his secretaries that he thought one of Chang's examination essays was laughable. The prefect's son, however, did not share his father's opinion of Chang. Chu Tsang-mei, in Yung-p'ing to visit his father, was struggling with examination studies and asked Chang for guidance.[d] Here was a different and far more attractive kind of student-teacher relationship. Chang had in his time been a "disciple"; now it was his turn to be a "master." It was probably soon afterward that he wrote to Chu Tsang-mei an eloquent letter, self-consciously in the manner of Han Yü to Li I, explaining the long and difficult (and glorious) task of self-education.

The true gentleman, the letter stated, will seek to live a life devoted to the *tao*. This does not require the sort of preoccupation with self-cultivation preached by the Sung philosophers—a preoccupation with the notions of man's moral nature, "rectifying one's mind," and "making one's thoughts sincere." The *tao* is everywhere and can be grasped equally well through a life devoted to writing or to scholarship. All branches of study and all specialties, when properly understood and pursued, are focused on the *tao* and need no further justification. The proper course for the student, therefore, is to recognize his own natural gift and develop it courageously:

Should something be esteemed by the world yet be not in accord with your inclination, do not give it a second thought, even though it be a matter as imposing as Mount T'ai; should a thing be in accord with your inclination yet be something valued lightly by the world, do not let yourself neglect it, though it be as minute as an autumn gossamer. Because what you are working on is specialized, it will be easy for you to achieve results; because you are indifferent to praise and censure, your understanding will be deep. Follow your natural talents and take those men of antiquity who are close to you in endowment as a standard.[12]

This is a variation of the claim of much of Ming philosophy, that the *tao* is to be found within one's own nature. But what is dis-

---

[d] HY, p. 56. *I-shu,* "wai-pien," 3.26a, "Notes of 1796." "Tsang-mei" was the younger Chu's *tzu*. He had been at some time a student of Chu Yün. See Ch'ien Mu, ed., "*Chang Shih I-shu* I-p'ien" ("Items Omitted from *The Remaining Writings of Chang Hsüeh-ch'eng*"), *T'u-shu Chi-k'an* (Szechwan), II (June 1942), 36, "Another Letter to Chu Hsi-keng" (1799).

covered within oneself is not, as it was for the earlier Neo-Confucianists, a set of moral values and impulses common to and valid
for all men (though Chang perhaps would not deny this). It is, to
be sure, the basis for a contribution to the sum of what is valuable,
but one that is in itself unique and individual.

These soothing sentiments must have pleased Chang's young
friend. And what a satisfying way to even the score with the prefect of Yung-p'ing! Chu Tsang-mei had come to Chang, rebelling
(as Chang had once rebelled) against learning to write *pa-ku*. But
Chang was not really letting him off. "The object of examination
studies is to get yourself known by others," he says gently, "and
yet in genuine learning you cannot simply accept what the world
values. And so you are afraid you cannot distinguish yourself in
both ways." But, Chang insists, even Confucius or Mencius, had
they lived today, could not avoid studying for the examinations;
and actually, the conflict Chu fears need not exist, for "I have never
heard of a person who had really achieved some understanding in
his learning whose examination essays were not fluent and beautiful." Here Chang sounds more like Chu Hsi than Han Yü.[18]

In the spring of 1783, possibly before his correspondence with
the younger Chu, Chang made a trip to Peking. There he was
stricken with a severe illness. Shao Chin-han came to his aid, took
him into his own house, and hired a doctor to treat him. During
Chang's convalescence he and Shao had a welcome chance to talk
and often stayed up until midnight discussing intellectual matters.
At this time, Chang stated his intention to write, after Shao had
finished his projected Sung history, a history according to his own
ideas, keeping it to five hundred thousand words. How serious this
intention was it is difficult to say. Certainly for some years it was
a plan for the distant future.[14]

While Chang and Shao were talking history in Peking, things
were happening in Yung-p'ing. Chang's friend Ts'ai Hsün, whose
bluntness had angered many around him, found himself removed
as magistrate of Luan-chou. Soon after, it was discovered that the
magistrate of a nearby district had mishandled tax funds and then

tried to cover it up by maneuvers that (it was charged) had been suggested by Ts'ai. An imperial investigating party was sent to Yung-p'ing, where Ts'ai's enemies were happy to make damaging accusations. The case came to the personal attention of the Emperor, who was still extremely sensitive about the exposure of official corruption and embezzlement in the case of Kuo-t'ai, the governor of Shantung, the preceding summer. In the fifth month, in an angry and impatient edict, the Emperor accused Ts'ai of knowingly abetting the crime. He was subsequently condemned to death.[15]

How much of this unhappy course of events Chang witnessed is difficult to determine. His association with Ts'ai was close, and by this time well documented in his own hand; he may have made his trip to Peking (where he had influential connections) partly out of caution. Or—more likely—he may have been seeking help for his friend.[e] If so, he failed. Ts'ai was now in prison awaiting execution. But he and Chang were destined to meet again.

After his recovery, Chang returned to the academy at Yung-p'ing (it now must have been a very different place for him) and continued his teaching. His students continued to dissatisfy him; he wrote to Chou Chen-jung that he found them, as usual, poor intellectual company, and that he could not discuss profundities with them. By autumn, however, most of them had left to take the examinations, and Chang wrote, "I am all alone here and have roughed out additions to my *Wen-shih T'ung-i.*" He mentioned two essays, " 'If Your Words Are Everyone's' " ("Yen Kung") and "The Teaching of the *Odes*" ("Shih Chiao"). These essays, both concerned with the motivation of good writing and the history of literary genres, are related to the literary and pedagogical ideas of

[e] Liang Kuo-chih, though perhaps still cool toward Chang, would certainly have come to his aid. Chu Yün was dead, but his brother Chu Kuei (1731–1807) was in the capital in 1783. He was Supervisor of Imperial Instruction and a close friend of Prince Yung-yen, who was destined to succeed to the throne. Chang was always on warm terms with Chu Yün's son Chu Hsi-keng. For the Kuo-t'ai case see *ECCP*, p. 150, and my "Ho-shen and His Accusers" in Nivison and Wright, eds., *Confucianism in Action* (Stanford, 1959).

Chu Yün (which Chang was now amplifying as his own) and to the recently written *Chiao-ch'ou T'ung-i*. In a note on his writings of this year, Chang tells us that, working from the seventh month into the ninth, he drafted for his *Wen-shih T'ung-i* seven essays, totaling eighty-nine paragraphs, as well as three unparagraphed essays—in all, more than twenty thousand words. He adds, curiously, that he went over the essays indicating their structure in five colors of ink, using yellow erasing powder to make changes. As soon as he had finished a paragraph, he noted the time of day and the state of the weather, so that in rereading his work later, he would be able to recapture his moments of inspiration.[16] For the autumn season he felt a particular sympathy. "My writing activity," he wrote five years later, "is greatest at the end of autumn and the beginning of winter. I can get close to the lamp, and the rhythm of the season is most conducive to feeling."[17]

In the winter of 1783, Chang left his position at Yung-p'ing. Apparently at this time he was engaged to compile a history of the Yung-ting river, for the river intendant Ch'en Tsung.[f] Then, probably through the influence of Liang Kuo-chih, he was made head of Lien-ch'ih (Lotus Pond) Academy in Pao-ting, and moved his family, now approaching twenty in number, to that city.

Here Chang remained for three years. One would think that he would have found this position an attractive one. Pao-ting was not Peking, but it was the provincial capital of Chihli and of some importance. It was on the main road to Peking, a stopping place for travelers going in a number of directions and close enough to the city so that Chang could make an occasional visit. The Lien-ch'ih position, furthermore, had been one of the positions he had tried and failed to obtain after his disastrous journey to Honan in 1781. But Chang was not happy and wrote later that he stayed only

---

[f] HY, pp. 58–59. Chang says that he was asked to write this history "in 1783–84." The Yung-ting River flows through Yung-ch'ing; possibly therefore Chou Chen-jung interceded for Chang with the river intendant. The completed work, *Yung-ting-ho Chih* (20 *chüan*), was not published, but the manuscript is in the Palace Museum Library in Peking (see the biography of Chang by Hiromu Momose in *ECCP*, p. 39).

because he could find no way of leaving.[18] It does indeed seem that Chang was depressed, for little of his significant writing was done during these years.

Chang arrived in Pao-ting to find a friend there before him— but a friend in circumstances that could have done little to improve Chang's state of mind. Pao-ting, as capital of the province, was a place of detention for criminals, and here, imprisoned since 1783, was Ts'ai Hsün, serving a life sentence, as commutation of his original sentence of death. Chang believed strongly that Ts'ai had been guiltless of any intentional wrongdoing, and now he paid him frequent visits in prison, where he found him, in spite of his misfortune, in considerably better cheer than himself. Ts'ai had his imprisonment terminated after four years, and died shortly after in 1788, when Chang had already moved on to new employment.[19]

Chang must have had a relatively comfortable income during this time. At some time during his stay in the provincial capital, probably in 1786, he edited a book for the lieutenant governor. And in the autumn of 1785 he was able to finance a printing of the popular moral and religious tract *T'ai-shang Kan-ying P'ien*— an act of piety in memory of his father and grandfather, who had thought highly of it.[g]

There are occasional indications in Chang's writings of this period that life was not wholly joyless in Pao-ting. Friends from nearby would occasionally come over to spend the evening with Chang. He describes a walk taken on a January night in 1787 with Chang Wei-ch'i (the fellow *chin-shih* who had helped him when he had been robbed six years before), Wei-ch'i's adopted son, Chang's son Hua-fu, and a few others. The weather had cleared

g HY, p. 63. *I-shu*, 29.12b–14a, "Postscript to the Printing of the *T'ai-shang Kan-ying P'ien*." Evidence of Chang's own interest in the "reward and retribution" doctrine of the *Kan-ying P'ien* is found in several short tales included at the end of *I-shu*, 18. The lieutenant governor, Liang K'en-t'ang (a native of Ch'ien-t'ang, Chekiang, *chin-shih* of 1756), had been in danger of severe punishment in 1782 as a result of the prosecution of Ho-shen's henchman, the Shantung governor Kuo-t'ai; he had served briefly under Kuo-t'ai and of course had not dared to make charges (*Kao-tsung Shih-lu*, 1154.18b, 21b–22a). Of all this Chang was no doubt aware. Liang became governor-general of Chihli in 1790.

after a heavy snowstorm; the evening stars were scattered in the sky and the moon was bright. Just the evening, suggested Wei-ch'i, to visit the old Lotus Blossom Pond. After they had walked for some time, Chang and Wei-ch'i sat down to rest and chat, watching the younger members of the party climb on the bridge and in the grottoes. Chang said to his friend, "Now I am almost fifty, and although I don't feel that my youthful zest has left me, I always give way to youngsters who are still under thirty and don't try to keep up with them." And Wei-ch'i admitted that he, too, was slowing up a bit—though he still had a few years before reaching Chang's age. Chang was possibly forty-eight by our way of counting and certainly not yet frail. But he was mellowing a little; we sense this in the armchair quality, the master-to-disciple tone, of much of his writing of the next few years.[20]

But Chang had not mellowed enough to lose his taste for his favorite form of enjoyment—a sharp and lively argument. Chou Chen-jung tells us that he came over from Yung-ch'ing on one occasion (shortly before Chang left Pao-ting permanently) to see his friend. The two presently found themselves arguing about the best method of teaching students to write, a subject on which both men had written in the past and on which both had firm views. Chou believed that one should start one's students using the T'ang and Sung essayists as models; Chang took the opposite position. Words flew and tempers rose. When Chang Wei-ch'i came in with a fourth friend, Chang did not even pause to greet them. The newcomers joined in, and the battle went on until Chang, overhearing some servants making fun of them, burst out laughing. The evening ended in a drinking bout.[21]

The year 1787, however, was an unhappy one for Chang and his family. Just three days after the moonlight walk in the snow, Liang Kuo-chih died. Soon after, Chang was forced out as master of Lien-ch'ih Academy. He had to move his family out of their quarters at the Academy to an inn, and before the year had ended two of his household died, including his fifth son. Sometime in the spring, hearing that men in his examination group were being selected for office, he went to Peking, only to be robbed there by night prowlers and thrown again upon the support of friends.[h]

Finally, when he was on the point of getting a magistracy, he changed his mind and declined it. We can guess his reasons. Chang himself says that he realized his talents were academic, not administrative, and that he was actually terrified lest he succeed in getting an appointment. He must have noted with great apprehension the quandary of petty officials during the ascendency of Ho-shen, and he must have recalled the unhappy outcome of his father's career. Certainly the sad end of his friend Ts'ai Hsün must have been much in his mind. Indeed, he writes, all of the minor officials he had known in Yung-p'ing had suffered some misfortune or other. Having made his decision, Chang returned to Pao-ting, and soon after that went south, leaving his family to follow later.[22]

Possibly it was not just the fear of an administrative career that prompted Chang's departure from Peking and Pao-ting at the end of 1787. It may also have been the hope of obtaining private support for his writing and research. At any rate, it was during the decade following this decision that Chang was drawn into the talented circle around Pi Yüan (1730–97), one of the most important patrons in the eighteenth century. A native of Kiangsu, Pi was both an able administrator and a scholar. He had been active in the suppression of several of the internal rebellions that marked the latter part of the century. He had distinguished himself, especially in the field of military supply, in the second Chin-ch'uan war in Szechwan (1771–76) and in the 1781 and 1784 Mohammedan risings in Kansu, which took place while he was governor of Shensi. From 1785 to 1788 he was governor of Honan, and from 1788 to 1794 governor-general of Hupeh and Hunan. Although in both these positions Pi had to contend with flood and famine, this was a period of relative internal quiet, a period that preceded the

---

[h] HY, p. 61. *I-shu*, 23.34b. Early in 1787 Wang Chieh (1725–1805), who had been associate examiner in the metropolitan examination of 1778, became a Grand Secretary. This fact may have caused Chang to suppose that he had a good chance of an appointment.

outbreak of fighting with the Miao aborigines of Kweichow in 1795 and the devastating rebellion of the White Lotus secret society in Hupeh in 1796. Pi was to die in camp in the course of the struggle with the White Lotus sect, a struggle that was to drag on, draining the resources of the state, until after Chang's own death.[23]

It was during this calm before the storm that Chang was most closely associated with Pi. They met in 1787, when Pi was still governor of Honan. Chang, armed with an introduction from Chou Chen-jung, visited Pi Yüan in K'ai-feng and tried to enlist his support for an ambitious project, which Chou had thought might interest Pi—a *Critique of Historical Writings* (*Shih-chi K'ao*), a massive study of historical bibliography that would require the extended labors of a number of scholars.[24]

In the letter he presented to Pi at this time, Chang recommended himself boldly. Then he pointed out the fact that his intended benefactor had already surpassed the famous patrons of old in attracting men of talent. "This being the case," Chang continued, "if I do not obtain a place at your side, where I can spew out the strange things within me, later on those who judge these matters will say it is indeed unfortunate that your story should be so incomplete—that one who so loved talent should not have had me in attendance, and that I, with my eccentric qualities, should not have had the restraining influence of your good judgment!" And he submitted with the letter copies of his Yung-ch'ing history and the "Rules of Compilation" for the Ho-chou history.[25] Ten years later Chang alluded to this event in a poem:

> I knocked at his gate and bowed, but had not the
> sense to be ashamed;
> I flaunted a letter, recommending myself without
> modesty.

In spite of his presumptuous letter, Chang was liberally received. Pi accepted the *Shih-chi K'ao* idea, and early the following year obtained for Chang the headship of Wen-cheng Academy in Kuei-te prefecture in Honan. Chang went on to Kuei-te, sent for his family, and started work on the *Shih-chi K'ao* at once.[26]

Chang's proposal seems to have been formally presented in a memorandum entitled "Essential Considerations in Compiling a Critique of Historical Writings" ("Lun Hsiu Shih-chi K'ao Yao-lüeh"), written about the beginning of 1788. In this proposal Chang reviewed what he considered to be the general inadequacies of existing work in historical bibliography. Few of the Standard Histories, he noted, have essays on bibliography; the reason for this is that their compilers did not have competent specialized bibliographical studies available to them (as Pan Ku, for example, had Liu Hsin's *Ch'i Lüeh*). A specialized work in the field of historical bibliography is therefore greatly needed. Chang continues:

The *Critique of Classical Studies* [*Ching-i K'ao*] of Chu I-tsun [1629–1709] is a very great achievement. After establishing which books were extant and which were lost, Chu proceeded to draw from bibliographical comments in many works, and from time to time used his own judgment to ascertain what was correct. His successors in the study of classical writings all rely upon him. If his organizational scheme is sometimes incomplete, it is because the creation of something new is difficult; and if his scope is limited to the category of the Classics, it is because historical writing is so vast that one man's strength is not enough to master this, too. And so there was obviously nothing for him to do but wait for a successor. Herewith I propose to compile a *Critique of Historical Writings,* essentially following Chu's pattern, with minor adjustments.

Next, Chang gives us a step-by-step outline of the way he would approach such a work: he would carefully distinguish different traditions of historical writing; he would treat separately fragments of earlier works embedded in later books; he would make a comprehensive study of the Classics (in ancient times, Chang believed, there was no distinction between Classics and history) and also of the categories of philosophy and literary collections, and would select from them titles of interest to the historian to be included in the critique; he would give proper attention to local histories and genealogies; he would indicate editions of all works in detail; and finally, he would clearly identify those books that had been proscribed, explaining why they had merited destruction. This was clearly, in Chang's mind, to be a work of great importance.[27]

Apparently Pi established an office for the compilation of the *Shih-chi K'ao,* for Chang's correspondence of this time indicates that he was supervising and directing research in which a number of scholars were cooperating, including Wu I (1745–99), Ling T'ing-k'an (1747–1809), and Hung Liang-chi. The work apparently got under way early in 1788. A letter to Hung dated April 6, 1788, gives a rough idea of the procedure that was followed. Chang writes:

I have now gotten some respite from official protocol, banquets, and calls [at Pi's headquarters at K'ai-feng], and from now on I shall be working steadily on the *Critique.* I have skimmed through the *History of the Ming* and the section on philosophers in the *Ssu-k'u* catalog and have gained a good deal of understanding from this, adding new comments.

Hung, it appears, was to work on the historical section of the *Ssu-k'u* catalog (the Four Categories catalog of the recently completed Imperial Manuscript Library), while Chang was to work on philosophers and literary collections. In addition, said Chang, they would have to go very carefully through the whole Sung encyclopedia *Sea of Jade* (*Yü Hai*) and not limit their attention to the section on historical bibliography for which this encyclopedia had always been famous. Later in the year, they would all get together to organize their material and set up a general plan for further work.[28]

What is of particular interest, both in Chang's proposal to Pi and in his method of procedure, is his assumption that a critical bibliography of historical writing should cover far more than what was conventionally regarded as history. Chang stresses this point in a letter dated June 26 to Sun Hsing-yen (1753–1818), who seems to have been a corresponding participant in Peking. In the *Shih-chi K'ao,* he said, he was not restricting his attention to books conventionally classified as history, but was investigating Classics, philosophers, and literary collections as well. "As I see it," Chang wrote, "anything in the world that has anything to do with writing is historical scholarship. The Six Classics are simply six kinds of history used by the sages to transmit their teachings. The different schools of literary and philosophical writing all derive from history," though these traditions are no longer identified with their origins.[29] This outright identification of the Classics as "history" is one of Chang's most famous theses and is stated axiomatically at the beginning of Chang's essays "The Teaching of the *Changes*" ("I Chiao"), which may already have been written by this date. The view is a result, or at least a consistent part, of Chang's theories on the origin of writing, the nature of the Classics, and the history of different traditions of writing—theories he had already expressed in the *Chiao-ch'ou Tung-i* and "The Teaching of the *Odes*."

There is no indication of work on the *Shih-chi K'ao* in the following year, and it seems fairly obvious that both Chang and Pi Yüan were sufficiently occupied with other matters. Chang's time was taken up by various projects. In the spring of 1788 (possibly under the stimulus of his work in historical bibliography) he re-edited his *Chiao-ch'ou Tung-i,* making extensive changes in it. Also at Kuei-te he produced ten new essays for the *Wen-shih T'ung-i.*

The titles for most of these are not known. One, however, was an essay entitled "The Teaching of the *Rites*" ("Li Chiao").[i] This was still another speculative reflection on the evolution of classical disciplines, similar to "The Teaching of the *Odes*." It also indicates that, by this time, Chang had well in hand the series of essays of this type that now begins the *Wen-shih T'ung-i.* It is close in thought also to "The Teaching of the *History*," which Chang wrote four years later.

Although this period seems to have been a very productive one, Chang was not able to remain long at the Wen-cheng Academy. In the fall of 1788 a flood in central China prompted the court to shift Pi Yüan, the flood and famine expert, to the governor-generalship of Hu-kuang. With Pi's removal from Honan, Chang lost his backing in the Kuei-te position and was obliged to relinquish it. In the winter we find him in nearby Po-chou, Anhwei, enjoying the hospitality of the magistrate P'ei Chen, who had been a friend

---

[i] One other essay, "So-chien" ("Points of View"), can be dated this year (HY, p. 67).

since Chang's Peking days. Chang moved his family once more, first putting them up in P'ei's official residence and later moving them into a private house.[30]

In the spring of 1789 Chang, obviously needing income, wandered on south to T'ai-p'ing. There he found one of Chu Yün's former students, Hsü Li-kang, now education commissioner. Chang stayed three months. Hsü had undertaken to compile a genealogy of his family. The project had proved too much for him, so when Chang arrived Hsü welcomed the opportunity to turn it over to a specialist. After much work, Chang found that he didn't have the free hand he wanted, and a number of theoretical pieces on family history written at the time are probably the result of his impatience. Forced then to find new outlets for self-expression, Chang turned to purely philosophical matters. In late spring, new essays for his *Wen-shih T'ung-i* poured forth in a veritable flood. On his way back from Tai-p'ing in the sixth month, he passed through Yang-chou and visited Shen Yeh-fu, who had a large part of Chang's recent writings copied. Back at Po-chou later in the year, he started work on a local history for P'ei Chen, which he finished in the spring of 1790.[31] After this, he once more enjoyed the patronage of Pi Yüan, and for several years had fewer worries.

Chang has written that these years of teaching and wandering were very difficult. There were times when he had his back to the wall—in 1781 after being robbed near Fei-hsiang, and perhaps in 1787 after being abruptly dismissed in Pao-ting and then robbed again in Peking. Yet the Pao-ting position, while it lasted, must have provided a comfortable living; Liang Kuo-chih obviously could afford to pay a tutor well; and in Yung-ch'ing Chang was offered more commissions than he could accept. Perhaps Chang pleads distress too easily—especially when writing to his patrons. After all, if he were really desperate, could he not have tried a little harder to get a government position?[j]

---

[j] It is Professor Paul Demiéville's view that Chang complains too much about his condition in life, for "all he had to do, after all, was to accept a post in the provincial administration, to which his degrees entitled him." Demiéville, p. 173.

Chang had good reasons for hesitating to present himself for a magistracy. But did he need one? In a poem in 1797, Chang wrote —rather imprecisely—that during the ten years beginning (apparently) with his move to Yung-p'ing in 1782 his earnings were "about 20,000," presumably silver *liang*. An average annual income of 2,000 *liang* would have allowed Chang to live very comfortably, and to have saved for the future as well. It was approximately the income of a prefect in the mid-nineteenth century, and nearly six times as much as an academy master could make at that time.[k] Yet Chang included this information in a list of the vexations and tragedies of his teaching years. He was obviously complaining. At the time he wrote, to be sure, he was looking back on his years of greatest earning power, years that should have provided for his old age. But Chang does seem to have been a person not easily satisfied, in this as in other ways. It may be that in him a hypersensitivity about his role in the world—of which we will see more—was reflected in an extravagant style of living.

He maintained a larger family than a man of his station required. By this time he had a second concubine (née Tseng) and, of course, still more children.[l] When he moved to Yung-p'ing in 1782, he had a family of about ten persons. But his sons probably married young, had children of their own, and were not self-supporting. The household for which Chang was responsible climbed, as a result, to twenty persons. With his responsibilities rapidly

[k] See Chang Chung-li, *The Income of the Chinese Gentry* (Seattle, 1962), pp. 14, 94. It is true that in the last half of the eighteenth century there was prolonged inflation. Hung Liang-chi said in 1793 that during the preceding fifty years, living expenses had risen nearly sixfold. See the essay, "Sheng-chi" ("Livelihood") in Hung's *I-yen* (*Opinions*) in *Chüan-shih-ke Wen Chia-chi*, 1.10a, *Hung Pei-chiang Hsien-sheng Ch'üan-chi* (Shou-ching-t'ang edition, 1877). For a translation, see Darlene T. Goodwin, "Selected Essays of Hung Liang-chi (1746–1809)" (unpublished master's thesis, Stanford University, June, 1961), pp. 25–27.
    Apparently the exchange rate of copper cash to silver was less favorable than it became later—800 to one in the middle of the eighteenth century as against 1200 to one in the middle of the nineteenth. See *Ch'ing Shih Kao, chüan* 130; and Chang Chung-li, p. 100. Chang's poem (*I-shu*, 28.51b) is addressed to Tseng Yü, an official he hoped would employ him to write another local history. See Chapter 9.
[l] HY, p. 147. Sons by this second concubine were Hua-lien and Hua-chi.

mounting, there can be little doubt that these years were trying for him. And although at his academies living quarters were occasionally provided, Chang's expenses were still abnormally high because he had to move so frequently. In the four years from 1787 to 1790 he moved no less than five times, "with all the household including the sick and the dead. In the midst of all the luggage, with the hens and the dogs, . . . and the books, we had to carry the coffins, chased through the waves of the rivers, through the dust of the roads." Some of the time the family may have suffered actual privation; in fact, six of the household died between 1780 and 1790, four of them apparently minors.[32]

In view of these facts, the amount and the quality of Chang's writing at this time is truly surprising. Some of his writing, of course, yielded good income, but essays in philosophy did not, unless cleverly disguised. Perhaps for Chang this sort of writing was partly a happy escape from just the preoccupations we might think would have encouraged it.

Chang's return in the spring and summer of 1789 to the scenes of his earlier life in Anhwei seems to have been an important period of reflection for him. His ideas about bibliography and literature had already taken shape; in historiography there were still interesting new ideas to come. But from Chang's taking stock of himself and his beliefs in 1789 came the writings that are of widest and most enduring appeal. The T'ai-p'ing essays, in particular, form a remarkably complete and coherent view of the life of learning and of the world as it appeared to a man of letters. They contain what is philosophically the most interesting part of Chang's thought, and they are stylistically among the finest pieces in his *Wen-shih T'ung-i.*

In May 1789, while he was at T'ai-p'ing, Chang wrote twenty-three new essays. Most of these can be identified with some certainty.[m] The list includes at least the following:

[m] Various manuscripts contain notes giving the date when most of these essays were "copied for preservation." For several opinions on the identity of those written at T'ai-p'ing, see HY, pp. 68, 71–72; WHL, p. 272; Ch'ien Mu, p. 422.

"On the Tao" ("Yüan Tao"). An essay in three parts, with the same title as the opening essay in the *Chiao-ch'ou T'ung-i*, but much longer. It is a speculative reconstruction of the history of civilization and of the state, and an analysis of the validity and nature of the Confucian tradition.

"On Learning" ("Yüan Hsüeh"). In three parts. An examination of the nature of traditional knowledge; it is an continuation of the preceding essay.

"An Explanation of the Classics" ("Ching Chieh"). In three parts. An elaboration of Chang's conception of the Classics as set forth in the *Chiao-ch'ou T'ung-i*.

"The Meaning of the Word 'Historian'" ("Shih Shih"). An argument that the scholar or writer, in order to justify himself, must be concerned with problems of the present day.

"Historical Commentary" ("Shih Chu"). An essay recommending that histories be accompanied by notes prepared by the authors.

"On Conventional Judgments" ("Hsi Ku"). An analysis of the process of forming and refining moral judgments, which concludes with an admonition against over-dogmatic judgments of right and wrong.

"The Analogy of Heaven" ("T'ien Yü"). An attempt to state the historical laws governing the development of learning and thought from the analogy of the development of astronomical theories.

"On Teachers" ("Shih Shuo"). A discussion of the relationship between student and teacher in the transmission of different skills and kinds of learning. (This essay, like "On the Tao," is a rejoinder to an essay by Han Yü.)

"One's Grant of Years" ("Chia Nien"). On the problem of the man of learning who tries to cope with the increasingly larger number of books in the world within the limited span of a lifetime.

"Collected Opinions" ("Shuo Lin"). On various problems of metaphysics, historiography, and literary theory.[n]

"Some Errors Corrected" ("K'uang Miu"). A miscellany of complaints: it is absurd to suppose that the titles to chapters in *Mencius*, *Lun Yü*, and other classics have any significance; absurd also to see numerological significance in the numbers of chapters in the various parts of the *Shih-chi*; and wrong to present one's ideas in the form of a fictitious dialogue if one names a real person as "questioner."

"A Criticism of Hypocrisy" ("Pien Ssu"). A logical analysis of an

[n] There is a reference in "Collected Opinions" (*I-shu*, 4.20b) to the essays "Ta K'e Wen" and "Shih T'ung," both of which were written in 1790; therefore at least a part of the "Collected Opinions" was written in that year.

ethical problem: why does the same language when used by two different persons sometimes conceal different intentions or reflect different states of mind?

"Chu and Lu" ("Chu Lu"), i.e., Chu Hsi and Liu Chiu-yüan. An analysis of the nature of the controversy between the two principal opposing points of view in Neo-Confucian thought; a defense of Chu Hsi and a criticism of various attitudes toward him, particularly that of Tai Chen.°

"On the Difficulty of Being Understood" ("Chih Nan"). "Knowing" another person is not a matter of knowing his name and being familiar with his manner and appearance, but of reading what he writes and understanding why he says it. This ability is so rare that the writer must despair of being understood by some reader in a later age.

"My Feelings About Being Appreciated and Employed" ("Kan Yü"). Chang's protest of his indifference to fame and position.

"The Essence of Literary Art" ("Wen Li"). The problem of learning to write and of transmitting appreciation for good literary style from teacher to student.

"On Breadth and Economy" ("Po Yüeh") is a three-part essay sometimes counted in this group. It is a very beautiful restatement of Chang's ideals of the life of learning; in thought it is closely related to the others, although it seems to have been written at the end of the year.ᵖ

These essays took up the central historical thesis of the *Chiao-ch'ou T'ung-i* and developed out of it, or rationalized in terms of it, a theory of the life of learning and a sophisticated philosophy of history. They amplify Chang's view of the nature and purpose of writing and his justification of the life of the scholar. The T'ai-p'ing essays are beautifully written and show a clarity of thought that anyone familiar with the Chinese classical prose essay would admire. Chang was delighted with his own work. "In all my life," he said, "I have never written anything better than these."[33]

° Ch'ien Mu (p. 422) believes this essay to have been written before Tai's death in 1777, and assigns the supplement to it ("Chu Lu P'ien Shu Hou") to 1789. I have followed HY (pp. 83–84) in assigning the supplement to 1790.
ᵖ This essay was sent to Shen Tsai-t'ing (son of Shen Yeh-fu) in a letter written about the end of the year; the essay, as it now stands, refers to this correspondence.

5. Art and Substance

The ancients said, "If something is not beautifully expressed, it will not be widely read."
— *Answers to Objections . . .* 1790

In Antiquity art and substance were one.
— *The Teaching of the Odes . . .* 1783

In 1790, Chang Hsüeh-ch'eng was past fifty and had been writing for nearly three decades. But most of the essays he had just written remained unpublished for nearly half a century. Chang was not, as we might suppose from this, one of those authors whose writings are rejected by one publisher after another. In eighteenth-century China, publishing was not usually a commercial enterprise. One might write a novel—surreptitiously—or edit a collection of model *pa-ku* essays in the hope that a printer would take it on as a business venture, but Chang is not known to have produced works of this kind. The sorts of things he wrote had to be published privately (if at all) at his own expense or at the expense of a patron who would hire the copyists and blockcutters to do the job. A writer, then, had to find a patron whose fortunes were steady and whose loyalty was unshakable, and at this Chang had not been very successful. Chou Chen-jung had published his history of Yung-ch'ing. But a work like the *Chiao-ch'ou T'ung-i* had to remain among his notebooks. There were, of course, no magazines, newspapers, or professional journals.

There were, however, means of publication other than the ones we readily think of. Chang's most important writings were essays and letters, two kinds of writing that were very much alike. Letters were written to be passed around, copied, and eventually published. Some writers wrote them as a way of using up the random notes and pearls of wisdom that they were unable to incorporate into their essays. It was not unheard of for a writer to publish his letters to an acquaintance even while that acquaintance was still living and without his permission.[a] Essays, once written, were often copied by several friends, then sent off by post to still more friends to be copied again, passed around, and discussed. Chang's writing did enjoy this kind of distribution, and in this way he became moderately well known and carefully read by those whose opinion he valued. Certainly a number of Chang's essays of 1789 were quickly circulated in this manner.

Therefore, when Chang met Tuan Yü-ts'ai for the first time (early in 1790 at Pi Yüan's headquarters in Hupeh), Tuan already knew him by reputation. Tuan was a philologist best known for his studies of the Han dictionary, *Shuo-wen*; he had also edited the works of Tai Chen, now dead, for whom he had the deepest respect. These were not promising common interests. But Tuan, who knew of the *Shih-chi K'ao* undertaking, expressed admiration for Chang's work in history, so Chang showed him the manuscripts of more of his essays. Tuan admired the profound passages in them. But he also noted that some of them showed more than a trace of the parallel style of *pa-ku*. Chang was apparently quite upset by this criticism, and wrote to his younger friend and admirer Shih Chih-kuang about it. "The only thing that matters in one's writing is whether what one says is right!" he exploded. "Surely there's nothing really essential in the distinction between ancient and modern prose! Granted that parallel sentences are common in the modern prose style, but surely parallelism wasn't invented by writers of modern prose!"[1]

Why should Chang have been so nettled? Because, for one thing, he knew that what Tuan had said was quite true. His prose often

---

[a] Arthur Waley, *Yuan Mei*, pp. 112–13. In 1797, Hung Liang-chi published a letter he had written to Chang a decade earlier, criticizing some of his ideas about the organization of local histories. Chang was quite indignant; but in the same year he himself wrote Sun Hsing-yen a long letter containing both intellectual and personal criticism, and submitted a copy of it to a mutual friend, Yao Nai (and probably to others), for editorial comment. And in 1796 Chang published a small selection of his own writings, some of which were letters to living friends. See HY, p. 125.

does have the artificial quality of the examination essay, with one
long sentence followed by another that artfully and exactly mimics
it. This style does become tedious and may account in part for the
fact that recognition for Chang has come slowly and late. As a
young man, Chang had hated having to learn to write *pa-ku*. This
was the traditional attitude of youthful rebelliousness, and Chang
always felt himself a rebel. This attitude had its noble rationale: to
concentrate endlessly on mastering a petty and tedious technique
in order to advance oneself in the world was to degrade the great
profession of writing, a profession that should be approached with
sincerity, not self interest. It was to corrupt oneself. It could be expected to stifle the naturalness of one's expression and make it impossible for whatever might be of value in one's inner nature to
pour forth on paper. It could (and did) subtly tempt one to distort
one's thought to fit the artificial requirements of style.

Chang, knowing this, had gradually made his compromises,
passed his examinations, and spent more than a decade teaching
other young men to do the same. He had reason to feel, uneasily
and probably subconsciously, that he had not been true to the ideals
of his youth. And so, even though Tuan volubly admired Chang's
thought, his criticism stung. But Chang had not just become old
and sensible; he had, in fact, changed his views about *pa-ku* for
philosophical as well as practical reasons. Even in 1783, one of his
essays contained almost grotesque praise of the institution of examination-essay writing. Later, he wrote to Shao Chin-han that
he had, indeed, been inclined in youth to sniff at the view that "you
cannot write ancient prose unless you study *pa-ku*," and to ask,
"Did Ssu-ma Ch'ien, Pan Ku, and Ou-yang Hsiu ever write examination essays?" But, Chang went on, he had come to see that
this way of thinking was mistaken.[b]

[b] For each age has its literary ways, and one must recognize that one lives in the
present, not the past ("To Shao Chin-han, on Literary Art," *I-shu*, "pu-i," 39b–
42b). This letter will be discussed further in Chapter 6. No one, to my knowledge,
has dated it, but in content it is close to Chang's thinking in 1789 and following
years. Chang printed it in 1796.

On Teaching Students to Read and Write

As a teacher of Chinese classical prose composition, whose success would inevitably be measured by that of his students in the examinations, Chang had to concern himself with teaching techniques. What he has to say on the subject is illuminating, for it shows us the standard pedagogical methods that teacher and student had to accept or resist, and it shows us, in addition, Chang's conception of the relationship between technical artistic skill and substantial literary value. In 1785, at the Lien-ch'ih Academy in Pao-ting, Chang found himself with a group of students who were not only trying to master the examination skills but also planning to become teachers of writing. So he wrote for them a statement of teaching methods in an essay entitled "On Teaching Students to Write."[c]

Chang takes it for granted in this statement that the student must eventually be taught *pa-ku,* although there is genuine danger that such instruction might extinguish in him any latent capacities to write anything worthwhile. Chang discusses the value of such latent capacities in a surprisingly modern way. The things a child writes before he has been taught to be skillful, Chang says, sometimes have a natural and wonderful quality that he cannot attain again later. In the same way, the first characters a child attempts to draw are sometimes close to archaic seal-form in their unspoiled artlessness; they lose this quality when the child becomes adept. What a young student is first exposed to is very important, for it sets his habits of expression. If he has to spend long hours learning the techniques of *pa-ku,* there is a danger that he will never develop anything more than a certain mechanical cleverness of thought and style; as a result, he will never have any good ideas. Therefore it is better to start students writing ancient prose, which "contains the *tao* and yet is free in form," rather than *pa-ku,* which is "in essence of a low order and very exact in form."[2]

---

[c] *I-shu,* "pu-i," 1a–11a. The theses in this essay were surely the substance of Chang's argument with Chou Chen-jung in 1787.

The prevailing pedagogical absurdities of his time are revealed in the methods Chang attacks in this essay. It was apparently usual to start training a student in *pa-ku* immediately, and customary to take up in order the various formal parts of the examination essay. First a student was drilled in composing disembodied examples of "broaching the theme." Then his teacher moved him on to the part of the essay called "taking up the theme," and so on. If you were learning to talk, Chang asks derisively, would you study beginning to speak for a while, and then move on to stopping? Or if learning to breathe, would you spend a few years on exhaling, and then take up inhaling? Chang feels that a student should be taught from the beginning to form ideas and express them in complete compositions, even if his compositions are at first only a sentence long. After the student has really learned to say something, he can be taught the techniques of *pa-ku* as one way of expressing himself.[3]

The student's training does, of course, have to have an ordered sequence. Chang thinks the student should be started with a careful study of the *Tso Chuan*. (This is what the young Chang had studied, when out of sight of his writing master.) The *Tso Chuan* would give him the background for Confucius's ideas, and at the same time would show him how ideas and citations from the basic Classics can be used in critical or hortatory discussions of events and problems. The student should then practice writing such discussions for himself. Then, after this relatively easy beginning, his teacher should have him make a study of the different kinds of persons in the "Spring and Autumn" period, collecting material on them as is done in the classified biographies in the Standard Histories. In his writing practice at this stage, he should use as models the comments and appraisals at the ends of the biographies in the *Shih-chi,* and at the beginnings of the tables and monographs in that book. The virtue of these models is their variety. They offer the student no obvious form to copy: some are philosophical, others are chapter summaries, others introduce new material or classical

quotations. In them the student will read a mixture of brilliant and
ordinary functional language. And this, Chang says, will be good
for him, for if a student is confronted with a set of models of uni-
formly elegant writing, he will come to think that study and writing are two different occupations; his writing will then be "flowers
without fruit."[4]

At every stage, then, the student is given something solid to
write about while he is being trained in literary expression. And in
this essay writing, the student should not be allowed to apply explicit forms; he should, however, be led to use the sort of material
that he will have to use later in writing *pa-ku*. The student should
ultimately move on to the writing of historical narratives—the most
difficult of all, Chang thinks, because here the writing must be
completely subservient to the direction taken by the events, without
formal guidelines of any kind.[5]

The importance of *ku-wen* (ancient prose) and its connection
with historical writing were ideas of the T'ung-ch'eng school of
literary art. The stress Chang places on the connection in his discourse on teaching methods is another evidence (it will not be
the last) of the influence of T'ung-ch'eng ideas on his thought.[d]
Chang, who was probably first exposed to T'ung-ch'eng critical
theory in Peking, spent several of the most productive literary
periods in his life in Anhwei, for generations the home of this
literary school.

In fact, four years later, when Chang was writing in Anhwei,
he dealt with these literary questions again in a delightful essay,
"The Essence of Literary Art" ("Wen Li"). In it he asks not only,
"How does a student learn to write?" and "What is it that he has
learned when he learns this?" but also, "How does a student learn

---

[d] The connection appears again in a letter to Wang Hui-tsu in 1796 (HY, pp. 120–
21). Present-day "fashions," Chang thinks, place too much value on ascertaining
facts and not enough on expressing one's ideas about them; the solution is to turn
to ancient prose, which means studying historical writing. Han Yü's error was in
making his models the Classics rather than history, failing to understand that the
Classics actually evolved into history.

to appreciate good writing?" and "How does a teacher teach him?" These questions were constant preoccupations of Chinese literary theory from Sung times on, and it was natural that they should be dealt with in Chang's discussions with his friends. But Chang's treatment of them in this essay focused on two important commitments of T'ung-ch'eng criticism: the literary merit of the Ming writer Kuei Yu-kuang (1506–71) and the value of Ssu-ma Ch'ien's *Shih-chi* as a model of ancient prose style.

Chang's essay was inspired by a literary conversation that probably took place in T'ung-ch'eng in the library of a friend, a local man of letters named Tso Mei.[e] In his friend's house, Chang happened to see a manuscript copy of the *Shih-chi*. Opening it, he discovered it to be carefully marked in several colors of ink. Tso explained that it came from the literary school of Kuei Yu-kuang. The symbols in color, he said, were supposed to indicate various points of style, structure, and "spirit" that would instruct a student in the principles of *ku-wen*. He added that this manuscript had been passed on to his family in a private tradition. He hastened to assure Chang that while he had used it in his youth, he had long since outgrown such things.

This exchange prompted Chang to make some critical comments on Kuei and other Ming writers. In his essay, he praises Kuei because he resisted the false archaisms made popular in the writing of his day by Wang Shih-chen (1526–90) and Li P'an-lung (1514–70); and he admits that Kuei, a writer of *pa-ku*, was as competent in his medium as Ssu-ma Ch'ien and Han Yü had been in theirs. Chang feels that Kuei's interest in the *Shih-chi* and other classic examples of ancient prose has had great influence on present-day writers of modern prose. But unlike Ssu-ma Ch'ien, Kuei did not really have

---

[e] Tso Mei was evidently a writer committed to the T'ung-ch'eng tradition. He was a student of Yao Nai and was indirectly related to Liu Ta-K'uei (1697?–1779), another well-known member of the school. There are brief appreciations of Tso and other members of his family in the literary collection of Fang Tung-shu (1772–1851), a later T'ung-ch'eng writer (*I-wei-hsüan Wen-chi*, 1868, 10.8a–b, 10b–11a). Tso's writings are listed in *An-hui T'ung-chih* (reedition of 1877), 223.21a.

anything to say. He is a bit superficial and facile, and has merely grazed what is nearest the surface in the *Shih-chi,* without probing its depths. In doing so, he has set a precedent for mere stylistic imitation.[6]

The manuscript Chang saw was apparently a version of Kuei's *Shih-chi P'ing-tien.* (The "critical punctuation" of texts used as models of style was fashionable in Ming literary circles.) Kuei, opposing Wang Shih-chen's use of archaic language, praised the "Eight Essayists of the T'ang and Sung," especially Ou-yang Hsiu and Tseng Kung. The T'ung-ch'eng school of Fang Pao and Yao Nai esteemed this text of the *Shih-chi* and thereby showed its feeling that artistic prose writing and historical writing are very closely connected. One modern critic has said that Kuei did not "value flavor [*hsing-wei*] without regard for moral significance [*i-li*]," but regarded learning (*hsüeh-wen*) as the basis of style; "as a consequence, the ancient-prose school in the Ch'ing came to have a connection with the philosophy of Chu Hsi."[7] Since all of these attitudes are close to Chang's, perhaps we may assume that in politely criticizing Kuei here, he is censuring a failing in a locally admired writer he otherwise thinks well of.

These specific criticisms of Kuei lead Chang to make some general ones about writing. Artistic writing should be a genuine expression of a writer's thoughts and feelings, and an interest in style that leads him to do anything else is a vice. It is absurd to try to express in one's writing a feeling one doesn't have: "A gentleman of wealth and status, even in a drunken reverie, would be unable to utter the words of a shivering beggar; a man in sickness and distress, even in the midst of a lavish banquet, would be unable to change his plaintive tone for expressions of joy and laughter." Yet literary art is important, for the ability to write well is necessary if one is to communicate one's learning, and the philosophers Ch'eng I and Ch'eng Hao of the Sung were wrong to belittle it.[8] But what is good writing? How does the student learn to recognize it, let alone produce it?

Good writing essentially requires the reader to apprehend its excellence for himself. It is like the flavor of food and drink or the warmth and lightness of clothing: the person who eats the food or wears the clothing understands it for himself, but it is hard for him to explain it to others. If you want to explain to a person the nature of clothing and food, you must show him a piece of roast meat and let him taste it for himself, so that he may appreciate its flavor; or show him a fur garment and let him try it on, so that he may appreciate its warmth and lightness. . . . But you are making a mistake if you try to convey the flavor of the food by spitting it out of your mouth into his, or if you try to convey the warmth of a garment by grabbing him and enfolding him in the one you are wearing.[9]

This brings Chang to the central problem posed by the colored marks on the *Shih-chi* manuscript: of what use is any such attempt to convey the principles of style to another, so that he not only recognizes them but also values them and knows how to use them? Chang finds that it is only the formal side of art that can be explicitly taught, and not the inspiration that directs it. The formal aspect is not so obvious, however, in ancient prose like the *Shih-chi*. "Therefore, when the ancients talk about writing, they often speak of the value of reading books to nourish the spirit, of the importance of having a wide knowledge of the past and a thorough understanding of the Classics, of the advantage of personal study under teachers and a close association with friends, and of the methods of choosing helpful material. This is the correct method." Marking up texts with private symbols (as Kuei Yu-kuang marked up his *Shih-chi*) can aid one's memory, but the symbols are of no use in conveying understanding to another. "A father cannot teach them to his son, and a teacher cannot pass them on to his students."

Good writing results, it seems, when in appropriate circumstances one expresses what one is, if one has become the right sort of person. Learning to write, then, is a form of Confucian self-cultivation. The great literary critics—Lu Chi, Liu Hsieh, Chung Hung—understood, too, that the essence of good writing can only be suggested. One cannot produce it by imitation. The use of stock symbols in poetry, for example, is to be deplored. Why, Chang asks, if someone longs for another and thinks of him while looking at the moon, does it follow that the moon always signifies longing for a distant friend?[10]

The teacher can teach the fixed rules that apply to regular poetry or *pa-ku,* but there are no fixed rules for the rhythm of the old poetry and the principles of ancient prose. Here the teacher must aid the student to understand intuitively not only the art of writing but also its meaning. The meaning of a piece of writing cannot be exhausted by examining it from a single point of view; it will mean one thing to one person and something else to another. One cannot interpret for another, for the second person would surely miss the real feeling in the writing. And if you proclaim your interpretation as the only right interpretation, even if it is followed by others, it would not be recognized by the author as his own.[11]

In his feeling that the teacher can, at most, help the student to understand and that this understanding is an appreciative response to the thing understood, Chang shows his debt to Ch'an, to Wang Yang-ming, and to the Taoist side of the Confucian tradition. As we shall see, direct experience and intuition play important roles in his theories about knowledge and historical writing. But in both the "Essence of Literary Art" and "On Teaching Students to Write," Chang is most concerned with expressing his antipathy for a preoccupation with mere externals of style. A piece of writing must have an "object," something to say; literary art is important when it is used to further this "object." But true art is never a matter of turning out, as the social occasion demands, a poem in this mood or an essay in that form.

In Chang's work, especially between 1783 and 1789, there is much that deals with the problem of good writing and with literary tradition. In the many ways he approaches these matters, we find him always concerned with the problem of the relationship between what a writer says and how he says it, or as Chang often puts it, between "literary art" (*wen*) and "substance" (*chih*). In 1783, while he was teaching in Yung-p'ing, his mind seems to have been especially alive to such theoretical literary problems. In his writings of that year, I find at least three distinct lines of reflection to which the "art vs. substance" conception is relevant: first, the implications, for the history of belles lettres, of Liu Hsin's theories of the derivation of intellectual and literary traditions from the age of the Classics; second, the problem of the importance of individual authorship; and third, the nature of the art of the poet. Let us examine what Chang says about each of these matters.

The Heritage of the Odes

There are a handful of essays that develop in detail Chang's idea that post-classical writing is derived from the Classics. These essays on the "teachings" (*chiao*) of the Classics are at the beginning of the present *Wen-shih T'ung-i.*[1] The second essay, "The Teaching of the *Odes*" ("Shih Chiao"), was written in 1783. It is one of the best examples of what Chang considered the historical analysis of writing to be. But Chang's reasoning is tortuous, in the traditional manner of Chinese scholarship, and one must keep in mind that it was not written for Western readers. He starts by deliberately stating rather enigmatically a set of theses:

Chou declined and culture decayed, the *tao* of the Six Arts ceased, and the philosophers raised their voices against each other. We may say that by the age of the Warring States, the permutations of literary art were complete; by the age of the Warring States, writing was a specialized occupation; by the age of the Warring States, the literary types of later times were all developed. Therefore, if we examine writing of this period, we may see the reasons for literature's rise and fall, its flowering and decline.[12]

f Chang's essay titles are derived from the well-known passage that opens Chapter 26 of the *Record of the Rites* (*Li Chi*): "Confucius said, 'When you enter a state, it is possible to know what the people have been taught.'" If such and such qualities of intelligence and character are observed among people, this is due to the "teaching" (*chiao*) of this or that Classic. (The Classics whose "teachings" are thus characterized by Confucius are, in order, the *Odes, History, Music, Changes, Rites,* and *Spring and Autumn.*) The particular influences that Confucius is said here to assign to the several classical traditions have little or nothing to do with Chang's thought. But the conception of the Classics in these essays is continuous in his mind with Confucius's (and Ou-yang Hsiu's) idea that in antiquity "government and teaching were one." For this reason, I have consistently rendered *chiao* as "teaching." Here, one must take the word as meaning "tradition" or "cultural influence."

Chang proposed to examine the writing of the period of the Warring States (402–221 B.C.) and to show three things: first, that all of it derives from the classical traditions (the Six Arts); second, that the literary genres of later times are all found in this period; and third, that for the most part the literature of this period derives from the "teaching of the *Odes.*" The critical purpose of this historical analysis is the same as it was assumed to be in the *Chiao-ch'ou T'ung-i*:

> Only when a person understands that the essential types of literature [*wen-t'i*] were complete in the period of the Warring States, can I discuss with him the writing of later times; only when he understands that the various ancient philosophical schools originated in the Six Arts, can I discuss with him the writing of the period of the Warring States; only when he understands that the writing of the period of the Warring States developed largely from the teaching of the *Odes,* can I discuss with him the writing in the Six Arts; only when I can discuss with him the writing in the Six Arts, can we leave writing [literary expression] and see the *tao*; and only when we can do that, can we hold up the *tao* and criticize thereby the various traditions of writing.[18]

The extreme semantic instability of Chang's philosophical vocabulary must be noted here. One of the most vexing words in Chang's vocabulary (and in the writings of many Chinese literary theorists) is the word *wen*—"writing," or "literary expression." The whole point of the passage just quoted depends on this word having two meanings: "writing" in the ordinary sense, and "writing" in an esoteric sense as the visible expression of the *tao. Wen* is culture itself ("Chou declined and culture [*wen*] decayed."). It is art (*wen*) as opposed to substance (*chih*). It is the metaphysical principle of ornamentation or elegance in the universe (or in the history of an age) as opposed to the principle of simplicity (again, *chih*). If we see this, we can begin to see why the *wen-jen,* the Chinese literary man, takes himself and his art so seriously. His hand and brush are for him the instrument through which the *tao* is "poured out" on paper, through which the essence of the cosmos takes beautiful form, and by which civilization advances or declines.

Chang continues: The literature of the Warring States is seen to derive from the Six Arts when it is understood that the *tao* includes all truth and value, and that the classical disciplines have expressed this truth and value completely. Hence, in the writings of the philosophers, Chang argues, anything that is sound and valuable must be covered in the classical disciplines, even though the ancient philosophers themselves were not aware of it. Lao Tzu, for example, with his interest in *yin* and *yang,* and Chuang Tzu, with his use of image and metaphor, are both in the tradition of the *Classic of Changes.* Shen Pu-hai and Han Fei Tzu center their thinking upon rewards and punishments, and hence derive from the discipline of the *Spring and Autumn.*[9]

It is this already familiar kind of essentialist argument that Chang uses to show the derivation of writing from the *Odes.* Anything like the *Odes* in some basic respect must, to that extent, be of its tradition. In part Chang's idea is a sequence of non sequiturs helped along by the mercurial semantics of the word *wen*: one aspect of the tradition of the *Odes* is the graceful, beautiful presentation of whatever the writer or speaker has to say. In the Classical Age, when all knowledge of government, society, and the world was contained in the offices of Chou, knowledge needed no conscious artistic expression; for "in antiquity, art (*wen*) and substance were one." But with the decline of culture (*wen*) at the end of the Chou period, it was necessary for the schools of philosophy that inherited the pieces of this tradition to express (*wen*) this knowledge gracefully in order to gain acceptance. In this curious sense, all writing (*wen*) of that age, considered in its literary aspect as *beautiful* expression, can be assigned to the tradition of the *Odes.*[14]

Chang's next move must be to prove that artistic writing of later times also derives from the tradition of the *Odes.* In a sense this follows without argument from Chang's concept of derivation (*liu*

---

[9] *I-shu,* 1.20b. Apparently the *Spring and Autumn Annals* is said to deal with reward and punishment because it was thought that Confucius in writing it delivered "praise and blame" by his choice of data and mode of narration. But I do not think that this view of the *Spring and Autumn Annals* is important for Chang. See Chapter 8.

pieh): the *Odes* are artistic writing; therefore, all artistic writing derives from the *Odes*. Chang, however, has more to say on this subject. First, he says, consider the writings found in such literary collections (*wen-chi*) as the *Wen Hsüan* (Chang, and perhaps everyone, assumed the *Odes* to be the ancestor of such anthologies). Next, disregard the part of these writings that can be discounted as belonging to some other discipline. What is left is true artistic writing (*tz'u-chang*). Next Chang argues that all "literary types" in this kind of writing are prefigured in the writings of the late Chou.[h] By "literary type" Chang means something different from what we might expect. Two pieces of writing may be quite different in form —one perhaps an essay, another a philosophical dialogue—yet Chang will see them as the same type if, for example, both are essentially arguments from historical example.[15]

The notion that it was not until the age of the Warring States that writing as such first became a specialized profession is implicit in the conception of classical antiquity that Chang outlined in the *Chiao-ch'ou T'ung-i*. In that age, writing was always a part of the operation of government. There was never a case where "writings were the compositions of a single person."[i] In this conception of ancient civilization as a time when writing wrote itself and the writer never attached even his name to his work, Chang finds the "*tao* with which to criticize the various traditions of writing."

But if the writing of classical antiquity was anonymous, what of the books (such as the medical texts ascribed to Huang-ti) that bear the names of men of antiquity? These were assuredly not writ-

---

[h] This idea was not Chang's alone. It was also held by Yao Nai, the well-known writer of the T'ung-ch'eng group in Anhwei, and is stated by him in an introductory section in his anthology *Ku-wen-tz'u Lei-tsuan*, finished (but not published) in 1779. It is quite possible the two men had talked about this idea, or that it had had wider circulation. See Shen Jen, "*Wen-shih T'ung-i* Nei-p'ien Hou-an" ("Notes to the First Series of the *Wen-shih T'ung-i*"), *Hsüeh-hai Yüeh-k'an*, I (1944), 54.

[i] Chang's friend Chou Chen-jung objected to this thesis in "The Teaching of the *Odes*," thereby showing, whether he realized it or not, that he found the whole of Chang's philosophy unacceptable (or perhaps simply failed to grasp it). See HY, p. 57.

ten by the men whose names they bear, Chang holds, nor are they forgeries. They represent instead oral traditions associated with these famous men, traditions which, after the break-up of the golden age, had to be written down to be preserved. Here is something that sounds at least partly right. For the *Kuan Tzu,* the *Yen Tzu Ch'un-ch'iu* and the *Sun Tzu* (and we might even lengthen the list to include *Mencius* and *Chuang Tzu*) were certainly not written by the men named in their titles; yet scholars of literal mind are surely confused about the significance of these books if they people Chou antiquity with a host of crafty forgers.[16]

The necessity of reducing oral tradition to writing, Chang says, made writing a specialized occupation in the age of Warring States. That age, the age of the so-called philosophical schools, was the age of "private" writing at its best because all writing served some particular end. But at the same time, the writing of that period had within itself the seeds of its own decay. Formerly nothing had been written except that which needed to be immediately expressed or communicated. Now it was possible for men to claim authorship for their work, and to try to produce writings that would excite praise simply as works of art.[17]

All post-classical belles lettres, Chang states, are in the tradition of the *Odes*—an oral tradition of poetry that embraced the entire literature of emotive expression. For "although in antiquity there were no private writings, there were always spoken words that expressed personal feeling." The expression of personal feeling now emerges in Chang's thinking (though he seems unaware of this) as an additional aspect of the tradition of the *Odes,* equal in importance to the aspect of literary beauty.

It is said that the ancient sages governed by means of "rites" and "music": this oral poetry of emotive expression was the "music" in their government; the "rites" were the official traditions of law and technical knowledge. The two are respectively the ornament or art (*wen*) and the substance (*chih*) of the civilization of antiquity. When the golden age ended, "rites" gave rise to various practical-minded "philosophers," whose teachings concerning terminology, law, military art, agriculture, and *yin-yang* theory derived from state offices. "Music," on the other hand, accounted for the "perverse theories" and "wild talk" of the "hundred schools" of speculative thought, and for the "elegant metaphysical discussion and logical speculation" that was concerned with "empty principles"; these were really "just expressions of personal feeling," and hence derived from the *Odes*.[18] Writing, after its ancient beginnings, is thus distinguished by whether it has factual, "practical" content or merely expresses feeling. It is rather startling to find Chang, in the course of such extraordinary reasoning, dismissing metaphysics in the manner of a logical positivist. But he does not pursue this idea closely, to try, for example, to pinpoint a distinction between what a piece of writing says and what attitude it expresses. The distinction serves him instead as a vague classificatory concept for identifying "traditions" of writing, rather than as a criterion for use in close criticism and analysis.

Literary Collections and Philosophers

Chang's objective in this analysis of the history of literary essences was to discover standards of literary value in antiquity that he could apply to the criticism of literary collections (*wen-chi*). Here his complaints are similar to those in the *Chiao-ch'ou T'ung-i*. The *wen-chi* as a literary institution developed by devouring specialized disciplines ("schools," *chia*) that are defined, as *wen-chi* is not, by content:

Classical scholarship has ceased to be a specialized discipline, and literary collections have come to contain discussions of the meaning of the Classics. Historical scholarship has ceased to be a specialized discipline, and literary collections have come to contain biographies. Philosophy has ceased to be a specialized discipline, and literary collections have come to contain philosophical essays.[19]

What is left in a literary collection, after the writings of other disciplines have been removed, belongs to the tradition of the *Odes*. If this is true, it is clear that this tradition must include prose as well as poetry; indeed, the distinction ceases to be important. Rhyme is not essential to the expression of feeling, and it does not necessarily indicate that a piece of writing belongs to the tradition of the *Odes*. Chang gives examples of writings in verse, both classical and post-classical, that are not emotive and therefore not derived from the *Odes*. "The good literary critic holds it his principle to study the motivation of the writer, and must not be bound by considerations of form." Here is another quite sophisticated idea emerging from Chang's strangely structured argument.[20]

These reflections on poetry lead Chang to a consideration of *fu*, a genre for which the prose-poetry distinction has always seemed unsatisfactory. He finds that *fu* as a genre has developed from the *Odes*, even though *fu* are often unrhymed. But writings in the *fu* form are sometimes of a different sort; some, such the *Shih Lei Fu* and its expansions, are collections of information worded in a way that makes them easily memorizable (Chang suggests elsewhere that the function of rhyme, and of literary art itself, was originally to aid the memory). Furthermore, *fu*, properly speaking, have something of the character of the writings of the ancient philosophical schools: they are informed with an idea and are not "art without substance," like later poetry; they can be differentiated into genetic types according to content, and are so treated by Liu Hsin. This reflection gives Chang an opportunity to disagree with Liu Chih-chi: it is a mistake to exclude *fu* from biographies in the Standard Histories; the *fu* of the Han court, for example, are as valuable an expression of the thought of that time as Tung Chung-shu's replies to the Emperor Wu.[21]

The blindly formalistic approach to belles lettres Chang finds most objectionable in literary collections, whether they are anthologies, such as the *Wen Hsüan*, or collections of the writings of a single person. The essays of the ancient philosophers, it can be shown, first circulated separately and were not assembled in collections, in spite of the fact that all such writings of one man or school were closely related in thought and content. Is it not more dangerous, then, to classify, merely according to form, the much more varied literary pieces in a literary collection without carefully analyzing their content? Chang concludes his appraisal of literature with a long and highly sarcastic criticism of the *Wen Hsüan*: it is the most important repository of ornamental writing and the archetype of all literary collections, yet it is an extreme example of the formalistic vice he deplores. He gives example after example of the inconsistency and superficiality of its classifications.

He says at the close of "The Teaching of the *Odes*" that he has written another essay discussing these matters, and since the *Wen-shih T'ung-i* does contain an essay entitled "Literary Collections" ("Wen-chi"), which is, in fact, referred to by name elsewhere in "The Teaching of the *Odes*," it is possible that it was one of those essays written in 1783.[22] He suggests, in "Literary Collections," that the *wen-chi* convention of editing writings developed historically out of the Chou and Han practice of grouping together in single books the writings of the ancient philosophical schools. The ancient philosophical writings and the literary collections of later times came into being at similar stages in the downward dialectic of literary change: "When government and teaching separated and the philosophers appeared, we have the transition from the public to the private principle in writing.[j] When a man's words came to be set apart from his actions and literary collections came into fashion, we have the dividing point between sincerity and artificiality." In the philosophical books, however, the principle underlying the grouping of the writings of the various schools was community of subject matter and of tradition; it was not authorship, for the philosophical books contain writings of more than one man in a school. Some, such as the *Han Fei Tzu,* contain chapters discussing inci-

---

[j] The significance of the shift "from the public to the private principle" will be evident shortly. Chang's assumption here that classical utopia was characterized by a union of government (*chih*) and teaching (*chiao*), together with his use of the concepts "rites" and "music," and his opposition of the *tao* and *wen* in "The Teaching of the *Odes*," indicates that he had been reading—rather freely—Ou-yang Hsiu's preface to the "Monograph on Rites and Music" in the *New Tang History* and Chu Hsi's essay on it. See Chapter 6.

dents in the life of the philosopher that could not have been written by him. These chapters show, through his "acts," why his "words" are what they are.[23]

This conception of the writings of the ancient philosophical schools suggests to Chang what is wrong with *wen-chi*: the trouble lies in treating writing as a thing of value in itself; the *wen-chi* separates "words" from "actions"—that is, from the historical context of events, both biographical and intellectual, which give meaning to an author's writings. It classifies pieces of writing capriciously according to accidental characteristics, thus suggesting to the literary world that the substance of a literary piece is of no importance. As it now exists, the *wen-chi* is guilty of the same "encyclopedism" that Chang objected to in scholarship, particularly in historiography; in history, facts are valued without regard for their meaning and significance; in the *wen-chi*, writings are valued without regard for their content and motivation. Chang would therefore include in a *wen-chi*, he later explained, both the events of the author's life and an account (and perhaps the writings) of those who were influenced by him and those who criticized him. Chang seems to think that such a treatment of an author will bring out in his writings the qualities Chang sees in the writings of the ancient technical and philosophical schools. These qualities will then become the generally accepted value of scholarship and writing.

Chang admired the writing of the age of philosophers. He was close to them in temper. Especially was he close to Han Fei Tzu. He has Han Fei's sense of organization of ideas, his willingness to take an idea and argue it out, uncompromisingly, to stark conclusions. He has covert legalist sympathies. In one of his essays ("Some Errors Corrected") of 1789 Chang, to a degree, admits his fealty. Han Fei was rough with Confucians. But, after all, he was a legalist, so why not? Chang admires him for the sharpness and depth of his thought, and for the beauty of his style. It is all right, he says, for later writers to admire Han Fei for his style, but not for his "character," i.e., for the substance of his thought. The Han philosopher Wang Ch'ung, Chang thinks, went too far in using Han Fei as a model, following him in attacking Confucians even though Wang himself was a Confucian.[24]

This is a bit embarrassing. Chang's fundamental literary principle was that good writing is the product of a man of cultivated mind, of good character. With Han Yü (and Mencius) he believed that a good man will be a good writer, and a bad one won't. Chang should have rejected Han Fei's stylistic excellence as spurious; or if he could not, he should have insisted (as he did in "The Teaching of the *Odes*") that the *tao* is in him somewhere anyway. His difficulty in applying his critical principles in this case may simply indicate that those principles were wrong. But it may also be (as I shall try to show later) that Chang had simply not thought out carefully just what it is that stands in the relation of "substance" to good literary art.

Symbolism and the Changes

Chang ought to have more to say about literary expression. And he does; but what he has to say does not alleviate the foregoing difficulty. A fragment—but a fascinating fragment—of Chang's literary theory brings us to his exploration of another of the classical disciplines in a major essay, "The Teaching of the *Changes*" ("I Chiao").[k] In the third part of this essay Chang argues that the essential genius of the *Classic of Changes* (and of the whole literary and philosophical tradition of which it is the fountainhead) is symbolic representation. There are, he says, two kinds of symbols (*hsiang*)—natural and artificial. The concept of a natural symbol is a difficult one, but perhaps here Chang is making the distinction sometimes made by semanticists between *signs,* mere phenomena, which we come to associate with other phenomena, and *symbols,* the signs and images we use or construct for communication. We should remember, too, that for a Chinese of Chang's time (and for

---

[k] This essay, which now opens Chang's *Wen-shih T'ung-i,* has three parts. In the third part Chang summarizes the argument in "The Teaching of the *Odes*" and refers to that essay. The "I Chiao" itself is referred to in the essay "The Teaching of the *Rites*" ("Li Chiao"), written in 1788. The "I Chiao" seems therefore to have been written between 1783 and 1788.

our own ancestors as well), the notion of nature communicating with man was not at all strange, and of course such a nature would use natural signs for its symbols. The *Classic of Changes* contains both natural and artifical symbols, though it is, of course, essentially a key to the "symbolic" aspects of the actual world. Chang's meaning, I assume, is that the *Changes* uses metaphorical language (artificial symbols), and at the same time is concerned with the interpretation of the hexagrams, which as produced by the manipulations of the diviner are themselves meaning-laden natural phenomena. These interpretations in turn direct us to see special significance in other natural phenomena in our immediate situation.

But, Chang insists, artificial symbols, the images poets and mystics use, are in the last analysis just as "natural" as natural symbols. The workings of the human mind are conditioned by emotion and through emotion are dependent upon human circumstances, which in turn are dependent upon the operation of the great universal forces, *yin* and *yang.*[1] For this reason, artificial symbols themselves are causally dependent on the natural world. This dependence of artificial symbols ("mental constructions," *jen-hsin ying-kou*) upon nature allows Chang to maintain that all symbolic writing and thought is generically related to the tradition of the *Changes.* He finds traces of this tradition in all kinds of ancient literature; obviously it must be found in most of what Chang, on other grounds, assigns to the tradition of the *Odes.* Chang uses this argument (as I noted in Chapter 3) to assign the whole of Buddhism to the tradition of the *Changes,* even though granting that in the ordinary historical sense its beginning was outside of China.

Did Chang, in his merging of natural and artificial symbols, have in his system of thought something like Jung's concept of archetypes? We don't know, for Chang has little more to say on the subject of symbols, except to insist that, because of the universal ten-

---

[1] Chang's philosophy contains no careful definition of *yin* and *yang*. Sometimes (as in "On the Tao," in 1789) he uses "*yin* and *yang*" as a collective expression for natural processes in history; sometimes (as in "Virtue in the Historian," 1791) they are psychological tendencies in the individual.

dency to represent the deepest feelings and insights symbolically, one must not laugh at anything—not even at the popular mythology of Buddhism—simply because it fails to make literal sense. "The Buddhists' description of Buddha as sixteen feet high with a richly adorned, golden-colored body, and their strange imaginings that no one has ever seen—the splendors of heaven, the torments of hell, the heavenly goddess scattering flowers, yakshas covered with hair—these things the Confucians criticize as absurd." But they fail to realize, he says, that the Buddhists are presenting their teachings symbolically, just as the *Classic of Changes* does when it speaks of such things as "dragons with dark and yellow blood." Buddhist myths in themselves are "mental constructions" like any symbols and are not intentionally deceptive. When unintelligent people began to believe the myths as fact, after the early tradition of Buddhism was broken, they were indeed being absurd; but Confucians, in attacking these beliefs, should realize that this is not what Buddhism really is. Indeed, Chang asserts, the best of Buddhist writings "come close to being superior to the philosophers."[25]

One question does seem in order about this theory of symbols in art and thought. Since Chang has linked literary symbols causally to nature, must we not suppose (as indeed both Jung and Freud do) that certain symbols, quite without the aid of traditional diffusion, will tend to recur with the same significance? It is odd that Chang's thought should have this implication, in view of his impatience with poetasters who cannot write of an absent friend without speaking of gazing at the moon. Chang didn't think of our question, but he would say, I think, that it is all right to let moon-gazing be your symbol, if you are led to it by real emotion, not by a desire to write in a commendable and conventional manner.

The Ideal of Non-Identity

Art is corrupted by man's desire to turn out a gem with his name on it, claim it as his own, and contrive that it will be something for which he will be given credit. It is the absence of this kind of attention to *wen* in high antiquity that leads Chang to see there the *tao* against which all of later literature is evaluated: "Waves are the wind of water, and wind is the waves of air. Dreams are the flowery delusions of the mind, and writing is the attempt to possess the *tao* for oneself. Still water has no waves, and quiet air has no wind. A perfect man has no dreams, and in perfect writing there is nothing of self."[m] This incredible ideal, that the craving for authorship is a vice, that perfect *wen* is attained only when the desire to possess the product of one's mind and hand is extinguished, is an ideal more to be expected in a religious mystic than in a literary critic. But it is what Chang thinks, or at least what he feels he ought to think. He explains his position and something of the view of literary history it implies in his second major essay of 1783, " 'If Your Words Are Everyone's' " ("Yen Kung").[n]

In relation to the idea of "literary art" (*wen*), this essay is almost entirely negative. In it Chang is, to be sure, led to comment on certain literary genres and devices. But essentially he is not concerned with what makes literary art good, but with what it is that makes any kind of writing valuable and "lasting," and he points out that mere literary skill may be used for a worthy end (for the *tao*) or for a base one. The dualism of *wen* and *tao* serves him here as it did in the essay on "The Teaching of the *Odes*." In antiquity they were not separate, and all was well. But in later ages it is otherwise. Chang begins:

The sense in which the ancients' "words were everyone's" was this: no one ever took pride in his literary work, thinking of it as "his," as something giving him personal justification. A man's aims were that the *tao*

---

[m] "Collected Opinions," 1789 (*I-shu*, 4.25a). Chang's logic slips at the end of this little piece of mystification. It should have ended with the paradox of Vimalakirti: the real *tao* has no *wen*; when one really grasps the absolute one does not express it at all. It would not be like Chang Hsüeh-ch'eng to say this, but this does show the religious-mystical direction in which Chang's literary ideal points.

[n] The title of this essay is a quotation from Ssu-ma Ch'ien's account (in the Shih-chi,* 10.3a) of the enthronement of the Han Emperor Wen-ti. Wen-ti, as prince of Tai, was invited to the capital to accept the throne. He and his councilor Sung Ch'ang were met outside the city by a group of capital dignitaries, one of whom at once sought to speak with the new Emperor privately. Sung Ch'ang intervened, saying, "If your words are everyone's [i.e., in the interest of all], then speak out before everyone; if your words are in your own interest, know that the ruler does not heed private interest."

be served. When he expressed himself, it was in order to make these aims clear. In his writing, he sought to do justice to what he had to say. His *tao* was in fact manifested in the world, and so his aims were always realized; it was therefore not necessary for his words to be in fact "his."[26]

Chang's essential point, then, is simply this: When you say or write something, it should be to express as well as possible that which is right or true, when this needs to be expressed. There should be no other purpose. In particular, it should not be to obtain credit for yourself for having written something elegantly, or for having thought of some striking idea. The important thing is that the ideas be right and the words those that are needed. And the right and the true are not yours; they belong to no one, or rather, to everyone.

This was the attitude the ancients had, and so they wrote without anxiety, "doing what was easy." The ancient writer, finding that someone had already said exactly what he wanted to say, used the earlier writer's words without hesitation, without acknowledgment, and, Chang insists, without plagiarism. These words are "his own words," for he and the earlier writer "have the same *tao*." And so Pan Ku quite properly used the texts of earlier writers such as Ssuma Ch'ien. For Pan Ku, a historian, the important thing was "meaning." So he simply used the "facts" and the "style" (the text) necessary to express this meaning. The obverse of this doctrine is this: if someone—your student, or someone who has talked with you or read your work—takes up your ideas and expands them, his words are "your own words," for again you have the same *tao*. The ancient writer was confident that this would happen and was not disturbed by it, for his concern was with the preservation and development of what is true and right, not with his own originality. This, Chang reminds us, was how learning developed and was preserved in the Han "schools," and the reason why ancient philosophical texts bear the names of men who did not actually write them. In these cases, individual authorship did not matter.

The modern writer, on the contrary, anxious to write something "imperishable" and having to rely on his own skill and intellectual cleverness to make his work survive, "does what is hard." Pretending to offer the world objective value, he is in fact offering it his vanity. In him, the *tao* is no longer joined with *wen*; the two are in conflict. True imperishability (*pu hsiu*), Chang thinks, is attainable with certainty only through this *yen-kung* principle, when the writer is willing to let his words be everyone's. Immortality can be counted on only in a milieu in which there are other authors who will use your work and incorporate it into theirs—as Pan Ku did with the work of Liu Hsiang and Liu Hsin. Chang seems to be saying of literary and intellectual immortality much the same sort of thing that Chuang Tzu said of physical immortality: Do not crave perpetuation of your personal identity. You will survive in what you become. Let it be enough that the *tao* continues.[o]

An example of the *yen-kung* principle is offered by Chang: in the *Classic of History* the phrase, "the king speaks to this effect," is repeated whenever the Duke of Chou issues an edict or proclamation in the name of King Ch'eng. It is wrong, Chang holds, to suppose that the Duke is reading words the King himself wrote. The Duke wrote the words, but they are nonetheless the King's because the King ordered and approved them. The minister Han Ch'i in the eleventh century was observing the same principle when he employed Ou-yang Hsiu as Han-lin scholar to write his state papers. Chang obviously would have been amused (rightly, I think) at the people in our time who sniff at the ghost-writing of political speeches. On the other hand, he surely would have condemned the ghost-writing of a doctoral dissertation or a book. There is such a thing as plagiarism, and it occurs whenever one falsely claims authorship to further one's own advantage. (Did Chang perhaps recall a certain old man of Yung-ch'ing?) This, he says, is to prostitute *wen* to "fame and profit."[27]

Obviously, the idea that one's "words" should be "everyone's" is incompatible with the idea of literary collections: the *wen-chi* institution is the very embodiment of the pernicious idea that one's words are one's own. And this is just why Chang thinks the meth-

[o] *I-shu*, 4.10b–11b. This austere position gets Chang into a serious epistemological difficulty. But I must postpone consideration of it until the next chapter.

ods of the ancient philosophical books are to be preferred: these books record the principles of a "school" (*chia*), not an individual's writings. A few years later he pointed this out to the literary profession, suggesting that if a man's literary collection is really excellent, there would be no harm in returning to this earlier method and including in the collection "writings done for you by others" —that is, by disciples or persons who share the writer's viewpoint.[28]

In spite of the deterioration of letters since ancient times, here and there the *yen-kung* ideal still persists in practice. Chang sees this principle, of course, in many official documents. He concludes his investigation of this matter by pointing out cases in post-classical and contemporary writing where, in some sense, the author's (or the speaker's) identity does not matter, and where in consequence the *yen-kung* principle is still in evidence, though unrecognized. Here we would expect Chang to mention, as he does, *yüeh-fu* poetry (poetry produced for state ceremonies in Han and later times). He sees the *yen-kung* principle also involved when a writer assumes the identity of a mythological or historical person to suggest by analogy his own problem or feelings—a practice Chang thinks is somehow derived from the ancient philosophers' use of anecdotes. An example of this is the often-read, bitter letter of Li Ling, the Han general who threw in his lot with his Hun captors, to his friend Su Wu, who had returned to China after many years on the steppe. Chang admits that Liu Chih-chi and many other critics have pronounced this letter a fake. But he does not believe it to be an ordinary literary deception. It was written in the Six Dynasties period by a southerner who was detained in the north and, feeling his circumstances to be like those of Li Ling, used this device to express feelings he did not dare to write about openly. Other extensions of this principle (and Chang can extend a principle almost beyond recognition) are the literary use of fictitious characters such as "Mr. Nothing" and "Mr. Nobody" in Ssu-ma Hsiang-ju's *fu* on hunting, or the use of deliberate anachronism in the case of nonfictitious characters.[29]

More surprisingly, Chang sees the *yen-kung* ideal in that much maligned literary form, the examination essay. The examinee, Chang says, has immersed himself in the Classics, in ancient literature, in philosophy, and in political economy. Having submerged himself in tradition, he accepts the discipline of an impersonal institution:

> Only the form of his writing is prescribed in the regulations;
> The thought he derives from the instruction of his teachers.
> He respects the three duties of human life;
> He conforms his knowledge to the rules of the essay.
> He observes a commonly accepted stylistic ideal;
> But he expresses to the fullest his own best abilities.
> Since an inner understanding of them guides what he says,
> Why should he hesitate to imitate the sages?
> Since this standard is rooted in his own heart,
> Why need he seek fame for his own ideas?[p]

As a young man Chang had groaned about *pa-ku* for the usual reasons—it forced him to spend his time on something preposterously artificial and kept him from his own intellectual interests. We know, of course, that Chang the postgraduate took a different view of the matter. Still, this is puzzling, for in talking about himself, in his advice to students, and in what he says about literary values, Chang stresses and continues to stress the importance of cultivating and expressing one's own ideas and responses; he continues to warn against preoccupation with forms, conventions, and "style." But now, because of his fear of the insincerity inherent in the desire for "fame," he sees in the stylistic discipline of the examination essay a virtue—it holds back a potentially self-serving individuality.

Chang earnestly and quite persistently held to his *yen-kung* prin-

---

[p] *I-shu*, 4.18a–b. Chang writes this (and all of the third part of "Yen Kung") in the *fu* style of irregular verse. The "three duties" are the duties to serve one's ruler, one's parents, and one's teachers. "Stylistic ideal" is a free translation of *i-fa*, a technical term in T'ung-ch'eng literary theory, which has drifted into Chang's vocabulary. As Fang Pao explains it, *i-fa* is the literary ideal that ancient prose should "have something to say," i.e., thought or content (*i*) and that it should have a style or form (*fa*) appropriate to this content. This dualism is, of course, the same "art-substance" dualism that runs through Chang Hsüeh-ch'eng's literary theory. See Kuo Shao-yü, *Chung-kuo Wen-hsüeh P'i-p'ing Shih* (*A History of Chinese Literary Criticism*), Vol. II (Shanghai, 1947), p. 361.

ciple; he was quite willing to apply it to himself. In a letter to Shao Chin-han a number of years later, Chang discussed this matter with Shao, who was always very careful not to divulge his ideas before publication. Chang said that he, on the other hand, in his travels about the country, had always talked freely with anyone about his insights and theories. The result, he admitted, had been that his ideas had been picked up and used by candidates taking examinations and by writers who disguised them and passed them off as their own. It annoyed him that they never got his ideas straight; but as for their claiming them as their own, he insisted he didn't care. He reminded Shao that years ago he had written, in his essay "Yen Kung," that one should not seek fame for oneself; all that mattered was that the *tao* be made clear to the world.[30]

We must take Chang at his own word here. But the fact remains that few Chinese have ever been more interested in their own gifts and achievements, in their own value in the world and in history, than Chang Hsüeh-ch'eng. To some extent, we are confronted with a man whose impulses are simply not in step with his beliefs. But the tension goes deeper, and can be discerned wholly within his beliefs. Examining *wen-chi* and reviewing the evolution of literature, Chang finds obsession with literary conventions and forms to be bad, for he sees in it the stifling of genuineness brought about by the egoistic craving for fame. But renouncing this craving now means for him that one must submerge oneself in impersonality, and accept the discipline of formal conventions (if sanctioned by tradition or authority), a discipline that will just as surely stifle genuine self-expression. This is a tension, but not an outright inconsistency. What Chang's philosophy requires (and indeed implies) is a subtler analysis of the "self" of the writer, an analysis that will allow him to deny the mere ego while affirming something more real and more basic.

Art and Substance in Poetry

There is one more subject to be explored before we leave the problem of literary value. Chang has, up till now, shown only a passing interest in poetry. Even though deriving literature from the *Odes,* he shows himself uninterested in the special characteristics and problems of poetic art—forms, rhyme, poetic diction, and tone; and in fact I think he is not much interested. Chang did write poetry. There are a few occasional poems from the trip he made to Shensi in 1763, when he was a student in Peking, and a few others, written when he was about sixty, notably the long autobiographical poem already discussed. Normally, however, one finds a great quantity of short occasional poems in a Chinese literary man's collected works. One finds almost none in Chang's writings. He had to write poetry in some fashion in order to pass the examinations; in 1757 the examination rules were sharply revised to give a substantial place to poetic composition.[31] This revision may have prolonged his struggles with the examinations. In any case, Chang knew that he was no poet, and often said so. Calligraphy, too, was beyond him (when he wanted his essays copied for preservation, he always turned over the task to others). These deficiencies constantly embarrassed him at parties, where petty verse-writing was a universally assumed social grace.[32]

It might then be supposed that Chang, with his anxieties about "empty words," would say nothing about the theory of poetry. Such austere consistency is too much to expect, although what Chang does say will interest the philosopher more than the poet.

One must distinguish Chang's view of the function of literary skill from his evaluation of belles lettres. Like many critics, Chang regards literary skill as an instrument for expressing truth (the *tao*) clearly; it is a necessary acquisition for any man of learning. Providing one does not make a fetish of it, it is a means to a morally valuable end. We have seen that this, the beautiful expression of anything, is one aspect of the tradition of the *Odes.*

But art per se is not a kind of writing. A kind of writing for Chang has a moral value of a different sort: it embodies the *tao*-aspect exemplified by the particular classical tradition from which it derives. Artistic writing (belles lettres) derives from the *Odes*; it includes some kinds of prose and most of poetry. It contains the *tao* of that particular discipline: its value is that it expresses personal feeling, and this is for Chang the other important aspect of the tradition of the *Odes*. In his recognition of this second aspect of the *Odes,* Chang would seem to be close to the opinion of a famous contemporary critic and poet, Yüan Mei (1716–98), also a native of Chekiang, who built a theory of criticism and a school of poetic writing on the claim that poetry, considered all the way back to its classical fountainhead in the *Odes,* should not be morally instructive but essentially the expression of personal emotion.*q* But when Yüan looked at the *Odes* and the poetic tradition with open eyes and accepted what he found, Chang, as his later writings testify, was outraged.

    Although Chang would in no simple sense say that poetry should be didactic, he still felt its value to be a moral one. In the same year "The Teaching of the *Odes*" was written (1783), Chang wrote a comment on the poems of his young friend Chu Tsang-mei, and in it attempted to analyze the creative processes of the poet: the poet should, he thinks, concentrate on the substance (*chih*) of a poem, and the style, the art (*wen*), will take care of itself. One stores up virtue (*te*) as one reads, daily becoming richer in one's grasp of words, ideas, and truths; and if a poet expresses his feelings only when there is something he cannot hold back, he will not have to try to write the poem with skill; it will come naturally. "There is no delight in forced laughter, there is no distress in forced tears. If sadness and happiness are not forced, then tears and laughter will be full without one's realizing it; surely this is the true relationship between study and writing."[33] From this viewpoint, a poem

---

q For Yüan, however, the distinction between prose and poetry is of basic importance. Poetry should express the feelings of the writer; prose should have a serious cognitive and moral function. See Kuo Shao-yü, "Yuan Chien-chai yü Chang Shih-chai chih Ssu-hsiang yü Ch'i Wen-lun" ("The Thought and Literary Theory of Yuan Mei and Chang Hsüeh-ch'eng"), *Hsüeh-lin,* VIII (1941), 63–64. Chang dispenses with the formal distinction and considers only the functions of writing significant.

can have a sort of didactic utility, for it will be a reflection of its author's intellectual and moral self-cultivation.ʳ Writing it will (one might put it) be a moral act and reading it therefore a morally edifying experience. Yüan Mei did indeed hold that a poem should express feeling, but argued that its purpose was simply to give pleasure. For Chang, however, the value of a poem will lie not only in the genuineness of its expression but also in the thing expressed. But what does the poem express? How does Chang's art-substance distinction apply here? In his comment on Chu's poems, Chang seems to be saying that the substance of the poem is the poet's cultivated feeling, and the art not something he *uses* to convey this, but rather the form in which the substance *appears*; art is thus inseparable from substance, as it was in the writing of antiquity. From this viewpoint a good poem simply could not be written accidentally by, for example, a monkey at a typewriter. Nor could it be written by putting words together according to some structural or semantic conception of verbal beauty, as a cleverly programmed machine might do. (If this happened, we would have to conclude the machine or the monkey had a moral and emotional character.) Chang would have to say too, I think, that a poem cannot be translated. For if the translation were not a poem, it would not be a true translation, since the art of a poem is inseparable from its substance. And if the translation were a poem, it would, by Chang's conception of poetry, be a manifestation of substance in the translator, not in the original author and his poem.

It is therefore quite disconcerting to find Chang saying, in the

---

ʳ Chang repeats this argument in "The Essence of Literary Art." The careful student of Chinese literary criticism will be able to trace Chang's ideas on poetry back to Han Yü, and ultimately to Mencius. Another source of Chang's thought is the "Great Preface" to the *Odes*. The "Preface" begins: "Poetry is the manifestation of motivation [*chih*, intention, concentrated purpose, or intensity of feeling]. In the heart [mind] it is motivation; expressed in words it becomes poetry." Motivation (*chih*) and substance (*chih*) are not the same word, but some of the meaning of the first *chih* has obviously been incorporated into Chang's "substance." For the complete text of the "Preface" and a rather different translation, see James Legge, *The Chinese Classics* (as reprinted in China, 1939), Vol. IV, "Prolegomena," p. 34.

preface to the poems of another friend, that the art of a poem can indeed be separated from its substance, and that this in fact is exactly what the critic should do in order to evaluate its content. The test of the excellence of a poem, Chang now says, "is for a translator to take the poem's ideas and express them in ordinary colloquial language," stripping away all of the poet's tricks of skill, his fine phrases, the niceties of rhythm and tone he uses in "old poetry," the rhyme and parallelism he uses in "regular poetry." If in this transformation it still shows outstanding qualities, it is really good; otherwise, it is "mere skill" and not true poetry.[34] We can assume from this opinion that Chang would reject the "spirit-harmony" (*shen yün*) theory of Wang Chih-chen (1634–1711), who saw the value of a poem as an ineffable quality produced by the author's language. This opinion, too, seems at first glance to reinforce Chang's view that the poem's substance is what is basic in it. But what has this substance now become? Poetry, Chang now finds, is at best bad prose, its art adding nothing to its value (indeed possibly deceiving the reader) and, fortunately, quite separable from its content, which Chang now sees as cognitive rather than emotive.

Chang took this second position in 1797, some fourteen years after the first, at a time when he had become rather impatient with poets. But there is more to this discrepancy than a change of mind or a lapse of subtlety in an older man. Chang's literary thought in 1783 was involved with a concept of substance that was treacherously ambiguous. Substance (*chih*) seems to be what is inside the writer, and art (*wen*) its natural or necessary expression in writing, called forth by the situation he is in. But what is inside the writer? His feelings and his moral dispositions. But also his knowledge and beliefs, which he acquires from his teachers or from his work and practical experience. When Chang sees ancient society as the historical enlargement of this ideal of writing, he sees it as a single whole: all its traditions and institutions express the one *tao*. And so he is able without violating his sense of unity to see *wen* and *chih* no longer as aspects of each other, but as parts of the perfectly integrated social and cultural whole. But they are, as we have seen, distinguishable parts nonetheless, and each the *urprinzip* of half of man's subsequent cultural history: *wen,* the "musical," beautiful, expressive, and emotive; and *chih* the "ritual," institutional, and factual.

Abstracted and distinguished in classical antiquity, the one can be conceived as the means of communicating the other, and any given literary object will exhibit both. But as archetypes moving through history they have no proper traffic, and Chang's business as cultural historian and bibliographer is to distinguish them where they have been confused. In this second sense, the content of *wen* is not the burden of a message communicated by it, but the quality of the writer's emotional temper or moral insight manifested in it. Here we have the latent tension between the two passages with which this chapter opens. Imbedded in Chang's strugglings with these concepts is a problem of great difficulty. In what sense and degree is a piece of writing universal, impersonal, a statement for man, "belonging to all"? And when is it intrinsically the expression of the one man who makes it, and of no other?

6. History and the Tao

The worthy man is one who learns from the sage; and the
gentleman is one who learns from the worthy man. But
the sage himself is one who learns from the common people.

—*On the Tao* ... 1789

It is said of Chinese philosophers that they are unsystematic. Sometimes this is said in praise, sometimes patronizingly; but agreement
is wide that the system-builders have lived in other parts of our
world, in India, Greece, Germany. Chinese philosophers are "practical," taking up problems as they arise, answering questions as
they are asked.

An opinion as widespread as this is likely to have some truth, and
so this one has. But it should not blind us to exceptions. Chang
Hsüeh-ch'eng is such an exception. In a sense, what Chang did was
to maintain the thesis that all philosophy should be practical and
piecemeal, and to work on this thesis until he had built it into a
system. Looking at the writings of his early fifties, we can see that
for at least two decades he had been obsessed with one idea, struggling to abstract it from the problems that must have first suggested
it to him, trying to relate it to more and more of his own experience, and finally attempting to incorporate into it everything he
knew and believed about history, the political and social order, the
life of learning and writing, himself, and his role. In his writings of
1789, one has the constant feeling that everything he says has a
necessary relation to everything else. I am convinced that Chang
had this feeling too, a feeling that he had finally put it all together.
And I am sure that this was why he was so excited about his writings in Anhwei that year.

I shall try to present Chang's thinking of 1789 in the way I believe he thought of it. The longest and most profound essay is "On
the Tao." Others seem to have been written to amplify and continue its arguments. Chang himself wrote a friend that this was
why he wrote his shorter "On Learning."[1] I shall therefore start
with Chang's argument in "On the Tao" and then bring in others
from the shorter essays. We find him, first, explaining how the *tao*
was "gradually manifested" in human history. Then he considers
how the world cultural order that resulted has gradually disintegrated. This leads him to ask what ought to be the role of the
individual writer, scholar, or thinker in the world as it is, and what
ought to be his relationship to others, to the state, and to the authority of tradition. In these ideas we can discern two main lines of
thought—one relating the man of intellect to the authority of the
state and tradition, the other considering him as a unique individual. I shall take up these ideas in turn, and then consider what
seem to me the unresolved problems in Chang's philosophy.

The Evolution of the Tao in History

What was there before Heaven and Earth? Like Hsün Tzu,
Chang makes no claim to know. When man came into being, the
tao existed in man himself, but he was unaware of it. The *tao* began
"taking form" in human history with the first human family and
continued as population increased and human society became more
and more complex:

As soon as three persons were living together in one house, they had to
open and shut the gates each morning and evening, and provide for the
morning and evening meals by gathering firewood and drawing water;
and since they were not one person, there had to be a division of work.
Sometimes each tended to his own business; sometimes they alternated
in turn. This was indeed a situation that could not be otherwise, and
from it developed the ideal of doing one's equal part and of keeping
one's proper place. Further, lest they do one another injury and quarrel
with one another, it was necessary to bring forward the one who was
most advanced in years to settle disputes. This also was an inevitable

situation, and as a result the distinctions of old and young and of honored and humble took form.[2]

But soon there came to be not just handfuls but hundreds and then thousands of people:

Then, with so large a number of people, there was need for direction, and so it was necessary to advance the one who was greatest in talent to manage the complex relationships among them. The situation became confused, requiring leadership and obedience among the people, so it was necessary to advance the one who was most vigorous in virtue to control the development of things. This also was an inevitable situation, and as a result there came into being ideas about setting up a sovereign, establishing teachers, marking off fields, and dividing up the country into provinces, along with the notions of the well-field, feudal investiture, and schools.[3]

Chang avoids saying what the *tao* is. But it manifests itself in all aspects of social life that develop gradually, and with at most only piecemeal planning, to mitigate or prevent disorder: the moral code ("concepts of benevolence and rightness, loyalty and filial piety"), laws, the division of labor, land tenure, education, political structure, culture. Chang's *tao* therefore seems to be the basic potential in human nature for living an ordered, civilized life, a potential that gradually writes itself out in history, and actualizes itself in what man must come to regard as right and true. The *tao* "comes from Heaven." But "Heaven" for Chang is really the order of nature, regarded with reverence. His *tao* therefore commands all the respect of a religious absolute, even though it is not supernatural. He insists that the *tao* must always, in itself, be distinguished from the "forms" it takes in history, yet one gains no idea of it except through these forms. The result is that Chang has an essentially religious reverence for the human moral order, yet at the same time he sees it as completely evolutionary and naturalistic.[4]

The *tao* lies embedded in and behind the historical process. The *tao* is the "why," the *so-i-jan,* behind particular events and things. But it is not itself a timeless model or standard of value outside of

history. It is not "what things ought to be," their *tang-jan*. Here
Chang quietly amends the Ch'eng-Chu philosophy in a very significant way. The "why-ought" distinction was a common one
among philosophers of the Sung. But Ch'eng I and his followers,
for example, regarded both *so-i-jan* and *tang-jan* as predicates of
"principle" (*li*).[a] Ch'eng I further supposes that his "principles"
exist before and after the material things whose principles they are,
whereas Chang always insists that his *tao* is inseparable from actual
things and institutions. It follows that for Chang the *tao* can never
be abstracted and explicitly formulated, and that the entire domain
of explicitly conceived human values and moral norms must be
assigned not to the *tao* itself but to the realm of changing material
existence. Apparently no moral norm in itself is absolute, although
the entirety of human values reveals the *tao* in the nature of man.

This conception of the relationship of the domain of value to the
world of fact becomes doubly interesting when we contrast Chang's
views with the alternatives presented by contemporary Chinese
philosophy. Chang both admired and denounced Tai Chen, who
is generally regarded as the foremost philosopher of the day. To an
important degree the two thought along parallel lines and were
concerned with the same problems. But in their manner and their
conclusions they differed significantly. Chang, a historian, wrote
imaginative essays on the history of culture. Tai, a philologist, systematically reexamined the psychological concepts of Mencian
ethics, using a method that was recognizably an application of a
philological manner to philosophy. Tai's method betrays his basic
persuasion: we must understand words to understand the sentences that we find in the writings of the ancient sages (the

---

[a] *Li* is in one way or another identified with the *tao* in virtually all Neo-Confucian
philosophy (see Angus Graham, *Two Chinese Philosophers: Ch'eng Ming-tao and
Ch'eng Yi-ch'uan* (London, 1958), especially pp. 11–14). *Li* is typically both one
and many; it tends, however, to be thought of as the "principles" of particular
things, and so as something easier to formulate explicitly. It is perhaps significant
therefore that Chang prefers the word *tao,* and uses the word *li* only rarely and
almost accidentally. But when Chang does speak of *li* (e.g., at the beginning of his
essay "Chu and Lu"), it is for him, like the *tao,* "inseparable from things." For the
Ch'engs and their followers on *so-i-jan* and *tang-jan,* see Graham, pp. 8, 29.

Classics), for these writings expound the *tao*. The *tao* and "principles" are not ineffable: they can be clearly known and expressed in words.[b]

Tai, like Chang, tries for a naturalistic accounting of the human moral order, but he starts from a more radical metaphysical base, and reaches more conservative conclusions. Where Chang recognized the *tao* and "matter" as distinct but inseparable, Tai openly flouted Sung doctrine and denied the distinction altogether. For him, the *tao* is simply the activity of things, "principles" simply their pattern, and human "nature" simply man's desires, emotions, and intelligence. Moral values and correct moral doctrine Tai, like Chang, derives from man himself, but by way of psychology, not history. Certain things are "natural" (*tzu-jan*) for man; doing them causes no uneasiness or regret. To this extent Tai, like Chang (and the *Classic of Changes*), sees the stuff of the *tao* in "man's everyday social activity."[5] But some men—the sages—had a more exact sense of the "natural" than the rest of us. As Mencius had said, their moral "taste" anticipated our own and was unerring, whereas ours in particular cases may not be.[6] With them the "natural" is perfected and becomes the "necessary" (*pi-jan*). Tai identifies this category of the "necessary" with moral principles, and in so doing not only reintroduces absolute moral norms in a very puzzling way, but also seems to restore under another description the very dualism he set out to overthrow. While disowning Chu Hsi, Tai obviously remains much closer to the Sung-Ming ideals of self-cultivation and classical study than Chang does, for the thrust of

[b] See Carsun Chang, *The Development of Neo-Confucian Thought,* Vol. II (New York, 1962), pp. 343, 378; and Tai Chen, *Meng Tzu Tzu-i Su-cheng,* section 13, in Hu Shih, *Tai Tung-yüan ti Che-hsüeh (The Philosophy of Tai Chen)*, Shanghai, 1927, appendix, p. 60. Occupied with his teaching and examinations, Chang probably never saw Tai's last and most important philosophical work, his analysis of concepts in Mencius (*Meng Tzu Tzu-i Su-cheng*). But Tai's basic ideas are already clearly presented in an earlier book, his *Hsü-yen,* which he had probably just finished when he and Chang collided in argument in 1773 in Ning-po. Chang seems not to have known the book by name, but he could hardly have avoided an acquaintance with the ideas in it. The *Hsü-yen* is the first of Tai's writings to openly attack the Sung school, and Tai's criticism of Chu Hsi was a good part of what Chang found upsetting in him. See Ch'ien Mu, pp. 328–29.

his argument is that "principles" are revealed in the persons of the sages, and that men should, by studying the Classics, look back to them for moral example and moral authority.[c] We will find something of this persuasion in Chang himself. His *tao,* however, is not set down in books, but revealed in time, and yields not rules but insights.

But Chang, too, as he develops his analysis of the *tao,* has to come to terms with the sages. The character of his gradual evolution of civilization remains essentially the same even after the fully organized state appears. But from that point the mythical and classical sage-rulers—from Fu-hsi, Shen-nung, and Huang-ti down to Yao, Shun, and the founders of the Three Royal Dynasties—play a central role; and Chang is led at once to consider how the action of these history-creators is related to that of ordinary men.

The mechanism of history remains the successive posing and meeting of needs. The ordinary man's role in this process is blind: life presents itself to him a series of "musts," a sequence of concrete things to be done. As he acts, he "sees nothing"; he has no insight into the *tao.* He simply "is what he is [does what he does] without understanding it." The sages, too, made history by responding to particular needs. Even for them, there had to be "first some need and then the satisfying of it, first some anxiety and then the expression of it, first some evil and then the remedying of it."[7] There is, however, a vitally important difference between the way the sage confronts things and the way the ordinary man confronts them. The sage does "see." But what does he see? Not the face of the *tao* itself, for "in the *tao* there is nothing to be seen." It is in the unreflective behavior of ordinary men that the *tao* manifests itself; and it is this behavior that the sage must look at to "see the *tao.*" The paradoxical consequence is that while the rest of us learn from the sages, the sage himself "learns from the common people." But

[c] This interpretation of Tai is mine (obviously I am not here attempting to do justice to the richness of his thought). But I have largely followed Ch'ien Mu in comparing him with Chang. See Ch'ien, pp. 340–41, 383, 385–86; and Hu Shih, *Tai Tung-yüan,* appendix, pp. 7, 60–61.

in so doing he shows no democratic humility. It is just that "if he is to seek the *tao*, he must seek it in its traces in the alternation of *yin* and *yang*," in the ebb and flow of man's life. Seeing this, he sees the needs, the anxiety, the evil that must be alleviated; seeing what *is* the case, he sees what he *must* do, and so performs his history-making acts of fashioning institutions and legislating.

Chang has said that this—the evolving problems of man's life and the accumulation of solutions from sage to sage—is the *tao* "taking form." Can we not then see in the sage's behavior, as we can in the ordinary man's, the *tao* in existence? Here Chang draws back: "The *tao* is so of itself, and the sage must do as he does. Are these things the same? They are not. The *tao* does nothing and is so of itself. The sage sees what he sees and must do as he does. One may, therefore, say that the sage takes the part of the *tao*; but one may not say that the sage and the *tao* are substantially the same."[8]

Chang, like Tai Chen, makes the sages' actions contrast with those of ordinary men as the "necessary" (in a new sense) contrasts with the "natural." But he is being very careful. What is he trying to avoid saying? He is trying, I think, to avoid giving the sages either too little or too much. His sages are men, and as men they think, choose, feel, and act. They "take the part" of the *tao*, but they are its free agents, not its unwitting pawns. Mankind's debt of gratitude to its great men is a debt really owed to them, and not to impersonal processes. The *tao*, for Chang, does not use Hegelian "cunning."

But Chang's sages are also men in the further sense that they are not divine; they are not the *tao* incarnate. The *tao* cannot be identified with the unfettered action of a conscious, planning human mind. A sage cannot "create" just anything. What he achieves is strictly limited by the possibilities of the historical moment. His institutions are not eternally valid, nor are his utterances the *tao* itself. This is obvious, Chang thinks, from the fact that the mode of governing, the laws and institutions tradition ascribes to the ancient sages (the Three Sovereigns, the Five Emperors, and the founders of the Three Royal Dynasties), are all different. But their methods were the same: they all suited action to need, so that "the *tao* was given form and gradually manifested." In this respect the earlier sages were indeed models for the later ones. The sages did not try to be original, "giving rein to their fancy, saying I must do so-and-so to be different from men of former times, or I must do such-and-such to make my fame equal to that of the former sages."[9] The sage's action is not arbitrary; it "necessarily comes about" from the "alternation of *yin* and *yang*." But it is necessary, quite plainly, not as a reactive part of the natural process—it is not itself the *yin-yang* movement that *is* the *tao*—but as a deliberate response to it. The sage sees what he sees and does what he knows he must.

This is important, for in pressing against paradox to characterize the action of the sage, Chang plainly means to characterize right action anywhere and at any time. He is up against that most difficult of problems, the place of deliberate human action in a world of necessity. He says in effect that action is right only when it is not arbitrary, for if it is, one is turning away from the *tao* to serve oneself. His talk about "sages" is his mythical way of talking about the role of great men in history. And his problem with them is to show how there can be great men in a history in which arbitrary action is never a meaningful part. Chang's answer is that the sage's field of action is so limited by circumstance that he can do but one thing; even so, the action in this field is his, and can be performed by no one who is not, like him, "endowed by Heaven with inborn knowledge."

Consequently, it is a complete mistake to try to compare one sage with another. Each is as "great" as the next, although their actual achievements, which are dependent on history, may differ in kind and in importance. As Chang pictures mythical history, the civilizing gifts of the sages to mankind—silk-raising, divination, schools and other institutions, rituals and laws—were in the long term cumulative, even though each succeeding ruler or dynastic founder made "changes and additions" as his times demanded. With the founding of the Chou state (1122 B.C., according to traditional dating), this process of the sage-assisted evolution of the *tao*-in-history reached a climax. The man standing in the line of sages at this time was not the founder of the new political power but its organizer. The man who really established the Chou political and social order was the Duke of Chou, regent of the second king. The Duke of Chou, Chang thinks, was the last of the civilization-creating sages. Standing at this point in time, historical possibility and historical need coincided in him (though he himself was unaware of his climactic role) : it was his task and his achievement to "survey" the work of past sages and to effect a grand synthesis of their institutions. Borrowing a metaphor from Mencius, Chang says that the Duke "summed up the full orchestra" of antiquity.

In achievement therefore the Duke of Chou was, up till his time, the greatest of the ancient sages. But there was still another sage to follow—Confucius. (Whether still others were, or are, to follow Confucius, Chang does not ask.) Confucius was a sage just like the others, and just as "great" but no greater than they were. Chang ridicules those who, through lack of understanding, think of Confucius as a divine being with a necessarily mysterious intellect. Confucius was a perfectly wise man but still a man; his greatness lies in the fact that he "studied the institutions of the Duke of Chou," which summed up all that was valuable for man, and passed on this knowledge first to his students and then to all men. Chang states that this does not mean that the work of Confucius was less important than that of the Duke; their achievements were "perfectly complementary" and yet quite different in kind, so that it is puerile to ask which is greater. One must instead understand their significance in relation to each other: "to understand the *tao*, one must understand why the Duke and Confucius were what they were."[10]

Chang's labor over this, if we glimpse ahead, is startling. For the battle between political conservatives and "Westernizers" a century later was to be fought for decades in just these terms. The conservatives were to hold up the position of the Duke of Chou in the Confucian tradition, maintaining that Confucius merely "transmitted" the wisdom of antiquity, adding nothing new to it. The reformers, thrusting at this total defense of the past, were to make Confucius into a semi-divine being, even an object of worship, and were to find in him double meanings, intimations of novelty, prophetic visions. Two of their prime targets were classics that Chang especially prized, the *Tso Commentary* and the *Rituals of Chou*; their bête noir in post-Confucian antiquity was the man Chang most admired, the bibliographer Liu Hsin (whom the reformers were to make out as a master forger). It may be that even before the threat of the West brought the problem into the open, this opposition of views as to the nature of the Confucian tradition was already taking shape and being argued. It may be that Chang was speaking to a present issue, not merely anticipating a future one. But it is also undoubtedly a fact that in the late nineteenth century both the reformers and their opponents were reading Chang Hsüeh-ch'eng. And for the moment we have the impression—though the impression will be shaken—that it was the conservatives' position Chang was preparing.[d]

Chang's discourse on Confucius and the Duke of Chou is not, as it may seem to be, a disappointing descent from philosophy into hagiography. For just as the opponents in the dispute to come were at root concerned not with the relative merits of Confucius and the Duke but with the questions of what to value and what to do, so too was Chang setting out not just the hagiographic ground plan of that dispute but its real ground plan. If we are to understand the *tao,* we must understand why Confucius and the Duke of Chou are what they are. But what are they? "Only the Duke of Chou and Confucius lived in a time when the law had so accumulated and the *tao* was so complete that neither could be added to. The Duke

[d] The political reform movement of the late nineteenth century grew out of a radical persuasion in Confucian scholarship already in evidence in Chang's day. This view held that certain versions of the Classics which in the Han Dynasty had existed only in manuscripts of Han date were in fact authentic, although they had been largely unrecognized by Confucians since that time. For the attention given Chang's ideas by these "new text" scholars and their opponents, see Chapter 10.

of Chou put together all of this achievement in order to put this *tao* into *practice,* and Confucius made a complete study of this *tao* in order to make his *teaching* shine forth clearly."[11] Again, "The Duke of Chou 'summed up the orchestra' of the tradition of *government* [chih], while Confucius displayed the highest excellence of true *teaching* [chiao]."[12] For Chang, the Duke stands for action, for government; Confucius represents knowledge, doctrine. And "in government there is a display of actual deeds, whereas doctrine displays mere theoretical statements" (i.e., empty words). This is why it is dangerous to glorify Confucius above the other sages. People who "extol Confucius as superior to Yao and Shun" come to "overemphasize 'human nature' and 'fate,' while slighting actions and achievements, and so the political achievements of all the sages have come to seem unequal to the academic discussions of Confucian scholars."[13]

There is another distinction between the Duke and Confucius that adds to the implicit authoritarian thrust of this argument. Chang's vision of antiquity remains what it was in the *Chiao-ch'ou T'ung-i*: in the ages down to the Western Chou state, the cultural and political orders were one. Officials were teachers; the Classics are simply what Confucius was able to preserve of the documents kept by these officials. As Ou-yang Hsiu had said in describing this vision of the past (Chang uses, but doesn't acknowledge his phrasing of the idea), government and teaching, *chih* and *chiao,* were not separate. The Duke of Chou was the last sage to inhabit this stage of history and the last sage to be a ruler. Confucius "had virtue but lacked position." And this is why he did not act, why he "transmitted but did not create," why he did not devise new institutions but simply studied and taught the values and ways of the past. To propose something new one has to be in a position of power to "demonstrate" it, to order that it be put into practice; Confucius couldn't "teach others with empty words," for "without demonstration one will not be believed." So Confucius "never devised his own theories."[14]

To be entitled to propose anything new to the world, it would seem, one must be a ruler, or at least have some kind of "position" giving one the moral right to act. Otherwise one may only "transmit" the received doctrine. But Chang's authoritarianism, as we will repeatedly see, is so structured that it can turn abruptly into its opposite. "Position" turns out to be a very broad concept. Chang, as a historical specialist, usually managed to think of himself as having enough position to justify any amount of originality. And if position was doubtful, there was always the necessity of one's historical situation. Chang's own new ideas always caused him anxiety: they had to be justified somehow, or they would be "empty words." But we actually find him (in a letter defending his writings of this year) berating typical Confucian scholars for following Confucius and the Classics blindly. This, Chang says, "is why learning has not advanced since antiquity." Instead, we should see that Confucius's age and its limitations are not ours. We should not copy Confucius "in what he simply had to do," endlessly purifying the Classical texts, but should "study what he studied," i.e., "the ways in which the world is ordered, and the everyday institutions of human society."[15]

The Disintegration of the Tao in History

Confucius's role as a sage was to "transmit," not to "create." Not only was this all he could do (without position), it was also what history demanded of him. For after the ancient world order described in the *Rituals of Chou* came to an end, "officials ceased to be teachers" and ceased to preserve the ancient learning. Confucius saw this, and saw that if ancient wisdom was not to be lost to posterity, steps must be taken. So Confucius edited and preserved the documents of the ancient kings in the form of the Classics. In doing so he "simply considered that the *tao* of the ancient sages and kings cannot be seen, and the Classics are just the material embodiment [*ch'i*] of this *tao* which can be seen. Men of later times who have not themselves seen the ancient kings ought, he thought, to use these material objects ... in order to grasp in understanding the invisible *tao*." The Classics, then, are not books that expound the *tao* but the matter (*ch'i*) that exhibits it, for "the *tao* can no more be abstracted from the material world than a shadow can be separated from the shape that casts it." It follows that the *tao* must be grasped intuitively in the Classics, which are not simple rule books for all time: "the domain in which the truth of these Classics is to be applied always differs."[16] Indeed, the Classics by themselves, Chang thinks, are not sufficient to reveal the *tao* fully. For what they do reveal, they reveal by showing what has been and what has happened in the past. Ultimately it is history itself, the course of events, that reveals the *tao*, and obviously the Classics cover only a part of this. And so from time to time the labors of the historian are needed to enable us to complete our understanding. In doing this, his work preserves the virtue of the Classics: it does not state the *tao* in "empty words" but exhibits it "in doings and in things."[17]

But what Confucius was doing was quickly misunderstood. His work was necessary in the first place because government and teaching had separated. The immediate result of this separation of knowledge from action was a private property in ideas. The traditions of learning that had been kept up in government offices were now, in distorted form, continued by "private" rival schools of philosophy. The Confucians (the scholars, *ju*), as one of these schools, in self-defense took the Classics to themselves and treasured them as "books that record the *tao*," the *tao* of *their* school as opposed to others. In doing this they made a double mistake; they mistook the nature of the Classics, and they supposed that the *tao* was theirs. But the *tao* belongs to everyone. Here Chang's purpose becomes clearly distinguished from that of Han Yü, to whose essay "On the Tao" Chang's own is in a way a rejoinder. Han defended the Confucian tradition against Buddhism and Taoism. Chang is trying to isolate and expose the roots of discord in an intellectual world in which Buddhism and Taoism are no longer threatening.[18]

Chang's "On the Tao" closes with a tight analysis of the development and nature of modern intellectual dissension. The analysis is conceptual, not historical. In antiquity it was easy for men to grasp the *tao* whole, for it was never presented abstractly by the ancient official-teachers, but always in its manifestation in "things" that could be seen and easily understood. The end of the classical utopia has placed an enormous epistemological burden on man. Scholars of later times, not having the living tradition of antiquity to work in, must engage in laborious classical research to grasp even a fragment of that tradition: they must work many times harder than the ancients to understand only a fraction as much—not because men have deteriorated in ability, but because the world has changed.[19]

This epistemological handicap means that to accomplish anything at all, the modern scholar must specialize in a narrow range of work. This presents two difficulties. First, the *tao* itself cannot be cut up; no one kind of approach to it is adequate. The specialist, therefore, unless he has a strong sense of the importance of what he does not work on, has a distorted idea of the classical tradition. Second, once the *tao* is not comprehended as a whole by man, a kind of logic of individuation sets in. This happened at once in antiquity with the appearance of rival philosophical schools, only one of which was the Confucian. Each group is held together by consciousness of its identity in contrast to other groups, but once its attention is diverted from these rivals, it in turn splits up according to the special interests of sub-groups within itself, and the same sort of rivalry develops between these—and so there was as much partisanship among the Han schools of classical scholarship as there had been among the Chou philosophers.[20] Looking broadly at post-classical times and not just at the Han, Chang sees three types of scholarship in the study of the Classics: textual study, philosophical analysis, and the philological study of technical detail. These have to exist, but those using them forget that all are necessary. And so "as different paths of thought more and more divide, the *tao* is more and more lost sight of."[21]

One remedy for this situation is for each specialty to be aware of its own limitations. Another remedy, Chang says, is for the writer to follow exactly the methods of that earlier and greater kind of creator, the sage-ruler: "first some need and then the satisfying of it, first some anxiety and then the expression of it, first some evil and then the remedying of it." It is the historian, Chang thinks, who best realizes this ideal.[22]

But this proposed self-discipline suggests to Chang another way intellectuals divide against each other. The alternative to doing what Chang urges is to use impressive language just to make a reputation for oneself—to pursue the cult of *wen*. And the cult of expression for its own sake contrasts in turn with two more fundamental functions of intellect (which are, Chang says, its *yin* and *yang*): preserving knowledge of the past and gaining insight into the future—the two basic ways to grasp the *tao*. The first is the historical or philological study of *fact*, the second the philosophical inquiry into universal *principles*. Ideally all three—*wen*, facts, and principles—go together, so that truth "shines forth" through facts, and both are well expressed. But this is not the way men have behaved: there are philologists, literary men, and philosophers, and each group disparages the others. And worse, the process of division sets in once again, so that each of these three modes of work is subdivided into bitterly partisan schools (such as the schools of Chu Hsi and Lu Chiu-yüan in philosophy), where scholars and literary men follow first one fashion (*feng-ch'i*) and then another.[23]

With this depressing conclusion, Chang closes his major philosophical statement, "On the Tao." The essay quickly circulated among his friends. Few of them liked it. Shao Chin-han was dutifully appreciative and wrote a comment in praise of it. But Shih Chih-kuang, whom Chang visited in Hupeh in the winter of 1789–90, expressed disappointment that it was not like Chang's other essays; it seemed to him to be "in the Sung manner" and not "fresh and new." Chang's son I-hsüan brought back similar reactions from Peking. Defending his essay in a letter to a friend, Chang admitted that he had indeed used an old title.[e] But his pur-

---

[e] "To Ch'en Chien-t'ing on Learning," winter of 1789, *I-shu,* 9.39b–41b.

pose was not, like Liu An's in *Huai-nan Tzu,* to talk of Taoist mysteries; it was not, like Liu Hsieh's, to discuss principles of literary art, nor, like Han Yü's, to attack Buddhism. He was actually doing something completely new—attempting to diagnose and prescribe a cure for the intellectual dissensions of his age.

In the same letter, Chang spoke of another essay in circulation, "On Learning." This, he said, he had written primarily to develop further certain ideas in "On the Tao." And at about the same time (the winter of 1789) he sent a third essay, "On Breadth and Economy," to Shen Tsai-t'ing (the son of his old teacher Shen Yeh-fu) with a long covering letter, which was, as we shall see, a very important philosophical statement in itself. All of these materials deal in different ways with the intellectual dissension problem and the scholar's duty in relation to it.

The arguments in "On Learning" and "On Breadth and Economy" can be presented briefly. In the former, Chang proposes that all knowledge (he means knowledge of what is right, of "standards") comes originally "from Heaven," in a special sense. Chang accepts the view that some people are naturally superior to others, and that it is necessary for those whose understanding is more limited to learn from those whose understanding is greater. Heaven —that is, nature—establishes standards through "virtues," which are a natural human endowment, and through social relations of status or "position," which are part of the natural order. Perfect understanding of these is possible only for the sages, upon whom our moral knowledge ultimately depends. These views are curiously like Tai Chen's. But Chang gives them a twist in the direction of his own interests: what we must do is study the words and deeds of the great men of history, men "whose natural virtues were the purest and whose natural status was the highest," and then we can "apprehend for ourselves" the natural standard and exhibit it in our actions. This process must be the essential part of our moral education. The reading of books, he says, is only a means to action.[24] This remark suggests the early Ch'ing philosopher Yen Yüan (1635–1704).

The relation of "knowledge" to "action" together with an associated problem, the relation of "thought" to "learning," concerns Chang in what follows. In later Neo-Confucian thought, a curious proportion seems to exist among these four concepts: to attempt to *know* without working with things or *acting* out what one is learning is to try to advance by the power of the mind alone; *learning,* on the other hand, as distinct from reflective *thought,* involves moving outside one's mind, coming into contact with things, objective facts. The learning of the ancients, Chang says, consisted of both study and practice and was the same for all; it "never lost sight of actual things," but when "the official and teacher were separated and the theories of the philosophical schools arose," different schools of learning became known by the names of the men who led them. This was the undoing of learning. Chang's next remark is aimed straight at contemporary classical scholarship: "the defects of the philosophical schools were due to thought without learning; the defects of traditional scholars arise from learning without thought."*f* He closes by noting regretfully that the examination system, devised as an expedient to encourage classical learning after the breakup of ancient culture, has ended by supplying a false motivation for it; and he deplores those of mediocre talent who imitate the great scholars and writers, not thinking of what end their wide learning and literary skill is to serve, but merely following the intellectual fashion of the day.[25]

In the essay "On Breadth and Economy," Chang talks about the seemingly conflicting values of breadth of scope and specialization in the life work of a man of learning. We should distinguish, he

---

f Chang was tremendously excited when he hit on this formulation. In the letter to Ch'en already cited, he said he felt that in this remark he had really gotten at the "neck and loins" of the matter. He had written the essay hastily, and fearing that he was subconsciously quoting something he had read, asked all of his friends about it, but none had seen it. Chang adds, "Whenever in my *Wen-shih T'ung-i,* I unwittingly express a view which is the same as that of some past writer, I always indicate the earlier man's words, to show that I am not plagiarizing." (WHL, p. 273a.) In the present case Chang does make acknowledgment to Confucius, Lun Yü* 1.13a (2/15).

says, between mere "industry"—the sort of effort made by a man preparing for the examinations, whose purpose is served by such works as Wang Ying-lin's encyclopedia *Yü Hai*—and true "learning." True learning must be focused and guided by basic interests springing from one's own nature.[26]

Superficially, this seems to be an ideal of learning different from that held in antiquity, when all went through the same curriculum of study. But, Chang points out, the universal understanding possible for a man in antiquity is no longer attainable for the modern scholar; their situations are basically different. The modern scholar can concern himself with only a small part of the knowledge that the ancient scholar would have acquired easily in childhood. So strongly does Chang press the difficulty of recapturing the learning of the ancient past that we must begin to wonder (as I suspect Chang must have) how any knowledge of that past is possible.

Specialization is the solution to the modern scholar's dilemma. This is all the more so, thinks Chang, because intellectual tempers differ. There are, in the broadest terms, those who tend to grasp intuitively the significance of things, to see things in large wholes, and there are others who are naturally interested in detailed matters of fact. Chang was, as he wrote his sons the following year, a person of the first type. But "there is for each man some kind of work to which he is by nature inclined and which he can pursue effectively; thus each man can achieve something of his own."[27] "Learning consists in making your own achievement," Chang insisted, "and you should not be ashamed because you lack an ability that someone else has."[28] Chang admitted that this imperative of recognizing one's own nature has something in common with Wang Yang-ming's idea of "innate knowledge," but Wang, he held, was simply continuing the thought of Mencius.

Specialization, however, ought not to imply a limitation of vision or relevance in the scholar's work. All special disciplines are part of the whole body of truth. In general terms, there have been three types of intellectual activity to which scholars in later times have applied themselves — philosophy, philology, and literary art. So

Chang had said in "On the Tao," and so he had written to Chang Ju-nan as long ago as 1766.[9] "If a man applies himself to one of these three, it is inevitable that he will slight the other two. If he understands that his own specialty is but one part of the *tao*, and does not suppose that the other two are to be disregarded, he will be not far from the true way."[29]

In "On the Tao," Chang discusses the scholarly strife generated by the conflict between different intellectual fashions, or tendencies (*feng-ch'i*). Chang explains this concept in detail in a letter to Shen Tsai-t'ing written in the winter of 1789, and in his essay, "The Analogy of Heaven."

In this essay, Chang's Heaven has a dual nature; it is, as Tung Chung-shu and Han philosophy conceived it, the sky above with its celestial bodies and their movements, and it is also the "great source of the *tao*," the sum total of the forces operating in history and human life. "Heaven," he says, "is undifferentiated and nameless." The various constellations, the sectors into which the sky is divided, and Tung Chung-shu's cycles, are "simply arbitrary concepts employed by astronomers to organize their calculations." At first, Heaven was simply the necessity of the natural order. Men did not think of human activity as falling under this or that concept, but simply acted as they had to. Then men became conscious of time and process as an alternation of "elegance" and "simplicity" (*wen* and *chih*, Chang's art and substance, but also cyclical historical forces in Han philosophy); eventually Heaven came to be even further differentiated as traditions of learning, historical achievements, literary art, and philosophic thought. This occurred because men's attentions were focused in different directions by the needs

---

[9] In both cases Chang's idea is like T'ung-ch'eng theory, which emphasized this three-way classification. Later Chang seems to have modified his position, perhaps in reaction to Yüan Mei, who ridiculed "philology." In the essay "Shih-hua" (probably written in 1798) Chang posits another triad: learning (*hsüeh-wen*), writing (*wen-tz'u*), and philology (*k'ao-chü*). *K'ao-chü* must be present in any kind of *hsüeh-wen*, but what a man specializes in to make his mark must be something more individual. Chang feels that Yüan is being silly in speaking of the philologists as a "school" (WTJ, p. 288).

of their times, "and it was necessary to name these tendencies arbitrarily in order to indicate their direction." In later times men let themselves be guided by these concepts, attaching themselves to one tendency or another, and the result has been conflict between "Han learning" and "Sung learning," between the philologues and the writers, between "moral cultivation" and "study." Adherents of one side condemn the other, and in so doing reveal their lack of understanding. Their own concepts of what they are doing and where they stand are offences against the natural order of things, which embraces all such oppositions.[30]

Chang then returns to his examination of the astronomer's knowledge of the physical heaven. Various systems were used in antiquity, the system of one time often differing considerably from that of another. It was inevitable that later chronologers would refine or supplement or change the work of earlier ones, for since heaven is formless and the astronomer's conceptions necessarily arbitrary, no one system can describe heaven; in the course of time it will show greater and greater error in its predictions. If the nominalism in Chang's view were not so extreme, he might here be close to a notion of hypothesis or natural law. But at this point he drops astronomy and makes an analogical jump to the history of learning and thought. Just as the systems of astronomers are practical constructions to fill a need, so is the work of the great intellects of history shaped to fit the needs of their times. Here Chang is talking not about the Classical Age, but about post-classical history: the Neo-Confucian tradition of the *tao*—the Duke of Chou and Confucius, Mencius, Han Yü, and the Sung school. The work of each of these great men is, like the work of successive astronomers, a correction of the tendency or fashion in learning that preceded it.

When such an emphasis is begun, it may temporarily be a valuable readjustment of balance. But human nature is such that the new tendency will eventually be carried to excess, and "men who love fame [or are blinded by their conceptions—*ming*] will eagerly follow fashion in learning, which amounts to fighting fire with fire, or water with water." A fashion that has ceased to be productive and must be corrected is like an astronomical system that may at first have been an improvement on the one it super-seded but has eventually come to show great predictive error of an opposite kind. In thought, as in astronomy, "when an extreme is reached, and it is not counteracted, it will be impossible to attain what is central and correct."[31] Thus, though human understanding has changed throughout post-classical history, it has not progressed. Instead of advancing, civilization forever zigzags about an imagi-nary center, moving from one extreme to another. But why, with the example of astronomy (in which the Chinese had made prog-ress) before him, could Chang not conceive of civilization as in-definitely perfectible? One reason was that he could scarcely con-ceive of concepts, even those of the astronomer, as being *approxi-mations* to truth at all. Since nature—Chang's Heaven—is form-less, any formula for dealing with it must be a distortion.

Another reason was Chang's rich familiarity with the history of his own civilization, and the ingrained habits of evaluating it that he shared with all Chinese literary men. The picture he had of the past would have made unreasonable any supposition that historical changes in man's learning, thought, and values could be progres-sive. It was almost an unquestionable assumption that the Chou state idealized by Confucius contained a social order that could not be improved on, even if it might be argued that something as good, or nearly as good, was possible in a different form. The idea of the best as a mid-point between extremes, of history as the field of dominant forces succeeding one another, overcoming and being overcome in turn, as in the procession of the Five Elements or the "virtues" of the dynastic lines—these deep-rooted conceptions in-evitably informed Chang's imaginings.

He was able, moreover, to fill out the general scheme he had in mind in a rather plausible way: the *feng-ch'i* (fashions or tenden-cies), he thinks, are three in number, following one another cyclically in a fixed order. This idea he elaborated in his letter to Shen. Chang explained that after the ancient society, in which the *tao* was realized all at once, broke apart in the separation of government from learning, men were capable of grasping only a part of the *tao* in any one age. This means that in a given age, some one fashion will dominate men's minds, as a sort of Zeitgeist. The three *feng-ch'i* are philology, literary art, and philosophical speculation; they recur in this order endlessly in history. They are expressions of three elements in the human makeup: learning (*hsüeh*), artistic talent (*ts'ai*), and understanding (*shih*). These elements are the mature development in the individual of three elementary faculties possessed by all men from birth: memory, expression (*tso-hsing*), and intuition. While the elementary bases of the fashions are present in all natures, natures do differ, as Chang stressed in "On Breadth and Economy." One man will be naturally drawn to one kind of work, another man to another. These differences in men are reiterated in the broad differences in historical ages. In history, the first of the tendencies can be seen in the scholarship of the Han, the second culminates in the literary art of Han Yü and Ou-yang Hsiu, and the third appears in Sung philosophy. This in turn has been superseded, and the Ch'ing has introduced a new age of philology.[32]

It is not to be supposed, Chang cautions, that an individual's talents will correspond to the fashion of his time. There is danger, "when praise and disapproval are influential and the inclination to fame strong," that he will disregard his own nature and follow fashion, thus falsifying his intellectual life. The duty of the true man of learning, Chang urges, is to understand his own place in history and then determine his course. If the fashion of his time is new and creative, and in the ascendant, it is his part to join it and support it. If it has passed its zenith and people are pursuing it merely for fame, then he "ought to note what the world is neglecting" and supply the lack. Chang apparently does not see the difficulties that might arise when the outer needs of history and the inner imperatives of an individual nature conflict. Today, he thinks, it is classical prose style that especially needs attention (literary art succeeds philology in the cycle). But in a sense, the fashions can be reduced from three to two, i.e., to learning and writing, since principles (the concern of philosophy) have no independent status. And since writing in turn should not be an end in itself, he proposes that "if we can pay attention to writing and still keep learning basic, we can hold on to the present fashion, and yet later on this fashion will not be corrupted."[33] Chang's grand conception fizzles out.

Chang's theory of fashions, proceeding from both metaphysical and psychological necessity, is the final refinement in his conception of the disintegration of the *tao* in post-classical history. But Chang has still more to say about intellectual strife. More than anything else, he was concerned with the philosophical quarrel within Neo-Confucianism between the adherents of Chu Hsi and those of Lu Chiu-yüan and Wang Yang-ming, and with the denunciation by contemporary philologists of both camps. Just as ancient harmony came to an end with the separation of knowledge from action, so is harmony among modern scholars threatened by the same cause under another aspect: the speculative abstraction of "principles" from actual facts and tangible realities:

The principles of Heaven and Man, nature and fate, are all contained in the Classics. The Classics are not the words of any one man, and yet the basic principles in them always form a single whole; the reason for this is that these principles are expressed in terms of concrete situations and objects, not in "empty words." If teachers and scholars, in explaining these principles for posterity, would simply express them in terms of concrete situations and objects, then there would be no quarreling among schools of thought.[34]

With these words Chang begins the essay on the schools of Chu and Lu, which contains his criticism of the philosophical divisions in Neo-Confucian China.

The Ch'eng-Chu and Lu-Wang philosophies he saw as inevitable expressions of the particularizing and generalizing aspects of man's intellectual nature, aspects that he considered equally valuable. Trouble arose, he thought, with the later followers of Chu and Lu, who quarreled with one another and assumed opposing philosophical positions simply to be different. These persons, whatever their position, are really imitators of Lu and Wang and not of Chu Hsi; for philosophical speculation, Chang argues, is the characteristic of Lu and Wang, whereas the distinguishing aspect of Chu's tradition is careful scholarship. Chu has no true imitators—because "empty words are easy, but real learning is difficult." Chu's true successors have been the solid scholars (such as Ku Yen-wu and Yen Jo-chü in the early Ch'ing) who "naturally had no time for partisan bickering, and of course did not follow the vagaries of intellectual fashion."[35]

Chang deplores the unqualified dogmatism of the self-proclaimed orthodox, those who "think highly of ethical abstractions and very little of actual achievement, who disregard scholarship and literary skill entirely but uphold one or two ideas in Chu's notes in order to attack Lu and Wang angrily, as though they could not suffer them to exist. They think they are carrying on Chu's tradition, but they are just downgrading Chu Hsi, who had a comprehensive grasp of all history and a complete understanding of the universe, to a rustic ignoramus, haughty and self-righteous."[36] But even those who are true successors of Chu are open to criticism. "There was in our time a man who belittled Chu Hsi, yet actually was a product of Chu's tradition." He was a man of real scholarly ability and intelligence, but "unfortunately he had more cleverness than understanding"; in attacking Chu he failed to understand his own historical position. Do we think the less of the astronomers in the *Classic of History,* Chang asks, because later astronomy has superseded them? This man "was forgetful of his origin." Yet "there are few men now who love learning but lack true understanding who have not succumbed to his influence."[37] Chang's appraisal of Neo-Confucian learning ended with this sharpening of his old disagreement with Tai Chen, now twelve years dead.

The Role of the Intellectual

From the foregoing, we see the great seriousness with which Chang regards the profession of writing and learning: he even describes the necessity that justifies the writer's work in the exact words he uses to characterize the historical necessity that called forth the creative actions of the sage-ruler. This can only imply that the writer is the very instrument through which the *tao* takes form. In a world of contentious scholarship, a world that pursues now this and now that fashion to excess, the intellectual's duty is to understand and to restore a proper balance.

Since the life of learning is so serious a matter, it must be pursued effectively. But how is this to be done, in view of the enormous range the subject matter of scholarship has come to have? A similar question had led Wang Yang-ming and Yen Yüan to question the value of books. In the essay "One's Grant of Years" ("Chia Nien"), Chang recalls an acquaintance who had posed just this question: "Although books have become very numerous in modern times, man's span of life is no greater than it was in antiquity. And so, this man argued, it follows that human capability is not what it was of old. To be sure, if a scholar had a life span of five hundred years, he could go through all the books now in existence to his satisfaction; but after a thousand years the number of books will have doubled, so that then it will take another thousand years to read them."[38] Chang rejects the complaint as absurd. Learning, he suggests, has no value in itself; it is valuable only in relation to the needs of a knowing mind, just as food has value only in relation to the needs of a body. Man, like other animals, has an allotted span. "His period between heaven and earth is one hundred years; and his mental powers and physical energy are sufficient to supply the needs and wants of this length of time."[39] He rejects, it would seem, Chu Hsi's ideal of universal knowledge on the very Neo-Confucian ground that the end of learning is self-cultivation.

But this is not really quite what Chang wants to say. He had written Chu Tsang-mei a half-dozen years earlier, saying then, also, that a life of study is as valid a way to seek the *tao* as the Sung philosophers' "rectifying the mind." But he had said then, and he continued to believe now, that the intellectual's moral task is to specialize on what his nature fits him for, the better to contribute what he can to learning. But what does he contribute? Some new addition to a growing body of knowledge?

Here we must ask some questions. In Chang's conception of history, human culture developed from inscrutable beginnings until in Western Chou it reached perfection, so that the *tao* had somehow gotten completely expressed in the world. Following this, history for Chang is a long decline from harmony into conflict, from man's total grasp of reality to factionalism and abstraction. In this perspective, the intellectual's contribution seems to be not to bring forth something new, but to bring back by specialization (for this is the only way he can do it), part of what has been lost, devoting himself completely to the study of the perfection that once existed.

But this is not what Chang thinks either. In presenting his theories of history, I have bypassed two problems. First, if it makes no sense to speak of principles apart from things, if the *tao* is always enmeshed in matter as shadow is attached to form, how is it possible to speak of the *tao* as completely manifested? There is no *tao* anterior to and apart from what *is*. Chang's apparent reason for bringing his progressive phase of human history to a close—that the *tao,* so to speak, got used up—doesn't work. Again, the process by which the *tao* takes form, the pressure of needs on human actors, is one that can hardly be thought to stop; indeed, it is just this pressure that continues to prompt and justify the writer in what he does. Chang implicitly acknowledges what I am pointing out, I think, when he argues that the writing of history is continuous with the tradition of the Classics. But whatever may be implicit in Chang, what he explicitly says is that historical development reached perfection with the Duke of Chou.

The second difficulty is the obverse of the first. What caused the apocalyptic change that started history on its downward course? Why did "officials cease to be teachers"? Chang leaves this completely unexplained. There seems for him to be something irreducible in basic change, a necessary mystery about it: "when government and learning separated and could no longer hold together, this was the doing of Heaven." These things "are so without our knowing why."[40]

It might help us to understand why Chang thought this way if we can see what he would have had to say if he had not. If he had seen the *tao* as developing continually in time, he would have had to see the context of a given moment in history as justifying whatever fills it. The Eastern Chou disintegration might then have appeared as a necessary prelude to a more glorious stage of the *tao* in history in the world empire, and the Emperor Ch'in Shih-huang as, unwittingly, moving the *tao* onward; the makers of history would then become, not sages who "take the part of the *tao*," but Hegelian world-historical individuals who move history forward by pursuing their own ends. And on such a view, the present, since in it the *tao* has reached the stage it has reached, would owe no apology to the past. Or, unbearably, Chang might have held that what tradition affirms to be bad really is bad, and that this, too, is the form the *tao* sometimes takes. This Chang could not say. It was necessary for Chang to pronounce the world order of Chou perfect (not seeing that it suffered from that gravest of imperfections, nonexistence), and having done so, to leave subsequent basic change at root incomprehensible. For to have done otherwise would have left him with an intolerable problem of evil. He is in the familiar position of the philosopher who posits an absolute as the ground both of the good and of the real.

But in the end, logic forces its way out. We repeatedly find Chang, having stated his conception of post-classical history, continuing to think as though he hadn't. This undercurrent of his thinking is nowhere more evident than in his essay, "The Meaning of the Word 'Historian.'" In this essay (we may disregard its title) Chang argues that the scholar's work must be of practical political and social use, here and now. But what is extraordinary is the way Chang justifies this view. To disregard the present and concentrate entirely on the study of the classical past, he argues, is the same kind of intellectual mistake one makes when one is preoccupied with "empty words," looking for the *tao* apart from "actual facts." With this twist, Chang virtually turns Ch'ing philology on its head.[41]

Why did Chang want to say this? It is clear that he is saying not that the Classics are to be ignored, but rather that hunting for the *tao* in them is mischievous unless the scholar also pays close attention to present ways and institutions. In his essay "The Teaching of the *Rites*" ("Li Chiao," 1788), he had argued that the philologist's approach to the rituals of antiquity is not enough. In the first place, philologists are chiefly interested in petty ceremonial detail (*ch'ü li*) rather than basic political institutions (*ching li*). And they are interested not in grasping their function and significance but in describing them exactly. This is merely "learning that treasures the past." What is needed is "learning that knows the future," learning that "seeks the basic essence of the ancients in order to enlarge the mind," learning that grasps intuitively the fundamentals of ancient institutions in order to "determine what is right for the present time." This calls for an equally careful study of present institutions, Chang now says. For (we read this in his "Collected Opinions") the past and the present are essentially alike; the *tao* of the one is the *tao* of the other.[42]

This is the view of Hsün Tzu, who thought of the early Chou (somewhat unrealistically) as his own "present" age. He thought of that age very much as Chang did: everything of value in the more distant past was contained in it. Chang now appears to see his own present in just this way. The present configuration of social and political institutions is the result of the total historical process, and it is the reality upon which the scholar's understanding of what is meaningful in the past is based. The scholar has access to this basis of understanding through observing society as it works— "the daily operation of social principles" — and through "documents." "The documents kept by government clerks are where the institutions of the state are preserved, and are actually the real evidence of historical change since Yao and Shun." One knows the past in the present, Chang seems to say. "Disregarding the present and seeking the past, ignoring daily social practices and pursuing the subtleties of scholarship" is like "ignoring *ch'i* and seeking the *tao*" by itself. It is in other words to seek knowledge without looking at what really exists.

But it is not only epistemologically necessary for the man of learning to be concerned with what is and not just with what was, it is also his duty. "In ritual the time is paramount," Chang quotes, and this means, he thinks, that "you should honor the institutions of the rulers of your own time." (We find this same sentiment in Confucius, who "followed Chou" in preference to Hsia and Shang because its institutions were "now in use.")[43] A scholar seriously interested in the classical past, and not just fleeing from reality, will pay close attention to the political institutions of the present ruling authorities and to current social practices. He can, indeed, be sure that the underlying principles he discovers there will be identical with those in the Classics. But "if a man talks about loving antiquity but lacks a knowledge of his own times, if he talks about classical scholarship without having an understanding of documents, his writing will be mere embroidery and his learning a guessing game. No matter how great his ability, it will certainly be of no practical use."[44]

There is, it seems to me, an extraordinary conception of the present imperial state implied in this expression of Chang's philosophy. It is in effect the living body of the *tao* in history. Chang expresses again, as he had in the *Chiao-ch'ou T'ung-i,* a compulsive admiration for Ch'in, the dynasty that "made officials be teachers."[45] His authoritarian political impulses are strong here, as they were when he stressed that Confucius did not "create," having no "position." And the same kind of historical thinking underlies both expressions of his thought: it is the historically valid act that is genuinely significant; only it can bring forth real novelty. But now, in demanding that the scholar concern himself with his own age, Chang is urging a view that could be revolutionary.

Authority and the Individual

Chang's call to the scholar to see the institutions, the state, and the rituals of his own day as important, fully as important as those of antiquity, was really both revolutionary and authoritarian. In the manner of the ancient legalists, he is saying that one cannot, at least not literally and in detail, use the past to criticize the present. The present exists, and one must accept it. A past practice revived in the present could not be what it had been. Its context would be different and so it would have a different significance.

This in fact is exactly what Chang did say in the letter to Shao Chin-han, probably written about this time, on that sticky topic, the writing of examination essays. In this letter, we will recall, Chang disowned his own earlier impatience with *pa-ku*. Each age has its forms, and there is nothing the individual can do about it. Early writers we admire, he says, may not have written *pa-ku*, but they did observe the officially sanctioned literary forms of their own times. It is folly "to neglect the present and turn back to the past," to copy the past literally, "being aware only of the past and forgetting the ground you now occupy" in history.[46]

Chang's strong disposition to accept and respect institutional and political authority is made more evident if we look again at his notion of the "unity of government and teaching" in antiquity, and notice how this conception in Chang has changed from what it had been in Ou-yang Hsiu. For Chang, the separation of government and learning is the alienation of the entire world of the mind from the state as the organized whole of things, and therefore from what is actually going on, from problems that matter. This has been a calamity for learning. He has no fears of, or fears about, government. For Ou-yang Hsiu and those who shared with him the earlier Neo-Confucian holistic vision, *chiao* (teaching or doctrine) also embraced the whole of the life of the mind in antiquity, the whole of culture. But they thought of it as the transforming influence of "rites and music," conceived as the soul and moral glue of society. The separation of *chih* and *chiao* for them was a disaster for both: government became soulless, morally corrupt, and corrupting, maintaining order through force and rigid system rather than education, while "rites and music" became lifeless, unreal, and meaningless, interesting only to the antiquarian.

The concern of the early Neo-Confucian vision, in short, was the reform of government and society by reviving within them the Confucian moral tradition. Chang's concern is the reform of the intellectual and literary world by reintegrating this world into that which is really important, the existing institutional and political order.

Respect for authority has always been, to some degree, normal rather than exceptional for a Chinese thinker, especially for one of Chang's time. A universal form it takes is respect for the great men and great writings of the past, at least when anything really important is at stake. In his essay "On Learning," we saw Chang argue that for the most basic knowledge one is dependent on "those who knew first." In "On Teachers" he makes a distinction between such basic knowledge and knowledge of lesser importance. Chang's "On Teachers" is a criticism of Han Yü's essay of the same title. In his essay Han argues—and this Chang approves—that in choosing a teacher a student should be interested in what the teacher knows, not in his status.[47] But, says Chang, this does not mean that the student has complete liberty of choice. The individual cannot know in advance the validity of what he is learning, so it becomes all-important for him to get his knowledge from the right source, from a teacher who represents a valid tradition. Just as the sage ultimately derives his knowledge from nature (or Heaven), so the authority of teachers, Chang thinks, is divinely ordained: "All men obey Heaven's commands, but Heaven is without sound or smell, and so the ruler governs them; all men are given birth by Heaven, but Heaven does not give birth to creatures individually, and so parents give them birth; all men study and learn from Heaven, but Heaven does not make repeated specific instructions, and so teachers instruct them." The people have three authorities; they are rulers, parents, and teachers, and to serve these three is to serve Heaven.[48]

This at least must be true of man's knowledge of the *tao,* which is that "whereby man is man." A teacher who communicates knowledge of such basic importance cannot be chosen at random or by caprice. There are, of course, teachers who are not of this sort. In the case of persons who teach the Classics or correct one's literary efforts, and who have come by their knowledge only by chance, then "if I follow A and cannot complete my study, there is no objection to my leaving him and proceeding to B: if A will not tell me the answer, B may be questioned." But, Chang continues,

Interpretation of the Classics passed on from teacher to teacher, and principles of compilation deriving from a tradition of historical scholarship, are all embraced by what the *tao* really is.[h] The ancients did not represent what they said completely in writing, and did not express their thought completely in speech. Outside of what was written on bamboo or silk, there was a "mental tradition"; and when something is transmitted orally, it is necessary to understand the source of the tradition. It is not merely that genealogical lines of scholastic descent should not be confused. This being the case, it is imperative first to choose the right man and only then to receive his teaching. If one chooses the wrong person, then it follows that one has no proper source for what one receives.

The role of intuition in the transmission of learning increases the authority of tradition by making the student more completely dependent upon this tradition for his contact with the sages of the past, "who created our virtues and arts, which we actually receive

---

[h] It must be granted that when he is not attending closely to the philosophical problem of the nature of the *tao,* Chang lapses into ordinary ways of talking about it. Here, the *tao* seems to be something that can be taught, authoritatively if not explicitly. In "The Teaching of the *Odes*" (see Chapter 5) it is something that can be "seen."

from no other source." Chang feels that one owes to these men and their traditions a loyalty that makes it absurd for a student to make his own judgment of a true teacher of the *tao*. But traditions have long been broken, and Chang finds none who can claim to be teachers of this sort; his teachers are the great men of history themselves. With this intense, emotional commitment to the past, it becomes irrelevant to ask if we can accept literally the instructions of men of old; for "does a son in serving his parents actually consider their worth and virtue, or consider ancestral precedence in paying honor to his grandfather?"[49]

We might suppose from this almost passionate statement that a man's dependence on his teacher, and through him on the authority of tradition, is total. But we will find that Chang is led by this same mode of thinking to say almost exactly the opposite: that the really great work of the mind is done by the men whose originality and intellectual power mark them as completely individual. To see how this happens we must examine not the theories Chang states so much as the assumptions he makes.

A basic concept in Chang's *Chiao-ch'ou T'ung-i* is the concept of a school (*chia*) of learning. This concept develops throughout Chang's thought, bringing into a common focus a multitude of other attitudes: a conviction that the scholar's work should matter and should be pursued effectively, a conviction of the importance of tradition and of the irreducible function of intuition in learning. These attitudes are linked to Chang's theories of history and literature through the concept of *chia-hsüeh* (the learning of a school or family). One cannot render this expression quickly, for it assumes values for all the meanings that the word *chia* can have for Chang and for the sources of his thought. *Chia* are individual books of history by single authors in Liu Chih-chi;[50] they are the bibliographic categories of Liu Hsin and the ancient philosophical schools from which they are derived; the schools, in turn, derive from the families of the (hereditary) offices of Chou. Even idiomatic usage shapes the concept: *ch'eng chia* is to establish one's family or fortune, to succeed, to make a mark for oneself. Ssu-ma Ch'ien, justifying his writing of the *Shih-chi,* said he had hoped "to fathom the relationships between Heaven and Man, to understand the historical changes of past and present, and fashion a work of my own."[51] Ssu-ma Ch'ien's phrase is *ch'eng i chia chih yen,* in which Chang sees much more than its semi-colloquial meaning of "to write an original work" or "to arrive at an original point of view." He thinks of Ssu-ma Ch'ien also as drawing together knowledge and insights of many kinds into one unique intellectual discipline, a "single school" (*i chia*). Through Ssu-ma Ch'ien the concept is connected again with the family, for the *Shih-chi* was "family learning" in the sense that Ssu-ma Ch'ien, his father, and his grandson all worked on it. In fact, *chia-hsüeh,* Chang thought (and said with greater emphasis later), is the key to the excellence of ancient historians.

In the essay entitled "Historical Commentary" ("Shih Chu"), the only one of the identifiable T'ai-p'ing essays to deal specifically with a problem of historical method, he develops the *chia-hsüeh* concept at some length: ancient learning (specifically history) was passed down through a family of hereditary officials, and one had to go to the proper authority to receive instruction in it. The philosophers who followed had disciples to pass on their learning; in the Han, Ssu-ma Ch'ien's work was "transmitted to members of his family." And "as for Pan Ku's *Han Shu,* after Pan's death all the scholars of the day were unable to understand it completely, so finally Ma Jung humbled himself at the door of Pan's younger sister and received her instructions; only after that was his learning brought forth." This esoteric character of the ancient *chia-hsüeh*— the notion that certain kinds of knowledge must be had from the proper source—suggests Chang's ideas in "On Teachers," but it is more directly related to his belief that certain kinds of knowledge can only be apprehended intuitively. "In the specialized learning of the ancients, there always had to be an unwritten transmission from one mind to another" (*fa-wai ch'uan hsin,* an important concept to which we must return later). "What was not touched in their writings, they gave verbally to their disciples, and the disciples together practiced and transmitted their heritage and so passed it on to posterity."[52]

The ancient *chia-hsüeh* served to transmit and preserve historical insights, making possible "caution and strictness in the selection of facts," avoiding just that encyclopedic complexity that Chang saw and deplored in Ma Tuan-lin. In time, such traditions deposited their knowledge in the form of commentaries to texts, but the traditions were ultimately broken. It is the point of Chang's essay that the modern historian, with no hope of a tradition to continue his distinctive learning, should accompany his own work with a commentary explaining his text and indicating his sources, a practice that would have the added advantage of promoting honesty in scholarship.[53] This, like his ideas on indexing, is a striking example of how Chang, starting with the most unlikely assumptions and proceeding by the most devious logic, could somehow arrive at positions that seem remarkably modern and that we are constrained to applaud.

The *chia-hsüeh* concept is here most closely connected with Chang's theories of historiography, but it is related to all his ideals of learning. The ancient traditions have been broken, but, Chang thinks, it is still possible for a modern scholar to master the learning of the ancients (even as Chang does in his historical analysis), and by the very force of his own unique understanding (*pieh-shih hsin-ts'ai*) to gain insight into it; in effect he can reestablish the direct connection of mind with mind that characterized ancient tradition, and in his work he can "form a school by himself," as did Ssu-ma Ch'ien. In other words, he assimilates the learning of the ancients and then produces himself a body of work that is a unique contribution ot the world's knowledge and a monument to his genius. It is for precisely such an achievement that Chang praises Cheng Ch'iao.[54] Shao T'ing-ts'ai also, said Chang, combines literary and intellectual excellences that can be found in other famous writers of the past into a unique amalgam—thus he "establishes a school of his own" (*tzu ch'eng i chia*).[55] But is this not as it is with the poet who reads to widen his acquaintance with ideas and styles, and then lets his poems be his own expression of his own feeling? What has happened is that a familiar idea in literary criticism, Chang's as well as others', has been drawn here into the concept of *chia-hsüeh,* and becomes an ideal for the scholar and literary artist alike.[i]

Chang's suggestions for the improvement of literary collections, *wen-chi,* now become clearer: they are to be reorganized and reconceived to cover both substantial contributions to learning and expressive writing, and will present the writings of a man in terms of a new value, that of uniqueness. This was the characteristic of the writings of the ancient philosophical schools from which *wen-chi* developed. It is perhaps significant that Chang intended his *Wen-shih T'ung-i* (which now includes only his essays) to include the writings of his entire lifetime. The sum of his work then was not to be a *chi* but a *chia*—not a collection of writings but a sustained effort to deal with an integrated group of problems, to advance theories and illustrate their application. Those writings that were deemed unworthy were to be discarded.[j]

It is clear that Chang's ideal of individual excellence is related to his appraisal of himself. In fact, in one unguarded moment we find him ascribing to himself that "unique understanding" which appears to be the distinguishing mark of genius.[56] Although Chang recommends following a specialized field or tradition of learning

---

[i] Chang's language is itself drawn from earlier Ch'ing literary criticism. A poet was said to *"tzu ch'eng i chia"* if having assimilated the art of earlier writers, he recreated it in writing that expressed his own individuality; cf. Aoki Masaru, *Shina Bungaku Shisō Shi (History of Chinese Literary Theory),* Tokyo, 1943, pp. 182–83.
[j] Chang Shu-tsu, "*Wen-shih T'ung-i* Pan-pen k'ao," in *Shih-hsüeh Nien-pao,* III (1939), 73–74. Chang may, however, have modified this intention after changing the title of his *Chiao-ch'ou Lüeh* to *Chiao-ch'ou T'ung-i* (which could not very logically be included in another *t'ung-i*). The close relation of the *chia* idea to Chang's criticism of *wen-chi* was dealt with in Chapter 3. It may be seen again in Chang's appraisal of Shao T'ing-ts'ai: "His writings are called a *wen-chi,* but if you consider their substance and meaning, they are between philosophy and history." HY, p. 24.

for itself alone, with no thought of achieving fame, nevertheless the psychological motive that impels him to value specialization is his conviction of his own genius, his compulsion to accomplish by himself something that is distinct and unique.

We have seen Chang proceeding in various ways from the view that division and partisanship in human thought are deplorable—a view anchored in Chang's resistance to the intellectual pressures of his time—to the view that what is valuable and important in human thinkers is their differences. This latter view, I suspect, is rooted in Chang's conviction of his own worth. But in whatever way he reaches it, this conviction that human minds are different takes on a life of its own, and leads him to fascinating areas of speculation.

One brief example, which is astonishing in a writer of Chang's time and place, opens the essay "A Criticism of Hypocrisy" ("Pien Ssu"). Here Chang's problem is to discover why a man's words do not always express what is in his mind. One cannot directly fathom what is in a man's mind; speech, however, is the "sound" produced by the mind, and so to understand a man we should study his speech. Yet all men in their speech assume the values we approve as good, but some men are in fact not good. It follows that the speech of some will be deceiving, and "will not come from a sincerity of intention." This means that words must always be studied not for what they say but for what they reveal or conceal about the motives of the speaker.[57]

Moreover, language itself cannot express all there is to express, for "The total number of statements possible is not very large. (Although the permutations of words are infinite, the number of principles [*tsung-chih*] expressible is limited; therefore I say the number of statements is not large.) Men, however, are infinitely varied in character. But since the statements they can make are limited in number, it must be that some statements, though corresponding to different characteristics in different people, are nevertheless the same."[58] It would be easy to press Chang with further questions, and one may regret that he did not continue this promising start by raising them himself. What, for example, is a *tsung-chih*—a principle? What examples could he give of two different combinations of words that express the same *tsung-chih*? But short and inadequate though the argument may be, the mathematical mode of thought involved—the placing of a finite against an infinite set—and its application to language comes to the reader of Chinese philosophical literature as a distinct surprise.

In two other arguments Chang stresses even more persistently the differences among minds.

In 1788 an acquaintance (a certain Mr. Liu) gave his study a name, calling it "The Hall of Preserving the Self" (Ts'un-wo-lou). For the occasion, Chang wrote a short essay on the concept "preserving the self." "My self has a future and a past; it is not something that lasts long." In what sense, Chang asks, may one "preserve" this self? Not by trying to preserve one's life, but by employing one's perception and one's mental faculties "so that in one's emotional makeup and in the reason one is endowed with, one attains, in some degree, that which is right."[59] Chang's thought, I think, is that in so cultivating myself I realize in myself a value that is universal and not limited to what is here and now. This seems to be what he is saying, too, in his "Collected Opinions" of 1789–90: "The *tao* is public [*kung*, universal, objective]; study of it is private [*ssu*, particular, subjective]." What one must do is "study" to try to realize the *tao*. That is, one must make full use of the element of "Man" in one's constitution, i.e., one's powers of perception and other faculties, to realize the element of Heaven in one's nature, i.e., the qualities of uprightness and fairness, which are "rooted in the universality of what is natural."[60]

This exercise is obviously not quite study in the ordinary sense, nor is it just a matter of being true to one's conscience. Chang's discourse on "preserving the self" continues: "A man in the course of his life lives through many, many changes, and what he calls 'myself' likewise undergoes many changes. Each man of course lives his own life, and each man's life is unlike that of any other. And even the experiences of one life differ one from another." It follows that not only is each self different from every other but also that each temporal self-state is unique. "My present self then surely must not be my past self. And how can I be sure that my future self will be like my present self?" How then can one isolate one's "real" self, the self that is "clearly identifiable" amid the flux of existence? One must face the fact, Chang thinks, that "where my thought goes, there go I," and that this "I" must change from year to year and even from day to day "without my realizing it." All one can do then is to examine oneself constantly and honestly, "casting away one's past prejudiced self [one's outworn opinions and dispositions?] and then what remains will be one's true self."[k]

In this almost Buddhist (and almost Humean) criticism of the ordinary notion of the self we see how far Chang's restless intellect can push the idea of the uniqueness of the individual, though even here seeking in the individual something common to man. But what is this contrast between the real and the unreal self? Chang's philosophy often seems to require a clearer distinction between the ego and the "true self." This is particularly true of his literary theory, in which he condemns self-serving but affirms self-expression, and then (in "Yen Kung") seems to suspect that self-expression is a kind of self-serving. Here we find Chang feeling his way toward such a distinction without, however, relating it to the problems that require it.

The individual appears in a different perspective, however, when Chang asks not how he can identify himself but how he can be identified by others. Chang asks this question in his essay "On the Difficulty of Being Understood," and in asking it stumbles into problems of the greatest difficulty.

[k] HY, pp. 65–66. Chang's "Where my thought [*ssu*] goes, there go I" seems virtually identical with Liu Tsung-chou's thesis, "Thought [*i*] is the lord of the mind." See Huang Tsung-hsi, *Ming-ju Hsüeh-an*, Cheng-chung Shu-chü (Shanghai, 1947), *chüan* 45, p. 521. Liu's idea is denounced by Fang Tung-shu, a T'ung-ch'eng writer and student of Yao Nai, in his essay "On Heaven" (*I-wei-hsuan Wen-chi*, 1.1b).

"Really" knowing a person, Chang thinks, means not just being able to recognize his features and his mannerisms, and being able to name him. What you must be able to do is to recognize his mind. This is much more difficult, and it is something you can do only if you are the person to do it. We have examples of successful understanding of one mind by another in Confucius's understanding of King Wen, the author of the *Classic of Changes,* and in Ssu-ma Ch'ien's understanding of the poet Ch'ü Yüan. In the first case, a sage understood a sage and shared the same kind of "grief." In the second, a worthy man understood a worthy man and shared his "motivation." But there must be many who are not as fortunate as King Wen and Ch'ü Yüan.

Chang's problem specifically is this: When can you be said "really to understand" an author when you read his writings? He appears to assume that at least you must be in some sense like him. But this can hardly guarantee that you will understand him, for Chang's standard for understanding is impossibly high. Really understanding another mind means being able to *recognize* it unerringly, as you would a face. Chang cites the eighth-century literary connoisseur Hsiao Ying-shih, who read the "Lament on an Old Battlefield" by the T'ang writer Li Hua, without being told that Li had written it. Hsiao said slowly, "Li Hua could have done something as good as this." "And so," Chang says, "people have always said that Hsiao ... had a genuine appreciation for fine writing. But words are rooted in the mind, and minds are as unlike as faces. Hsiao was not able to conclude as soon as he had seen the essay that Li definitely had written it. ... So we cannot call this real understanding."

The difficulty is so great, Chang laments, that a man of truly distinguished mind cannot hope to be fully understood after his death. Thirty or forty per cent of the thought of Ssu-ma Ch'ien and Pan Ku remains beyond our reach, even with the aid of all the old commentators. Why is this the case? "It is feeling [*ch'ing*] that distinguishes men from trees and rocks. What is important about feeling is that by shared experience men understand one another." A man who isn't understood, accepted, or successful in his own time may hope to be understood after he dies. But he had better not hope too much, for the person who understands him must share both his principles (*li*) and his mode of existence (*shih*), must establish contact both with his tangible "effects" and with his mind. And for one person to do all of this is not likely.[61]

If Chang is saying that understanding another is just a matter of being able to recognize his work and call off his name, he has obviously been misled by taking his mind-face analogy too literally. We understand better than he could that a man's phrasing, vocabulary, or word-rhythm may betray his identity just as surely as his fingerprints. It is conceivable that a machine might be capable of this kind of recognition. Chang surely means to employ a far richer concept of recognition that this. I think he would want to say that Hsiao would have shown that he "really understood" Li Hua, not just by being able to name him with confidence, but by being able to name him with the right kind of confidence, sensing in the man's work his complete personality in all of its dimensions, intellectual and emotional. If this is what Chang is saying, he is not being absurd.

But what he says still contains a mistake. When we fully understand a person, we understand not just his attitudes, emotions, and feelings but also his thoughts, his ideas. Chang's inordinate demand that to understand a person, we must be able to recognize him in what he writes makes it seem that his ideas are a part of him, uniquely. And is this not just what Chang has said before? ("Where my thought goes, there go I.") Is it not also just what is pointed to in his likening minds to faces? Ideas for Chang seem to be grimaces on inner faces. How then can I ever know what your ideas are? I cannot think them for myself, for my grimaces will always be mine, never yours. Chang seems to have stripped away from the notion of understanding another person the perfectly good sense it ordinarily has. His difficulty here is a form of the difficulty that leads him to contradiction when considering the content of a poem. It may make sense to hold, as Chang wants to, that a poem, to be more than a mere exercise in technical cleverness, must be an expression of the poet's developed *personality,* a personality that is surely his and his alone. Chang says this and then forgets it, allowing himself to talk of poetry as if it were cognitive utterance. Now he seems to reverse this mistake in insisting on a concept of understanding so restrictive that grasping a person's *thought* becomes a matter of recognizing him for the unique individual he is.

But Chang is not really worrying, as I am, about communication. He is interested in sympathy. He wants someone to read him, if not now then after he is gone—someone who, reading him, will see how he felt, see what he believed, and see, the way he saw, that it is right. And he knows, while he hopes, that it can never be.

Some Remaining Problems

I have been pursuing Chang's thought beyond the point where it can still be described as a system, and must now examine certain remaining problems generated by it. It is to Chang's great credit that, to some degree, he recognizes these problems himself and attempts to work out solutions. These moments of recognition and the attempts at solutions are exciting reading, for they show Chang's mind stretched to the limit of its resources. And humility and prudence require that I admit that I have not always been sure that my own mind is elastic enought to keep up with him.

The first problem will have occurred to the reader. Chang's conception of an intellectual world divided among partisans of this or that viewpoint, dominated first by this, then by that fashion, is related in a simple way to his conception of the man of special gift or insight. Chang feels himself to be one of these persons. People like himself (or Cheng Ch'iao) are subject to reproach by those whose point of view is warped by bias or fashion. Fashion exerts a tyrannical pressure upon the individual, both tempting and intimidating him into conforming, seeking the approval of others, and betraying himself. Yet Chang seems to be not at all afraid of what we would consider the greatest threat to the freedom of the individual mind, the restraints of an authoritarian state and of traditional orthodoxy in thought.

But traditional orthodoxy presents itself to the individual as a limitation on his freedom of thought only when he feels that he cannot deviate from it without being criticized by others. To those who demand blind conformity to the authority of the past, Chang is indeed opposed. They are mere partisans. The attitude he urges (e.g., in his essay on the schools of Chu and Lu) is that one should respect one's intellectual origins, and that this respect is quite consistent with constructive criticism, indeed requires it. For those who go to the opposite extreme of unrestrained criticism of the past, Chang has much the same advice. He chides a nameless critic of Cheng Ch'iao (probably Tai Chen) for simply writing Cheng off intemperately. A sensible attitude toward Cheng, Chang urges, would be to respect his greatness while trying to correct his mistakes—to be, as he puts it, a "worthy minister" to him.[62]

His attitude toward the state is a bit more difficult to deal with. Chang approved of the censorial function of government, but (though he was more enthusiastic about it than most would be) this viewpoint is not surprising in a Chinese writer. We do find in him—though quite rarely—extravagant praise of the Emperor and his reign. But perhaps this is to be expected. I have taken the view that although the Manchu regime was very authoritarian, the eighteenth-century literary man accepted it, and that Chang Hsüeh-ch'eng accepted it wholeheartedly. Some will think this view simple-minded. Faced with overwhelming power, men typically become devious; this has been especially true in China. When Chang praised the state or indirectly justified actions that we now condemn, he may have been just assuming protective coloring. For we will find that later in his life when the political climate had changed, Chang spoke out vigorously on political questions.

This view of Chang's expressed attitude toward the state, however, dismisses too much of his philosophy as mere pretense. The importance he gives to the state in the world of the intellect is implicit in his concept of the ancient world order and the relationship of thought to reality. In working out his ideas, Chang may have been guided by a subconscious wish to believe, for the best reasons he could find, the things he felt compelled to say. This is a universal characteristic of the human psyche, and one that probably every political power has in some degree utilized. It may also be that Chang, by nature stridently independent, struck out at what he safely could, at intellectual factions and fashions, and took the part of authority in order to be all the more perverse. For in his milieu, his protest of Neo-Confucian orthodoxy was itself a gesture of revolt.

Chang never questioned what a man should do if he found himself conscientiously compelled to accept a view condemned by the state or obviously inconsistent with the sages. Was he then constitutionally unable to be clear in this part of his thought? On the contrary, a letter to Ch'ien Ta-hsin (of uncertain date) makes it clear that he was aware of the problem. Chang had evidently included copies of some of his essays with the letter. On these he comments, "In my labors in literary and historical criticism and in bibliography, I may perhaps have achieved something new, but in my arguments there is much that runs against popular taste, and I would not want these essays too widely known. It seems to me there are two important things to be careful about in writing, first that one's judgments of right and wrong be in accord with the sages, and second that one say nothing that is offensive to rulers and parents." These things "the principles of Heaven" do not allow. But "a man who even in a general way is explaining the fundamental ideas of what is right [*ta-i*]" and who has understanding of what writing is about will "surely not offend in this way."

Nonetheless, Chang continues, "popular fashions and preferences are always one-sided." And this makes it inevitable that even the values and pursuits of outstanding and intelligent persons will be tainted by this limitation. A writer is not doing his job unless he sees this and tries to correct it. Yet if he does do this, "he must inevitably take a stand against the tendencies of his time, and the tendencies of one's time are more to be feared than the punitive powers of the police." Even Han Yü, Chang points out, had to be careful about spreading his criticisms of Buddhism. But now the danger from the disapproval of influential persons is worse than it was in the T'ang Dynasty. Other people in writing books try to keep in step with the values of the present age. Chang on the contrary feels he is writing for the ages, and this, he says, is why his views are "not understood."[l] It seems clear from this that wherever we might expect Chang to see the authority of the state as an obstacle to his free expression, he himself sees the danger in the prejudices of his contemporaries.[m]

Chang saw another, more difficult problem in the relationship between original insight, orthodoxy, and conventional opinion. Is it not possible, even likely, that in particular cases all three will concur in the same judgment? To take a simple paradigm case: suppose that a man, thinking things out for himself, comes to the conclusion that the ancient emperor Yao was a good man and that Chieh, the last king of the ancient Hsia dynasty, was an evil man. But this is just what tradition has always affirmed; it is also what everyone says without thinking, simply because it is the approved thing to say. Even in a case like this where the conclusion reached is the same, Chang says that it is better to think the matter out for oneself than to accept the prejudices of others. But what *is* better about it?

This problem Chang confronts in an essay, "On Conventional

[l] *I-shu,* 29.58b–59b. Yao Ming-ta assigns this letter to the year 1772, when it is known that Chang corresponded with Ch'ien and sent him some of his essays. HY, pp. 25–6; see Chapter 2. But a note in one manuscript states that it was "copied for preservation in 1798," and in it Chang refers to Ch'ien Tsai (a vice-president of the Board of Ceremonies) as already dead. Ch'ien Tsai died in 1793. Probably Chang sent this letter in 1796 or later, together with a copy of his selected writings published that year. See also Demiéville, p. 172 n.
[m] Chang's view here, that authority and individual expression do not conflict, is perhaps unconsciously reflected in one of his ideas about learning to write. A student needs to place himself under the discipline of a teacher, not for the purpose of learning the man's particular style but for the discipline itself, which Chang thinks will help the student toward self-development. See *I-shu,* "pu-i," 44b, "Letter to Shih Chih-kuang on Literary Art."

Judgments," which is superficially innocent but actually exasperating. We can imagine how an answer might go: it is better to think things out for yourself, even though you often reach conventional conclusions, because it is always possible that your conclusions will be different; if they are, you are more likely to be right because you have reasons for your conclusions. But Chang doesn't say the obvious thing, perhaps because it would suggest the possibility of unsettling improvements on traditional orthodoxy too. In fact he doesn't even raise the question how you tell whether a judgment is the right and not the wrong one.

What Chang does instead is to consider the uttering of a judgment of approval or disapproval, praise or blame, as itself a moral act, and then to concentrate on the attitude of the man who makes the judgment. In so doing, Chang cautions the individualist as well as the man who accepts his judgments ready made without thinking. One ought to think out the judgments one subscribes to and see what their ground is, for the making of judgments, exercising "our innate disposition to approve the right and condemn the wrong," does not in the full sense consist simply in pronouncing what is right and wrong; it consists, in a particular case, in starting with "problems that are subtle and minute" and clarifying them, starting in doubt and ending in certainty. But the man who does his own thinking should not puff himself up with pride. It is natural for him when he comes upon a problem, "to form his own subjective view of what is the wrong and the right of the matter and to treasure this view, considering it an original insight into a subtle point." But if he analyzes his problem diligently, he will see that it involves nothing really new, but simply leads back to views that he and everyone else have always taken for granted. If he doesn't pursue his "original insight" this far, he deserves to be laughed at, for others will see that his view is obvious even if he doesn't.

Even though such a labor of thought will only lead a person back to obvious conclusions, he has still done something important. "For-

merly he did not understand the reason for the rightness of his
moral views; now he does. . . . Consequently what he sees now does
differ from what he saw then, although what he aserts is actually the
same." Chang is saying in effect that one has a duty to be thoughtful. It is tempting to look here at what he does not say. There are
those who have argued that a person does not really make a moral
judgment unless his judgment is "universalizable," unless, that is,
he is prepared to accept with all of its consequences the moral principle under which his judgment falls. But this kind of analysis belongs to systems of ethics that are concerned (as Chang is not)
with distinguishing correct judgments from mistakes.

What Chang really wants, I suspect, is that a person shall, so to
speak, be able to "particularize" his judgment and have a vivid
sense of the actual situation, both as a whole and in all of its concrete detail, which lies behind his judgment and makes it right.
In the ideal case this sense would come from immediate experience.
But the person who has this sense will not be able to speak easily;
he will be too close to the thing itself for words to be adequate.

There is, of course, no need to discuss our judgments of Yao and Chieh.
But a man who had experienced the benevolence of Yao would be almost unable to talk about Yao; yet he would be just the man who would
truly appreciate Yao's goodness. And the man who had suffered under
the tyranny of Chieh would be virtually unable to criticize Chieh explicitly; yet he would be just the man who would really know how bad
Chieh was. Even our judgments of Yao and Chieh, which have been
taken for granted through the ages, we find to have originated with
those who were almost unable to discuss and criticize them, and only
afterwards did these judgments become generally established as obvious. Therefore, he who really knows what the good and the bad are
will not be able to utter his judgment hastily.

With this Chang returns once again to an old theme. The person
who is too eager to take sides does not really understand things.
"That Yao was good and Chieh was bad, . . . that the Duke of Chou
and Confucius should be honored and differing views criticized,
that the school of Ch'eng and Chu is correct and the school of Lu

and Wang is one-sided—with these judgments I do not disagree. But the person who accepts them as obvious and utters them glibly I know to be one who does not have real understanding."⁶³ What Chang is suggesting, it seems to me, is that one who is too quick to pass judgment, to say the accepted thing, is really only uttering "empty words."

In the foregoing essay Chang never faces a problem we would like him to face: when is one justified in being sure that one's understanding is adequate in content and not just in tone? When can one be sure one is right? Epistemological questions are not favorites with Chinese philosophers, but Chang's system of thought does contain serious implicit problems about knowledge, and in places Chang glimpses these and tries to cope with them. His anxieties about moral judgment point to the nature of these difficulties. Here he was chiefly concerned with judging people (and their views and acts) belonging to the distant past. Such judging requires, of course, that one know something of the past. Here there are problems lying in wait for Chang, and in some measure for any traditional Confucianist. How does one know what the past was? How are the thought and insight and experience of men of the past preserved, and if lost, how regained?

The problem is particularly difficult for Chang. As he stresses repeatedly (for example in "On the Tao" and "The Analogy of Heaven"), the ancient world order is inadequately understood when understood in pieces. It is the gestalt of the whole, the complete structure (*ch'üan t'i*) of antiquity, which needs to be grasped, and this is something that one can at best only "glimpse." Furthermore, as he reminds the reader in "On Breadth and Economy," the ancients were far better off than we are when we try to know antiquity. For we have to study texts, while they had the actual things and operating institutions around them throughout their lives. And there is finally in Chang's thought more than a suggestion of the idea that the *tao* cannot be "named," that what is ultimately right cannot be communicated in words. Concepts are for Chang copies of reality, and poor copies at best. Both the knowledge of particulars and the insight into the whole structure seem to need direct intuition.

It perhaps should not be surprising then that Chang when talking of the perpetuation of knowledge stresses the importance of a direct intuitional link, a "mental transmission," between teacher and student. Words by themselves won't do. Chang says in "Historical Commentary" that although the continuation of "specialized learning" involves spoken words, simply writing down what one might otherwise have said to one's followers seems at best a poor substitute for the direct contact of minds that occurs when a tradition is alive. *Fa-wai ch'uan hsin,* an "unwritten transmission from mind to mind," is a Ch'an Buddhist conception, referring to the wordless understanding that the Buddha conveyed in his "flower sermon," the understanding that links the series of Ch'an patriarchs. The existence of traditions conceived in this way is part of Chang's explanation of how what was known in the past can be known today.

But this mind-to-mind transmission of learning cannot account for knowledge of antiquity, for traditions of learning have long been interrupted. The details of ancient society can be reconstructed in fragments by laborious scholarship. But the grasp of the whole, the grasp of the significance of the details, requires something else. One answer to this problem is contained in a notion popular in Neo-Confucian philosophy since Han Yü, the notion of the "transmission of the *tao*" (*tao-t'ung*) from one "later sage" to another over intervals of centuries. If it is possible to make any kind of sense of this notion, one must suppose that the later recipient of the *tao* somehow establishes direct contact with the mind of an earlier sage, achieving the same sort of "mental transmission" Chang posits between teacher and disciple. And this is just what some Neo-Confucianists went so far as to claim. Ku Yen-wu finds occasion to sneer at those who claim they have authority for their speculations by virtue of a "mental transmission from the Two Emperors" (Yao

and Shun); Fei Mi, too, excoriates the idea as a completely illegiti-
mate way for philosophical conservatives to claim authority for
their doctrines.[64] Indeed this kind of claim to knowledge of the past
must be anathema to Ch'ing philology, itself a radically different
way of knowing. Yet Chang Hsüeh-ch'eng comes very close to this
notion of a direct leap into the minds of the ancients when he says
that the great men of history themselves are his teachers, when he
says that it takes a special type of intellect to grasp the overall picture of antiquity, or when he says that a man of great insight can
sometimes "see the essence" of the ancients.

But Chang does not go all the way to complete mystification. The
notions of insight and significance are obscure enough, but with
these Chang stops. And he claims, rightly I think, that one must
make some use of them, that a radical philology is nonsense. The
claim is made most clearly in another of his letters.[65] In it Chang
recalls Tai Chen's demand for thoroughness in classical study,
which had impressed him deeply as a young student. But now Tai's
position seems to him absurd. Tai would have it that one has not
"finished one's work" in reading, e.g., the *Classic of History,* until
and unless one understands all of the details of archaic astronomy
presupposed in parts of the book, that one hasn't really read the
Odes unless one has a complete knowledge of the ancient system of
rhymes. Perhaps Chang does not clearly see the paradoxical direction of Tai's argument (that one does not really understand
anything until one understands everything), but he seems to sense
it. Grasp of the whole, of the *tao* permeating and illuminating
everything, he implies, cannot require the grasp of every detail.
Such a standard would rule out even Mencius as a knower of the
ancient world order, not to mention such later intellects as Ssu-ma
Ch'ien, Han Yü, and Liu Tsung-yüan.

Tai and other philologists, however, in stressing the knowledge
of detailed matters of fact, were attracted to this kind of knowledge
because these seemed to be things one could be sure of. On the
other hand, insight (*hsin te*) seems to be completely subjective.
And there is nothing in Chang's system of ideas that allows him

to accept its renditions as subjective, as, for example, conjectures to be corrected; they seem to be valid as they stand.

This difficulty Chang does not help us with. But his thought leads to another difficulty concerning the subjectivity of understanding, which he at least sees. Consider what Chang must suppose to happen when the words of a man of antiquity are repeated or written down, quoted, passed on, and interpreted. The sages whose words are anonymously preserved in the Classics did not intrude themselves into what they wrote. Their words are "everyone's," produced as necessity demanded, called forth by the concrete problems they dealt with. Anyone who writes like this, Chang has argued (in 1783, in " 'If Your Words Are Everyone's' "), should be willing to have his words used and quoted by others without credit to himself. Such words are so to speak in the public domain, and in reading them we ought, it would seem, to have uncomplicated access to the meaning that is expressed in them. But Chang could not say this, and he saw that he couldn't say it. For, as we know, he also believed that what words do is to reveal (incompletely) the contents and characteristics of minds, and he believed that each mind, with whatever capacity for understanding it has, is in some degree different from every other mind. What happens, as everyone knows, is that "when worthy men transmit the words [the ideas] of the sages, sometimes the meaning is lost, and when ordinary men transmit the words of worthy men, sometimes the meaning is lost." What Chang has exposed is the problem, How can we be sure we understand past "words" at all?

Chang tried to dig himself out of this difficulty. We must, he argues in the same essay, admit that there is such a thing as correct interpretation, which we can contrast with misunderstanding. "When men have the same *tao* and their characters are in harmony, in the last analysis they will not go off in completely opposite directions." Even where writers use the words of the ancients to develop writings and arguments of their own, one must recognize a distinction between the man who quotes and twists the meaning for his own purposes and the man who simply and honestly draws the implications out of what he uses.[66] This seems to me to be good repair work as far as it goes; but showing that understanding exists is not the same as showing how it is possible.

Some of the theses to which Chang is committed, and which seem to bear on this problem, are far apart indeed. A sage and the best sort of writer are not interested in themselves but in the truth. It should not matter to them nor to us who is recognized as the author of their words. Their words, it seems, are for the ages, and for all. Yet even the Classics do not "state what the *tao* is" but somehow show it, by being the historically unique particular things that they are. And the writings of a great writer of the past are so individualized by his personality and circumstances, we find Chang urging, that we really need detailed chronological biographies to read them properly. "The appropriateness of words always depends on when they are uttered," so much so, he thinks, that sometimes the same words written at two different times by the same man will "in truth and worth be as far apart as heaven and earth."[67] And, of course, this is true.

Perhaps we have pursued Chang's thought into frontiers that, even for him, were quite uncharted.

7. The Historian's Craft

When jade is carved to make a vessel, the jade discarded is
not necessarily inferior to that which remains. The
jade-carver hews away without regret, because he considers
that which is flawless yet out of place no different
from that which is blemished.

— *Various Remarks,* published 1796

After leaving T'ai-p'ing and Hsü Li-kang's hospitality in the summer of 1789, Chang went to work on the history of Po-chou. Mean-
while, knowing that this source of support could not last, he
approached his old patron Pi Yüan. Pi, as governor-general of
Hupeh-Hunan, was now established at Wu-ch'ang in Hupeh,
where he was continuing his generous support of scholarship.
Chang wrote to him that he was in distress ("with my begging
bowl I go sighing from street to street asking for food"), and followed this plea with a visit to Hupeh. In the third month of 1790,
his local history finished, Chang traveled to Wu-ch'ang, where Pi
welcomed him once again and provided him with a residence.
Here Chang remained for the next four years. He took only one of
his wives with him, leaving the rest of his family in Po-chou. Later,
in 1793, he had them travel on—with his books, his coffins, and his
grandchildren—to his ancestral home in K'uai-chi in Chekiang.[1]

As a result, he was again separated from his family for an extended period of time. His sons were now in their twenties, and his
eldest, Chang I-hsüan, had tried the provincial examination in
Peking in 1788. It was probably a combination of this separation
from his family and an interest in his sons' education that prompted
Chang to write, in 1790 and 1791, seven delightful "family letters."
In these letters Chang reexpressed his personal philosophy of learning, with frequent references to his own interests and to incidents
from his early life. He strongly emphasized his interest in history.

"In history," Chang wrote, "I seem to have a natural gift. I feel that I have developed principles which have broken much new ground for posterity."[2] This interest and this gift were to be fully developed in the next five years. It was primarily as a historian that Chang joined Pi Yüan's group of scholars, and primarily as a critic of historical scholarship that he expressed himself in essays and letters during this period.

This did not indicate a change in Chang's scholarly temper, but rather a focusing of interests that had always been important to him—interests that had first appeared in his surreptitious attempt to compile a history of Eastern Chou, and which had been strengthened when, while assisting his father in the compilation of the history of T'ien-men in 1763–64, he had written "Ten Proposals for the Compilation of Local Histories." In 1765, his discovery of Liu Chih-chi had apparently so stimulated him that at this time he resolved to write his own book on the forms and principles of historical writing. In the next few years his interests turned toward bibliography and the history of learning, in which he was influenced particularly by the ideas of Liu Hsin. It is worth noting, however, that his interest in bibliography and literature was instinctively historical, and that his models of literary style were the great historians.

Chang's preoccupation with the purely literary aspects of writing has often been insufficiently emphasized, and even what he says about the development of historiography and much of what he proposes in the way of new historical forms can scarcely be understood without taking this preoccupation into account. But during the years from 1770 to 1790, when he was most concerned with the history of learning, with education, and the theory of literary art, he was also writing history intermittently. In 1773–74 Chang was compiling his history of Ho-chou, and wrote at this time that he felt that he, as a scholar and writer, should concern himself with the "idea" of history; during this period he had his debate with Tai Chen over the function and form of local histories. In 1778–79 he was writing the Yung-ch'ing history; in 1783 or 1784, he com-

piled a history of the Yung-ting River. And in 1788 his interests in
the writing of history and the history of writing came together in
the *Shih-chi K'ao,* a project that was to apply to history Chu I-tsun's
method of dealing with the bibliography of classical scholarship.
Chang's work on the *Shih-chi K'ao* had been suspended in 1789,
a year that was so productive in other ways, but at least one of his
essays of that year had dealt specifically with a problem of historiography—the handling of footnotes—and a significant part of
another ("Collected Opinions") had discussed problems of historical writing. Furthermore, during 1789 Chang was working at
intervals on a family history for Hsü Li-kang and on his history of
Po-chou.

The five years he spent at Wu-ch'ang, however, constitute the
one extended period in his life when he was constantly engaged
in historical writing and research. During this time Chang wrote
his most interesting essays on the nature of historical scholarship,
and on the history, form, and purpose of historical writing. The
most important of these are the following:[3]

"Answers to Objections" ("Ta K'e Wen"), 1790 or 1791, in three
parts; a dialogue between "the philosopher Chang" and a "guest" which
elaborates and defends views Chang had stated earlier in his "Defense
of Cheng Ch'iao."

"The Meaning of the Word 'General'" ("Shih T'ung"), 1790 or 1791,
a long essay in two parts; the first part traces the history of those genres
of scholarly writing to which the word *t'ung* (general, comprehensive)
could be applied, and the second discusses the particular problems and
advantages of a "general history" vs. a history that is restricted to a
single dynasty.

"Virtue in the Historian" ("Shih Te"), 1791; an essay discussing the
historian's attitude toward the events and persons he writes about, and
the critic's attitude toward the historical writings he evaluates. Chang
dwells in both cases on the danger of making unfair judgments.

"A Proposal for Indexes in Historical Writings" ("Shih-hsüeh Pieh-lu
Li-i"), 1792 or 1793; this essay proposes that an outline of the material
in a history be inserted after its table of contents.

"A Proposal for a Three Part Form for Local Histories" ("Fang-chih
Li San Shu I"), probably 1792; this essay proposes that a local history

should consist of (1) a *chih* or history in the ordinary sense, (2) a section of *chang-ku* or documentation, (3) a *wen-cheng* or literary anthology.

"The Teaching of the *History*" ("Shu Chiao"), probably 1792, in three parts; a synthesis of Chang's views on the development of historical writing, the relation of literature to history, and the general characteristics of a good history.

Though these essays were written over a three-year period, they are so clearly interrelated and so closely connected with the work Chang was doing that they can be intelligently examined only as a group and only in relation to Chang's research and personal history during this time.

Chang's Po-chou history is as much a part of his historical scholarship from 1790 to 1794 as his work at Wu-ch'ang. He had undertaken the *Po-chou Chih* with the sponsorship of P'ei Chen in the fall of 1789, and finished it in some haste the following spring because he was eager to get to Wu-ch'ang; nevertheless he was delighted with what he had accomplished. He wrote of it in some detail to Chou Chen-jung, and said expansively, "If this work were to be compared with the Standard Histories, it would have to be placed beside those of Ch'en Shou and Fan Yeh." He had slight hope that it would be noticed by his contemporaries who all had their eyes turned to the past, though later perhaps a true historian would recognize its greatness. But unfortunately for Chang's hopes, his friend P'ei Chen left his magistracy late in 1790, and the history went unprinted. It now appears to be lost.[4]

The history's original features, in which Chang took such pride, can only be inferred from the surviving prefaces to two sections. Apparently there were two distinct innovations: (a) A supplementary section entitled "documentation" (*chang-ku*), which displaced the six monographs (treating the six departments of government) in the Yung-ch'ing history; in this section Chang attempted to present not the actual documents, but the general structure of local institutions and supporting facts about them. (b) A "table of persons" (*jen-wu piao*), a device borrowed from Pan

Ku's *Han Shu*; Pan's "Jen-wu Piao" listed the names of all persons of historical importance down to the beginning of Han, arranging them chronologically and according to moral worth. Chang's adaptation dispensed with Pan's moral ratings, for he felt that Pan, in posing as a judge of all the great and small men of the past, had failed to show the "restraint" of Confucius in his *Spring and Autumn Annals*.

These two features are of interest because they illustrate an attitude toward historical writing that we have seen in Chang before. Histories, he thought, were getting to be too long and too complicated; they could not be easily read and understood, and as a result, they were in danger of being neglected and even lost. The histories most objectionable in this respect, as he and Shao Chin-han had agreed some years before, were those compiled during the Sung and Yüan. The "documentation" device and the "table of persons" (which Chang saw as applicable to any kind of history, not just to a local "gazetteer") would reduce this length and complexity. The former would take the description of institutions out of the history itself. The latter would provide an economical means for noting persons whose biographies were already available in the Standard Histories, and for giving some recognition to persons who deserved to be mentioned but didn't really require biographies.[5]

It is not easy to make sense of this. We can understand well enough Chang's feeling that an historical narrative ought to be intelligible, and his conviction that historical writing should convey a comprehensive understanding of the past. But his desire to limit the information in a history violates our notions of the value of historical writing; and his fears about such works as the Standard Histories becoming "lost" seem ludicrous in a country where printing had existed for at least eight centuries.

We must of course remember that in China printing was a slow hand process. Even in the last three centuries, many valuable books remained unprinted for generations and survived only by good fortune—for example, Huang Tsung-hsi's histories of Sung and

Yüan philosophy, and indeed the greater part of Chang's own extant writings. Chang's own local histories are ironic examples of how devastating time and indifference can be. Even among the Standard Histories, the *Old History of the Five Dynasties* owed its preservation only to the fact that it had been copied into the manuscript of the Ming encyclopedia *Yung-lo Ta-tien*. Chang of course knew this, for it was Shao Chin-han who had put this history back together again.[6]

But a rational concern for this danger surely would have led Chang simply to worry closely about the practical problem of getting his books printed. To understand his thinking, we must go back to his ideas on the history of writing, ideas he had found originally in Cheng Ch'iao's "Chiao-ch'ou Lüeh." Chang had admired Cheng for his ability to select and organize material in order to bring out its underlying meaning, and had contrasted him with Ma Tuan-lin who typified (he thought) the pointless and indiscriminate collecter and cataloguer of facts. From Cheng he had also gotten the idea that the bibliographer should clarify the different traditions of learning and writing by proper classification of books. In Cheng this idea was associated with the question —brought to his attention by both official and private Sung bibliography—why some ancient writings had survived to the present while others had not. For Cheng the explanation seemed (not unreasonably for one surveying the past from the perspective of the Sung, when printing was still quite new) to be that bibliographers had not done their job of keeping track of books and keeping them properly sorted out. Books succumbed to the onslaughts of time because, so to speak, confusion prevailed in the ranks. As long as specialized traditions of learning flourished and it was clear to what tradition a book belonged, the book would be preserved.[7] This idea had appeared in Chang's "Historical Commentary" in 1789, and was at least implicit in his *Chiao-ch'ou T'ung-i*.

If the preservation of a book depended on the continuation of a living tradition of learning, simplicity and readability seemed to Chang to be of crucial importance. A historian should not only bring out, by selection and organization, the meaning in his material but should also express his narrative well. We should perhaps recall here Chang's view that attention to literary art is needed if the values of the present age of philology are to be preserved; he was guided in his ideas about historiography by the instincts of the literary man at least as much as by those of the historian. He was perhaps influenced, too, by an old and familiar literary idea— one's writing is always improved if one can convey more meaning in fewer words. The Po-chou history's imitation of the "Jen-wu Piao" in the *Han Shu* incidentally illustrates the positive pleasure Chang seemed to take in being intellectually perverse, for he knew that this feature of the Han history had been almost universally condemned by Chinese historical critics.[a]

Chang's literary impulses impinged on his historical writing in other ways. In 1790 he reedited his *Ho-chou Chih-li,* reducing it greatly in length (this still survives). Then he turned his attention to his Yung-ch'ing history, cutting it from twenty-six chapters to ten. This he named the "New History of Yung-ch'ing." Chang wrote to Chou Chen-jung suggesting that it be printed, for then the two books could be regarded as a pair, "like the old and new histories of the T'ang."[8] The T'ang Dynasty and Yung-ch'ing district, Ou-yang Hsiu and Chang Hsüeh-ch'eng—a pleasant thought indeed. Chang had always held up Ou-yang Hsiu as a great master of literary art, and the revision of the *T'ang History* that Ou-yang supervised must indeed have seemed to Chang to exemplify the values he was after. It had that conciseness (compared to its original) so highly prized by the stylist, and seemed to prove the adage, "if a book is not well written it will not last long." For the *New T'ang History* had always been popular, while the *Old T'ang History* was, in Chang's time, just being rediscovered after lying forgotten by scholars for centuries.

In his revision, however, Chang may have been motivated by more than a desire to preserve his work. It is possible that he had deep anxieties about his reputation. "When a copy is made," he

[a] *I-shu,* 15.1a; HY, pp. 79–80. Cheng Ch'iao, whose view of Pan's "Jen-wu Piao" is typical, dismisses it as "not worth talking about." (*T'ung Chih Lüeh,* Kuo-hsüeh Chi-pen Ts'ung-shu edition, 4.556.)

wrote Chou, "I shall send it to you immediately, to redeem in some
degree my mistakes of a dozen years ago, which were due to my
immaturity in scholarship." He suggested that Chou might show
the revision to people in Yung-ch'ing. It would be excellent if
some patron could be found to print it. In any case, Chang said,
he would include a copy in his own works (it is in fact not to be
found there). We know what is in the Yung-ch'ing history, and
it seems clear that by this time Chang knew too. "It has been
twelve years since I wrote my history of Yung-ch'ing," he reflected,
"and eighteen years since I did the history of Ho-chou. Looking
at them now, I see many things I regret having written; and I've
come to understand that one ought not to go into print without
caution." Perhaps, he mused, in five or ten years he would feel the
same way about the writing he was doing now.[b]

A bit of Chang's work in 1791 exhibits the literary man as historian in another light. Chu Yün's son, Chu Hsi-keng, wrote to
Chang from Peking, asking him to write a biography of his father.
(We remember that Chang had already written an epitaph for his
former teacher.) Chang of course agreed, and later submitted to
the younger Chu a draft with some explanations. In the biography,
he pointed out, he had quoted in full one of Chu's literary pieces,
the "Wen-niao Fu." (This poem, written in the archaic style of
Chia I of the Han Dynasty, recounted the visit of four striped birds
to Chu's garden. The birds stayed for a week and showed no fear
of humans or animals. Chu describes them with a virtuoso display
of poetic diction.) In the phrasing of this poem, Chang added, he
had ventured to make a few changes. "But there is no harm in
this version existing along with Master Chu's original. In literary
art I take great pleasure in clarity; so when I came upon wording
that was obscure, here and there I quietly altered a word or phrase
to bring out the spirit of the piece. This is something for which
there is good precedent, and in no way indicates that the original
was unsatisfying and would stand only after editing."

[b] See Chapter 4, p. 84. I can only add that I have deepest sympathy for Chang in
this matter. But there seems to be no escape from his dilemma.

Then to sugarcoat the pill, Chang expressed his view that Chu's writing actually surpassed that of Ou-yang Hsiu. True, it was not as "vigorous," but then, the times were different. Chu, unlike Ou-yang, was not a remonstrance official and did not live in a time of misgovernment to call forth his talents, but lived instead in an age "when one who is a Yao and a Shun is on the throne, when generals and ministers all hurry about attending to their duties," and the world is in good order.[9]

But Chang's high-handed exercise of the historian's pen quickly raised eyebrows. Shao Chin-han, in Peking at this time, saw Chang's draft and wrote to him in protest. Chang defended himself with an argument from his "Yen Kung" essay of 1783: it's the thought in a piece of writing that counts; it is rather petty, therefore, to make a fetish of the author's actual words.[c] We smile. And yet Chang did have "precedent" for his tampering, as anyone who examines similar quotations in *Shih-chi* or *Han Shu* biographies can verify. It seems that Chang's perversity could as easily lead him to be behind his age as ahead of it. But he was not so very far behind his age. If we are surprised at his self-confidence in marking up the compositions of an old gentleman of Yung-ch'ing, or in rewriting a poem by his own deceased teacher, we should remember that an "editor" in old China had wide prerogatives. Often the posthumous printing of a man's writings (including perhaps Chang's) reached the bookstands only after the all too devoted care of one or more of these persons.

Nor was it only the writings of the dead that were "improved" in this way. In 1789 when Chou Chen-jung printed a collection of short biographies that Chang had written for some departed friends, Chang was quite annoyed at the changes Chou had made. His annoyance did not, to be sure, interfere with their friendship; and soon the irony of time reversed their roles. Chou died in 1792.

[c] WHL, pp. 274, 278. Chang stuck to his position on the "Wen-niao Fu" (cf. *I-shu*, 18.3a–4b; Chu Yün, *Ssu-ho Wen-chi* (Peking, 1815), 4.1a ff.). Several other biographies of Chu, including Chang's epitaph, are printed in the introductory chapter of Chu's works, but Chang's controversial biography is omitted. For Chang's letter to Shao, see *I-shu*, 9.15a–b.

Chang's eldest son I-hsüan, in Peking at the time, wrote his father of Chou's death, adding that the family would be grateful for a biography. Chang was deeply moved by the loss of this friend who had been so close to him. He wrote Chou's son at once, offering to write Chou's biography (which he duly composed) and to edit his writings as well; the rest of his letter was filled with editorial advice.[10]

In Wu-ch'ang, Chang went out of his way to disagree with other scholars. His friend Shao was at this time in Peking, but Chang corresponded with him frequently. In 1788 Shao had published his *Erh-ya Cheng-i,* a study of the ancient dictionary *Erh-ya,* which he had been working on for over a decade. Chang now wrote to him praising it effusively. But, Chang asked him, was he never going to write anything expressing his own ideas, anything that really mattered? "Your ancestor Shao T'ing-ts'ai once said that it is a principle of writing to be concerned with problems of the world," he chided. In Chang's view, apparently, his friend had not been able to make that essential distinction between true "learning" and mere "industry." And there was the Sung History Shao had set himself to do years before. How was it coming, Chang prodded. Shao's replies carefully avoided the subject.[11]

In 1790, also, Chang for the first time encountered Tuan Yü-ts'ai, a friend and admirer of Shao and self-styled disciple of the late Tai Chen. Although they had never met before, Tuan had heard of Chang, and wrote to Shao that he felt they had "long been friends in spirit." Tuan read a number of Chang's philosophical essays and generously exclaimed over them, writing to Shao in high praise of Chang's historical insight.[12] But (as we have already noted) he made remarks about Chang's style that nettled him. And Tuan's commitment to Tai Chen's memory must have entered into their relationship. Perhaps, indeed, Tuan was the "guest" in Chang's "Answers to Objections" of that year.

All of Chang's principal essays that year dealt with Tai or with Chang's disagreements with him—in particular their disagreement over the relative merits of Cheng Ch'iao's *T'ung Chih* and Ma

Tuan-lin's *Wen-hsien T'ung-k'ao.* In his defense of Cheng and criticism of Ma, Chang now attempted to define what could and what could not truly be called historical scholarship. He was further led to make (in "The Meaning of the Word 'General'") a detailed and reasoned statement of the nature and advantages of "general history" (*t'ung-shih*), which Cheng's *T'ung Chih* was supposed to exemplify. In a supplement to his essay on the two schools of Neo-Confucianism, Chang was much more explicitly critical of Tai. But his appraisal was not entirely adverse, for he did express admiration for Tai's philosophical writing. And in another essay he praised Tai's attitude toward Cheng Hsüan. Chang felt that he had shown the proper combination of respect and open-mindedness in criticizing the Han philologue.[13] Some of Chang's fellow scholars at Wu-ch'ang were undoubtedly supporters of Tai Chen, but it was not just this fact that stimulated Chang to pursue his differences with the dead scholar. Chang was quarreling with Ch'ing philology, and Tai, the great philologist of his age and the recognized leader of contemporary fashion, was an obvious target.

As we might expect, Chang pressed this quarrel at the most abstract level. This is why we find him repeating, in "Answers to Objections," his famous thesis that "the Six Classics are all history." This is also the opening phrase in the *Wen-shih T'ung-i,* and because of its prominent position, it has become the best known and most often discussed of Chang's opinions.[d] The remark has been widely misread as an exhortation to the historian to regard the Classics as source material.[e] Chang of course would have agreed to this readily enough. After all, he himself had said exactly this to Chen Sung-nien thirty years ago, and it was a view he never abandoned. In 1788 he had written Sun Hsing-yen that the historian's material includes the Classics and every other sort of writing. But in saying now that "the Six Classics are all history," Chang

---

[d] Occurring at the beginning of the opening essay, "The Teaching of the *Changes*," probably written between 1783 and 1788 (*I-shu,* 4.44b, 1.1a).
[e] E.g., Dr. Hu Shih (HY, pp. 137–38).

was not making a methodological point but a philosophical one. What he meant by the phrase was what he had said in "On the Tao" the year before, that "the Six Classics are all *ch'i*"; they are, as he had written in the Ho-chou history more than fifteen years earlier, "the documents of the government of the ancient kings."[14] And if one can see what the Classics really are, one can also see what values the traditions derived from them ought to have.

If we consider Chang's "Classics are histories" thesis in this light, we can distinguish two implications in it. The Classics are not "empty words." Like them, all writings should be in thrall to reality, to the necessities of the time. And like those nameless men who wrote the Classics, all writers should be concerned with what needs to be said, not with being authors. This first implication of Chang's idea is the foundation of most of his past philosophy and literary criticism and supports his view that the scholar, taking Confucius as his model, ought to be concerned with documents and "actual facts."

But Chang's thesis has another implication, present certainly from the time he first formulated it, and from the beginning of his vision of antiquity, but which he now stresses much more strongly. Not only are the Classics like the historical part of the library in being enmeshed in the world of fact, but also (as Chang had said in "On the Tao") histories are like the Classics. The Classics in documenting antiquity *illustrate* (though they do not state) the *tao* of ancient society. And when one sees that this is the nature of the Classics, one must admit that not only history but also other kinds of scholarship should be like this. Therefore, the scholar, and especially the historian, should be primarily concerned with the significance of the material he deals with. Merely recording facts or picking them apart endlessly is pointless unless the philologue's material "illustrates the *tao*." This of course was the point of Chang's criticism of Shao. It is a view that will lead Chang to insist, more and more, that the highest kind of scholar must be a man of insight, able to grasp the significance of things.

The idea that the Classics are history was not original with Chang, nor was he the first to state it. It had appeared earlier in

Wang Yang-ming, in the context of his discussion of the "unity of knowledge and action," and Wang, like Chang, argued that the *tao* and events are not to be distinguished—that the *tao* cannot be stated abstractly, and that the function of events as recorded in the Classics (specifically the *Spring and Autumn*) is to "illustrate" the *tao*.[15] In view of the strong influence of Wang's theory of the "unity of knowledge and action" on Chang's thought, it is to be presumed that the influence was there too when Chang pronounced the Classics history.

Chang's "Classics are history" idea, like many of his ideas, can be found in the writings of his contemporaries. The poet of the Garden of Ease, Yüan Mei—whom we have mentioned before and will need to mention again—also characterized the Classics as history. In his *Random Notes*, Yüan writes, "In ancient times, there were histories but no Classics. The *History* and the *Spring and Autumn* were both histories. The *Odes* and the *Changes* were writings transmitted by the ancient kings. The *Rites* were the laws established by the ancient kings. All are history."[16] Who influenced whom? Or were these ideas that were often exchanged when writers and students got together to talk? Perhaps the question is not useful. Chang's ideas formed an integrated whole. His "Classics are history" was not really different in its intended impact from the thesis he had resurrected from Liu Hsin (though he himself had put the meaning in it) that all types of writing and learning derive from traditions maintained by the hereditary royal offices of Chou, and are rendered visible in documents in their care. The Classics are vestiges of these traditions; they are surviving documents and so for the bibliographer (and the metaphysician) history.*f*

---

f Other possible sources include Su Hsün, Hu San-hsing, and Wang T'ung (see Shen Jen, "*Wen-shih T'ung-i* Nei-p'ien Hou-an," *Hsüeh-hai Yüeh-k'an*, 1.4 (1944), p. 52, and Demiéville, p. 181). Chang himself quotes Wang T'ung (*I-shu*, 14.12b): "The sages wrote three histories: the *History*, the *Odes*, and the *Spring and Autumn*." In 1787 or 1788 Chang had said, in his *Shih-chi K'ao* proposal, that "in ancient times there was no distinction between Classics and history" (*I-shu*, 13.36a). See also his essay of 1789, "Explanation of the Classics" ("Ching Chieh"), *I-shu*, 1.36a–b; and HY, p. 71. In "On Learning," Part II, Liu Hsin's thesis is cited explicitly as an application of the idea of the "unity of knowledge and action" (*I-shu*, 2.16a).

In Chang's thesis was crystallized his vision of the past, with all of its moral lessons. But his thesis did other, more practical work for him. He has said himself that he wanted to ward off the reproaches of classical scholars who might object to intellectual poaching by a mere historian. For Chang was a habitual trespasser in other fields of scholarship—in his philosophical essays as well as in his great projected critical bibliography of history, the *Shih-chi K'ao*. Furthermore, if the Classics are history, and if history, like the Classics, exhibits the *tao,* it should begin to share the Classics' prestige. Just as he had earlier sought to attach to the "gazetteer" the prestige of history in the great sense, so now he meant to invest history itself with the near-sacred character of classical writings.[17]

Chang had one more job for his thesis to do, one that interested him more than it can us, and surely more than it did his friends. If the Classics are history, he argued in 1792 (in "A Proposal for a Three-Part Form for Local Histories"), later historical writing derives its nature from the Classics; therefore we can see, by examining the Classics, just what a history should be. Chang explains how history derives from the Classics. The *Changes* did not continue in later historical form, beyond certain survivals in the Han Dynasty, because since antiquity there has been a general shift of interest from "the seasons of Heaven" (*t'ien-shih,* i.e., fate, astronomy, natural powers) to "the affairs of men" (*jen-shih*). The tradition of the *Classic of History* was "discontinued" and "merged" with that of the *Spring and Autumn*. The *Music* "perished" leaving no classical text, its tradition merging with the *Odes*. The three classical traditions that remained active—the *Odes,* the *Rites,* and the *Spring and Autumn*—survive in three modes of historical writing: the *Spring and Autumn* continues in ordinary narrative history; the *Rites* in collections of documents and institutional encylopedias; and the *Odes* in collections of literature, to be thought of as complementing histories in the ordinary sense and illustrating the *tao* in their own way. Ergo, a history should be a triad of three such works.[18]

This, too, is Chang Hsüeh-ch'eng. One wonders if he impressed many of his acquaintances primarily as an eccentric who argued hotly for contrived ideas of this kind.

Chang's interest in the definition of historical scholarship at this time may have been partly due to the fact that he was again working on the *Shih-chi K'ao*. We know that as early as 1790 he was back at work on this project, and that Pi had provided him with a small staff for it. One of his assistants (or collaborators) was a personal friend named Hu Ch'ien; and three others have been identified.[g] At Wu-ch'ang, Chang brought the *Shih-chi Kao* to within eight- or nine-tenths of completion. He never finished it, although he was able to work on it again for a time in 1798. It was probably never completed, and is now almost certainly lost. There does survive, however, a copy of the table of contents, together with a long essay explaining it, from which we can get some idea of the nature of the work in its nearly completed state. It had twelve main divisions: (1) decrees, (2) histories in annal-biographical form, (3) chronological histories, (4) historical criticism, (5) irregular histories, (6) astrology and chronology, (7) genealogy and chronological biography, (8) geography and local history, (9) documents and studies of institutions, (10) bibliography, (11) biography and miscellaneous narrative, and (12) stories and anecdotes. But there were ten times this number of sub-categories, with room for all of Chang's pet ideas about what counts as "history." In all, the work came to 325 chapters.[19]

But the enormous labor required by such a work was not expended for nothing, for it must have been a major stimulus to Chang's thinking during the years when he was writing the most

---

[g] Lo Ping-mien, "*Shih-chi K'ao* Hsiu-tsuan ti T'an-t'ao" ("A Study on the Compilation of the *Shih-chi K'ao*"), Part I, *Hsin-Ya Hsüeh-pao*, VI (Feb. 1964), pp. 384, 390. Hu Ch'ien, like Tso Mei, was a native of T'ung-ch'eng and a student of Yao Nai. See his biography in Fang Tung-shu, *I-wei-hsüan Wen-chi*, 10.11b–13a. Hu's life was in some ways like Chang's; he was a writer with influential friends who were able to get him academy posts and scholarly projects from time to time. His local historiography shows Chang's influence; unfortunately most of his personal writings are lost. His students were said to have had an especially warm regard for him. See *An-hui T'ung-chih*, 1877, 223.11a–b and Chu Shih-chia, p. 189.

interesting of those essays expressing his historiographical theories. One of the essays that seems clearly to have been written under the stimulus of this research was "Virtue in the Historian" in 1791. The essay begins with a criticism of Liu Chih-chi; one assumes from this that Chang had recently been rereading the T'ang historical critic, an assumption supported by another (relatively inconsequential) essay of that year, "On Reading the *Shih T'ung.*" Also, Chang's bibliographical "comments" of 1791 show that he was going over the T'ang essayists, especially Han Yü, with care, again probably in search of material for the *Shih-chi K'ao.*[20]

The *Shih-chi K'ao* was perhaps not Chang's principal work at Wu-ch'ang. When he first arrived, he found Pi's group working on a continuation of the Sung historian Ssu-ma Kuang's *Tzu-chih T'ung-chien.* Ssu-ma Kuang's long chronological history was a continuation, in the same style and form, of the narrative of the *Tso Chuan,* which, unlike the other classical commentaries to the *Spring and Autumn,* was a very detailed history of early China. The Sung Emperor had taken up the enterprise, and the work that resulted covered Chinese history to the beginning of Sung (960). Subsequently a number of historians attempted supplements carrying the narrative down through Sung and beyond, but Pi Yüan and other scholars did not regard these as satisfactory. His projected work was to be a new history, in chronological (*piennien*) form, of Sung and Yüan. Pi sought out the men of the highest talent to work on it. The writing had been going on for years before Chang took part. (Hung Liang-chi had been largely responsible for the early drafts.) Pi's efforts bore fruit; his *Hsü Tzu-chih T'ung-chien* is still greatly esteemed today.

Chang participated in the compilation of this history until 1792, when the completed version was submitted to Shao Chin-han for editing and revision. When Shao returned it, Pi sent a copy to Ch'ien Ta-hsin for corrections, accompanied by a letter Chang had written for him. The letter, which describes the compilation and criticizes the sources used, is a fascinating document of Chinese historiography. There is one interesting difference between the *Hsü T'ung-chien* and Ssu-ma Kuang's work: the original *T'ung-*

chien contained comments scattered throughout the text in which the historian made judgments of the men and events in his work. Pi Yüan, however, did not presume to do this. "In my humble opinion," Chang writes for him, "if the writing just straightforwardly follows the facts, the good and the evil will appear of themselves"; it is risky for the historian to judge his material, for unless he has the insight of a sage his remarks will not bear examination.[21]

This view was, I think, as much Chang's as Pi's. But Chang had other ideas that were too bold for Pi to accept. He explains them in the letter to Ch'ien, referring to himself in the third person. One was a pretty suggestion that Lü Tsu-ch'ien's anthology of Sung literature, *Sung Wen Chien,* be expanded into a *Sung Yüan Wen Chien* to "accompany" and "complement" the *Hsü T'ung-chien,* the one dealing with literature (*wen*), the other with events (*shih*). The second suggestion had much greater merit. Chang would prepare for the history a sort of outline index (*pieh-lu*), which would list "empresses, princes, generals, chief ministers, and high officers," and so on down to prefects and magistrates, with a reference after each name to the date under which it appears in the history.[22] Here Chang had in mind the organization of the historical encyclopedias called *hui-yao.* This proposal was the subject of Chang's essay "A Proposal for Indexes in Historical Writings" ("Shih-hsüeh Pieh-lu Li-i"), also written in 1792, but in the essay he extended the idea to the standard history form as well. For a history in annal-biography form, he suggested, one should prepare an outline of the main events, with references (including chapter and page) after each entry to any material bearing on it in other parts of the history—annals, tables, monographs, or biographies. In this way, Chang thought, both chronological and standard history could be improved by grafting onto one the advantages of clarity possessed by the other.[h]

[h] *I-shu,* 7.42a–49a. In the first half of 1792, Chang apparently put together a short book, *Chi-nien Ching-wei K'ao,* developing the idea of the "Pieh-lu" essay (to judge from its preface, *I-shu,* "pu-i," 46a–b). The book was published in 1806 by a certain T'ang Chung-mien, who misprinted Chang's surname, using the commoner character that is the surname of Chang's friend Chang Wei-ch'i. (HY, p. 93.)

It is likely that much of Chang's energy during these years was
taken up in the compilation of local history. For Chang's patron
Pi Yüan had long been committed to supporting local historiography; it has been estimated that as many as thirty-three local histories were compiled under Pi's orders while he was governor of
Shensi. It is not surprising therefore that in Hupeh he quickly
began to make use of Chang's experience with this form of historical writing. Pi probably was indirectly responsible for a number of the compilations Chang became involved in; and in 1791
the Board of History (Kuo-shih Kuan) in Peking ordered that
newly compiled local histories be submitted for its use, thereby
providing a special incentive to local officials disposed to initiate
such projects. The magistrate of Ma-ch'eng in Hupeh engaged
Chang to compile a local history for his district. Following this
Chang wrote, at Pi Yüan's request, two others—for Ch'ang-te prefecture in Hunan and Ching-chou prefecture in Hupeh (1792–93).
In 1792 he went over the manuscript of still another (of Shih-shou
district in Ching-chou), again at Pi's asking. And in 1793, Chang
gave advice on the compiling of the history of Kuang-chi district
(Hupeh) to Ch'en Shih, a friend since Peking days, when the two
had attained the *chin shih* degree in the same class.[i]

And in 1792, the year the *Hsü T'ung-chien* was finished, Chang
finished the greater part of the work on a general history (*t'ung-
chih*) of Hupeh province, a major undertaking which he had
probably started for Pi soon after arriving at Wu-ch'ang, and
which he completed in 1793 or 1794.[j] To compile a general history
of a province was an assignment of some distinction. Chang held
the title of editor in chief, and must have had a large staff and a
substantial salary. His status in fact may have had an unfortunate
effect on his sense of his own importance, for we are told that he

[i] WTJ, pp. 238–41, 248–49. Chu Shih-chia, pp. 142, 153–56. Chu Shih-chia offers
different dates of completion for some of these histories: the history of Ma-ch'eng,
1795; of Shih-shou, 1795; of Ch'ang-te, 1793–94. This history of Ch'ang-te was not
published.
[j] WTJ, pp. 261–62. Yao Ming-ta (HY, pp. 105–6) is of the opinion that the *Hu-pei
T'ung-chih* was not started until 1792.

treated his subeditors "like lackeys." One of these, however, enjoyed his full respect and confidence: this was his friend Hu
Ch'ien, who worked with him on this undertaking as well as on
the *Shih-chi K'ao*.[23]

Chang had never before been in a position to construct a history
of a whole province, and now with a patron behind him giving
him unlimited confidence, he let himself go. Its structure is outlined in "A Proposal for a Three-Part Form for Local Histories,"
which he wrote in 1792, probably to defend what he was doing in
the *Hu-pei T'ung-chih*. His *t'ung-chih* contained the prescribed
three parts: (1) a history proper (*chih*), employing the subdivi-
sions of standard history with a few innovations, such as a section
of maps; (2) a section of "documentation" (*chang-ku*), divided
according to the six departments of government; and (3) an anthology (*wen-cheng*). It also had a supernumerary section, called
for in the essay, entitled "assembled discussions" (*ts'ung-t'an*), a
catch-all for other important source material. The "table of persons" (*jen wu piao*) found a place in the history, and so did another innovation—the inclusion of essays on events and other impersonal topics in the section of biographies—which Chang had
made much of in "The Teaching of the *History*."[24]

Indeed, in this part of the work Chang expended the greatest
care and took the greatest pride. His *t'ung-chih*, moreover, treated
the province as a unit rather than as a collection of subordinate
entities, and one critic has praised it as a real history of an area
rather than a mere encyclopedia. This characterization should not
lead one to suppose that the Hupeh history was lacking in detail.
On the contrary, the history was extraordinary precisely as an expression of Chang's enlightened sense of the breadth of material
that deserves the historian's attention. Chang included maps
with boundaries in two colors, the present boundaries in black, the
ancient boundaries in red. Genealogies were supplied for local
families. The section on financial administration included such
details as the wages of yamen runners and the expenses of found-
ling hospitals. There were biographies of women as well as men,

giving recognition to nine girls with marked ability in art and literature. In appropriate places the history provided descriptions of occupations and gave the prices of commodities at various times. Chang explicitly recommended that the local historian always provide his readers with economic data of this kind. These features led Liang Ch'i-ch'ao to praise Chang's work as the finest of all Chinese local histories, and one of the outstanding works in the whole field of history.[25]

This work, when reassembled in 1797, totaled twenty-four chapters. It was not printed (we shall later see why), and present editions of Chang's works contain only four chapters. These are probably not just chance fragments because Chang later on copied from his *Hu-pei T'ung-chih*, as he had from some of his other local histories, the parts of the manuscript he valued and wished to preserve. But later historians of Hupeh province have either ignored his work or have known nothing of it.[26]

Chang was occupied with the *Hu-pei T'ung-chih* for another year or so, but it did not take up all of his attention. The energy and confidence he now felt in himself is evidenced in the range of his work at this time. He expressed this feeling in a letter to Shao Chin-han in 1792:

It seems to me that before this time of life, we were young and strong and perhaps had the capacity to do things, yet we hesitated to commit our empty words to posterity; and after this time of life, our spirit and strength will start to diminish, and we may feel that there are problems we cannot understand. Therefore, all in all, the literary activity of such as ourselves falls mostly into the period from fifty to sixty; moreover, we have done a great deal of reading by this time, and should in the course of it have gained considerable insight.[27]

These remarks were intended specifically to urge Shao to finish his Sung history, but Chang makes them applicable to himself as well. In this year Shao was in his fiftieth year, and Chang in his fifty-fifth.

In 1792 Chang was intensely interested in the formal aspects of historiography; he wrote three long essays on the subject, and, it appears, intended to do much more. In the letter to Shao just quoted, he mentions "The Teaching of the *History*" and the essay on a three-part form for local histories; he sums up the main arguments of the first, including the suggestions at the end of it for changes in the form of standard history.[k] These suggestions, he said, he was developing separately in an essay entitled "On Adaptability" ("Yüan-t'ung"). "The analysis is very minute," he wrote, "but I am in some confusion and find difficulty in finishing it; you must wait until I've prepared a draft." But no draft was forthcoming; Chang evidently found it too difficult to work out, for he never completed it.

It would seem, in fact, that his ambitions were running ahead of his capacities; for in the same letter, he again took up the idea, which he and Shao had discussed years before, of writing a new Sung history himself. But now he would no longer wait for Shao to finish his own:

The ancients say that expressing one's ideas in mere theoretical terms is not as effective as exhibiting them in actual achievements. I propose to write a history myself, using my own principles in order to make it evident that what I have set forth is not just talk. And so, in choosing among the histories for one to which I should devote my efforts, it seemed to me that the one most obviously in need of attention is the history of the Sung. But since the form I wish to use is different from that of Ssu-ma Ch'ien and Pan Ku, there should be no objection to my working on the same thing you propose to do.

But Chang finds that he does not know where to start, and so asks his friend Shao, a recognized master of Sung history, to give him a few suggestions:

---

[k] Chang here refers to "The Teaching of the *History*" as "recently written." But the content of the letter to Shao suggests that it may be a New Year's greeting. Chang was at least thinking out this essay earlier, for in 1789 or 1790 he reviewed a book, *Shih-hsüeh Li-i* (*Proposals for Historiography*), which discussed (unsatisfactorily, Chang felt) a number of problems reappearing in "The Teaching of the *History*," and in his review Chang says he has "a separate essay discussing these matters in detail." Chang did not know the author of the book, and I have not been able to identify him. (See *I-shu*, 7.38b–42a, and Ch'ien Mu, p. 422.) It is perhaps significant that Yüan Mei also wrote a short comment on this work. (Yüan indicates that it was written by a Master Nan-keng, apparently an aged friend.) Yüan's comment was already in print at this time, and is close to Chang's thinking. See p. 310, Note 16.

Would you from your long application to this, just indicate a few of the important tendencies and main topics—more or less like the chapter headings of Yüan Shu? Although I wouldn't necessarily follow your suggestions entirely, I would very much appreciate having your general outline to work with.... In this undertaking...I fear I shall be like Cheng Ch'iao in his *T'ung-chih*—there will be too much form and not enough matter to fill it out—but if you will offer your instructions, it may be that in the end I shall avoid serious offense.[28]

The essay "On Adaptability" was never finished, and it is likely that Chang's Sung history, which would have applied and illustrated its formal proposals, was never started. This we need not regret. What should interest us is, first, that Chang should have had such a grotesque preoccupation with form, and second, that he should have felt compelled to undertake the writing of a history of an entire dynasty, his knowledge of which was apparently quite uncertain, simply for the justification he would gain from applying the principles he was recommending.

But what, then, is the significance and the value of Chang's historiography? To this question we now turn.

8. The Metaphysics of Historiography

He who writes histories wants most of all to understand the
significance of what he treats. He does not, as does the keeper
of records, merely attend to the relatively unimportant problems
of fact and form of expression. Confucius has said, "If I were to
put what I want to say in empty words, it would not be as
penetrating and clear as it would be if I showed it in doings
and events." This is the fundamental principle of the historian.

—"If Your Words Are Everyone's" . . . 1783

It might seem strange to us that Chang should argue the advantages of adopting some formal device, such as his subject-index
scheme for the *Hsü T'ung-chien,* with the sort of seriousness appropriate to a proposal to change the laws of the empire. But Chinese historiographical critics have always regarded such formal
questions seriously; the reasons are in the nature of Chinese historical writing itself. A primary reason for the importance of form
was the tradition that the historian should allow the facts to speak
for themselves. This tradition discouraged him from specifying
the significance of a datum, from stating its relationship to other
facts. Getting the data down in the right order was consequently
of great importance; it was the historian's mode of explanation,
and the categories he fixed upon were his criteria of what was significant.

The historian's form was therefore not simply a matter of convenience, but an assertion about the actual structure of the world
of his interest, centered upon the state and the imperial authority.
Thus Chang feels that the historical bibliographer should at least
be able to adapt his categories of books to conform to actual traditions of writing, and in his local histories he recommends a division of text corresponding to the actual organization of local government. It seems probable that the earliest examples of standard
history, with their organization of material according to reigns

and strict time sequence, according to governmental functions, and according to groups of persons or families, reflect in a general way the Han conception of the world as an interrelated network of series of metaphysical categories—seasons, "virtues," governmental operations, types of persons, emotions (of Heaven and of the ruler), and so on. And so historical form weighs very heavily on the tradition of history writing.

But Chang's obsession with historical forms is partly the result of anxiety. For in his day, it was becoming increasingly difficult to think of the world in this schematic way. His world, as we discovered in the "Analogy of Heaven," is *formless*. If the writer imposes standard ready-made concepts upon the world, he always distorts it and inevitably pictures it inaccurately. This must be the case for the historian as well as for the astronomer. Chang is therefore concerned with modifying and making more flexible those genres of history that he finds too rigid and conventionalized. The facts, and the historian's insight, should prevail.

And yet Chang, while insisting that the true historian should organize his material as he thinks best, is nevertheless far from simply disregarding tradition. The conventionality of historical forms is something he cannot throw off. He does not want to abandon existing forms entirely, but simply to modify or to "correct" them; and to do even this much, he feels obliged to labor mightily to justify himself. This weight of tradition was due in part to the extraordinary seriousness of historical writing in China, which had from the start been thought of as a means of advising (and even criticizing) rulers, and was associated in its primitive beginnings with addresses to deceased royal ancestors and with the study of the heavens.[1] When Chang, for example, suggested to Pi Yüan his idea for a subject-index to the *Hsü T'ung-chien* (a device that would actually have provided users of the history with a great convenience), Pi hesitated because the original *T'ung-chien* of Ssu-ma Kuang did not have such a feature. And Chang, instead of challenging the relevance of Pi's objection, pursues his point by arguing that the Tsin commentator Tu Yü's edition of the *Tso Chuan* did have a similar device.[a]

In fact, Chang's improvisations in local-history form and his proposed changes in standard forms were attempts to modify conventions that had almost the character of unwritten law. This is why he felt compelled to discover precedents for what he did; this is why he felt that he should demonstrate his ideas about standard history rather than leave them stated in "empty words." Seen within Chinese ethical tradition and within the framework of his own ethical and political philosophy, Chang's situation was like that of Confucius, who, though he had "virtue," could not propose new institutions because he had no "position" of authority to put these ideas into practice. Chang felt that only as a practicing historian could he say how history should be written. And the reason is not (as Collingwood proudly claimed) that only a practicing historian can understand what historians do. The reason is that theory without demonstration in practice is like a name which names nothing or a promise unkept—a metaphysical anomaly.

Probably enough has been said of Chang's interest in the form of historical writing to make it plain that it would not be profitable to examine his proposals for possible contributions to historical science. The sorts of history he dealt with are no longer written, and even if they were, we would be under no compulsion to take

---

[a] *I-shu*, 9.14b, Pi Yüan's letter to Ch'ien Ta-hsin (written by Chang) on the *Hsü T'ung-chien*. This argument is thicker than it seems. Tu Yü was eight centuries earlier than Ssu-ma Kuang, and hence could claim greater prestige; moreover, the *Tso Chuan* is a classic, and was regarded by historical critics as the classical prototype of *pien-nien* (chronological) form, of which the *T'ung-chien* and its continuations are examples.

In the case of local histories, Chu Shih-chia (pp. 19, 43) points out two facts that must have heightened the importance of formal questions for Chang and his contemporaries. It was not until the Ming Dynasty that local histories came to be written for virtually every locality in China. This recent expansion of the genre led to much discussion in the Ch'ing about what its form should be. Also, the local history had come to serve as a quick and convenient briefing for an official newly assigned to a strange locality. Local histories served this purpose more efficiently if they were all more or less alike in structure.

his traditionalistic view of them—though we may usefully be able to discover through studying a person like Chang what the limitations of Chinese historiography are. His ideas about historiography are interesting, however, in ways quite unrelated to history—as a reflection of his philosophical and literary assumptions, the social pressures of his times, or even his personal prejudices.

We note, for example, that in all of his local histories Chang gives great importance to his treatment of what he calls "documentation," namely, a description of the institutional forms and workings of local government, and that he views the Classics as the documents of ancient government. He argues that a scholar, if his writing is to be useful—to the state—must study documents; he views history (at least ancient history) as a process of the development of social-political institutions, i.e., the growth of the state. The "documentation" in his local histories is an expression of a general attitude toward writing and toward government, an attitude that applies to literature as well: *wen-cheng* means literary evidence. Like the *Odes,* it is a kind of documentation; literature is evidence of how people have felt and reacted in particular situations, and acquires significance as it is related through the historian's use of it to the social-political whole.

Chang consciously and constantly tried to adapt the standard-history form of annals, tables, monographs, and biographies to local histories. This was simply one of Chang's attempts to make the "gazetteer" something more than a handbook of local information, to make it a respectable form of historical writing. This he felt compelled to do because such petty forms of historical writing as the local history or the family genealogy were the only kinds of compilation that most scholars in Chang's day could hope to engage in or direct. For Chang the obvious way to make the local history respectable was to attach to it the prestige of the history of a dynasty or of the entire state. It was for this reason that he argued with Tai Chen and others that a local history should be regarded not just as a work of local importance but as a fund of source material for higher forms of history.[2]

Viewed in much the same way, Chang's conception of the development of historiography is of extraordinary interest. He made one attempt to state his views in his "Answers to Objections" in 1790. In this dialogue with an imaginary "guest," Chang ("the philosopher") held that the *Spring and Autumn* is the beginning of historical writing and the key to what good historiography should be. "The meaning of the *Spring and Autumn* is brought out in its selection of facts. The principle of the selection of facts is not just to set down a complete account of every fact and achieve perfect form in one's writing; . . . its purpose is to show the principles governing Heaven and Man and to analyze and illuminate the Great Way." This motive will require the true historian at times "to be detailed where others are brief, disagree where others are in accord, give weight to that which others treat lightly, and be indifferent where others are careful." He must not be bound by "rigid forms and encyclopedic schemes," and if successful, he will in the subtlest problems "be able to reach an independent decision [*tu tuan*] with singleness of mind." When done his work will "naturally be able to 'stand with Heaven and Earth,' 'confidently face the spirits,' be in accord with past writings, and await the attention of a later sage." Chang's true historian is like the sage in the *Doctrine of the Mean* who has achieved perfect "sincerity," and with it spiritual omnipotence.[3] His work is *chia hsüeh,* and for Chang this concept has now been completely assimilated in the idea of individual genius (*i chia chih yen*) and specialized scholarship (*chuan chia chih hsüeh*).

With this ideal before him, Chang judges the Standard Histories. The first four—those of Ssu-ma Ch'ien, Pan Ku, Ch'en Shou, and Fan Yeh—he finds worthy to be called true histories, for each one is the work of an individual genius who was able to grasp the significance of material and bring it out by proper selection and arrangement. But the histories written in the T'ang and later dynasties by official bureaus of compilation are at best merely cataloged collections of data. They simply follow the established forms and are as rigid as the writings of common government clerks. They may indeed be useful as source material for genuine historical scholarship, but to rank them with the earlier histories is absurd.

Yet, Chang continues, so inverted have standards become that when a true historical genius does appear, such as Cheng Ch'iao in the Sung, a man who "loves learning, thinks deeply, and is able to make his own approach to the ancients . . . and displays a judgment that is uniquely his own," he is everywhere reviled.[4] This evaluation of Cheng seems strange, for the *T'ung Chih,* aside from its twenty monographs (*lüeh*), which it has been fashionable to praise, is so far from displaying the original genius Chang saw in it that its chief value today is in the correcting of now corrupt texts in the pre-Sung Standard Histories, of which it is in the main a meticulously faithful copy. But Chang is less interested in the facts than in his opinion that true history is the work of genius—the product of an intelligence that is able to grasp directly the "significance" of historical material.

Chang contrasts this intuitive insight of the true historian with other types of scholarly temperament, in much the same way he did in "On Breadth and Economy." He recognizes that there is not only the scholarship of ideas, of "independent decision," but also a kind of scholarship that calls for careful research into detailed matters of fact. Both of these kinds of scholarship call for "wisdom," although of opposite sorts. And there is still another kind of scholarly work—that which simply classifies and arranges facts as source material for the scholarship of "wisdom." This kind of work calls for "stupidity"; it is not expected to endure and need not display literary excellence. Thus the man who collects and catalogs material is not to try to determine what is significant, or to select from the material he preserves. The scholarship of insight or research cannot exist without this lower type of learning, just as "good grain cannot be had without dung and earth." But it is not to be called true *chia-hsüeh*: it is not specialized learning or the work of genius. These three types of work must be kept distinct, just as the ancient schools of philosophy (like the several senses)

are distinct in their spheres of perception, their grasp of the *tao*.
It is the fault of some writers who "classify and arrange" facts
that they do not know their limitations, and try to be what they
cannot be. This was precisely the fault of Ma Tuan-lin. In his con-
cluding discourse with his "guest," Chang analyzes the common
faults he sees in this lower type of learning.[b]

The deterioration of historiography is analyzed from a different
perspective in another essay of 1790, "The Meaning of the Word
'General'" ("Shih T'ung"). *T'ung* means far more than "general."
It is that unity and wholeness which for Chang characterized
ancient civilization and government. It is the synthetic understanding and comprehensiveness of ancient knowledge; and so
it is the attribute of a book that deals with its proper subject matter as an integrated whole rather than as a collection of discrete
parts. Chang sees the *t'ung* ideal continuing in classical studies in
such Han works as the *Po-hu T'ung-i,* and in the great early works
of commentary.[c] In historical studies, the ideal is exemplified in
Ssu-ma Ch'ien's *Shih-chi,* in the now lost *T'ung Shih* of the Liang
emperor Wu, and in the monumental T'ang and Sung works of
Tu Yu, Ssu-ma Kuang, and Cheng Ch'iao. But the classical tradition over the centuries disintegrated, yielding mere collections
of philosophical talk; and the *t'ung* ideal in historiography was
dissipated in such works as Ma Tuan-lin's, which are mere collections of data.[5]

---

[b] *I-shu,* 4.45a–50a. What Chang says here about the type of scholar who merely
classifies and arranges facts is inconsistent with remarks he makes elsewhere. In a
letter to Huang Chang (a great-grandson of Huang Tsung-hsi), he argues that such
a scholar must understand the idea (*i*) of historical writing, so that the material he
collects will be useful to the true historian. (HY, p. 86.) On the other hand, Chang
is sometimes so impatient with the cult of dead facts that he dismisses all of philology as mere "industry," lacking insight and so not true "learning." See *I-shu,*
29.82a–84b, "Letter to Chang Cheng-p'u."
[c] Chang attempts to prove, here and in his "Notes of 1795" (*I-shu,* "wai-pien,"
2.17b), that Pan Ku's digest of the proceedings of the classical conference in the
White Tiger Hall is properly called *Po-hu T'ung-i* and not *Po-hu T'ung,* as usually
supposed. His real reason for this view is his constant desire to best Liu Chih-chi.
In his preface to the *Shih T'ung,* Liu says that the *Po-hu T'ung* suggested his title
to him. Chang, of course, uses *t'ung-i* and not *t'ung* in his own titles.

Having attended to the fundamental *begriff* of the matter, Chang then considers the properties of a history that is general or comprehensive in form (here Chang is thinking of historical writing covering not just one dynasty but many in succession). A comprehensive form presents certain dangers to the historian. He will be tempted to copy verbatim from the various histories that were compiled during, or shortly after, the period he is dealing with. But he has opportunities for greater clarity in presenting his material. He can avoid much duplication, straighten out contradictory accounts of periods of dynastic change, give continuous treatment to families, intellectual traditions, civil institutions, and border states whose histories are not necessarily coterminous with any official Chinese dynasty.

Chang prefers this kind of history chiefly for the opportunity it gives a gifted historian to exercise his own distinctive understanding and his own impartial judgment. Chang observes that a historian writing of events recently past, or of a dynasty just superseded, must step carefully when he comes to matters that are still politically sensitive. "For this difficulty there is really no remedy." But the writer of a general history escapes this, for he deals with a greater sweep of time: "When events are separated from the present by several dynasties, then historical writing can be almost completely impartial, and the real truth can be ascertained." Furthermore, the general-history structure allows the great historian to employ that special insight which is his mark of genius, to develop his own *chia-fa*. This is his real justification for taking a multitude of records and histories of smaller scope, and reworking them into a new comprehensive whole:

When all the facts are available in existing historical presentations, what is the value of doing the work over again? Just that the profession of a specialist has its own essential guidelines. For example, Cheng Ch'iao's *T'ung Chih* exhibits a vast understanding in its analysis of concepts and a unique viewpoint in its discrimination. The ancients cannot claim to have anticipated him, and his successors have been unable to improve on him. Although the facts he deals with are no different from those found in older books, ... the idea of a school of philosophy is embodied in his historical sensibility. His work will ultimately be imperishable.[d]

In "The Teaching of the *History*," Chang attempts to explain why historiography developed the way it did, what has gone wrong with it, and what might be done to rectify matters. He now finds history to have begun, not with the *Spring and Autumn,* but with the *Classic of History.* But the two Classics do not have two separate traditions: the tradition of the *Classic of History* was broken off and then merged with that of the *Spring and Autumn,* so that all later history derives from this common tradition. Yet here Chang has shifted his emphasis, for whereas the *Spring and Autumn* was significant because of the genius of Confucius who "concerned himself with its meaning," the *Classic of History* was an anonymous and formless accretion of material. It did not follow even a bare chronological form, and had no "fixed character" whatever, its chapter titles being simply what the subject-matter called for. Consequently he now sees the development of historiography as concerned not so much with the genius of historians as with the growing fixity and complexity of forms of historical writing itself.[e]

In the golden age of the three ancient dynasties, Chang says in the first of the three parts to this essay, there were established rules (*ch'eng fa*) for record-keeping, whereas there were no fixed genres (literally fixed names, *ting ming*) for historical writing. After the golden age the situation was exactly reversed—there were fixed genres for historical writing, but there were no established rules for record-keeping. "Now, when there are no established rules for record-keeping, selecting material is difficult; when there are fixed genres for writing, completing a work is easy. When completing a work is easy, then art [*wen*] dominates substance [*chih*]; when

[d] *I-shu,* 4.38b–39a. In this discussion, Chang also lists six "conveniences," two "advantages," and three "defects" of general history. For translations, see Lien-sheng Yang, "A Theory about the Titles of the Twenty-four Dynastic Histories," *Harvard Journal of Asiatic Studies,* x (1947), 47; also, HY, pp. 87–89; and *I-shu,* 4.37a–b. For *chia-fa,* see Chapter 3, p. 64. On the embodying or "lodging" of an "idea" in one's work, see p. 235, Note *h.*

selecting material is difficult, then falsity confuses truth," and when this happens, "historical scholarship perishes, even without appearing to do so." The development of forms ultimately ruined historiography.[7]

Chang explains how this occurred with an elaborate theory in the last part of his essay. Record-keeping and historical writing, Chang holds, are opposite and complementary activities in historiography. One is the regular business of official recorders; the other can only be performed by a man of insight and genius. Each has its "virtue." That of record-keeping is the "square" (i.e., exactness and "wisdom"); its function is the preservation of knowledge, and its concern is with the past. That of historical writing is the "circle" (i.e., flexibility, insight, "spirit"); its function is the intuitive apprehension of the significance of facts, and its orientation is to the future. All true histories exhibit both "circularity" and "squareness," though one of these virtues may predominate. Thus the character of Ssu-ma Ch'ien's *Shih-chi* is essentially "circular," that of Pan Ku's *Han Shu* is essentially "square." Historical forms, which at first were loosely structured (as in the *Classic of History*), have by stages become more and more precise. The first stage of development after the *Classic of History* was the *Spring and Autumn* and the *Tso Chuan* (considered as a unit), which had a simple chronological arrangement with a division between the main text (*ching*) and the commentary (*chuan*). The next stage was the *Shih-chi,* which was broken up into categories—annals, monographs, and so on. Finally came Pan Ku's *Han Shu,* which was restricted in scope to a single dynasty. With the last, the standard-history form was established, and for over a thousand years writers, finding it suited their needs, continued it without change.[8]

But the *Han Shu* was not a piece of record-keeping, and still had in it something of the "circle"; yet in simply imitating its form, later historians have been blind to this aspect of it. "They have lacked a power of discrimination and judgement.... On the contrary, as if following forms prescribed in the examinations, they have slavishly dared not make the slightest change, or like mere clerks handling records, they have been unable to leave out anything. If we look for the characteristics of the 'square' and 'wise' in later histories, we find they contain redundancies and mistakes, and are difficult to rely on; if we look for the characteristics of the 'circle' and of 'spirit,' we find they are tangled and spilling over, as vast as the ocean, and cannot be read and remembered." These books are the victims of their own structure.[9]

Yet the history of historical writing itself suggests a remedy. The development of form in historiography is not a one-way process: it is cyclical. For after the standard-history form had long been used, Ssu-ma Kuang appeared and was dissatisfied with its rigidity; therefore he returned to the straight chronological form of the *Tso Chuan*. And following him, Yüan Shu (1131–1205) found even this unsatisfactory, and rearranged the *Tzu-chih T'ung-chien* according to topics. The *T'ung-chien Chi-shih Pen-mo*, which "names its chapters for events and has no constant form," is thus "circular," and in the tradition of the *Classic of History*. Yüan's history was, Chang feels, not a work of genius, but his method was good.[10]

Chang himself would "strike a mean between art and substance, follow the 'idea' of the *Classic of History*," and incorporate the best features of the *Shih-chi* and the *Tso Chuan* "not simply from a desire to make changes but in order to remedy the worst defects of the standard-history form." Specifically, he would preserve the "basic annals," and treat everything else as a kind of commentary to them; therefore each chapter would be either a biography of an individual, or a discussion of an event, or a treatment of whatever kind of subject matter the particular history might call for, and would be titled accordingly. For "histories are books that record facts; facts exhibit innumerable variations and are not uniform. If the text of a history is to follow the facts in their twistings and turnings, it must name the chapters for the facts and not be restricted by an invariable form." This was the idea that Chang had intended to spell out in his essay "On Adaptability," and to apply in his Sung History.[11]

But the Sung history seems to have been scarcely more than a fancy in his mind, and the whole set of notions just described is actually more the work of a Neo-Confucian metaphysician than that of a historian. Chang feels that rigid forms are inimical to good history because he assumes that the real world is "not uniform," but infinitely varied. He is registering the suspicion, general in Neo-Confucian thought after Wang Yang-ming, of the violence done to "actual facts" by preconception and abstraction. And yet he plays freely with metaphysical entities both conventional and of his own devising, for Neo-Confucian philosophical language and the habit of thinking in this language had by no means died out in the age of philology.

A conspicuous example of an argument that appears to deal with a technical problem of historical method but is actually philosophically motivated is Chang's long discussion of words (*yen*) and events (*shih*) in "The Teaching of the *History*."[e] It had been rather traditional in Chinese historiography to regard words (edicts, memorials, and literary pieces by famous men) and events (the actions of rulers or the deeds of great men) as antithetical types of material. There was even a notion, appearing in the *Li Chi,* that in ancient Chou the words and the actions of the sovereign were recorded by two distinct officials; and there was also a (not implausible) theory among Han scholars that the *Classic of History* was essentially a record of words, whereas the *Spring and Autumn* was essentially a record of events.[f] In order to make

---

[e] Elsewhere English idiom has required me to translate the word *shih* as "fact" or "facts." I am not quite sure what events and facts really are or whether they must differ.

[f] For speculations about ancient record-keeping, see *Li Chi,** 9.1b; *Sui Shu,** 33.3a; *Han Shu,** 30.8a; and *Wen-hsin Tiao-lung,** 4.1a. The last two also offer the suggestions concerning the two Classics, as does Cheng Hsüan's commentary to the *Li Chi. Chang* particularly criticizes Liu Chih-chi for holding this view of the *Classic of History* (*STTS,* 1.2a; *I-shu,* 1.10b).

these two Classics part of the same tradition, Chang has to over-come this distinction, which he does by arguing that the *Spring and Autumn* and the *Tso Chuan* should be regarded as a unit, and pointing out that the *Tso Chuan* contains an abundance of what pretend to be the actual words of persons in the narrative.[12]

But this does not reveal his real interest in the matter. Later his-torians and critics (including Liu Chih-chi, whom Chang has a fine opportunity to disagree with here) had held that words and events should be dealt with in separate parts of a history.[13] To this Chang strongly objects: Words, as historical utterances, are them-selves events; and events are complexes that always involve words. To keep them separate, he argued, would be to make a metaphysi-cal mistake, which in turn would make it impossible for the reader to apprehend the full significance of either words or events. State-ments and literary writings, he feels, are not to be dealt with in a vacuum, or accorded any absolute value for the truth they express or the stylistic virtues they display; for these statements have no stylistic value apart from what they express, and what they express is meaningless apart from their historical context.[14] Here, Chang is showing in one more way the impact upon his thinking of the "unity of knowledge and action."

As this last problem in "The Teaching of the *History*" might lead one to suspect, that essay, like the Po-chou history, is saturated with literary ideas. A striking indication of this is the association of the deterioration of historiography with the ascendency of art over substance. It is not a mere coincidence that this should sug-gest Chang's earlier view that the writer of a poem should con-centrate on substance and let art take care of itself. It turns out, in fact, that Chang's whole conception of the development of histori-ography is paralleled in the contemporary criticism of poetry. For example, in the preceding century Ku Yen-wu had insisted, in his famous book *Jih Chih Lu,* that the best poems are those which have no titles (but are designated only by their first lines or first words), and are therefore not created to fit any fixed notions or preconceived purposes of the writer. This is the way, Ku argued, that the best poetry—the poetry of the *Odes*—was written. Ku went on to explain why modern poetry was so inferior:

In the poetic writing of the ancients, the poem comes first and then the title; in modern poetry the title is first set and then the poem is written. When the poem is written before the title is chosen, the poem will be rooted in feeling; when the title is chosen before the poem is written, the poem will follow external objects.[15]

Similar ideas were expressed by Yüan Mei. A poem, Yüan held, should have no set title, for if it has, it is not genuine, but only an attempt to move the emotions upon preconception. "A poem without a title is heavenly [natural] music; a poem with a title is human [artificial] music." The poetry of antiquity, Yüan thought, is in this respect superior to later art. When the practice of writing poems to set themes was introduced in Han and Wei, "feeling" diminished. The nadir of this progress of artificiality was reached in the T'ang examination system, which demanded the composition of "regular" poems on lines extracted from older poets.[16]

For Chang, historiography also approached its worst in the T'ang and Sung, when compilers used conventional forms "slavishly, as if following forms prescribed in the examinations." For Ku and Yüan the best and earliest poems had no set titles; for Chang the best (and earliest) history had no form, and hence had no conventional titles for its parts, only names that reflected their subject matter, their substance. For Yüan it is inner poetic feeling that disappears as poetry deteriorates; for Chang it is insight that is stifled by the conventionalization of historiography.

These ideas are related not only to literary theory but also to attitudes in contemporary classical scholarship. The situation, as Chang conceived it, was that historians had become the victims of historical form, so that "their works are cumbersome and the meaning of the facts is obscured"; historians should therefore look back to the *Classic of History*, to the stage of historiography before form had developed. Chang compared this to the situation in classical scholarship, "where commonplace teachers have actually become so immersed in the commentary that they obscure the significance of the Classics." Therefore, "when a Classic is obscured by explanation, one should look at the original stage of the tradition before there was any explanation; and when history has become imprisoned by rules, one should investigate its beginnings before there were any rules."[17] The reasoning which here leads Chang the critic of historiography back to the beginnings of his tradition is the same reasoning that led Ch'ing classical scholars from the Sung commentaries back to those of the Han, and from the Han commentaries back to fresh interpretations of the Classics themselves.

Chang's view of the history of historiography is also closely related to his own idea of the history of belles lettres. The development of historical form has had the same sort of bad effect on historiography that the development of literary genres and the formal classification of a man's literary productions in collections (*wen-chi*) has had on literature. The one leads to the collecting and cataloging of facts as valuable in themselves, to a mere "attempt to be complete in every detail" without regard for the significance of the whole; the other leads to neglecting substance, to making style and beauty ends in themselves, or worse, to making the gaining of a reputation the sole motive for writing.[18] As Chang had said in "On the Tao" and in "On Breadth and Economy," the fetish of facts and the fetish of style are of a piece in absurdity.

More than this, Chang's contention that words should be regarded as events was a way of saying (among other things) that literature itself is a kind of "history." It should be recalled that in deploring the appearance of literary collections in the Three Kingdoms and Six Dynasties, Chang had said, possibly as far back as 1783, that the development of *wen-chi* was due to the separation of words from actions. As so often in Chang, the problem was to find some way in which words could be other than "empty." His recommended remedy in this case was to edit a man's literary work so that his writings document his life and thought, and include biographical material, criticisms, and continuations of his thought in other writers. Chang's models for this idea had originally been

the ancient philosophical books such as the *Han Fei Tzu,* which
he believed were the historical antecedents of *wen-chi.* But such a
transformation would be to make literary collections in effect "histories of single individuals."

This is the view Chang took of *wen-chi* in his "Collected Opinions" of 1789, and again in 1791 in an essay on two chronological
biographies of the T'ang essayists Liu Tsung-yüan and Han Yü.
As histories of individuals, *wen-chi* are at the base of a hierarchy
of historical types. Above them are histories of families (composed
of individuals), then histories of localities (in turn made up of
families); at the top are histories of a dynasty, that is, of the whole
world. Lower types should be progressively more detailed, so that
they may be used by the compilers of higher types.[g] Thus *wen-chi*
are not only "histories" in themselves but also source material for
history of broader scope. It follows that each kind of history, even
the humblest, has a unique value; it contributes something to the
total picture of the world achieved in standard history. Chang's
hierarchy of histories can perhaps be regarded as an application
to historiography of his thought, expressed in a letter to Chu Tsang-
mei years before, that the special work of every man of learning,
honestly performed, is an expression of the *tao* and a contribution
to the understanding of it.

Just as he objected to conventional literary collections of individuals, Chang objected to literary anthologies that were simply collections of beautiful specimens of art, cataloged by some superficial
set of formal or generic concepts. This view, first expressed in 1783,
appeared again in "The Teaching of the *History.*" Anthologies,
Chang thought, should be regarded as companion volumes to his-

---

[g] *I-shu,* 4.20b, also "wai-pien," 18.13a. In his essay on the biographies of Liu and
Han, Chang writes (*I-shu,* 8.16b–17a): "*Wen-chi* are histories of individual persons. Family histories, histories of localities (*kuo*), and histories of dynasties will
draw upon them for evidence." Chang discusses this hierarchic conception again
(with local histories particularly in mind) in his "Proposal for the Establishment
of Departments of Local Historiography in Local Governments" (*Chou Hsien Ch'ing
Li Chih K'e I*); here, however, he regards biographies as the "histories of single
persons" (*I-shu,* 14.19b).

tory. They must exist because literature, which is historically important, cannot possibly be adequately represented in histories themselves. Hence his proposal for a *Sung Yüan Wen Chien* (Literary Mirror of Sung and Yüan) to go with Pi Yüan's *Hsü T'ung-chien* (which Shao Chin-han would have had Pi call the *Sung Yüan Shih Chien,* "Factual Mirror of Sung and Yüan"). This is, indeed, the idea behind the *wen-cheng* (literary evidence) section in the local histories; Chang had been recommending this device since his school days in Peking. These ideas seem a little strange, for it is hard to reconcile them with Chang's own objection to treating words and events separately within a history.

Chang was aware of the difficulty himself, and had always argued that really pertinent poetry and prose should be included in the narrative portion of a local history and not relegated to the *wen-cheng.* Chang's critical ideas may not be entirely consistent when considered as proposals for historiographical method, but what is consistent in them is the idea that words, including belles lettres, are empty and of no interest unless they are interesting historically. Words as utterances and happenings in time are important to the historian; in written or printed form they are historical documents. Chang says in "The Teaching of the *History*" that literary anthologies are "spring flowers," while what are conventionally called histories are their "autumn fruits."[19]

Chang has said that when art overwhelmed substance, history writing suffered. But art is important to the historian nevertheless. When he put together his Po-chou history in 1790, Chang felt strongly that a history cannot perform its function of communicating clearly an understanding of the past and present to future readers unless it has literary quality. This consideration of literary skill as an aspect of historical writing is part of a more general theory that is concerned with identifying the qualifications of a good historian and discovering how these qualifications can be exercised in writing history. For part of this theory Chang was in debt to that other earlier and equally famous historical critic, Liu Chih-chi of the T'ang Dynasty.

The theory is neat and already partly familiar. Liu Chih-chi had made a famous remark: the good historian, he said, must have talent, learning, and understanding. Chang added to this idea. Mencius, he found, had characterized the *Spring and Autumn Annals* in the following way: it dealt with certain *facts* (*shih*), i.e., the historical events of the times of Duke Huan of Ch'i and Duke Wen of Tsin; it recounted these facts in the "historical" or plain *style* (*wen*) of writing; it also contained certain *meanings* (*i*). We have seen the daring use to which Chang put this simple analysis. His cyclical progression of fashions in intellectual history is, as he had said to Shen Tsai-t'ing, simply a recurring preoccupation with these three elements. And Liu's qualities of the good historian are the basic qualities of man's developed intellectual nature, which these fashions reflect. When adequately exhibited in the historian, these qualities enable him to deal satisfactorily with the three aspects of a history noted by Mencius. With talent he masters literary art and is able to write his book. With learning he disposes its facts. And with understanding he "decides its meanings." If this puzzles, an analogy Chang uses in an essay written the following year adds color but invites more questions. Any history is like a living organism: its facts are its bones, its style (the writing itself) is its skin, and its meaning is its vital spirit.[20]

What sort of entity then is a history? More, apparently, than a string of words that the author's studies have enabled him to put together for us to interpret; it is something containing invisible things within a visible "skin." As theory-builders often do, Chang seems to expect us to accept a striking figure as a substitute for clarity. We would like, especially, to know more about these meanings that get "decided" by the understanding historian, for it does seem that Chang is directing our attention to them as most important.

But Chang goes on without satisfying us. Always welcoming a chance to declare his independence of Liu, he held that one more quality should have been required of the historian. It is essential that any analysis of the historian consider his "virtue," that is, Chang says, the "workings of his mind." This was the substance of the essay "Virtue in the Historian," written in 1791. The historian, Chang feels, must take great care not to let the hidden "workings of his mind" lead him astray. And he again voices his anxiety, expressed in his "On Conventional Judgments" two years before, about men's failure to reflect on the danger of being thoughtless.

Everyone knows that he should praise Yao and Shun, and condemn Chieh and Chou Hsin; respect for the "kingly way" and contempt for the deeds of those who ruled by force is commonplace among Confucians. And as for calling the good good and the evil bad, praising right and despising wrong, everyone who wants to write something lasting has this intention. But we must always be concerned with the workings of our minds; and the reason is that when Heaven and Man are associated together, the distinction between them is very subtle, and this is not a matter in which our puny intelligence can be relied upon."[21]

All men, save Confucius (who was a sage and the only perfect historian), have some tendency to personal bias in their judgments. The insidious seductive power of human emotion is such that a man cannot trust his intelligence to tell him when he is being fair. In the language Chang uses, the language of the Neo-Confucian metaphysic of morals, that which is "Man" in the individual—his tendency to impetuousness, shortsightedness, and lack of restraint —becomes confused with the "Heaven" in him, the part of his nature that yields the moral law, the universal *tao* that enters into his being, insofar as he is sober and fair. The best a historian can do is to be conscious of this limitation in himself, and be wary of judging the men and the historical events he discusses.[22]

This suspicion of judgment is one of the basic motifs in Chang's thinking. It appeared in his appraisal of Neo-Confucian controversy and of Tai Chen's criticisms of Chu Hsi; and in 1789 he had written an entire essay on the analysis of moral judgment, reaching the conclusion that a too sure assertion always betrays a lack of real understanding. Writing for Pi Yüan, he advised historians against making explicit judgments; adapting Pan Ku's "table of persons," he shunned Pan's pose as moral judge. It is not, as we shall see, a consistent doctrine in Chang that the historian should not judge, but it is nevertheless a persistent attitude, revealed both in theoretical analysis and in almost trifling details. It is, I think, a basic correlate to Chang's concept of the relationship of knowledge to existence, of the historian to the kind of world it is he grasps.

But the matter is not simple. Chang is quite ready to criticize others—perhaps paradoxically—for their lack of caution in criticizing others. An important part of Chang's criticism of Liu Chih-chi in particular is on the score of the fallibility of his judgments. The essay "On Reading the *Shih T'ung*," written, like "Virtue in the Historian," in 1791, takes Liu to task for judging an earlier history (the *Sung Shu*) unfavorably on grounds which, Chang held, admitted of no judgment at all.[23] And he more than once sniffs at Liu for his criticism of Ssu-ma Ch'ien.[24] One suspects a certain intellectual jealousy in this attitude of Chang's, but the particular cast to his criticism of Liu is, I believe, not accidental, and is a key to the profoundest difference between them.

That Chang should have found fault with Liu is not surprising. Liu was regarded as the greatest writer of historical criticism, and his *Shih T'ung* had recently been reedited and reprinted with commentary by P'u Ch'i-lung.[25] In 1774, ten years after Chang had first read the *Shih T'ung*, he had stated what seemed to him to be his justification for claiming a unique position for himself in the tradition of historical criticism: Cheng Ch'iao had understanding, Tseng Kung had learning, and Liu Chih-chi had understood method, but his own concern was with the basic idea of the discipline of history. In 1790, again, Chang had protested in one of his family letters that "people have actually likened me to Liu Chih-chi, not understanding that Liu talks about historical method, whereas I talk of the idea of history; Liu discusses compilation by an official bureau of historiography, while my proposals have to do with historical writing by a single author."[26]

The differences between the two critics were actually more complicated than Chang makes them. Chang, for his part, had had an extraordinary amount to say about historical method, whether "method" is taken to mean the way a history should be organized, or the way a historian should process his material, or the way he should gather it. Again, it is perhaps true that Liu had thought of his book as a technical manual for official historians, and while Chang never held more than a nominal official title, Liu himself was for much of his life an official compiler. But Liu was actually highly dissatisfied with his position, and looked nostalgically back at the Six Dynasties and earlier times, when a historian was a private author responsible to no one.[27]

And Chang was in fact partly indebted to Liu for his own ideas about individual scholarship and "independent decision" in the historian. What Chang did was to try to make Liu appear different from himself in ways that corresponded to what Chang regarded as good and bad in historiography. Liu had worked in a bureau of compilation and dealt with problems that must arise if the civil service is the context of historical scholarship. He represented, for Chang, the bureaucratic historiography of the T'ang, Sung, and Yüan, which had (he thought) produced enormous catalogs of data subjected to a mechanical classification, insensitive to the real nature and significance of these data. Chang, for his part, was concerned with an amorphous idea of the historian's craft and subject matter, an idea that condemned just this sort of formal rigidity, was inimical to rules, and could be realized and applied only by a man whose qualities were unique, who fitted no bureaucratic job description. The state must keep its records and wait for him to appear. He could not be an "official historian," for there could be no such office.[28] Such a man would have to have an intuitive sense of the significance of his material, an understanding that would enable him to exercise his "individual judgment" as to its "meaning." And yet Chang's historian is not to judge, not to praise or criticize. What is Chang really saying?

Chang's "judge-not" attitude does not, indeed, inhibit him from passing out, with a heavy hand, judgment of other men, past and present, in his essays and letters. These to be sure are philosophy and not history (though it is not clear to me why this should make a difference). But some of the things Chang says about historical writing itself seem at first to point the other way, toward a historian who will normally point out what is good and what is bad.

In the first place, it is certainly true that Chang saw the object of historical study, the course of events in man's past, as morally significant. The moral order is revealed in it and only in it, and we must therefore turn to the record of the past to learn what this moral order is. Chang as practicing historian occasionally offers praise in the conventional place at the end of a man's biography. And when as a young man he counseled Chen Sung-nien on these matters, we remember, he took the explicit position that "praise and blame" (*pao-pien*) should be retained in historical writing, though kept under restraint. This, to be sure, was probably before his philosophical vision of antiquity had clarified; and this may be important, for his anxieties about judgment are at least in part a feeling that taking sides is to express a "private," subjective view, to utter "empty words."

We find Chang talking about praise and blame later, in one essay written after he reached his characteristic conception of antiquity. In " 'If Your Words Are Everyone's' " (the section preceding the passage that begins this chapter), he has the good historian simply setting down bare facts, and the idea or moral significance of praise and blame is "silently lodged therein." Chang's manner of speaking leaves it unclear whether this "significance" is imputed by the historian or recognized by him. But here we press for a distinction Chang wouldn't have needed. We think of evaluation and description as two necessarily distinguishable properties of language. In Chang's tradition, to avoid saying anything unpleasant about a person was a common form of flattery;

and so, for Chang, to make it clear whether a man and his actions were good or bad was simply to give all the facts about him.[h]

At one time Chang actually entertained a naive popular view of history as a drama of reward and punishment. In 1785, when he financed a publication of the Taoist *T'ai-shang Kan-ying P'ien* (*Treatise of the Exalted One on Response and Retribution*) in his father's and grandfather's memory, he wrote in a preface to this popular moral tract that his father had intended to write a commentary to it, and had entrusted the task to himself. Chang never did the commentary, but did think carefully about what it should be like. A recent commentary by Hui Tung (1697–1758) Chang found praiseworthy as a piece of scholarship.[29] But something else, he said, was needed for the encouragement of ordinary men. So he proposed to write a commentary supplying historical arguments to support the book's theses. He would take material recorded in histories and biographies and "explain the causes of changing fortune," organizing this explanation around the "main developments of the rise and decline of families and states" in earlier ages:

Then I would cite cases where blessings have come to the good and ill fortune to the wicked, where the response between Heaven and men has been exact to the last detail [i.e., where men's fortunes granted by Heaven have been exactly in proportion to their deserts] in order to demonstrate that the book is true. And then I would bring out cases where the good have not necessarily been blessed nor the evil punished, where the cosmic movement has sometimes not worked evenly, and yet ultimately the good have not lost nor the evil succeeded—cases that oblige us to exercise deeper thought and analysis—so that I may show that everything works out in the end."[30]

If Chang could have considered such an undertaking, even in a relatively self-contained moment of piety, I think we must recog-

---

[h] Thus Chang speaks of "not covering up flaws" as "the *Spring and Autumn*'s idea of providing standards for the world [*ching shih chih i*]" (HY, p. 50). In speaking of the idea (significance?) as "silently lodged" in a history (*I-shu*, 4.7a), Chang uses a conception of painting theorists, who speak of "lodging one's conceptions [*yü i*]" in one's work of art. See James F. Cahill, "Confucian Elements in the Theory of Painting," in A. F. Wright, ed., *The Confucian Persuasion*, p. 133.

nize that he remains very much within the age-old Chinese tradition of the historian as moralist.

Nevertheless, one must make an important distinction. There is, on the one hand, the historian who points out the moral lessons of history by pointing to the ways historical events have rewarded and punished. Chang and most Chinese apparently believed that there is in the order of things reward for the good and punishment for the evil (though Chang's friend Hung Liang-chi questioned even this).[31] On the other hand, it is quite another matter for the historian himself to sit in judgment on the past and mete out reward and punishment in the form of praise and blame, condemning or approving this man or that act, requiting evil by seeing to it that the evil man is scorned by posterity. This is the function of the historian implied by the older, pre-Sung conception of Confucius as a "throneless king." ("Confucius wrote the *Spring and Autumn*," said Mencius, "and rebellious subjects and wicked sons were struck with terror.") Han Yü in the ninth century and Ouyang Hsiu in the eleventh, for example, assumed this to be the historian's role and both attempted to play it. But if Chang had this conception of the historian, his empty plans for a commentary to the *Kan-ying P'ien* do not show it; and for Chang, Confucius was no "throneless king" but only a subject "without position." Chang did, to be sure, write biographies of virtuous widows. But if one wrote local history one could not afford not to.

It is more difficult, however, to reconcile Chang's cautions about judgment with the things he has to say about "meaning" in historical writing. For to make his point that meaning is the most important of the three basic ingredients in a history, Chang appealed to Mencius's comment on the *Spring and Autumn*: "Of its meaning, Confucius himself has said that it was with this that he was concerned." He thus appears to invoke explicitly the tradition of Confucius writing the *Spring and Autumn Annals* as a vehicle of moral teaching. And at one time at least, Chang did explicitly accept the view that Confucius wrote the *Spring and Autumn*, using the text of the official chronicle of Lu.[32] In this remark from

Mencius that Chang was so fond of citing, the meaning or meanings are presumably the goodness or badness of persons and acts implied by the text; if Confucius wrote it, they have to be his judgments of those persons and acts. In consonance with this idea, the dominant Confucian historiographical tradition, beginning with the most ancient commentaries to the *Spring and Autumn,* had held that Confucius expressed praise and blame by his choice of what to record and by his choice of words. The good historian should do likewise, tradition directed, giving praise where praise is due and not hesitating to criticize even when wrongdoers are men of power. And the praise and blame need not be only implicit. In the *Tso Commentary,* the *Shih-chi,* and later histories we find explicit evaluative comments regularly included in the historian's text.[i] The literary critic Liu Hsieh in the sixth century had felt that the historian's duty was "to cover coherently and systematically an entire age, taking the whole world as his burden, and pronouncing final judgment of right and wrong."[33] Liu Chih-chi took this tradition for granted, criticized it, but criticized it only to improve it. He was uttering a commonplace when he stated that "the meaning of the *Spring and Autumn* is its punishment of evil and its exhortation to good."[j] Has not Chang Hsüeh-ch'eng at the outset placed himself squarely in this tradition of the judging historian?

Perhaps not quite. For our real task is to find out what meaning in historical writing is for Chang, not what it may have been for

---

[i] Chang himself much admired the comments of the "Grand Historian" in the *Shih-chi,* though he seems to have thought of them especially as models of style (see Chapter 5 and Chang's "On Teaching Students to Write," *I-shu,* "pu-i," 5a–b). Chang occasionally includes comments of this kind, with words of praise, at the ends of some of the biographies in his local histories, e.g., Part III of the *Hu-pei T'ung-chih Chien-ts'un Kao,* biography of Ku T'ien-hsi. (*I-shu,* 26.1a ff.)

[j] *STTS,* 20.16a. See also *STTS,* essays 9, 24, 25. There is one other kind of meaning that an ancient tradition (in the Han Dynasty) ascribes to the *Spring and Autumn.* The book according to this tradition was written by Confucius to present allegorically his vision of an ideal world order. (This idea became important again in the political thought of the "new text" school in the nineteenth century.) But Chang could not have thought it had this meaning, since he maintained that Confucius did not "create."

the *Spring and Autumn* tradition of Han and T'ang. Chang's categorizing habit of thought will be our best help. His three dimensions of a history are correlated with threes in other domains, and it is not unreasonable to expect these domains to shed light on one another. In his essay "On the Tao," Chang gives us something useful: "Mencius said, 'Principles delight our minds just as fattened meat delights our mouths.' But principles may not be stated in empty words. One needs wide study to make them real and literary skill to express them," and the ideal is always to combine these three elements together.[34] As Chang knew, Mencius's "principles" denoted that rightness in action and judgment to which man was supposed to be innately inclined. Certainly Chang's "meanings" at least include moral ones. By saying that wide study "makes them real" Chang does not of course say that a life devoted to books is a virtuous one. Wide study yields a harvest of facts, and facts grant existence to meanings or moral "principles." And so Chang praises the historian as one who supplies us with narratives of events, "and principles shine forth therein."[35] This historian does not, presumably, consider an act and then, mentally measuring it against a principle, deliver praise or blame.

An example will help. If it is a principle that "one shouldn't accept office if one has served under a preceding dynasty," a Confucian "praise-and-blame" historian will narrate any cases of double service in such a way that it is evident he disapproves of the person and his act; he may also say that he disapproves and why. Chang would seem committed, on the other hand, to finding and recounting cases of this kind of "disloyalty" in order to show that the principle is true, so that its truth is self-evident from the facts. When is a moral principle true? We have seen that Chang is quite willing to entertain the straightforward idea that its truth is borne out if violating it leads to misfortune. But this is misleading. Chang surely did not think of doing history as a program of confirming moral hypotheses. Confucius did not claim that he was testing his principles against historical data. He said rather that he was "revealing them in actions and events" because this was the only way to make them clear, to get them across. To state them, to preach, would have been to use empty words. Whether Confucius ever uttered these words Ssu-ma Ch'ien puts in his mouth is irrelevant. This is a part of *Spring and Autumn* lore which we know Chang felt to be identical with his own point of view.[k]

But it must be admitted that what Chang does mean by "meaning" he never tries to state exactly, and surely he often has something much vaguer and grander in mind than this. Confucius in writing the *Spring and Autumn* was using "matter" (documents and facts) to "illustrate the *tao*," Chang thought, and any scholar should want to do the same.[36] Presumably for Chang this is the "meaning" in that Classic. Indeed, illustrating the *tao* is the function of all the Classics, when they are conceived of as "history." If the meaning of Chang's data is their "illustration of the *tao*," then Chang's concept of meaning depends upon his concept of the *tao*, which in "On the Tao" in 1789 he had seen as the indescribable, only intuitively apprehendable "why" (*so-i-jan*) behind what happens and what is. It is this "why" that the highest kind of intellect should always try to grasp.[37] But if Chang insists that the *tao* (and a fortiori, "meaning") is indescribable, cannot be grasped in a "name," a concept abstracted from "actual things," it is apparent that it cannot be a definable moral concept by which actions and persons may be judged. Such a moral measure for judgment would be at most not the *tao* but the sage's sense of what he must do as he takes the *tao*'s part; and sages differ. In the ordinary case it would be what Chang calls the *tang-jan,* the "ought" of things, that which men at any particular time experience as necessary or obligatory. It would be simply the judger's sense of what is necessary, and so not

[k] Perhaps Chang would say to this matter what Wang Yang-ming surely would have had to say: that as soon as you recognize a historical event for what it really is, you have in the recognizing seen what is involved in "principle" and already approve or disapprove. (Cf. Wang's remarks in *Ch'uan Hsi Lu,* Part I, on seeing a beautiful color or smelling a bad odor, in explaining the unity of knowledge and action, W. T. Chan, p. 10; for the complete citation see p. 310, Note 15.)

the *tao* itself but just one more datum in the temporal process, which is the "trace" of the *tao*.

For Chang, history will resist the kind of explicit pinning down that conventional moral judgment attempts, just as it resists the other categories of conventional historiography. History—what has happened—is just what it is and nothing else; and all conventional labels and sorting-bins are something else. Only the intuition of a genius can bridge this gap between thought and the world. If this analysis is right, Chang's "meaning" is very close to his "idea" of history (which is, he says, what all his work is about, which distinguishes him from Liu Chih-chi and his "method"). This "idea" seems to embrace not only the "idea" beyond the rules of method (and so beyond formulation) that guides the historian's craft, making it adequate to the "significance" of the things he studies, but also this significance itself. And so he urges upon the historian the example of Ssu-ma Ch'ien, who was "fond of learning things, thinking deeply about them, mentally (intuitively) understanding their idea"—their "significance."[1]

Dare we go further in identifying the unidentifiable?

The "meaning" of a history cannot be the *tao* itself, if we take Chang seriously when he says the meaning is the work's "vital spirit." It is part of the history, not of the world. But the *tao* in the world, like the meaning in a history, seems to be an organic cohesive principle holding all together. Chang's *tao* in the historical process "comes from Heaven," from the nature of things, including the nature of man. Chang's meaning in historical writing "comes from the Heaven" in a human being, the better side of the his-

---

[1] "Answers to Objections," *I-shu*, 4.45a. The term *i*, here rendered "idea" (also "significance"), is pronounced exactly the same as the term rendered "meaning" (sometimes "principle"). But the two terms are usually interchangeable only at the cost of good sense. In the present example, *i* is the "significance" of the things the historian writes about. (For *i* as the historian's guiding "idea" see Note *b*, p. 219.) *I* is thought, the movement of the mind, and intention in Liu Tsung-chou (see Note *k*, p. 177) and in Ch'eng I (see Angus Graham, *Two Chinese Philosophers*, London, 1958, pp. 61–63). Perhaps in Chang it is, so to speak, what the historian, or his writing, or what he writes about, "intends" or tries to do. See also Note *h*, p. 235, for the "idea" of the *Spring and Autumn*.

torian's nature wherein he participates in the universal moral order.[38] Meaning is perhaps a moral conception still, but not one that is usable in the ordinary way. From what Chang says about historical writing, and from the way he as a philosopher deals with historical problems that interest him (such as the history of genres of writing), it seems a reasonable suggestion that the meaning exhibited in the historian's work is his intuition of the totality of things, into which the various parts of his subject matter fit to form a unified and organic whole. And having apprehended his material in this way, the historian is to present it in such a way that the reader likewise can grasp it easily as a whole. He must not write too much; he must include all and only those facts that are "meaningful." The ability to do this is the mark of historical genius: "Only one who apprehends the essential character of past and present, and who understands the principles by which the world is ordered, can gather his material together as in a net, and shape it so that there is nothing missing and nothing included that should not be."[39] A historical genius who can do this and see this is emancipated from formal restrictions, and is able to grasp his material's significance exactly for what it is, and "decide independently" how to manage it exactly as its nature demands. The ideal of genius, which Chang sees in the *Spring and Autumn,* and the ideal of formal freedom, which he sees in the *Classic of History,* here meet.

In Chang's late Neo-Confucian metaphysics, the *tao* cannot be separated from things. To try to abstract it is to fail to see things whole, to fail, in one's seeing, to be a part of the whole, to use "empty words." The symptom of this is always conflict and animus. So much Chang had said in "On the Tao." In "Virtue in the Historian" he tries to explain exactly how this illness develops in the writer. A historian has to deal with facts. To do this he must write. To write well he must respond to his subject matter as a human being, instinctively approving and disapproving, sympathizing. His emotional responses eventually build up, get out of balance, overcome his judgment, so that "when he writes, he injures meaning and opposes the *tao* without realizing it," thinking he is being objective but actually being partial. Not only have historians not been cautious about this danger but their mistaken conception of their tradition has made it worse. The *Shih-chi* is a book that critics have recognized—rightly—as writing of the finest. Ssu-ma Ch'ien they have supposed—wrongly—to have been writing for spite. (They have even thought that he "slandered his prince," says Chang indignantly.) "And so critics have regarded Ssu-ma Ch'ien as an expert in slander, and have thought that innuendo is the historian's most powerful function." This, Chang thinks, completely perverts the tradition of the *Spring and Autumn* in historiography and makes the historian's craft an instrument of just the sort of depraved denial of authority Chang feels Confucius was attacking.[40]

It is important to see that Chang's is an ideal for the historian very different from the ideal that prevailed before Neo-Confucian thought had fully developed. If Chang thought that he himself still stood squarely in this earlier tradition, he was surely mistaken. The old tradition of the historian as critic was a heroic one, in ideal if not always in fact. It was a tradition of unhesitating political criticism, and although the historian in this tradition was always supposed to defend legitimate imperial authority, it was sometimes his duty to criticize its use and to attack de facto holders of power, even at the risk of life. This duty was a part of the conception of the loyal servitor as a giver of good counsel to his prince, even if that advice were infuriating. The historian as servitor was to be guardian of the right; and this is why Liu Hsieh says of him that he "takes the whole world as his burden." To Liu Chih-chi, "virtue" for the historian could have meant only one thing: courage to state the historical truth, regardless of personal danger and no matter who in authority might be displeased. This ideal had its own mythology. There was, for example, in the *Tso Commentary* the famous story of Nan-shih, the "historian of the south": Duke Chuang of Ch'i (553–48 B.C.) had been done away with by the general Ts'ui Ch'u, who subsequently executed three official historians for entering in the official record that "Ts'ui Ch'u murdered his ruler"; on hearing this, Nan-shih, so the account goes, set out for the capital of the state and turned back only when he learned that a fourth historian had succeeded in making the record stand.[41] This classical story was a commonplace, and there are frequent allusions to it in the *Shih T'ung*, but Chang Hsüeh-ch'eng scarcely ever mentions it.[m] The story simply did not fit into his philosophy.

This absence was not, I believe, due to any conscious fear of official censure. Chang was not lacking in courage. The chief uncertainties in his life were economic; and yet by frequently expressing opinions which were either unconventional or downright eccentric, he consciously ran the risk of "shocking people," and thus making himself unacceptable to possible patrons or employers. Indeed, it might be argued that Chang evinces the older tradition of the historian as critic in his censure of "fashion," which he regarded as the intellectual decadence of his own time. But while he often dealt severely in his writing with the aping of intellectual fashion and with conventional narrow-mindedness that could not recognize a true man of genius, such as Cheng Ch'iao—or himself—he nevertheless tended to regard the state as the ally of the true historian: the state preserves books, keeps documents, curbs objectionable writing, and reserves a special place for the historian's work. While the genuine historian must have an insight that resists official definition, his task is made easier when the source material with which the government can provide him is in good order—when there are "established rules" for record-keeping. His difficulty arises only when "fixed concepts" have become so ingrained in the thinking of men of letters that he is hampered in expressing himself. Both Chang and Liu Chih-chi talked of the "independent decision" of the true historian. But in using this phrase, Chang's emphasis was on originality and uniqueness of perception, which called for the historian to make up his own mind about the meaning (in Chang's sense) of his material, without being bound to *conventional* perspectives. Liu, on the other hand, was arguing that a really good historian does not have to be an *official* in order to

---

[m] One such mention is in the Ho-chou history (*I-shu,* "wai-pien," 18.55a). But Chang completely avoids the traditional point of the story here.

write; some of the greatest of ancient historical writing was done by men who did not hold office and did not have to put up with petty bureaucratic restrictions. "Wherefore, a man of profound understanding, realizing that this is the case, retires quietly and closes his doors, bringing to completion his own books, simply deciding matters for himself."[42]

Liu was a member of the bureaucracy, and he hated it. Driven to frustration, he lashed out with raw courage at those above him. Chang shunned official position and did not have to contend with its vexations. We shall see presently that he saw much about him in the official world that angered him. Yet we find him saying that his is an age of "good order," with generals and ministers "hurrying about attending to their duties." The state for Chang was the visible part of the iceberg of history, which is the very embodiment of the *tao*. Confucius had said that "when the *tao* prevails in the world the people do not even discuss it." For Chang the *tao* prevails in the existing political and institutional order of things by definition. With such a view criticism of that order would seem to be almost unthinkable. Yet we must remember that Chang's cautions about judgment were directed essentially at conventional brainlessness. His is a flag of independence as well of orthodoxy, and he remains unpredictable.

9. Last Battles

The scholar who has his own special discipline always works
alone to implement his ideas. Though his colleagues attack him,
he doubts not. Though the whole world condemns him,
he looks not back.

—*Answers to Objections . . . 1790*

Chang's thinking about historiography, considered against the
background of subsequent events at Wu-ch'ang, is significant on
two counts. First, it is clear that he regarded the historian as a man
of genius and extraordinary importance, a man whose needs should
be served by lesser scholarship and by local functionaries. Second,
Chang had precise ideas about how history—particularly local
history, in which he regarded himself an expert answerable to no
one—should be written; these ideas were an integral part of his
entire philosophy, and in defending and applying them he was by
intellect and disposition unable to show respect for contrary opinion. In view of this, it is not surprising that in his work on his general history of Hupeh, which dealt with local matters and persons
and in which there was necessarily a certain amount of local interest, he should have aroused opposition, and then should have proceeded to infuriate this opposition.

If Chang's own accounts are to be taken, he worked on the *Hu-
pei T'ung-chih* under considerable difficulty. As in the case of the
Po-chou history, he was pressed for time; and in spite of Pi Yüan's
support, he was beset with criticisms that further dissipated his
efforts. Persons from whom he sought material were vague and
devious for personal reasons; district clerks were lazy and slow to
produce documents. He wrote later to his friend Ch'en Shih that
the *wen-cheng* or anthology gave him the greatest difficulty. He
made the selections of prose himself—"but poetry, *fu,* and verse

in general is where I fall short, so I turned the selection of it entirely over to others." His assistants, unfortunately, were incompetent and corrupt. The worst poetry he expunged, but "villains and deceivers bribed the clerks to add things; it was indeed beyond imagination." The blame was partly his, Chang admitted, for not checking up on them. But people kept coming like a swarm of bees, bringing their poems to him, relying on influence to have them included. If Pi Yüan couldn't fend them off, how could he? The best he could do was to limit poetry to the last two of the four collections of the anthology, deliberately reserving the last for the worst poetry (this section was designated "recent poetry") on the principle that a house cannot be kept clean unless it has a privy. Later when influential persons were gone, he suggested, the blocks for this fourth collection could be destroyed.[1] Still, these difficulties with the local poets did not matter too much, for "history's main concern is politics, and verse is not really of importance."

Chang is nowhere more supercilious and disdainful of the rest of intellectual creation than here. His surprising remark that history deals mainly with government and that poetry "is not really of importance" was made under conditions that might lead us to discount it, especially in view of its gross inconsistency with his opinion of a year or so before that all literature is of great interest to the historian. Apparently, however, it reflected his present attitude. In the same letter (probably written in 1794) from which this remark is quoted, he compares the writing of the lofty historian with that of the mere literary man. Chang represents himself as a historical theorist who has "never expressed many theories about literature," and who feels that an understanding of purely literary matters hardly qualifies a person to discuss such an important and far-reaching subject as historiography. "When the literary man writes, his only fear is that his writing may not really come from himself; but when the historian writes, his fear is that his writing will come from himself."[2] It may be that Chang's attitude toward literature (or at least poetry) was at this point significantly changing. These remarks are certainly consistent with the suspicion expressed in "Virtue in the Historian" that personal feelings are a source of bias in the historian; his disgust with "recent poetry" suggests the sort of invective which, in conversation at least, he may already have been directing at Yüan Mei.

It is obvious that Chang was not disposed to soothe the tempers of those he had dealings with, and it is therefore not surprising that his attitude should have made him the center of mounting tension at the viceregal secretariat at Wu-ch'ang. The climax came early in 1794. The *Hu-pei T'ung-chih* was at this time being readied for the printer. But in the third month Pi Yüan had an audience with Emperor Kao-tsung, who was making an imperial visit in Tientsin. Pi left Chang under the direction of the Hupeh governor Hui-ling, a Manchu and a military man, who had recently been governor-general of Szechwan. Hui-ling's dislike for Chang's writings presented others with an opportunity to discredit him. A certain Ch'en Tseng (*chin-shih* of 1780 and a native of Chia-hsing, Chekiang) approached Chiang and requested a recommendation for the job of "editing" the history. Chang consented, thinking that this would merely involve correcting errors in wording and copying. But Ch'en, supported by his superiors, proceeded to criticize the structure of the entire work and to recommend that it be completely redone. Pi, on his return, reasserted his support of Chang and had him write a formal reply to Ch'en's criticisms ("Po Ch'en Tseng I"), and with that the incident might have passed.

But in the autumn (eighth month), Pi was denounced for failing to give advance information on the budding revolt of the White Lotus secret society. As punishment, he was fined and demoted to the governorship of Shantung. This development threatened to deliver the situation again into the hands of Chang's enemies. But this time Chang's friend Ch'en Shih persuaded his employer, the prefect of Wu-ch'ang, to intercede, with the result that the *T'ung-chih* drafts were turned over to Ch'en himself for further editing. Ch'en, a native of Ch'i-chou in Hupeh, was a local historian who, besides the local history Chang had helped him with, had compiled a more ambitious work, *Old Accounts of Hupeh (Hu-pei Chiu-*

wen). He frankly admired what Chang had done with his Hupeh history. The *T'ung-chih* was never published, however, and Chang, now without Pi's monetary support, was obliged to leave Hupeh and return to his native K'uai-chi, where his family had been since 1793.[3]

This was a tragic turn of events for Chang, for he had been counting heavily on a quite different outcome to his work in Wu-ch'ang. In 1793 he had admitted, in a letter to an acquaintance in Peking, that he had come to Hupeh with great hopes of saving something for his retirement; apparently it was his understanding with Pi Yüan that this "something" would be forthcoming when his books were finished. "Then," wrote Chang, "I will go home and make temporary disposition of my father's coffin, and use what remains to provide myself with a plot of land and a roof over my head, enough to keep alive a family of a few persons."[4] All this had now slipped from his hands. From this time until the end of his life Chang was forced to drift about, in Chekiang, Kiangsu, and Anhwei, seeking support from a number of patrons without meaningful success. Early in 1795, Pi Yüan was restored to his position as governor-general of Hupeh-Hunan, but Chang did not return to Wu-ch'ang. Because of an uprising of the Miao tribes in Kueichow and Hunan, Pi, who was an experienced supply officer and the responsible administrative official in the area, had no time for literary patronage.[5]

Chang spent the first half of 1795 in K'uai-chi, tidying up his library, inscribing family portraits, and writing prefaces, enjoying his status as a local literary man who had gone forth into the world, earned distinction, and returned home. But he was also reading and exploring. Though his life since childhood had been spent in other parts of China, most of his close friends were men from Chekiang. He always had a strong feeling of identification with his native region, and he was aware of the intellectual greatness of its past. At least one earlier Shao-hsing writer, Shao T'ing-ts'ai, he had read with admiration. But now, apparently, Chang began to probe more deeply and methodically into his intellectual roots. He had scarcely noticed Ch'üan Tsu-wang (1705–55) of Ning-po. In 1795 he found and read the manuscript of Ch'üan's literary collection, and was both impressed and disturbed. The breadth of Ch'üan's knowledge of Southern Ming history amazed him. But Ch'üan had pronounced Shao T'ing-ts'ai a rustic, and Chang concluded that Ch'üan was lacking in literary sensibility.[a]

For Huang Tsung-hsi Chang already had a deep respect. He had noticed that Shao T'ing-ts'ai had known Huang and had quoted him. And perhaps he had noticed that Huang's point of view was often broadly similar to his own. But in his most important earlier writing on Neo-Confucian thought and on the history of historiography—such as his essay on the schools of Chu Hsi and Lu Chiu-yüan and "The Teaching of the *History*"—he had not found occasion to mention Huang. Now, however, Chang began to notice him. A random entry in his reading notes of 1795 lists "Sun Ch'i-feng, Huang Tsung-hsi, and Li Yung" as "three great Confucianists of the K'ang-Hsi era." (Perhaps we may infer that Chang had been reading Huang's *Ming Ju Hsüeh-an*, for Sun wrote a similar history of post-Sung philosophy.) In Shao-hsing Chang got acquainted with Huang's descendents. Writing to Hu Ch'ien in 1796, he mentioned his discovery of Ch'üan Tsu-wang, and observed, "There's Huang Tsung-hsi—although he's well known, there are still many of his works that are not printed. In the house of his descendant Huang Chang, the former director of studies of Chia-shan, I saw a *Yüan Ju Hsüeh-an [Documentary History of Yüan*

---

[a] HY, pp. 118–19. WHL, p. 249a. *I-shu,* "wai-pien," 2.31b–39a (especially 2.38b), "Notes of 1795." This date is not certain, for some of these notes were written as early as 1791. Ch'üan's literary collection (*Chi-ch'i T'ing Chi*) was not printed until 1804 (*ECCP,* pp. 204, 276). Chang apparently did not know of Ch'üan's extensive work (unprinted until 1888) on the *Shui Ching Chu* (*Classic of Waterways,* with commentary by Li Tao-yüan, d. 527). A famous controversy has developed about eighteenth-century research on the *Shui Ching Chu*: accusations have been made that Tai Chen, in his editions of the text (1775–76), plagiarized an unpublished work by Chao I-ch'ing (1710?–64?) of Hang-chou; Chao was a close friend of Ch'üan and exploited discoveries for which he gave Ch'üan credit (*ECCP,* pp. 76–77, 205, 970–82). I find no indication of any knowledge of this in Chang, though Chang does accuse Tai of two rather trivial instances of intellectual dishonesty (*I-shu,* 2.31a–b).

Confucianism] in several dozen big volumes, which had been compiled by him. It brings together an unrivalled amount of material on the Yüan Dynasty." Chang had evidently seen a part of Huang's *Sung Yüan Hsüeh-an,* which was not published until 1846. His excitement was justified, but it seems clear that he was only now beginning to realize fully how important Eastern Chekiang historical scholarship actually was.[6]

Chang had been wandering too long to settle down at once. Indeed, probably he could not afford to. In the winter he was off again, to visit his old friend and teacher Shen Yeh-fu, now retired in Yang-chou. Here he helped Shen with his family genealogy; Chang wrote the preface and a number of biographies. Apparently he still had some relationship with Pi Yüan, because while in Yang-chou that winter he wrote on Pi's behalf an epitaph for a certain Chang Sung-p'ing. This incident illuminates both the literary side of funerary custom and Chang Hsüeh-ch'eng's personality. The Chang family supplied him with a large quantity of material to work with. But when Chang opened it he found nothing but fluff —occasional poems, lists of guests at parties, and so on. What could one write about a man whose life had been so empty? Chang solved the problem by composing a very short prose epitaph (*mu-chih*), then adding an inordinately long eulogistic ode (*ming*) at the end; the odes, of course, did not have to contain any facts. But custom unfortunately dictated that the ode should be very short, and the prose biography relatively long. The Chang family was upset and Chang, criticized, was also upset. To justify himself Chang wrote a theoretical essay on epitaph-writing, citing precedents among T'ang writers to show that what he had done was all right. What Chang was expected to do in this case, we may assume, was to draw freely upon his imagination and his knowledge of literary models for incidents to record in his subject's life. He lamented this all too common biographical practice in a critical essay ("Ten Faults in Classical Prose") probably written shortly after his dealings with the Chang family.[7]

It was probably from Yang-chou that Chang wrote a letter to

Juan Yüan, the now world-famous classical scholar, who had just been appointed commissioner of education in Chekiang. Chang wrote to him about collecting antiquities in Chekiang, an activity Juan might be interested in pursuing in his leisure time (in fact he was very interested). Formerly, said Chang, there were many good libraries in the province and a strong historical tradition; many of the scholars who worked on the Yüan and Ming histories came from this area, and there were better historical collections here than elsewhere. "But now all is scattered and lost! Thirty years back, book buyers in Peking bought up many books from old families here, but in the last decade they have paid no attention to us. I've heard that foreign ships, for example from Japan and the Ryukyus, have come and bought many books for which they have paid high prices. The authorities have not watched carefully, and this may have much to do with it."[8] Chang's relations with Juan were to continue to be cordial.

Chang returned to K'uai-chi again in the spring of 1796. He wrote at this time a number of family biographies, and a preface to a pair of historical reference works by Wang Hui-tsu. Wang, seven years older than Chang, had been a friend of Chu Yün, and had known and admired Chang since their first meeting in Peking in the spring of 1769. Wang had retired to his home in nearby Hsiao-shan in 1793, and was now bedridden with partial paralysis. But he was still writing, and his autobiography *Ping-t'a Meng-hen Lu* (*Traces of Dreams from a Sick-bed*) supplies an occasional detail of Chang's last years. At this time Wang was training Chang's second son Hua-fu in the profession of judicial yamen clerk. We find Chang, for his part, offering Wang friendly advice about the education of one of his sons.[9]

Chang wrote sixteen essays in 1796. One of these, "Virtue in the Literary Man" ("Wen Te"), is one of his best known. This essay, like "Virtue in the Historian" written five years earlier, dwells on the danger of bias in judging writings of the past. Chang now presses this view almost to the point of complete historical relativism:

If we do not understand the times in which the ancients lived, we ought not to criticize their writings indiscreetly. And even if we understand their times, if we do not understand their personal situations, we still should not criticize their writings. . . . The Confucian principle of sympathy is that "what you do not wish done to yourself, you should not do to others." This is a great principle indeed.

Writers of the past had their own points of view, which are as likely to be right as ours; and our danger of misunderstanding them is great. Chang gives examples to show that their opinions were the only possible ones for them to hold. *Tout comprendre, c'est tout pardonner.* This attitude is no more than is implied in "On the Tao," where Chang stated that the writer is justified when he says what he must. But this is the most appealing and humane expression in Chang's essays of his aversion to dogmatic and unreflective evaluation of the past. His argument, as might be expected, is supported by examples from the history of historiography, but the point of the essay is to caution the critic of any kind of writing whatever.

Like "Virtue in the Historian," this later essay addresses itself to the man of letters not only as a critic but also as a writer. Its relativistic sense is only part of its thesis. We have noticed that for Chang, and probably for most Confucians, becoming a good writer is dependent on becoming the right sort of person; it is ultimately a moral matter. "Virtue in the Literary Man" supports this theme. It is not enough, Chang says, for a literary man simply to "cultivate his virtue," in advance. He must have the right sort of attitude and exercise the right sort of self-discipline when actually engaged in reading and criticizing, or in producing his own art. When reading and criticizing he must have sympathy, consciously putting himself in the other person's place. When writing, he must have reverence (*ching*) for the springs of creativity in his own nature. The process of creation is so important that the writer must when engaging in it "calm his mind and restrain his spirit," lest fancy and passion at the moment of composition taint what he writes. It is this combination of sympathy and reverence that makes up "virtue" in the literary man.[10]

Early in 1796, Chang had printed in a limited edition a small selection of his essays and letters under the title *Wen-shih T'ung-i*. Of this printing he wrote in the spring to Wang Hui-tsu:

> I really had no choice but to develop the criticisms advanced in my *Wen-shih T'ung-i*, and in so doing I have cleared away confusion that has surrounded historiography for a thousand years. But I am afraid that these arguments might startle the world, horrify common folk, and be severely criticized by people who do not know me; so for the time being I have chosen some essays that are close to present ways of thinking and might be tolerably received. I will print only a few for the inspection of those associates whose judgment I value; but I still do not want to have them shown to everyone.

Apparently this last structure was taken seriously, for the edition has disappeared. From other sources, however, it is known that it included the first eight sections of the present *Wen-shih T'ung-i*, i.e., "The Teaching of the *Changes*" (three parts), "The Teaching of the *History*" (three parts), and "The Teaching of the *Odes*" (two parts). By way of confirmation Chang writes elsewhere of the essays in this selection: "By their titles they would appear to deal with the Classics, but actually they discuss history." This was the only work of Chang's published during his lifetime to bear the title *Wen-shih T'ung-i*.[b]

This printing of a few of Chang's literary pieces (probably only about two dozen items) was a very limited venture. He may have done it merely to have something to show to prospective patrons. His major works—the *Hu-pei T'ung-chih*, still unprinted, and the *Shih-chi K'ao*, still unfinished—were certainly much more impor-

---

[b] HY, p. 121. *I-shu*, 9.26a–b. Other parts of what is now the *Wen-shih T'ung-i* had, of course, been printed. The *Ho-chou Chih* had been printed and not distributed, though Chang retained copies of the prefaces. His "Biographies of Friends Who Died Around 1780–81" and the Yung-ch'ing history with prefaces has been printed by Chou Chen-jung. The selective *Wen-shih T'ung-i* of 1796 included several letters to Shao Chin-han, Shih Chih-Kuang, and others, a number of other essays, among them the proposals for a three-part form for local histories and for departments of local historiography in local administrative centers; and probably also " 'If Your Words Are Everyone's,' " "Collected Opinions," and "On the Difficulty of Being Understood." See HY, p. 123, and Ch'ien Mu, pp. 425–26; also Chang Shu-tsu, "*Wen-shih T'ung-i* Pan-pen K'ao," in *Shih-hsüeh Nien-pao* III (Dec. 1939), 72.

tant to him. Chang had hoped that things would quiet down at Pi Yüan's headquarters, so that he could go back to Hupeh (the manuscripts remained there with Pi, for nominally, of course, they were his) and see his books through to publication. In particular, he wanted to finish the *Shih-chi K'ao*. But now, with the Miao disturbance still in progress, the long-brewing White Lotus rebellion broke in full force. Chang worked alone in K'uai-chi on the *Shih-chi K'ao* as well as he could, waiting.[11]

While he was so occupied, his old friend Shao Chin-han died in Peking, at the age of fifty-four (*sui*). The news must have reached Shao's home quickly. Chang was grief-stricken. It was, as he wrote to Hu Ch'ien, more than a personal loss: Shao was extremely talented; his household possessed many books of Sung and Yüan times, and he knew many unwritten verbal traditions inherited from his learned ancestors. "I urged him to train a scholar to carry on his learning, but he said he hadn't found the right man. I urged him to write down what he knew, but he said he hadn't the time. And now it is forever ended!" Ended, also, was the idea of a Sung history the two had discussed, and a history of Shao-hsing they had planned to do together. Several years later (1800) Chang performed the final office of writing a biography of his dead friend.[12]

Late in 1796, Chu Kuei (1731–1807), the younger brother of Chang's former teacher Chu Yün, was appointed governor of Anhwei. This appointment was actually a demotion from the governor-generalship of Kwangtung and Kwangsi, and he was opposed by the powerful Ho-shen.[c] Nevertheless he was highly regarded by Emperor Kao-tsung (now in nominal retirement) and was a personal friend of the new Emperor Jen-tsung. He was a man worth cultivating, and Chang had a strong claim to his attention.

As soon as he learned of Chu's appointment, Chang wrote to him, discussing his difficulties in completing the *Shih-chi K'ao*.

[c] Ho-shen may actually have engineered the demotion. See my "Ho-shen and His Accusers," in Nivison and Wright (eds.), *Confucianism in Action* (Stanford, 1959), p. 240.

"Now my credit is exhausted," he said, "and I have nothing left to mortgage.... All I can do is follow the road with my begging bowl...and hesitatingly wait for unexpected official patronage." He asked Chu to recommend him to the Ta-liang Academy in Honan or the Lien-ch'ih Academy in Chihli, adding that if Chu helped him now, his credit for patronizing the *Shih-chi K'ao* would be as great as Pi's. He included for good measure a copy of his recently printed essays. The appeal apparently bore some fruit, for by the end of the year he was in An-ch'ing visiting Chu, remaining in Anhwei well into 1797. Spring found him reading examinations in An-ch'ing and T'ung-ch'eng.[13]

In T'ung-ch'eng, he consulted with Yao Nai, asking him to criticize a piece of his recent work. He showed Yao a long letter addressed to Sun Hsing-yen, his former associate in the *Shih-chi K'ao* project. One doubts that Chang ever sent Sun this letter, for while its tone is friendly, it contains rather harsh criticism of a book Sun had recently published, as well as personal criticism of Sun himself.[d] Chang urged upon Sun his view that there were no "private" writings in the age of the Three Dynasties (Hsia, Shang, and Chou) and showed (often sensibly) how this assumption invalidated a number of Sun's statements about ancient books. Chang went on to suggest that Sun's book and his basic ideas and values would have been clearer if Sun hadn't tried so hard to display his erudition, and he declared that Sun had been too intemperate in criticizing other scholars by name. (To this counsel Chang added a fascinating note: "My own writings are also tainted with this defect, only not as badly as yours. I now realize my mistake and have edited out much of this.")

[d] HY, p. 125. WHL, p. 286b. While Chang was in Anhwei this year (1797) he wrote a number of things critical of Sun Hsing-yen: "A Comment on the Essay 'Human Nature' " ("Shu Yüan Hsing P'ien Hou") (Ch'ien Mu, p. 428, dates this 1800); several letters to Chu Hsi-keng (then in An-ch'ing); and probably also an essay "On Being Different" ("Pien I"), which in thought is close to parts of Chang's "On the Tao" and "On Conventional Judgments." In "On Being Different," Chang may also have had Hung Liang-chi in mind (WHL, pp. 286b–287a, 289b); I think this essay is one of Chang's best.

Chang concluded his letter: "Gentlemen are known by the company they keep. It was all very well for you to print those appraisals by various people in your book, but why did you include that 'Letter to Mr. So-and-so on Philology'? The man is a menace to public morality, who thinks the Classics encourage desire and license." What was Chang talking about? The book in question was Sun's *Wen-tzu-t'ang Chi,* a collection of letters and other literary and scholarly pieces of writing. It was first printed in 1794, and then sent to a number of well-known men of letters for criticism. Then, in 1795, Sun reprinted the book with their comments at the beginning. Chang was not one of those whose criticism was asked, and perhaps this annoyed him. As for the offensive "Mr. So-and-so," there was only one person Chang talked about this way: this "menace to public morality" was the poet Yüan Mei, a wealthy and pleasure-loving old man, who was lionized by high officials and courted by generals and princes. The very thought of this man infuriated Chang.[14]

Perhaps Chang, who had always been difficult with other people, was now getting worse. Hung Liang-chi addressed two poems to Chang, one in 1789, the other in 1794. One speaks of Chang's difficulties with Liang Kuo-chih in 1780, and both dwell on sharp animosity between Chang and Wang Chung. The tone of both these poems is friendly, even though Hung is quite realistic about Chang's difficult temperament. In 1797, however, Hung printed his literary collection, *Chuan-shih-ko Wen-chi,* containing an old letter to Chang, in which Hung had criticized some of Chang's ideas on local history. Chang was stung by having this made public, and complained bitterly about it in a letter to Chu Hsi-keng.[e]

But Chang sometimes could manage to get along with those who might help him. We may observe in Chang's present movements how a needy old scholar, who was difficult but undeniably talented, could be passed around. Chu Kuei had presumably found

---

[e] In 1797 Chang wrote an essay in rejoinder to Hung, "Ti-chih T'ung-pu," picking apart one of Hung's historical works. HY, p. 125.

Chang a temporary job reading examinations. At the same time Chu introduced him to Lieutenant-Governor Ch'en Feng-tzu. In the spring of 1797 Chang wrote a preface for Ch'en's poems (the one in which he suggests that the critic must translate a poem into ordinary speech)./ In the summer Ch'en supplied Chang with a letter of introduction to one Tseng Yü, a salt comptroller in Yang-chou, Kiangsu. Tseng, who enjoyed playing the patron of litera-ture, considered retaining Chang to do a local history of Yang-chou. Chang stayed on, but when he left at the end of the year the project still had not materialized. On his departure there was an exchange of poems between the two. Chang presented Tseng with a long autobiographical poem, "An Expression of My Feelings," and Tseng reciprocated with a poem in praise of his guest, which is at the same time a character sketch:

> Master Chang is so endowed by nature
> That both in virtues and defects he is far from common. . . .
> His appearance is quite unimposing,
> And he is always the object of popular amusement.

Chang was red-nosed, hard of hearing, and constantly suffered from headaches. But Tseng was still able to say,

> Though his senses are only half existent,
> His intelligence is marvelously active.
> Whenever he essays to express himself in writing,
> His discussions of learning go straight to the truth.

And he goes on to praise Chang's scholarly attainments, conclud-ing:

> Thus, if you judge a man by his appearance,
> You will confuse a phoenix with a pheasant.

/ Chang's social obligations in An-ch'ing were responsible for other odd bits of writing. One such curiosity is a preface by Chang for a treatise on geomancy by one of his hosts. Chang, of course, had to defend this occult science, and argued (here he was right) that it was recognized in Classical antiquity. WHL, p. 287b. HY, p. 124. The preface is the piece, "T'ien-yü Ching Chieh-i Hsü."

Tseng closed by thanking his guest for coming and urging him to return when he could.[15]

In the seventh month of 1797, Pi Yüan died in camp in Hupeh. His death ended Chang's hopes for further help; now he would have to salvage what he could of the Hupeh history. It was probably at this time that he edited "for preservation" the incomplete manuscript of the *Hu-pei T'ung-chih* in his possession—a step that must have meant that he had despaired of its ever being printed.[16]

As for the unfinished *Shih-chi K'ao,* Chang still had hope. His friend Hu Ch'ien was working in Hang-chou for Hsieh Ch'i-k'un (1737–1802), lieutenant-governor of Chekiang, on a critical bibliography of classical philology, the *Hsiao-hsüeh K'ao,* conceived, like Chang's work, as a continuation of Chu I-tsun's *Ching-i K'ao.* Hsieh had long been friendly with Hu, who had been helping Chang with the *Shih-chi K'ao* a few years earlier, and also with Ling T'ing-k'an, who had been one of Chang's associates when the project first started in 1787. He must have been well informed about what Chang was attempting, and he could be expected to be interested.[g]

Hu now apparently persuaded his patron Hsieh to take up the *Shih-chi K'ao* as soon as the *Hsiao-hsüeh K'ao* was finished. Probably Juan Yüan and Chu Kuei (whom Chang consulted) lent at least moral support to this plan. And undoubtedly this is why Chang abandoned the prospect of a local history of Yang-chou and left Tseng Yü at the end of 1797. Thus in the summer of 1798 Chang found himself once again an editor in charge of an office of compilation. His associates included Hu Ch'ien once more, Ch'ien Ta-chao (1744–1813, specialist in Han history and brother of Ch'ien Ta-hsin), and several others. Chang collected the *Shih-chi K'ao* manuscripts from Pi Yüan's home in Kiangsu, taking

---

[g] HY, pp. 124, 132, 139. Lo Ping-mien, "*Shih-chi K'ao* Hsiu-tsuan ti T'an-t'ao" ("A Study on the Compilation of the *Shih-chi K'ao*"), Part I, *Hsin-Ya Hsüeh-pao* VI (Feb. 1964), 383, 390. Hsieh and Ling were both students of the calligrapher and poetry critic Weng Fang-kang (1733–1818). Hu had met Hsieh while working for Weng in 1786.

them to his new patron. The group set to work on the historical bibliography of the Ming Dynasty during the summer and fall. Perhaps now, at last, the great work could be finished and published.[17]

But Chang Hsüeh-ch'eng was always his own worst enemy. The disdainful and unbending historian of Wu-ch'ang had not changed. His inevitable personal difficulties with those around him were aggravated this time by a conviction that the approach the others wanted to use was too philological. But Hsieh Ch'i-k'un, unlike Pi Yüan, seems to have taken a close and continuing interest in what was going on. We have noted that Chang's friendship with two other early *Shih-chi K'ao* collaborators had turned sour. Both Hung Liang-chi and Sun Hsing-yen were friends of Hsieh, and he began to turn to them for advice, which often turned out to be strongly at variance with what Chang wished to do. Chang was boxed in, and soon saw his editorship becoming purely nominal. Furthermore, Chang's rancor against Yüan Mei had gone beyond sinister remarks in his letters. He was now writing uninhibited diatribes against the old poet, and one can only imagine how he must have been talking. But Hsieh had been friendly with Yüan too; and as Chang's obsession began to be apparent to him he could hardly have been pleased.[18]

Even worse, there was talk that Chang, by removing the *Shih-chi K'ao* manuscripts from Pi Yüan's house, had fraudulently taken possession of a work that rightfully should be credited to a dead man in order to ingratiate himself with a new patron. The firmest of Chang's relationships began to dissolve in this poisonous atmosphere. Working on a biography of Shao Chin-han, Chang asked Shao's second son, Shao Ping-hua, to make available to him some of Shao's unpublished manuscripts. The son became evasive; Chang persisted; the son stopped answering letters. Chang then heard that Ping-hua was spreading the *Shih-chi K'ao* innuendo, professing a fear that Chang wanted to "steal" his late father's papers also, and use them to advance himself further with the lieutenant-governor. Chang was aghast, and seems at once to have suspected that Sun and Hung were whispering in the young Shao's ear.[19]

Finding Hsieh turning against him and his situation becoming progressively more impossible, Chang gave up. Realizing that he would probably never finish his work, he apparently at this time prepared a long explanation of its guiding principles ("Shih-k'ao Shih-li"), which with the table of contents is all that is now known to exist.[h] With the coming of winter Chang was again moving about, making another visit to Tseng Yü the salt comptroller.[20]

Chang was sixty, and he was not to live to a great age. We see him nearing his end, unsuccessfully trying to finish, put in order, and preserve what he had been able to accomplish, alienating the very people who might help him. But he did not, in his last years, fade gradually into oblivion; on the contrary, his life came to a close in a burst of literary fireworks.

His lifelong polemic temper now broke all bounds. He had met Wang Chung in 1772, and for a number of years had thought highly of him. But for some reason his impression changed abruptly when he encountered Wang again in Wu-ch'ang, and an antipathy between the two had existed since 1790. In 1792 Wang's *Shu Hsüeh* (*An Account of Learning*) had been published, a work that exhibited some daring departures from orthodox scholarship. In 1798, four years after Wang's death, Chang attacked him in two essays. In "Writing Must Have a Basis" ("Li-yen Yu Pen"),

---

[h] This dating of the "Shih-k'ao Shih-li" is my conjecture. Chang complained about Shao Ping-hua's charges against himself in a letter to Chu Hsi-keng in 1799. This matter is clearly reflected in the "Shih-k'ao Shih-li." In it, Chang does not claim credit for himself for the work already done on the *Shih-chi K'ao*. He states very carefully that he had intended to write a continuation of Chu I-tsun's *Ching-i K'ao*, but when he discovered that Pi was already working on one, he discarded his own plans. But when Pi died, Chang wrote, "his work was not finished, and since it was truly a work whose loss would deprive literature of a classic, I went to his house and sought and obtained what was left. I have revised the scheme of organization, relying partly on the original text but adding embellishments until I was satisfied. I would not presume to conceal the creative labors of my predecessor." This statement contradicts what Chang himself had said of the *Shih-chi K'ao* in letters over the past ten years. It is clear, under the circumstances, why Chang made it; but at least one modern student of Chang has taken it at face value (cf. Fu Chen-lun, "Chang Hsüeh-ch'eng *Shih-chi K'ao* T'i-li chih P'ing-lun," *Pei-Ta T'u-shu-pu Yüeh-k'an,* 1.1 (1929), 19–33, especially p. 20).

he criticizes the *Shu Hsüeh* on the grounds that it is an unorganized mass of philology and conventional occasional writing, without order or principle. Chang declared that Wang, while not lacking ability, "unfortunately has an overdose of keen perception and not enough real understanding. He forces himself to discuss learning without knowing how to make use of his natural abilities, and he gets at what only appears to be the truth, never the real truth."[21]

Such criticisms are not altogether unreasonable. Wang's book is in fact only a collection of pieces. The book for which Wang's title would have been appropriate was a book he was never able to write, though he did have the imagination to conceive it. It was actually to have been a speculative intellectual history, following a conception almost identical with Chang's own. One of Wang's sons has preserved an outline of the unwritten book, and a biographer offers a glimpse of its guiding idea:

Ancient learning was kept in government offices. Men occupied these offices from generation to generation, and so the officials perpetuated this learning. But once the officials failed to keep up their work, then specialized traditions of learning deteriorated.

It is strange and rather sad that Chang, with all of his anxieties over "the difficulty of being understood," should have had little but disparagement for a man who was intellectually so close to himself.[22]

The second essay, "Criticisms of the *Shu-hsüeh*" ("*Shu-hsüeh* Po-wen"), contains some arguments that have merit, but it is, on the whole, intolerantly conservative. For showing measured sympathy and objectivity toward the ancient Mohists, Wang is denounced as "fond of extravagant talk." Another criticism is rather curious. Wang had tried to do something with the account, in the *Rituals of Chou*, of the ancient officer of marriage (*mei-shih*), who "orders young men and women to be brought together in the second month of spring and does not prohibit irregular unions" —obviously a rather difficult text. Wang had it meaning that the officer "orders a census of young men and women," explaining that the usual prohibitions would be suspended to punish parents, if they failed to arrange marriages for their sons and daughters at the proper age. Chang found this cautious rationalization offensive, however, and tried to clean up the passage with a laborious interpretation of his own.[i] But Chang's "Criticisms" gave greatest space to an essay by Wang on modern marriage customs. In his essay, Wang had urged that a wife's obligation of lifelong loyalty to her husband does not begin until actual marriage (i.e., that the initial exchange of betrothal presents is not binding). To this Chang indignantly charges that Wang would "eliminate the distinction between Po I and the robber Chih."[j]

But these criticisms seem tame compared to the fury Chang poured upon Yüan Mei, perhaps the most interesting of his contemporaries. Yüan was one of the most successful literary men of his time. Actually a learned man with serious interests in history, he is better known as a poet-critic who practiced his belief that an important function of poetry is simply to delight the heart, and that the poet should freely express his emotions. Yüan passed high in the examinations (his model *pa-ku* essays enjoyed a brisk market), and retired early to the life of ease that his literary ability placed within his reach; and if his pleasures were not always sanctioned by Neo-Confucian strictness, he enjoyed them with quiet dignity. He was author of a witty cookbook and a book of entertaining ghost stories. He taught poetry writing, and among his students (this was thought especially outrageous) were a fair number of talented ladies. Yüan was from Chekiang, and a full generation older than Chang. But he had left his roots behind and settled

---

[i] HY, pp. 116–17. *I-shu,* 7.4a–5a. This curious statement in the *Chou Li* must have caused proper Confucians considerable embarrassment, and various attempts were made to patch up matters by emending the text (cf. Édouard Biot, tr., *Le Tcheou-li ou Rites des Tcheou,* Vol. I, Paris, 1851, pp. 307–8).

[j] Wang's essay is quoted in part in HY, p. 117. Wang cites two unhappy cases of early betrothal, in which the prospective grooms turned out to be less than desirable. In each case the girl insisted on going through with the agreement. Both marriages ended in tragedy. Interestingly, the first of Wang's two cases was the marriage of Yüan Mei's younger sister. The whole sad affair is described by Arthur Waley, *Yüan Mei: Eighteenth Century Chinese Poet* (London, 1956), pp. 36–38.

in Nanking, where he died early in 1798. Chang, in a collection of notes of that date, took note of his demise as follows:

There has lately been a shameless fool who prided himself on his licentiousness, poisoned the minds of young men and women, and deluded everyone by engaging actors and putting on plays about heroes and fair ladies. South of the Yangtze, many women from important families were lured by him; he enhanced his reputation by soliciting their verse and printing their compositions. He ceased to have any regard for the distinction between men and women, practically to the point of forgetting their physical sex![23]

Chang followed this outburst with an essay criticizing Yüan, which he presented to Chu Kuei. It contained an exposé of Yüan's account of a conversation between himself and Chu; Chang asserted the conversation could never have taken place, and that Yüan had fabricated his story by plagiarizing other writers.[24] There are several other undated writings attacking Yüan in Chang's collected works; it is not unlikely that they belong to this year.[k] No evaluation of Chang's character as an old man can be complete without taking into some sort of consideration the following piece of raillery from his postscript to the printing of Yüan's *Poetry Talks (Sui-yüan Shih-hua)*:

He [Yüan] neglects the *Changes*, the *History*, the *Rites*, the *Music*, the *Spring and Autumn*, and values only the Mao tradition of the *Odes*; and even in that work he ignores the ceremonial odes [*ya* and *sung*] and extols the popular songs [*kuo-feng*]. And among them he disregards those that bear on government and popular customs, and esteems only those that deal with love between the sexes. And with regard to these poems, he criticizes the interpretation that the poets were writing satire and proposes that they are actually expressions of men's and women's own lustful feelings; he carries this to the point of holding that references in them to the picking of orchids and the giving of peonies don't have any important significance. And he points

---

[k] "Fu Hsüeh," on studies for women; "Fu Hsüeh P'ien Shu-hou," a comment on the first essay; "Shih-hua"; "Shu Fang-k'e Shih-hua Hou"; and "T'i Sui-yuan Shih-hua." The last three are all directly or indirectly concerned with the *Sui-yuan Shih-hua*, Yüan's critical study of poetry. All five are in the "inner series" of the *Wen-shih T'ung-i* in the Chia-yeh-t'ang edition.

out that Confucius copied these poems into the *Odes* to refute the theory that poetry must have serious relevance.[1] In the past when people of low mind have advanced evil theories, they have merely made forced interpretations of doubtful statements in the ancients to their own advantage; but there has never been anyone who, in broad daylight and beneath the warming sun, has dared to go to this extreme in denying the precedence of the Classics, doing away with sanctity and law, and indulging in such perverse, depraved, obscene, and licentious ideas!"[25]

"The picking of orchids and the giving of peonies," it must be explained, are symbolic gestures between lovers in the "Songs of Cheng." One can hardly deny a certain vigor in this criticism; Chang's ability as a stylist was if anything enhanced by the violence of his prejudices. But it is one of the strangest anomalies of Chang's old age that such heated denunciation could follow so closely the counsel of tolerance in "Virtue in the Literary Man."

Chang is probably as famous in China for his criticism of Yüan Mei as for anything he has written. And modern opinion, inevitably, sides strongly with Yüan. As a Classic the *Odes* makes us impatient; we want to read it the way Yüan did. His encouraging women to write and publish wins our sympathy at once, as does his interest in drama. And so Chang seems to us exposed at last as a bigot, caught helplessly, for all of his intellect, in the toils of an outmoded conservative view of life. But explanations can never be quite as simple as this. And some defense of Chang is not necessarily impossible.

Chang claimed repeatedly that Yüan was a braggart and a liar.

[1] Chang was not just upset about Yüan's "libertine" views. His ire was directed specifically at Yüan's thesis that a poet should not try for "relevance (*kuan-hsi*) in his verse-making. Yüan's actual position is that it is disastrous for the poet consciously to try to make his writing relevant, i.e., to make it "illustrate the *tao*," for the result will be that each writer will "form his own subjective conception of the *tao*," without really getting to the truth. See Ku Yüan-hsiang, Sui-yüan *Shih-shuo ti Yen-chiu* (*A Study of Yüan Mei's Theory of Poetry*), Shanghai, 1936, pp. 156–57, quoting "A Second Letter to a Friend on Literature." (See *Hsiao-ts'ang Shan-fang Wen-chi,* 19.16b–18a.) The matter is curious because, like a number of other things in Yüan, this could almost have been said by Chang himself.

Yüan did like to brag. He was constantly telling stories that showed himself to great advantage, and he did occasionally embellish the facts.*ᵐ* We are amused by this, but Chang wasn't. Nor was he amused by other aspects of Yüan's character. In the essay Chang gave to Chu Kuei, he mentions that he once happened to pick up a volume of Yüan's letters that were for sale. The contents were disgusting: "judgments of feminine beauty, appraisals of concubines for other men, sly flattery, accounts of tasting food for men of eminence, procuring, retrieving concubines who had run away," and more. We need not doubt this; the letters exist.[26] In his *Poetry Talks,* complains Chang, Yüan "even goes so far as to encourage perversion, saying that since the *Rituals* honor a virtuous woman but do not praise a chaste man, there should be no objection to taking a beautiful man as a concubine." It is not surprising to find Yüan saying this, when we consider his social environment; this was the way he and his peers behaved. But Chang was indignant: "This is just the bawling of an animal! Yet he boldly puts it in his *Poetry Talks!* The man ought to be executed and his book burnt!"[27] Perhaps we may not all object so strongly; but it is at least not absurd that Chang did.

Chang wrote an essay arguing that a girl's education should be chiefly concerned with decorum and the molding of character; he did not think she should be encouraged to write verse. Yüan had "advanced" ideas about women: it was all right for them to write

---

ᵐ One possible case of this is Yüan's claim of friendship with the poet T'ung Yü (discussed by Waley, pp. 150–51). Yüan claimed that T'ung, who was critical of most poets, was highly impressed with Yüan's own work. According to Yüan, T'ung painted a picture of a plum branch on his deathbed and inscribed on it a poem to Yüan, asking him to write a preface for his poems. Subsequently, Yüan says, he did write the preface and edit T'ung's collected works. Chang angrily claimed (in his comment on Yüan's *Poetry Talks*) that this was a brazen lie; T'ung was not intolerant of others' poetry, but he had no use for Yüan and his kind. T'ung, it should be noted, was from K'uai-chi, and according to one account (*Wen-hsien Cheng-ts'un Lu*; see *I-shu,* "fu-lu," p. 4a), Chang studied under him when young. WHL (265b–266a) cites a note by Chou Tso-jen that seems to support Chang's opinion. It does seem that T'ung and Yüan were friendly, but the collection Yüan claims to have edited does not exist, and Yüan was even confused as to the identity of T'ung's native place.

poetry, and all right for them to study with a man. But Yüan also had views about women that were not as enlightened as we might expect: "A wife," he wrote, "must be loyal to her husband until death, but it is all right for a man to have concubines. Why? This was the ancient sage kings' way of sustaining the *yang* and restraining the *yin*. Dogs and pigs may not eat man's food, but man may eat dogs and pigs. Why? This was the ancient sage kings' way of honoring the pure and dishonoring the coarse."[28] Chang, too, took it for granted that the world is a man's world, but at least he respected women. Consider his Yung-ch'ing biographies. Consider his opinion (to a friend in 1797) that even singing girls—who sometimes deserve praise for their character—should be represented in historical anthologies of poetry, if the historian is to be fair to all.[n]

Chang also had strictly intellectual objections to Yüan. In what Chang considered a piece of flippant metaphysics, Yüan had said that literary art is to be identified with the *tao*; in contrast, philology (*k'ao-chü*) was matter (*ch'i*). But really, said Chang, both are matter, while the *tao* is the reason one uses them.[29] Yüan, who had no gift for philology, was constantly criticizing it (and was in turn criticized for this by his friends); but this was not what bothered Chang. Yüan, he thought, had no true conception of art. Art itself is not the *tao*. The ideal in literary art, Chang argued (following Li Po) is "purity and genuineness" (*ch'ing chen*). The writer who is faithful to this ideal gains inner understanding through learning—Chang must mean the word in a partly moral sense—and then expresses his attitude in poetry or prose without thought of writing skillfully. When he does this, even one who devotes all his efforts to style will not be able to equal him. Yüan,

---

[n] WHL, 286a. On biographies of women in histories, Chang held that any woman whose life was worthy of remembrance should be included (and not just widows who don't remarry). Further, he maintained that their own names should be given, and not just their husbands' names. In one case, he recommended including a biography for a prostitute who saved the city of Ta-ming, in the late Ming Dynasty, by surrendering herself to besieging rebels. See Chu Shih-chia, pp. 391–92, and *I-shu*, 18.52b–53b.

Chang thinks, is an enemy of learning and of self-cultivation; he just gives vent to his own vulgar feelings. Yüan's inner substance (*chih*) is already dead, so there is nothing for his art (*wen*) to cling to. "He just tries busily to excel in verbal skill. This is like a cockatoo or a chimpanzee imitating human speech."[30]

In part, I think, Chang's anger at Yüan is the anger of a man watching another he cannot reach. Yüan was successful; his company was sought after. Pi Yüan was his good friend. Chang was awkward; he couldn't write poetry, and was embarrassed and defensive about it. Chang's attitude, however, was caused by more than petty jealousy. Yüan, he felt, was a shameless flatterer. "He is always meeting persons of power and importance and ingratiating himself with those of high reputation and eminence."[31] Yüan was indeed "always meeting persons of power and importance." He was on intimate terms with some of the highest officials and generals in the empire, and they were not a savory lot. The notorious Ho-shen exchanged poems with him. Ho-shen's brother Ho-lin and General Fu-k'ang-an, a member of Ho-shen's inner political circle, were both admirers of Yüan. Sun Shih-i, another figure in this corrupt clique, was his patron. Another less august member of this company was General Hui-ling, who had derailed Chang's Hupeh history in 1794.[32] How Chang may have fitted these things together we can only guess.

In any case, history was to give Chang a much more suitable object for his indignation than Yüan Mei. In the first month of 1799, the senile Emperor Kao-tsung died, and Emperor Jen-tsung, who had bided his time during his father's three-year "retirement," immediately arrested the latter's favorite, Ho-shen, forced him to commit suicide, and confiscated his great wealth. Steps were taken to halt corruption: the Emperor forbade the practice of giving gifts to himself, and it is said that with this the market price of pearls and jade plummeted. There was an open invitation for denunciations of the fallen chief minister.[33]

The aged Chang, who in the course of his life had not been guilty of even the most innocent political act, now sent off numer-

ous letters to the highest officials offering lengthy advice on matters of state.⁰ In a "letter to Those in Charge of the Government, on
the Problems of the Present Time," he analyzed the state of the
country with clarity:

The most important problems at present are these: first, the problem of
rebels and bandits; second, the problem of treasury deficiencies; and
third, the problem of the management of the civil service [i.e., of official
corruption] ... Although the problems are divisible into three, they
are essentially one. Deficiencies and rebellion are related in that they
both originate from laxity in the management of the civil service."

And what was the cause of this deterioration in the civil service?
The cause, said Chang, was Ho-shen, for under his influence bribery and corruption had become universal:

Public funds have flowed from the treasuries until now they are bone
dry; and the cause of all this is as plain as the nose on your face. From
1780 through 1798, Ho-shen dominated the government, and for almost
thirty years, officials high and low have covered up for one another, and
have thought only of grasping for bribes and of personal gain. At first
they nibbled away like worms, gradually taking more and more until
they were gulping like whales. In the beginning, their embezzlements
could be reckoned in hundreds and thousands of taels, but presently
nothing less than ten thousand would attract notice. Soon amounts ran
to scores of thousands, then to hundreds of thousands, and then to mil-
lions.... High officials, corrupted by avarice and accustomed to extravagance, came to regard a present of ten thousand pieces of silver as
if it were no more than a casual present of a box of food.

To force ordinary officials to make good these treasury deficiencies is not the answer. They cannot cope with this situation. Realizing the extent of the deficits, they will only try to juggle accounts,
but this just leads to more corruption. Pressure on them will
merely drive them to plundering the people. But rebellion cannot
be dealt with until the rebel leaders have been deprived of their
main excuse, that "officials have forced the people to rebel." But

⁰ A number of these letters were addressed to Wang Chieh, who had been one of
Chang's examiners in 1778. Wang was at this time the senior member of the Grand
Secretariat.

the lost money must have gone somewhere, and the guilty ones should be discovered and punished:

These are the persons who have gnawed away at the state, distressed the people, and instigated the present revolts.... What they have stuffed their greedy purses with are the public funds and the people's substance. Are they to be allowed to bequeath these injuries to others, while their families and descendants remain prosperous?

Chang then analyzed the state of corruption that developed at the end of the K'ang-hsi period and the steps taken to meet it by the Yung-cheng Emperor Shih-tsung. Imperial economy set an example to the officials, and the property of the worst offenders was confiscated. If the new Emperor will only follow this example, he urged, the treasuries will be filled and the civil service reformed; it will be easy, then, to end rebellion, once its cause has been removed.[34]

Kao-tsung had consciously compared his reign to Kang-hsi, and it was natural for Chang to do the same, in hopes that history would repeat itself. Chang's advice (which did correspond to the policy that Jen-tsung, in a half-hearted way, actually followed) was based on a typically conservative analysis of the situation: evil in the state is at root a moral problem. Its manifestations are all interrelated; its solution is to be found in economy, punishment, example, and an administrative act that will correct the source of the difficulty. Still, it is an honest piece of thinking and a credit to its author's good sense. There is subtle irony in Chang's call for the confiscation of the property of implicated officials, for among the first to be affected by such action was the family of his late patron Pi Yüan.[p]

Once stimulated to public utterance by his indignation against Ho-shen, Chang expressed himself on other matters with considerable originality. He recommended that the Censorate be made responsible for studying national finances and economic condi-

[p] Arthur Waley (pp. 96–97) has said of Chang's patron that "the means by which Pi Yüan accumulated his fortune were not always very scrupulous, but it cannot be denied that he put it to good use not only in helping impoverished friends to exist but also in paying for the printing of their works."

tions, and for evaluating proposals relative to political economy. He also suggested recasting the examination system in order to stimulate solid learning (*shih hsüeh*): the lowest examinations would deal with the meaning of classical texts; those for the degree of *chü-jen* would allow a choice of specialties in either classical exegesis or poetry; and the metropolitan examinations would return to something like the T'ang system—examinees would have a choice of such specialties as the classical books of ritual, the commentaries to the *Spring and Autumn,* the Three Histories (*Shih-chi, Han Shu, Han Chi*), mathematics, law, or the *hui-tien.* There would be a standard program of study in these special fields, and examinations would be given at the end of three or five years. Candidates would still have the option of proceeding according to the old system if they wished.[35] In making these revolutionary proposals, Chang no doubt recalled his own bitter experience with a system that demanded talents he did not have or did not care to cultivate. Suggestions of this sort had been made by others, too. Ku Yen-wu had analyzed the examination system in his *Jih Chih Lu,* and had suggested that a return to the T'ang system of special examinations in history would produce men "versed in the essence of government," which would "surely be of advantage to the state." Even Chu Hsi had suggested making the examinations less literary and more specialized, and had urged that history, geography and political institutions should be important subjects.[36] Chang, however, believed strongly that scholarship, if it is to be worth anything, must be specialized, that it must be something the scholar has a special aptitude for, and that the work of the scholar and writer must be of practical use to the state. His suggestions for the reform of the examination system were a final and logical outcome of these ideas.

We know little of the last two years of Chang's life, except that he was poor and in failing health. In 1800 he wrote his biography for Shao Chin-han, and said in it, "My eyes are now failing, and I cannot write; my sickness daily grows worse, and I fear that I shall not remain long in this world. . . . I have dictated the substance of this, asking my son I-hsüan to write it."[37] Possibly in the same way he wrote one of the last of the essays to go into the *Wen-shih T'ung-i*—the "Intellectual Tradition of Eastern Che-kiang" ("Che-tung Hsüeh-shu"). In this statement he discussed the position of the Eastern Chekiang historical school in Ch'ing scholarship, tracing its beginnings through Wang Yang-ming back to Chekiang philosophers of the Sung. It was in this tradition, Chang now saw, that he himself stood. In taking this stand, he stated, for the last time, his view of history and the Classics. Men of antiquity recognized history, not Classics. They were concerned with man and his world, and not with empty talk about ideas. "The learning of Eastern Chekiang, when asking about 'human nature' and 'fate,' always investigated history. This is the reason for its greatness."[38] Sometime during 1801 he turned over the drafts of his writings to a friend, Wang Tsung-yen of Hsiao-shan, and asked him to edit them. In the eleventh month of that year he died.[39]

10. Late Praise

A century hence, we too will be men of old. Let us therefore
put ourselves in their place. How then will it fare with us?

—Ten Criticisms of Sun Hsing-yen ... 1797

"When Chang Hsüeh-ch'eng was young," writes one biographer,
"he was afflicted with an ulcer in his nose. In middle years his hearing was impaired. And in old age he was plagued with headaches
and blindness in his right eye.... At the end of his life both poverty and sickness assailed him. Truly he had the ill fortune of the
literary man at its worst!"[a] Certainly Chang was often not happy,
and sometimes miserable. But he did write, and there were moments when he knew the elation of achievement. What had he
achieved in his lifetime? What had he done or written that should
make the study of his life and writings worthwhile for us?

From his own point of view, or that of a contemporary at the
beginning of the nineteenth century, Chang's life might have
seemed largely a failure. The economic condition of his family
had not improved since his father's dismissal from office. Chang
himself had attained the *chin-shih* degree, and knew and was
known by virtually all of the outstanding literary men of the
later part of the eighteenth century. But his relationships with
them ranged from gradually cooling friendship to open enmity.
And of his sons, apparently only one, Chang I-hsüan, succeeded in
the examinations, and he went no further than the degree of *chü-
jen*. A pitiful letter written by Chang I-hsüan when he was an old
man of more than seventy to Chang Hsüeh-ch'eng's friend Chu

---

[a] Shen Yüan-t'ai, in *Pei-chuan Chi Pu* (WHL, p. 287b). According to Hung Liang-
chi, Chang was deaf in his left ear. HY, p. 36.

Hsi-keng revealed that for years he had been unemployed and extremely poor, and had recently gone blind.[b] Chang's fourth son, Hua-lien, was a perpetual ne'er-do-well, who ran off with his father's original manuscripts. The second son, Hua-fu, fared better; his father had had Wang Hui-tsu give him a legal training, and he was employed as secretary in the office of the governor of Honan. While in that position, Hua-fu had printed in 1832–33 what is in effect the first edition of Chang's *Wen-shih T'ung-i* and *Chiao-ch'ou T'ung-i.*[1]

But this was already more than thirty years after Chang's death, and it was not until 1851, when Wu Ch'ung-yüeh (1810–63) included the two works in his *Yüeh-ya-t'ang Ts'ung-shu,* that Chang's essays gained anything like a wide circulation.[2] Most of his major works—the *Shih-chi K'ao,* the *Hu-pei T'ung-chih,* and various other local histories—remained unprinted and were partly or wholly lost. Most of Chang's letters, biographies, and essays on books remained unavailable until 1922. This delay in the appearance of Chang's works cannot be ascribed simply to the accident of his sons' fortunes, for after the disastrous robbery of 1781, Chang made a point of preparing multiple copies of all he wrote. Furthermore, he had a small group of admirers, each of whom had copies of various parts of his writings; of these, there were in fact a half dozen or more manuscript traditions.[3]

The inescapable conclusion is that the scholarly world was on the whole quite indifferent to Chang's work. It is true, apparently, that Juan Yüan (whom Chang knew personally) showed some interest in his essays on the Classics; and the scholar and philosopher Chiao Hsün (1763–1820) expressed admiration for the *Wen-shih T'ung-i.*[c] But Chiao, in praising him, wrote his name incorrectly, and it seems unlikely that either Juan or Chiao had any

[b] The letter is not dated, but its contents indicate that it was written in late 1830 or early 1831 (see *I-shu,* "fu-lu," 15a).

[c] *I-shu,* "fu-lu," 9b. There is somewhat dubious evidence that Juan Yüan or one of his family printed a group of Chang's essays under the title *Wen-shih Pien-su T'ung-i.* See Chang Shu-tsu, *"Wen-shih T'ung-i* Pan-pen K'ao" ("A Study of Edi-

conception of what Chang was trying to say. Chang, for his part, often showed an equal indifference to what others thought of him. His Peking friend Tseng Shen once advised him—obviously in vain—to think and act the way most people did. Chang wrote his sons that his interests were not those of others, "and so other educated men of my time have wholly neglected me and do not talk about me at all; but in my heart I have never regretted this." At a deeper level of consciousness Chang did regret it. But he saw his situation clearly. He had no disciples, he told his sons, to carry on his ideas after his death. To Chu Hsi-keng he confided that he knew it would take a century for him to be appreciated.[4]

Chang's intellectual views were not attractive to nineteenth-century scholars. He had, indeed, a philological viewpoint, in that his instinctive approach to a statement or a piece of writing was to explain it in terms of its background or its history; and he was, as much as anyone in his time, at least openly committed to solid learning and openly opposed to mere philosophical speculation. But Chang's notion of explaining something in terms of historical patterns did not interest most intellectuals of the Ch'ing. It was not until the end of the nineteenth century that this sort of interest in historical change reappeared in strength, and with it the beginnings of a new interest in Chang's ideas. In a more practical sphere, the technique and form of compiling local histories, Chang did have some influence; and his essay, "Studies for Women" ("Fu Hsüeh"), enjoyed a success that contrasted sharply with the rest of his work. It was printed separately in a number of anthologies and *ts'ung-shu* before the rest of his work appeared. This success at least brings out an important fact: that Chang's prejudices were widely shared. Wang Hui-tsu defended Chang's attitude toward Yüan Mei, and indeed some of Yüan's severest critics (it is claimed) were among his own students.[5] But it is a sad commentary on Chang's popularity that an essay such as the "Fu Hsüeh," reflecting the accentuated social prejudices of his last years, should have found the readiest acceptance.

Chang's reputation is no longer in this precarious condition; in China and Japan he is now considered one of the most important writers on the subjects of historiography and bibliographical method in recent centuries. This importance, to be sure, is not easily transposed from the context of traditional Chinese scholarship to that of contemporary thought. But Chang has also begun to be noticed for his insights about the historical past, and even for his moral philosophy. It is evident that he can be interesting in many different ways to modern students. How interesting, and in what ways? Let us try to look at Chang's thought in both historical and philosophical perspective.

Chang has an obvious value for the student of Chinese history. His intellectual and social world, in so many ways remote from our own, is part of the immediate historical background of modern China. Chang lived at a critical point in Chinese history, when Manchu power had reached its peak and was beginning to recede, and when economic developments were subjecting both the Confucian literati and the common people to increasing pressure. Chang was sensitive to this situation, and expressed in his writing the social prejudices and political attitudes of the educated class in reaction to such matters as the literary inquisition and the corruption of Ho-shen. The record of his intercourse with other literary men and his criticisms of them (though they are often unfair) are an invaluable aid in reconstructing the intellectual history of the eighteenth century.

But may we only draw historical inferences from Chang? Can we not locate Chang himself in the scene, as belonging to some identifiable group or current, and not merely as giving depth to our historical perspective? If we try, we will find Chang exasperating.

Chang was impatient with "search for evidence" scholarship as a way of life, and his opposition was often biting. But he thought of it as a fad, not a school; his opposition was qualified with respect, and it left open to him a variety of alternative positions. In defining his own alternative he saw himself as a bold, speculative type of thinker rather than a cautious cultivator of small details, and he recognized in this an affinity between himself and Wang Yang-ming. But the affinity was psychological not scholastic. Wang's thought influenced Chang deeply: it shaped his picture of antiquity and his ethical and literary ideals; but the influence was derivative and indirect, not the influence of master on follower. Whenever Chang compares the two rival schools of Neo-Confucian philosophy, he is careful to give first honors to Chu Hsi.

Then shall we say that Chang was a member and champion of the Chu Hsi "school"? We cannot. If we can speak of a Chu Hsi school in the early and middle Ch'ing, we must identify it with the stern moralism, the obsession with psychological self-purification of such men as Chang Po-hsing and Lu Shih-i. Chang does not deny value to this type of thinking; in fact he hardly notices it. He was a moral conservative, but his own personal philosophy was one of intellectual self-expression. When he discussed Sung philosophy, he was usually critical of what seemed to him its one-sided abstractness.[6] And if we carefully compare Chang's basic philosophical outlook with that of Chu Hsi and Ch'eng I, we see profound differences. Chang's celebrated identification of the Classics as "history" implies a far-reaching modification of the basis of Ch'eng-Chu metaphysics, the dualism of the *tao* and "matter," of principles and things. Wang Hui-tsu unconsciously expressed the common Chu Hsi mode of thought in a piece of advice he offered to professional local-government aides: "When you have time, you should read history; for while the Classics speak of the principles of things, the histories record the actualities."[7] It was just this habitual separation of principles from actualities that Chang, again and again, had pronounced a dangerous confusion. As he said boldly in one letter, a man cannot be said to have genuine "learning" unless he has grasped "the unity of the *tao* and matter" (*tao-*

ch'i ho-i).[8] In this Chang is like Chang Tsai (whom he ignored), like Wang Fu-chih (who was unknown to him), and even like Tai Chen (whom he denounced).

The T'ung-ch'eng literary school in Anhwei has a stronger claim on Chang, however. The school's theoretical sweep, its self-expressive tone, and its cult of "old prose" style in a world of *pa-ku* appealed to restive students of writing; it seems to have become popular in Peking in the 1760's, just at the time Chang was a student there. Chang spent some time in Anhwei as a student, and returned to that area to do his most important philosophical writing. In Hu Ch'ien and Tso Mei he had close friends from T'ung-ch'eng, friends who had studied with Yao Nai and were probably committed to Yao's ideas. Much of Chang's thinking parallels the T'ung-ch'eng viewpoint—his impatience with philology, his loyalty to Chu Hsi, his art-substance analysis of literary value. But Chang's conception of thought, writing, and research as the three basic intellectual ways of life, while also a trademark of T'ung-ch'eng theory, was probably a very widely held idea (Chang himself believed this to be the case).[9] Chang nowhere acknowledges a debt to T'ung-ch'eng writers. He was patronizing toward their esteemed Kuei Yu-kuang. He seems to have been aware of Fang Pao only as a writer of *pa-ku*.[10] He knew and respected Yao Nai, but in a very ordinary way. And in condemning the strident partisans of Chu Hsi he seems to be criticizing a conspicuous T'ung-ch'eng characteristic. In literary matters, Chang himself acknowledged that his major debt was to Chu Yün.

Then (since he says so himself) perhaps Chang belongs to the Eastern Chekiang historical school. There is more to support this claim than the fact that he admired Shao T'ing-ts'ai, and the fact that he grew up and was educated in a family of Shao-hsing literati. There are broad similarities between Chang and Huang Tsung-hsi. Huang, for example, did not doubt the value of scholarship, yet held speculative thought to be both permissible and necessary if a person also engaged in some kind of solid work. Chang similarly justifies his theoretical essays on history by appealing to the fact that he has actually written histories. It was this notion that at least partly liberated Chang from the effects of the general suspicion in his time of "empty words." Huang regarded Sung philosophy and Ming philosophy as each valuable in its own way, and so did Chang. Divergent points of view, Huang thought, all reveal something of the nature of mind, which was for him, as it had been for Wang Yang-ming, of ultimate importance. The *tao* is like the sea, and the various schools of thought like the rivers that flow into it. It was in this way that Huang rationalized his interest in the history of philosophy.[11] Chang's attitude was somewhat different: all types of learning, he held, though incomplete in themselves, are justified because each makes a unique contribution to the understanding of the *tao;* but partisan schools of thought, in breaking up the primal unity of truth in the golden age, and in treating the *tao* as their own private possession, isolate the *tao* from reality and falsify it. But this departure from Huang's liberality is the kind of difference that easily develops within a single tradition.

Both men had a primary interest in history, together with a particular conception of its nature and value: both saw in history the verification of philosophical truth. And both had a very broad conception of the scope of history. Huang assumed that the historian must deal not only with philosophy but also with literature. His enormous *Ming Wen Hai,* a collection of Ming literature which he compiled (along with a now lost collection of Ming historical documents entitled *Ming Shih An*) as source material for the offical history of the Ming, suggests Chang's idea that collections of literature are historical works, which should be compiled to co-exist with and supplement narrative histories.[12] Chang's recommendations for recasting literary collections immediately suggest Huang's manner of handling Sung, Yüan, and Ming philosophers in his *hsüeh-an.*

Chang could easily have derived these features of his thinking from Huang, but there is no evidence that he did. If similarities are to argue for derivation, we may as easily argue that Chang was a late member of the north Chinese "school" of Yen Yüan and Li Kung, the so-called seventeenth-century pragmatists. Chang like Yen believed that empty talk about human nature and fate should be shunned in favor of useful work and experience, and that one should specialize in something one can pursue effectively. Where Chang stressed that in antiquity government and learning were one, Yen himself, arguing for the same values, had insisted that "for the sages, education and government had the same end."[d] There may, indeed, be tenuous personal connections. And with the Chekiang background the connections are more than tenuous. But they serve to establish a climate of opinion, not an esoteric filiation of ideas.

Chang's interest in Huang came late, after his chief writing was done. The ideas they share may well be Chekiang common stock (one can imagine many an evening's conversation with Shao Chin-han, another "member" of this "school"), but they do not appear to be historically traceable. If Chang were a member of such a school, one would expect him to be constantly quoting Huang and his philosopher-master Liu Tsung-chou, and frequently prais-ing the historians of the Wan family and Ch'üan Tsu-wang. In-stead, he respects Liu and Huang but usually leaves them alone; he virtually ignores the Wans, and he criticizes Ch'üan. To talk of an "Eastern Chekiang School" as including Chang Hsüeh-ch'eng is to fall into Chang's own historical-essentialist manner of speaking. Influence there may be, but Chang's self-identification with a special Chekiang tradition was a lifetime's afterthought.

Chang in short was his own man. He thought of himself as un-classifiable, even indescribable. He was constantly afraid of seem-ing to be a merely derivative thinker. He decried partisanship, and he praised writers who read widely, were receptive to many in-

---

[d] Yen Yüan, *Ts'un Hsüeh (On Learning)*, *Chi-fu Ts'ung-shu* edition, 1.1a. Ch'ien Mu (p. 401) points out that Chang warmly praises the writings and opinions of Fei Tzu-heng (b. 1664, son of the Szechwan philosopher Fei Mi, *ECCP*, p. 240) in his "Comment on the *Kuan-tao-t'ang Wen-chi*," *I-shu*, 8.19a–24a. Ch'ien notes that the younger Fei exchanged letters on philosophy with Li Kung.

fluences, and reached their own individual syntheses. This is what Chang himself set out to do, and this is what he did.

But a writer who "creates his own school," Chang recognized, may end without followers. This was indeed Chang's immediate fate. His work was not completely ignored, however; the *Shih-chi K'ao* did have a potentiality for interesting philologists. Notwithstanding Chang's anti-philological, holistic, and essentialist way of doing bibliography, his programs for examining a multitude of sources and digging lost works out of other texts were bound to be appreciated by philologists. And in fact another attempt was made to finish the *Shih-chi K'ao*. After Chang's death, a certain P'an Hsi-en (*chin-shih* of 1811, d. 1868) obtained the manuscripts, perhaps through Ling T'ing-k'an, who had been his teacher. In 1846, P'an was director general of the Yellow River and the Grand Canal for Kiangsu, and with this position was able to finance a continuation of the compilation. But the times were unsettled. P'an was dismissed and work again stopped.[13]

Shortly after this, the devastating T'ai-p'ing Rebellion inundated the Yangtze Valley from Hupeh to the sea, covering the part of China in which Chang had spent his most productive years. It is probable that this was the immediate cause of the loss of much of his unpublished writing. The *Shih-chi K'ao* is probably gone; and the local histories of Ho-chou, Po-chou, and Hupeh province now exist only in the fragments Chang himself saved. All of the smaller local Hupeh histories in which he had had a hand did survive, though there are only one or two known copies of the histories of T'ien-men, Ma-ch'eng, and Kuang-chi districts.[e] Chang's total contribution to the historiography of Hupeh was a massive one. But until recently it has gone unrecognized. The smaller histories are not in his name, and the 1921 edition of the *Hu-pei T'ung-chih* does not even mention Chang among earlier historians who have dealt with the province.[14]

---

[e] The history of Ch'ang-te was not published but is cited as a manuscript in the first printed edition of a history of that locality in 1813. It was presumably used by the compilers. (Chu Shih-chia, pp. 152–56.)

Nevertheless, Chang's ideas about local-history writing were sometimes noticed and used. A number of later local histories in Chekiang show his influence. Many scholars (even Hung Liang-chi and Sun Hsing-yen) praised his idea of including discussions of the works of earlier historians of the locality in his histories. His genealogical charts and, especially, his historical maps in two colors were much imitated. Hsieh Ch'i-k'un became governor of Kwang-si in 1799, and commissioned a general history of the province. Chang's Hupeh history was used as a model, no doubt because the Kwangsi history was really the work of Chang's former associate Hu Ch'ien. And the Kwangsi history in turn influenced others, notably the histories of Kwangtung and Kiangsi later in the nineteenth century.[15]

More important, if less tangible, were the faint beginnings of an influence of Chang's philosophical thought in the nineteenth century. Chang talked freely about his speculations while he lived, and passed his essays around; they were known by some, at least. And there were several manuscripts of his writings in Chekiang. Kung Tzu-chen (1792–1841) of Hang-chou was only a child when Chang was spending his last years in Hang-chou and Shao-hsing. But it is evident that elements of Chang's thinking found their way into the young man's mind. In 1814, at the age of twenty-two, Kung was involved in a history of Hui-chou in Anhwei. Like Chang as a young man, he wrote an advisory essay, stressing (as Chang had) that a prefectural history should be a source of material for provincial history. A year later he wrote a collection of political and philosophical essays showing Chang's influence more clearly. In the sixth essay of this group Kung surmises that "in the Chou and in earlier ages, the government at any time was identical with the learning of that time, and was initiated by the ruler of that time; ... committed to writing, it was what is called law, in other words, the *History* and the *Rites*; and the business of recording it was the function of the historian." Kung was obviously trying (without acknowledgment) for his own formulation of Chang's "the Six Classics are all history"; and in the same essay he saw in this idea Chang's principle that it must be the duty of the man of learning to use his abilities to serve the state, the ruler, and (Kung adds) the people. But, Kung complained, men today do not understand this; now, they are "blind to the difference between good and bad government, between pretense [art, *wen*] and reality [substance, *chih*]," even going so far as to "use the past to reproach the present," disrupting the unity of the state, so that "the benefits of kingly government do not penetrate to the masses, and the people's grievances do not reach the authorities."[16]

It is significant that Chang stimulated the young Kung to conscious political reflection, for after the strong emperors of the eighteenth century the Manchu despotism was weakening, and the scholar's tradition of political criticism was beginning to revive. We see Kung taking over two political implications of Chang's philosophy that were really incompatible: its authoritarianism, calling the scholar to accept his place in a unified scheme of things, leaving anything new to be proposed by those having "position"; and its modernism, calling him to serve the present age, reform its evils, and leave the past alone. Kung's circumstances eventually made this uneasy combination of values impossible for him. He was more and more painfully aware of the evils of his time—the opium trade, the weakness of the state, the absurdity of the bureaucracy—and continually frustrated in his attempts to get an effective post in the government. We find Kung therefore beginning to think of his own work and thought as a source of enlightenment for the future rather than salvation for the present, beginning to experiment with Buddhism, and becoming more and more interested in the growing "new text" movement in classical studies—turning to what for Chang would have been "empty words."[17]

What for Kung had been an inner conflict became, late in the nineteenth century, a political struggle. The radical wing of Confucian scholars had been slowly developing the contention (at least since the time of Liu Feng-lu, Kung's teacher) that the genuine Classics were those that had existed in the Han Dynasty only in "new texts," contemporary script; the other "Classics," as K'ang

Yu-wei (1858–1927) eloquently argued, had been forged by Liu Hsin, lackey of Wang Mang the usurper. K'ang revived Han Dynasty esoteric interpretations of the *Spring and Autumn,* and made them over into a theory of historical progress, in which Confucius reappeared as a divinely inspired prophet of a futuristic utopia. Thus radical classical scholarship blossomed into radical political reform. The reformers' image of Confucius was a complete negation of Chang's; so, too, was their concept of the Classics, their estimation of Liu Hsin, their vindication of political novelty. All this they knew. Chang and his age had taken for granted that "mere theory" must always bow before "real achievement." But the reformer T'an Ssu-t'ung (1865–98) stated flatly that he valued "knowledge" over "action," for action is impossible without an anterior theory of action. The Classics and the sacred texts of other nations, he found, sustain him in this view, for they advance new and untried theories for the conduct of society, and a modern man who does the same is of great importance to the world.[18] Liao P'ing (1852–1932) must actually have been reading Chang Hsüeh-ch'eng and taking issue with him directly. "The Six Classics," he wrote, "are empty words; they are not history"; and it is precisely this that makes them valuable. In contrast Chang Ping-lin (1868–1936), the reformers' articulate opponent, flung back at them Chang Hsüeh-ch'eng's own words: the Six Classics are all history.[19]

At least, and at last, Chang was being attended to. The political values his philosophy implied had come to be the central issue in all that mattered. But was he really the conservatives' champion and the reformers' antithesis? Not quite. True, Chang Ping-lin honored him by quoting him, and by supporting much of his view of tradition. But Chang had said that a scholar should devote his energies to the problems of the present time, correct present evils, and cultivate the skills to do so; and (though they had different evils in mind) the reformers surely honored him in this. He (and Kung) had said that one must not use the past to reproach the present; and in opposing traditionalism the reformers honored him in this too. One modern scholar, Ch'ien Mu, actually considers

Chang's "the Six Classics are history" to have an essentially reformist import.[f] And he is right in this sense: if one says, with
Chang, that the *tao* is embodied in the everyday functioning of
government and in man's most ordinary social acts, one will be
led to argue not only that the Classics are not abstract statements
of the *tao,* removed from existence, but also that there ought to
be no isolated elite of scholar-officials who are guardians of the *tao*
but otherwise lack any technical skill. The ideal of the scholar-
official as a "generalist," as a specialist only in a great classical tradition that guided him in the handling of human relationships,
was an ideal at the very root of conservatism.[g] But Chang Hsüeh-
ch'eng had insisted again and again in his essays on the *tao* that
human learning had actually begun as a collection of specialized
technical traditions of government functionaries. Chang's theories
implied a new conception of the intellectual as a technical specialist, just that conception which was eventually to require the aboli-
tion of the examination system.

But frank and general acknowledgement of Chang's stature as
a thinker did not come until after 1920. Naito's work, followed by
Hu Shih's, attracted wide attention to Chang in both China and
Japan. And Chang was not merely an object of academic curiosity.
As a pre-Western Chinese historian with highly original ideas
about his craft, Chang has played an important role in helping
Chinese historians accommodate themselves to new orientations
in historiography. Hu Shih found in Chang exciting lessons in
both historical and philosophical method which helped to give a

[f] Ch'ien Mu (p. 392) points to a specific connection between Chang and reformist
thought in the arguments of Pao Shih-ch'en (1775–1855) that local government
aides be included in the regular civil service, with opportunities for promotion all
the way to the top. Pao was one of many reformist-minded writers who themselves
held such unofficial positions. His idea was much discussed by reformers at the end
of the dynasty. Pao seems to have derived it from his own interpretation of Chang's
"The Meaning of the Word 'Historian.'"

[g] Etienne Balazs underlines this nonspecialist character of the scholar-official (e.g.,
Chinese Civilization and Bureaucracy, New Haven, 1964, pp. 16–17). It is well
analyzed and documented by C. K. Yang, "Some Characteristics of Chinese Bureaucratic Behavior," in D. S. Nivison and A. F. Wright, eds., *Confucianism in Action*
(Stanford, 1959), pp. 134–64.

Chinese stamp to what he had learned in the West.[20] Ku Chieh-kang has said that reading one of Chang's essays deeply influenced his own ideals as a young man.[21] Fung Yu-lan turned to Chang for important insights into the history of Chinese philosophy.[22] Interest in Chang has continued on the Mainland since 1949, where he has received the acclaim of popularizers as well as the sober criticism of intellectual historians. One author is especially delighted with Chang's conception of the broad scope of historical studies, as shown in the *Shih-chi K'ao*. Chang's acceptance of ordinary documents, economic data, etc., as material for the historian is "something earlier feudal scholars were unable to dream of."[23] Another study examines Chang's Classics-history thesis with great perception.[24]

Chang's fame is secure. Yet Ku Chieh-kang reacted to only a fragment of Chang's viewpoint; historians have seen his technique in isolation from its philosophical matrix; even Hu Shih misunderstood him; Fung, using him well, failed to see that his historical generalizations are "history philosophically considered," not history per se. Chang has not been well understood, and for most he has remained an object of scholarship, not a thinker to be seriously reckoned with.

May we ask more than what Chang meant and why he said it? May we ask whether he was right or wrong? This is not always easy. In some instances Chang's position is obviously commendable. He suggested a scheme for indexing books and recommended the use of footnotes in historical writing. Both proposals indicate that we are dealing with a man who has unusual imagination and intelligence. But we applaud these ideas because we already share them. Perhaps, then, it is not Chang's ideas, but his arguments in support of them, that might be important. But we usually find his arguments too bizarre, too dependent for their meaning upon Chang's own intellectual tradition, for us to assimilate them.

In other cases, we are unwilling to admit that the question of Chang's rightness even makes sense. For example, should local histories in fact have three parts, or not? We feel that this is an open question—a matter of convenience, not of essential rightness—about something that does not concern us. The question did concern Chang closely, and for him the question was not open. It had to be pried open, and why this was the case is the really interesting problem. The same observations could be made, I believe, of many of the things that Chang says about the forms of historical writing, and of virtually everything he says about bibliographical organization.

It can be argued that Chang's theories about the classical past are not serious historical hypotheses but are based on metaphysical necessity. But the ground (for him) of his ideas need not impair their truth. Fung believes that Chang was right in holding there was no authorship before Confucius, and that Chang's instincts were sound in seeking institutional origins for types of thought. We may well agree. In his criticism of the recent history of Chinese thought, Chang was seeking to establish values that really make no persuasive bid for our approval: the elimination of philosophical controversy and a respect for the authority of tradition without the disadvantages of orthodoxy. But when he insisted, as he did in stating his case against Tai Chen, that Ch'ing philology is not so much a revolt against the past as a historical development of Sung Neo-Confucianism itself, he made a highly fruitful suggestion. Intellectual history probably never exhibits the sort of discontinuity that some interpreters assume to have occurred in seventeenth-century China, and to suppose otherwise is to risk making the attitudes, methods, and objectives of Ch'ing scholarship far more like those of Western philology than in fact they were.

But what about the things Chang thought were true philosophically? Some of Chang's philosophical writing is only of philological or historical interest, and can hardly be transposed from its Neo-Confucian frame in such a way as to make it accessible to evaluation. But one matter that is provocative enough to be worth further thought is Chang's view, developed in "A Critique of

Hypocrisy" and "On Conventional Judgments," of the limited resources of language and the ethical implications of this limitation. Another is his ingenious analysis of historical writing into "style," "fact," and "meaning," and his inference that there are corresponding intellectual faculties in human beings, variously predominant in different constitutions and expressed with differing emphasis at various periods in history. Here Chang is saying the kind of thing that we must look at thoughtfully in any writer of any place and time.

Some of Chang's persuasions, although unlikely to appeal to us, may still be profitable to reflect upon. Chang's attitude toward the state and his justification of the inquisition are matters we cannot afford to dismiss as merely curious or treat as simply historically interesting. We of course must grant that authoritarianism is built into much of Confucian thought, and must grant, too, that Chang lived at a time when to demur would have been impossible. But these views do seem to be integral parts of Chang's philosophy. The situation is the reverse of what it was with his ideas about footnotes, for while few if any would support these views, the literary and ethical ideals on which they are based might seriously tempt our acceptance. The problem, I suspect, can be reduced to the question of how far Chang's political views can be disentangled from the other consequences in his thinking of Wang Yang-ming's "unity of knowledge and action."

In other cases— and these are the ones I feel to be most fascinating—the universal problem in Chang's thought is so well disguised (from our point of view) that we could easily miss it altogether. Who would expect a Chinese writer, telling the roll of the sage-rulers, to be probing the role of the great man in history and the way in which human thought impinges upon the world? Yet he does just this. Chang, to be sure, might not recognize our way of putting it. But is this not of a piece with our not recognizing his way of putting it? Such problems as this one are so puzzling in themselves that we must stop and attend wherever we find them considered; but how can it be that a universal problem of this kind can arise in such an improbable, nonuniversal context? Does this mean that it can't, really, be the problem I think it is? This puzzle, of a second order, which I am led to by reading Chang, is more vexing and perhaps more important than the first.

Or consider Chang's view of the Classics. How could there be anything for philosophy in the contention that the Chinese library categories of Classics and history did not exist in antiquity? Yet, one thing that Chang is saying in this strange way is that the Classics are not "writings that state what the *tao* is," and so he is implying that we cannot go to writings of the past in any simple way to fill up our tanks with truth. At best they can only, somehow, show us what is right by being what they are; they cannot tell us by what they say, for the form the *tao* takes at any time is a form for that time only. But a problem remains: how then can one come to grips critically with any past statement? For it must always at the same time be a historical datum. Words are everyone's, meaning-laden and universal, right or wrong, true or false. And yet words are events, the responses of individual minds to individual problems, just what they are and nothing else. Here Chang stumbled. And here I must hesitate; for this is of course the very problem I have just raised about Chang himself.

These fragments and puzzles are important. But Chang would surely have hoped that his thought might merit evaluation as a philosophy and as a whole, and I think we owe him the attempt. The system Chang gradually thought out includes a critical theory of literature (and a closely related theory of bibliography), a theory about the history of civilization leading into a personal philosophy of life, and a theory about historical writing. I am not adept at judging philosophies of life, and will say of Chang's only that I find his individualism and his counsels to intellectual humility and intellectual honesty very attractive. I think Chang was not always honest with himself, and was never humble, and these facts are mildly puzzling. Chang also disapproved of intellectual argument; I see why, but I see no point in a personal philosophy that condemns something one is so very good at. What of the other parts of Chang's philosophy?

Chang's central thesis about the evolution of literature—that it broke away from the primitive community and became "private" —seems, as a general theory of what happened, to be reasonable enough. It corresponds to a widely accepted picture of classical literature in the West, and to the evolution of music out of medieval religious and folk anonymity. But Chang's assumption that one can derive values from such a scheme does not tempt me, nor, often, do the values he derives. I cannot share his regret at the loss of the early oneness of the human community. And Chang seems to me to be simply wrong in holding that while one can say something about how good writing is produced, one can in the last analysis say nothing about what is good about it. But one basic insight informing Chang's (and Chu Yün's) literary point of view seems to me profoundly true. It is true, unfortunately, that a writer's literary impulses, his desire to make a pleasing or striking impression, are constantly at war with his instinct to be honest. This is especially true for the writer of history, for reasons that need penetrating examination. This matter deserves much more attention than we usually give it.

Chang's literary theories have genuine philosophical interest. Chang accepts the common (and plausible) Chinese critical view that the writer cannot validly (or possibly) entertain a state of feeling that his nature and situation do not authenticate. This view, as Chang presses it, is a valuable philosophical mistake, for it leads him directly to his "words-events" troubles and his difficulties in "On the Difficulty of Being Understood." If Chang did not have the imagination and capacity to make such mistakes, and to think about them persistently enough and clearly enough to make them recognizable, he would not be the philosopher that he is. Chang might be broadly described as a "motivationalist" in literary theory, just as he might be characterized as a "geneticist" in bibliography: in effect, he believes that to say something about the meaning and value of a literary work (or any kind of writing) we must (at least) give an explanation of that work in terms of the writer's background, circumstances, character, and motives. This position can easily lead to paradox, but there is surely something right about it. If the matter is controversial, this very fact demands that no thoughtful statement about it, however strange, be dismissed as merely curious.

Chang's philosophy of history is the part of his thought that will preoccupy most of his readers. In the last decade, the philosophy of history has enjoyed a spirited revival in England and America, and I will not try here to enter into the controversies that have resulted. It will suffice to try to show where Chang's reflections may be located in this field of inquiry.

It has been the usual practice in philosophy of history to distinguish between two classes of questions. Some philosophers and historians, such as Vico, Hegel, Marx, and Toynbee, have asked themselves whether history—what has happened—has a "meaning," whether viewed as a whole it exhibits a rational structure or a single process. Such partly metaphysical questions about what history really is have been labeled "speculative philosophy of history." A contrasting group of questions constitute what is called "critical philosophy of history." These questions concern not what has happened but the branch of knowledge that deals with what has happened: Is history a science or an art? How do historians explain? Is objectivity possible (or desirable) for the historian? Are there general historical laws? As this last question shows, the speculative and the critical philosophies of history cannot be neatly separated. But it is true that most recent philosophers have wanted to deal with the critical questions, and have felt that the speculative ones are rather suspect.

Usually Chang is asking speculative questions, reaching for the essence of things, discovering patterns of development and decay. His Chinese intellectual background offers him as wide a variety of ideas as would a Western one. The idea of cycles is as old as the concept of a dynasty. It was elaborated with a mad exuberance by Tung Chung-shu in the Han Dynasty. The dynastic concept does not preoccupy Chang, for his interest is entirely in institutional and literary change rather than in political and military events. But his picture of the history of "fashions" is cyclical, as is his concept of historiography turning back to its beginnings. He is able to see history (at least ancient history) as evolutionary and progressive, following the *Changes* but quite ignoring the *Changes'* strange notion of the hexagrams as the governing elements of the physical world. He is not tempted by the notion of history forever falling away from, and then reapproaching, an immutable ideal (a notion implicit in the type of Neo-Confucian metaphysics he rejects), but instead tends toward the Legalist view, that present needs must overrule appeals to explicit past models.

Perhaps Chang's tradition is too rich and powerful for full clarity of thought, for he also sees the postclassical history of culture as a devolution; and so in the end the classical age retains its prestige. His concept of history is the inverse of what Collingwood would call apocalyptic: he sees a linear development in one direction (upward), decisively changed by one great event—the separation of government and learning. Yet his attitude, as he appraises his own position, though indignant, cannot be called defeatist or pessimistic. Chang persistently calls to mind nineteenth-century German thought (in temper if not in detail) in the way his near obsession with an essentially metaphysical idea, the antithesis of "empty words" and reality, projects itself onto history and begins to yield to him a dramatic theory of man—a theory of civilization as first the expression of human needs, and then the estrangement of the cumulative cultural achievement from the state in the long history of human vanity. His conception has a kind of Wagnerian grandeur, which (in a very different intellectual world) might have given it an exciting future. In seeing history as a gradual manifestation of the *tao* Chang at once suggests Hegel and his absolute spirit. Yet Chang's *tao* does nothing, needs nothing, in no sense *uses* mankind to realize itself. Chang is like Vico in having his eyes fixed on the sequence of cultural modes; and like Vico again in being in the end tethered by a tradition that is virtually sacred.[25] One mode of thinking in Chang may not have an obvious Western counterpart. He has the instincts of an institutional historian; and so he often seems to be asking not what happens, but what exists. History becomes a kind of accumulation, an organic growth, the past the nucleus of the present, which contains the past in itself and reveals what it was. This way of thinking goes back to Confucius, who gave Chang his conception of the Chou as the summation of all earlier history.

Is there critical philosophy of history in Chang? Some of Chang's own problems will show that there is no sharp line between speculation and criticism. Chang's identification of the elements in a piece of historical writing is part of his noticing that there are writings in which only one of these elements predominates, and that these writings seem to fall into periods. Chang notices that institutions and values evolve in history, that all men feel their force; and some men (he himself, he thinks) can understand why and how this happens. Apparently there are two ways of apprehending and responding to historical reality (two ways of describing it?): the motivational and moral (as *tang-jan*) and the intellectual (as *so-i-jan*). We find something like this distinction in both Kant and Hegel, and there have been recent attempts to untangle the free-will-determinism puzzle along these same lines.

But there are obviously many questions Chang does not ask. Current Western interests such as the nature of historical explanation, or the question whether history is a science, belong to a cluster of philosophical problems that are simply not Chinese problems: the logical analysis of argument, the characterization of laws of nature, the problems of induction and confirmation. Chang does deal with problems we would have to call critical ones; but there is an important difference in his approach to them. Western critical philosophers of history have pretended that they are offering detached analyses of historical reasoning, disclaiming any intention to tell historians what to do in their own domain.

This curious posture is induced partly by the way Western universities happen to be organized, and partly by the idea endemic in British and American philosophy that philosophical analysis can never do more than cure philosophical confusions. Chang, too, has anxieties about giving "empty" advice to the historian, but he downs them by being a historian himself. With him, critical questions are also methodological ones.

This is surely true of his cautions about judgment and his examination of the nature of bias (though here Chang is concerned with much more than historiography.) It is true also of his question whether the past can be adequately known by the modern scholar; although here he means to reproach the philologists, he is also arguing that the historian must be a man of special insight, distinguishing him (as Collingwood and Hegel distinguish him) from the man who merely records or processes facts. Clearly, if Chang were asked whether history is a science or an art (if we could translate this question into his framework of concepts), he would have to answer that it is both. Chang is again both doing philosophy and proposing a way for the historian when he considers the purpose of the historian's work and how his subject matter serves that purpose. Though this is also a Western problem, here is where Chang's answers seem most Chinese. History yields moral enlightenment. But it yields this not by what the past says to us but by what it is, as an object of intuitive understanding. The Classics are history.

But Chang has his own kind of difficulty in passing from philosophy to history. For example, his speculative concept of the evolution of culture and institutions that begins "On the Tao" seems very promising. But Chang puts this forward as a philosopher, not as a historian, and then pursues it into Confucian ethics. The idea is not articulated as an explanatory concept for the historian to use, but merely results in his busy schemes for "documentation." Chang seems unable to think out the implications of his own concept of development. He shrinks from the usual way of seeing history as the story of great men's words and deeds, feeling

that the really significant events in history could not have been
brought about simply by someone's deciding that they should be so.
But he is not led from this to a consistent and thoroughgoing study
of nonpersonal historical causes. When he comes upon basic
changes in direction in history, too often he retreats into mystery,
appealing to such nonexplanations as the "seasons of Heaven" and
the "revolution of the ether," to account even for something like
the development of new forms in poetry.[26]

This failure of Chang's may be approached in another way.
Chang said that local histories must from time to time be rewritten. Chang also conceived the ideal historian to be a man of great
insight who, by selectively using documents and the work of earlier
historians, produces his own inspired account of the past, prefer-
ably in a continuous and comprehensive "general history." What
is this insight and why does the historian have it? We might suppose that the true historian, like a sage-ruler, appears on the scene
to refashion the past in a manner made possible for him by his
own position in time—that his "insight" is his own temporal point
of view, a view which was impossible earlier, and one which may
be superseded later. And how close Chang comes to saying this!
But his relativism in "Virtue in the Literary Man" is not directed
to the practicing historian; and it is in fact a warning about what
one must not say, not a claim that one's times justify one's point
of view. Local histories need to be redone, not because a later
historian will have a new way, valid for him, of looking at the
whole of the past, but because earlier histories were usually done
badly. Ideally, the historian could simply add his own chapter to
what has already been written. Even a mere continuation of a
general history (such as Pan Piao's continuation of the *Shih-chi*)
counts for Chang as general history.[27]

Why is Chang's great historian left with an insight that can be
used only in an obscure "illustrating of the *tao*"? If Chang could
have seen the historian's insight as what at his particular point in
time he is able to think, then Chang's own dreams as a philosopher
could have become his avowed business as a historian: document-

ing and describing the cycles of fashion, the separation of state and culture, the gradual development of institutions. His belief that the *tao* is revealed in the ordinary life of man could have moved him beyond the mere collecting of economic data to the task of delineating the patterns of economic development. Would Chang's envisioned history of the Sung Dynasty, and his unwritten essay "On Adaptability," have carried him beyond this block in his thinking? I feel that this was the direction in which he was moving. But apparently it was not possible for Chang to think this far. He remains at root a kind of historical mystic: his *tao* preserves its identity through historical change by being indescribable. His historical genius is to let the facts be just what they are, not making them fit any prejudice or preconception. Thus he adds his bit to a growing corporate work of history, picking up where the last great historian left off.

And so while Chang as philosopher of history does theorize about the causes and general trends of history, nevertheless he cannot tell historians to do this. On the contrary, he feels that when he writes history he is in some way atoning for the theorizing he allows himself as a philosopher. In the end, in spite of all Chang's jeering at philological blindness, his concept of the historian's craft is bound by the limitations of his age, the age of philology.

We see that Chang repeatedly thinks in a way which seems to lead toward radical positions, but always stops short before his thinking takes him too far. He thinks that poetry should be self-expressive; but in the end he remains very much a traditional moralist, and shudders at Yüan Mei, who follows the thought to its conclusion. The scholar should get his nose out of the past, be concerned with contemporary government. This is modernist and reformist. Chang shows that he really means it when the repression of the Ch'ien-lung era finally begins to lift, with the death of Kao-tsung and the fall of Ho-shen. But during most of his life his reformist impulses are expended in mere tinkering with the forms of historiography. It is not all tinkering. The "meaning" of history in the *Spring and Autumn* tradition is transmuted by

Chang, who counsels "restraint," and shuns a categorizing moral judgment. His meaning becomes an ineffable "significance." Yet it never quite loses its moral overtones. Yüan Mei, like Chang, saw the *Classic of History* as the fountainhead of historical writing, and as a work that forces no interpretations on the reader, "simply giving the facts and letting the meaning appear of itself." But Yüan took the final step, and openly ridiculed the idea that the historian should "praise and blame," pronouncing the *Spring and Autumn* to be simply a chronicle that existed before Confucius.[28] "The Classics are history"; they contain no explicit moral, Chang insists. This could mean that the Classics may be viewed quite naturalistically. Instead they lose none of their holiness, and other "actual things" begin to share it.

It would be a mistake too quickly to impute to Chang an intellectual failure of nerve. Closely examined, the traditionalism in his conclusions—on poetry, on the Classics, even on historiography —is discovered to be implicit in his premises. His times were not ours. To be sure, he is more appealing to us than he was to his contemporaries. He clashed with the philological movement, and at the same time resists classification in any of the conventional alternative ways. This seems to suggest that Chang was radically different from other thinkers in premodern China, that he was somehow an intellectual deviant, inexplicable in terms of native tradition. This is, of course, far from the case. Chang, like a number of other men in the seventeenth and eighteenth centuries—Ku Yen-wu, Wang Fu-chih, Huang Tsung-hsi, Tai Chen—tried in his own way to break away from the past, to think out new positions, to frame new problems, and to deal with old problems in new ways. And like the others he was ultimately unable to free himself from the bonds of tradition.

It is the structure of late Neo-Confucian thought itself—its suspicion of flat statement, its notion of intuitive access to truth, its emphasis on "actual facts"—that induces Chang's impatience with conventional opinions and leads him to his most original ideas. His personality caused him to take extreme positions that made him seem atypical. But for this very reason, often he reveals the intellectual assumptions of his times; views that others would hesitate to commit to "empty words" Chang states boldly. In his high regard for intuitive understanding, Chang shows his ties with a kind of thought more fashionable in earlier centuries. But in his announced esteem for solid learning, and in his paradoxical protestation, within a theoretical philosophy, of dislike of mere theory, he was saying what other men were thinking and saying it in a way that established the close connection between the values of his own day and those of earlier times. He himself is the best illustration of his contention, in his criticisms of Tai Chen, that the history of Neo-Confucian thought and learning is continuous, and that the Ch'ing study of "actual facts" is part of that history.

An invaluable way to look deeply into another world is to see it through a mind of the first order. Chang Hsüeh-ch'eng had such a mind, and we must be grateful. Could I address him, I should want him to know how useful he has become to other historians. But I should also want him to know that the things he felt and believed and valued have often proved worth examining. To understand him is not always easy; but if he will not demand too much of us, he need not despair. In my own attempt, I may indeed have said things about Chang that would anger him. But what I have tried to do surely would have pleased him. I have tried to understand him as a man.

Notes

Notes

See the Bibliographical Note (pp. 319–22) for an explanation
of abbreviated citations. An asterisk after any title
indicates *Ssu-pu Ts'ung-k'an* edition or (for histories) *Po-na* edition.

Introduction

1. Naito Torajiro, *Shina Shigaku Shi* (Tokyo, 1949), p. 238; *Kenki Shōroku* (Kyoto, 1928), p. 117.

2. I have analyzed the dissatisfaction with the system in more detail in my "Protest against Conventions and Conventions of Protest" in Arthur F. Wright, ed., *The Confucian Persuasion* (Stanford, 1960), pp. 177–201.

3. D. S. Nivison, "Ho-shen and His Accusers," D. S. Nivison and A. F. Wright, eds., *Confucianism in Action* (Stanford, 1959), pp. 235–36.

4. *Ibid.*, pp. 232ff.

5. Inaba Iwakichi, *Shin-chō Zenshi (A Complete History of the Ch'ing Dynasty)* (Tokyo, 1914), 2.1ff.

6. Sheng Lang-hsi, *Chung-kuo Shu-yüan Chih-tu (An Institutional History of Chinese Academies)* (Shanghai, 1934), pp. 85–91, 131–39.

7. See Wm. Theodore de Bary, "A Reappraisal of Neo-Confucianism," in Arthur F. Wright, ed., *Studies in Chinese Thought* (Chicago, 1953), pp. 81–111; also D. S. Nivison, "Introduction," in *Confucianism in Action.*

8. Hellmut Wilhelm, "Chinese Confucianism on the Eve of the Great Encounter," in Marius Jansen, ed., *Changing Japanese Attitudes toward Modernization* (Princeton, 1965), pp. 289ff., 303.

9. *I-shu,* 6.3a, "Literary Collections."

10. See Ku's letters quoted at the beginning of his *Jih Chih Lu (Record of Daily Learning)*, (Kuang-chou Shu-ku-t'ang edition); and Joseph R. Levenson, "*T'ien-hsia* and *Kuo* and the Transvaluation of Values," *Far Eastern Quarterly,* XI (1952), 449–50.

11. Chin Yü-fu, *Chung-kuo Shih-hsüeh Shih (History of Chinese Historiography)* (Shanghai, 1946), p. 256.

12. Mansfield Freeman, "The Ch'ing Dynasty Criticism of Sung Po-

litico-Philosophy," *Journal of the North China Branch of the Royal Asiatic Society*, LIX (1928), 94ff.

13. Quoted by Hou Wai-lu, *Chin-tai Chung-kuo Ssu-hsiang Hsüeh-shuo Shih* (*History of Modern Chinese Thought and Doctrine*) (Shanghai, 1947), p. 423. Nivison, "The Problem of 'Knowledge' and 'Action' in Chinese Thought since Wang Yang-ming," in *Studies in Chinese Thought*, pp. 132–33.

Chapter 1

1. HY, p. 1. WHL, p. 247. Chao Yü-ch'uan, "Chang Shih-chai Hsien-sheng Nien-p'u" in Hsü Te-hou, *Hsiang-chu Wen-shih T'ung-i*, Vol. I (Shanghai, 1927), p. 1a.

2. HY, pp. 1–3, 147–48. Naito Torajiro, *Kenki Shōroku* (Kyoto, 1928), p. 141. *I-shu*, 17.54b, "Family Record of Master Lo-yeh."

3. HY, pp. 1–2. *I-shu*, 29.12bff, "Postscript to the Printing of the *T'ai-shang Kan-ying P'ien*," 1785. *Liang Che Yu-hsüan Lu* (Chu and Ch'en edition, 1801), 22.51b–52b.

4. *I-shu*, 9.70a–b, "Family Letter No. 3," 1790.

5. HY, pp. 3–4. WHL, pp. 247–48. Chu Yün, *Ssu-ho Wen-chi* (Peking, 1815), 16.20a, "Funeral Ode for the Mother (née Shih) of Chang Hsüeh-ch'eng." *I-shu*, "pu-i," 44b, "Letter to Shih Chih-kuang on Literary Art."

6. *I-shu*, 22.36b, "Letter to Chang Ju-nan on Learning," 1766.

7. HY, p. 5. WHL, p. 248. *I-shu*, 17.42b–43b, "Family Record of Tu Ping-ho."

8. HY, pp. 5–6. *I-shu*, 22.36b, "Letter to Chang Ju-nan," 1766.

9. HY, pp. 6–7. *I-shu*, 9.70a, "Family Letter No. 3," 1790; 22.37a, "Letter to Chang Ju-nan," 1766; 9.73a, "Family Letter No. 6," 1790.

10. *I-shu*, 9.73a, "Family Letter No. 6," 1790.

11. Chu Yün, *Ssu-ho Wen-chi*, 16.20b. HY, p. 8. WHL, pp. 250, 252. WTJ, p. 253. *Liang-che Yu-hsüan Lu*, 22.51b.

12. HY, pp. 10–11. *I-shu*, 9.73a, "Family Letter No. 6," 1790.

13. For a history and description of the Kuo Tzu Chien, see Chang Yü-ch'üan, "The Kuo Tzu Chien," in *The Chinese Social and Political Science Review*, XXIV (1940), 69–106.

14. HY, pp. 11, 21, 147–48. WHL, p. 253. *I-shu*, 22.14a, "Comment on the Catalog of the Floating-Cloud-Hill Studio Library," 1795.

15. HY, p. 11. *I-shu*, 19.20b, "Biography of Tseng Shen" in "Biographies of Friends Who Died Around 1780–81."

16. HY, pp. 12–13.

17. *I-shu*, 15.11b–12b, "First Letter to Chen Sung-nien on Writing Local Histories."

18. *I-shu*, 15.16a–b, "Second Letter to Chen Sung-nien on Writing Local Histories."

19. *I-shu*, 15.14b, 22b–24a, 25bff.   20. *I-shu*, 15.10a–b, 17a–18a.

21. *I-shu*, 15.20b.   22. *I-shu*, 15.12b.

23. *ECCP*, pp. 198–99. HY, p. 15. WHL, p. 249.

24. HY, p. 15. See Chu Yün's delightful little essay on friendship, "Reflections on a Small Gathering in the Pepper Blossom Humming Boat" (Chiao-hua Yün-fang, Chu's studio), 1766. *Ssu-ho Wen-chi*, 5.20a, 21a. *I-shu*, 17.12b, "Biography of Feng T'ing-ch'eng."

25. *I-shu*, 29.66b, "Note to Wang Hui-tsu" (1795 or later).

26. *I-shu*, 23.14b–15a.   27. HY, p. 16.

28. *ECCP*, p. 696.   29. *I-shu*, 22.36a–40a.

30. HY, p. 15.

31. HY, pp. 19–22. WHL, p. 252.

32. HY, pp. 21–22. WHL, p. 253.

Chapter 2

1. HY, p. 23. WHL, pp. 254–55.

2. *I-shu*, 18.6b–7a, "Biography of Shao Chin-han," 1800.

3. Chu Yün, *Ssu-ho Wen-chi* (Peking, 1815), 11.1a–6b. *I-shu*, 18.6b, 10a. Shao T'ing-ts'ai's *Ssu-fu-t'ang Wen-chi* is reprinted in the collection *Shao-hsing Hsien-cheng I-shu*. Lu Ch'ien, *Pa-ku-wen Hsiao Shih* (*A Short History of Pa-ku*) (Shanghai, 1937), p. 77.

4. *I-shu*, 9.23a–24a. *ECCP*, pp. 637–39.

5. HY, p. 24. Naito Torajiro, *Kenki Shōroku* (Kyoto, 1928), pp. 135–36.

6. *I-shu*, 22.41b–42a. HY, pp. 22, 25.

7. The category *wen-shih* is used in the bibliographical sections of *Hsin T'ang Shu* and *Sung Shih*. Probably not relevant to its meaning for Chang is *Lun Yü*, 6.18. See *I-shu*, 14.29b–30a for Shao Chin-han on Chang's concept of *wen-shih*. The encomium of Liu occurs at the end of *chüan* 102 of *Chiu T'ang Shu*.

8. HY, pp. 81–82. *I-shu*, 9.68b–69a, "Family Letter No. 2"; the friend was Liu T'ai-kung (1751–1805).

9. *ECCP*, pp. 189–99, 637. HY, pp. 29–30. Ch'ien Mu, p. 415 (citing Shen Yüan-t'ai in *Pei-chuan Chi Pu*).

10. HY, pp. 27–31, *passim*. Chu Shih-chia, pp. 158–59.

11. HY, p. 31. *I-shu*, "wai-pien," 16.1a–b. The remains of Chang's *Ho-chou Chih* may be found in *I-shu*, "wai-pien," 16–18. The original *Ho-chou Chih* was in 42 *p'ien*. The *Chih-yü* was in 20 *p'ien*. But the "Chih-li" (rules of compilation) done first, which Tai Chen saw and which Chang later sent to Pi Yüan (in 1787), was also in 20 *p'ien*.

Chang was able to save printed copies of it. See HY, pp. 27, 29, 31, 62 and *I-shu*, 22.43b. In 1790 Chang extracted a *Hsü-lun* in one *chüan* from his *Ho-chou Chih-li* (the original *Ho-Chou Chih* was at that time already lost; *I-shu*, 9.44b). This is most of what survives.

12. *ECCP*, p. 697. Hu Shih, "A Note on Ch'üan Tsu-wang, Chao I-ch'ing and Tai Chen," *ECCP*, pp. 970–82, especially 971–72. HY, p. 29. Chang also may have seen Tai at Ning-po the preceding year, when Tai displayed great knowledge of astronomy. *I-shu*, 18.22a–b, "Biography of Feng Shao."

13. *I-shu*, 2.30b, Postscript to "Chu and Lu," 1790.

14. *I-shu*, 2.27b, "Chu and Lu" (1789); 2.31a–32a, Postscript to "Chu and Lu."

15. *I-shu*, 14.37a, "Account of a Discussion about Local Histories with Tai Chen."

16. *I-shu*, 14.38a–b.

17. HY, pp. 31–32.

18. WHL, pp. 258, 260. *I-shu*, 19.18a, "Biography of Lo Yu-kao," in "Biographies of Friends Who Died Around 1780–81."

19. WHL, p. 257.

20. HY, p. 33. *I-shu*, 18.25a.

21. HY, pp. 32–33.

22. HY, p. 35. *Kenki Shōroku*, p. 127.

23. HY, p. 35. WHL, pp. 256, 258.

24. *ECCP*, p. 501. HY, p. 36. WHL, p. 258.

25. Li Wei, "Ts'ung-yu Chi" (in which Li relates his recollections of Chu Yün), in Chu Yün, *Ssu-ho Wen-chi*, p. 32a–b.

26. WHL, p. 261. *I-shu*, 16.33b.

27. HY, p. 42. *I-shu*, 19.18a–b, "Biography of Lo Yu-kao"; 18.23a, "Biography of Feng Shao," 1790. See also D. S. Nivison, "Bukkyō ni taisuru Shō Gakusei no Taido" ("Chang Hsüeh-ch'eng's Attitude toward Buddhism"), *Indogaku Bukkyōgaku Kenkyū*, IV (1956), 492–95.

28. Naito Torajiro, *Kenki Shōroku*, p. 125.

Chapter 3

1. *I-shu*, 29.25a–26a, "Postscript to Drafts Written While Compiling the Po-chou History in the Winter of 1789–90"; 1.23a, 24b, 26b, "The Teaching of the *Odes*" (where Chang refers to parts of his "Chiao-ch'ou Lüeh").

2. The parts of *Ho-chou Chih* discussed are found in *I-shu*, "wai-pien," 17.3b–24a, 18.54b–62b. The *Chiao-ch'ou T'ung-i* (hereafter *CCTI*) occupies *chüan* 10–13.

3. Kang Wu, *Histoire de la Bibliographie Chinoise* (Paris, 1938), p. 5.

4. *I,** 8.2a–3a (Appendix II, 2).

5. *I-shu*, 10.2a–3a.

6. *I-shu*, "wai-pien," 17.3b-4a.

7. *I-shu*, 10.3a–b. Yen Shih-ku (581-645) was the T'ang commentator on the *Han Shu*. For Liu Hsin's ideas and liberal translations from the *Han Shu* "Monograph on Literature," see Fung Yu-lan, A Short History of Chinese Philosophy (New York, 1953), pp. 31–34.

8. *I-shu*, "wai-pien," 17.4b.   9. *I-shu*, 10.4a (*CCTI*, 2.1).

10. *I-shu*, 11.2a–3a (*CCTI*, 10.4).   11. *I-shu*, "wai-pien," 17.3b.

12. See Chapter 2, p. 43n.

13. Nivison, "Introduction" in Nivison and Wright, eds., *Confucianism in Action* (Stanford, 1959); also "Protest against Conventions," Wright, ed., *The Confucian Persuasion* (Stanford, 1960) pp. 189, 192.

14. Nivison, "Knowledge and Action" in Arthur F. Wright, ed., *Studies in Chinese Thought* (Chicago, 1953) pp. 117–34.

15. *I-shu*, 10.3b–4a (*CCTI*, 2.1); "wai-pien," 17.6b–8b.

16. *I-shu*, "wai-pien," 17.5a–6b.

17. *I-shu*, 10.5b–7a (*CCTI*, 2.5, 2.7).

18. *I-shu*, 10.10a–11a (*CCTI*, 4.1, 4.2); "wai-pien," 17.8b–10b.

19. *I-shu*, 10.5a–b (*CCTI*, 2.4); "wai-pien," 17.8a.

20. *I-shu*, "wai-pien," 17.8b, 18.57a.

21. *I-shu*, "wai-pien," 18.54b–62b.

22. *I-shu*, 10.4b-5a (*CCTI*, 2.3).

23. *I-shu*, 14.13a, "A proposal for a Three-Part Form for Local Histories." See also HY, p. 110.

24. *T'ung Chih*, 71, "Chiao-ch'ou Lüeh" (*T'ung Chih*, Vol. I, Wan-yu Wen-k'u edition, p. 831).

25. *I-shu*, 10.17a–b (*CCTI*, 9).

26. *I-shu*, "wai-pien," 17.11a–b.

27. *I-shu*, 10.14a–b (*CCTI*, 7.1).

28. *I-shu*, 10.15a–16a (*CCTI*, 7.3).

Chapter 4

1. HY, p. 43. WTJ, p. 215. *I-shu*, 18.17b–18a, "Biography of Chou Chen-jung." Chang organized the work into 25 *p'ien*; it is printed in *I-shu* as ten *chüan* ("wai-pien," *chüan* 6–15). Other editions include Chou Chen-jung's original edition of 1779, a reprint with supplements in 1813, and another reprint in 1930. (WTJ, *ibid.*)

2. Lei Hai-tsung, "Chang Hsüeh-ch'eng yü Lan Ting-yüan 'O-hsiang

Chi,' " *Ch'ing-hua Hsüeh-pao*, XII (1937) 619–30. (Lei was actually able to examine Chia P'eng's manuscripts.) In 1790 Chang reedited his own work, which he reduced to ten *p'ien* and called *A New History of Yung-ch'ing* (*Yung-ch'ing Hsin Chih*); this does not survive (WTJ, pp. 214–15), but it seems safe to assume that in this revision the Chia family received less space.

3. HY, p. 48.

4. WHL, p. 264. HY, p. 50.

5. HY, pp. 48–49. WHL, p. 264. *I-shu*, 17.15b (biography of Chang Wei-ch'i's father).

6. HY, pp. 50, 53, 58. The Ta-ming history was completed in 1785 (HY, p. 60).

7. HY, p. 54. *I-shu*, 23.33a, "Lament for Ts'ai Luan-chou."

8. *I-shu*, 23.33a; 29.9a–10a.

9. *I-shu*, 28.22a–23a.

10. For an excellent analysis of this esthetic tradition see James F. Cahill, "Confucian Elements in the Theory of Painting," in Arthur F. Wright, ed., *The Confucian Persuasion* (Stanford, 1960).

11. HY, pp. 51–53. WHL, p. 264.

12. *I-shu*, 9.31b.

13. *I-shu*, 9.30a, 33b. See my "Protest against Conventions" in *The Confucian Persuasion*, pp. 190–91.

14. HY, p. 55.

15. *I-shu*, 23.33b–34a, "Lament for Ts'ai Luan-chou." *Kao-tsung Shih-lu*, 1180.6b–7b.

16. HY, p. 55. *I-shu*, 29.28a–b, "Postscript to Drafts of the *T'ung-i* for 1783."

17. *I-shu*, 29.27a, "Postscript to the Autumn Workbook of 1788."

18. *I-shu*, 23.34b, "Lament for Ts'ai." WHL, p. 265.

19. *I-shu*, 23.33b–34b.

20. *I-shu*, 22.21b–23a. "An Account of a Visit to the Lotus Pond on a Moonlit Night."

21. *I-shu*, 19.31a, Chou Chen-jung, "Postscript to 'Biographies of Friends Who Died Around 1780–81.' "

22. HY, pp. 42, 61. *I-shu*, 23.34b, 35b, "Lament for Ts'ai"; 17.37a, "Biography of K'o Shao-keng"; 28.50b, "An Expression of My Feelings" (a long autobiographical poem, written at the end of 1797 to the salt comptroller Tseng Yü).

23. ECCP, pp. 370–623, 966.

24. *I-shu*, "pu-i," 30b, "Letter to Governor-General Pi" (probably late 1789).

25. *I-shu*, 22.42b–43b, "Letter to Governor Pi" (written in the winter of 1787). Hu and Yao argue correctly that the *I-shu* is in error in assigning this letter to the year 1789. See HY, p. 62.

26. HY, p. 62. *I-shu*, 23.34b, 28.51a.

27. HY, p. 63. *I-shu*, 13.34a–38b.

28. HY, pp. 63–64. *I-shu*, 22.29b ff.

29. *I-shu*, 9.42a–b.

30. HY, pp. 66–67. *I-shu*, 28.51a–b, poem to Tseng Yü, 1797.

31. HY, pp. 68, 73. Yao Ming-ta, *Chu Yün Nien-p'u* (Shanghai, 1933), p. 134.

32. *I-shu*, 28.51a–b (translation from Demiéville, p. 171).

33. HY, p. 68.

Chapter 5

1. This information is given in *Hsün-hsüeh-chai Jih-chi*, the diary of Li Tz'u-ming (1830–94). Li, who was a native of K'uai-chi, had seen an unpublished collection of letters written to Shao Chin-han (who in 1790 was still in Peking); several of these letters were from Tuan, discussing Chang Hsüeh-ch'eng. See WHL, p. 276b and WTJ, p. 268.

2. *I-shu*, "pu-i," 1b, 10b–11a, "On Teaching Students to Write," 1785.

3. *I-shu*, 1b–3a.   4. *I-shu*, 3a–6a.

5. *I-shu*, 7a–b.   6. *I-shu*, 2.35a–36b.

7. Naito Torajiro, *Shina Shigaku Shi* (Tokyo, 1949), p. 361.

8. *I-shu*, 2.36b–37a.   9. *I-shu*, 2.37a.

10. *I-shu*, 2.37b–38a.   11. *I-shu*, 2.38a–39a.

12. *I-shu*, 1.20a.   13. *I-shu*, 1.20a–b.

14. *I-shu*, 1.21a–b.   15. *I-shu*, 1.21b–22b.

16. Hu Shih has made the suggestion that Chang here holds a good idea for the wrong reasons. See HY, p. 116. The anonymity of the ancient philosophical books is a thesis that Chang argues in other places, e.g., in a long letter to Sun Hsing-yen in 1797. See Ch'ien Mu, pp. 444 ff.

17. *I-shu*, 1.22b–23b.   18. *I-shu*, 1.24a–b.

19. *I-shu*, 1.21b.   20. *I-shu*, 1.25a–26b.

21. *I-shu*, 1.26a–27a.   22. *I-shu*, 1.21b.

23. *I-shu*, 6.1a.   24. *I-shu*, 3.15b.

25. *I-shu*, 1.7a–8a.   26. *I-shu*, 4.3a–b.

27. *I-shu*, 4.3b, 9a–10b.

28. *I-shu*, 4.21b, "Collected Opinions" (1789).

29. *I-shu*, 4.14a–15a, 16a–18a. For the Li Ling letter, see also *I-shu*, "wai-pien," 2.10a, "Notes of 1795."

30. *I-shu*, 9.23a–24a. Ch'ien Mu, p. 416.

31. *I-shu*, 29.54a, "Letter to Censor Ts'ao Ting-hsüan on the Examination System," 1799.

32. WHL, pp. 281b, 289b. *I-shu*, 29.26b, "Postscript to the Autumn Workbook of 1788." Naito has reproduced a specimen of Chang's handwriting (a short note to Chu Hsi-keng) in *Kenki Shōroku* (Kyoto, 1928), opposite p. 112.

33. *I-shu*, 29.30a.

34. *I-shu*, 13.10b–13b, "Preface to the Poems of Lieutenant Governor Ch'en Tung-p'u" (i.e., Ch'en Feng-tzu 1726–99, lieutenant governor of Anhwei in 1797).

Chapter 6

1. *I-shu*, 9.39b–41b.
2. *I-shu*, 2.1a–b.
3. *I-shu*, 2.1b.
4. *I-shu*, 2.1a.
5. *I*,* 7.3b (Appendix I, 4).
6. *Mencius*,* 11.7b–8b (6A7).
7. *I-shu*, 2.2a.
8. *I-shu*, 2.2b.
9. *Ibid.*
10. *I-shu*, 2.2b–6b.
11. *I-shu*, 2.5a (emphasis mine).
12. *I-shu*, 2.5b (emphasis mine).
13. *I-shu* (Kuei-yang ed.), 2.4b.
14. *I-shu*, 2.6b–7a.

15. I-shu, 9.39b–41b, "Letter to Ch'en Chien-t'ing on Learning," 1789.

16. *I-shu*, 2.7b–8b.
17. *I-shu*, 2.11a–b.
18. *I-shu*, 2.9b.
19. *I-shu*, 2.10b.
20. *I-shu*, 2.10a.
21. *I-shu*, 2.10b–11a.
22. *I-shu*, 2.11a–b.
23. *I-shu*, 2.12a–13a.
24. *I-shu*, 2.14a–15a.
25. *I-shu*, 2.15a–18a.
26. *I-shu*, 2.20a–21b.

27. *I-shu*, 2.21b–22a. Ch'ien Mu, pp. 411–13.

28. *I-shu*, 2.18a.
29. *I-shu*, 2.22b.
30. *I-shu*, 6.10a–b.
31. *I-shu*, 6.10b–11a.
32. *I-shu*, 9.35a–36b.

33. *I-shu*, 9.37a–b; 2.27a–28a; 6.11a.

34. *I-shu*, 2.25a.
35. *I-shu*, 2.26a–b, 28a.
36. *I-shu*, 2.26b–27a.
37. *I-shu*, 2.28a–b.
38. *I-shu*, 6.14a.
39. *I-shu*, 6.14b.
40. *I-shu*, 2.8b, 1.11a.
41. *I-shu*, 5.6b–7a.

42. *I-shu*, 1.30b; 5.6b; 4.24b.

43. *Lun Yu*,* 2.5b (3/4). *Chung-yung*, 28/5. Chang's quotation is from *Li Chi*, No. 10, "Li Ch'i," 23.4a.

44. *I-shu*, 5.6b.

45. *I-shu*, 5.7a.
46. *I-shu*, supplement, 39b–42b.
47. *Han Ch'ang-li Chi*,* 12.1b–2b.
48. *I-shu*, 6.12b.
49. *I-shu*, 6.13a–14a.
50. *STTS*, 10.9a.
51. *Han Shu*,* 62.21a. *Wen Hsüan*,* 41.25b. *Shih-chi*,* 130.21b.
52. *I-shu*, 5.8a–b.   53. *I-shu*, 5.8b–10b.
54. *I-shu*, 4.40b–41a.   55. HY, p. 24.
56. In the essay "Ch'uan-chi" (*I-shu*, 5.13a). It must have been written after 1794 because in it Chang speaks of having compiled the *Hupei T'ung-chih* "some time ago."
57. *I-shu*, 3.1a. "Speech is the sound of the mind" is an aphorism from Yang Hsiung, *Fa-yen* (*Kuang Han Wei Ts'ung-shu*), 4.3a. With this and the following argument compare *I*,* 7.11b, and *Mencius*,* 3.8a (2A2).
58. *I-shu*, 3.1b.   59. HY, p. 65.
60. *I-shu*, 4.19a.   61. *I-shu*, 4.31a–33b.
62. *I-shu*, 4.41a–b, "In Defense of Cheng Ch'iao."
63. *I-shu*, 5.14a–15b.
64. *T'ing-lin Shih Wen Chi*, 3.1a–2b (*Ch'ing Ju Hsüeh-an*, 7.7a). Mansfield Freeman, "The Ch'ing Dynasty Criticism of Sung Politico-Philosophy," *Journal of the North China Branch of the Royal Asiatic Society* LIX (1928), 94–95; "The Philosophy of Tai Tung-yüan," same journal, LXIV (1933), 52–53.
65. To a relative, Chang Cheng-p'u; written probably in the winter of 1789 or in 1790, *I-shu*, 29.83a–b. Similar argument is found in *I-shu*, 8.32a–33b, "Comment on a School Text of the *Shuo-wen Tzu-yüan*."
66. *I-shu*, 4.12b–13a.
67. Ch'ien Mu, p. 416.

Chapter 7

1. HY, pp. 75, 104. *I-shu*, "pu-i," 31b, "Letter to Governor-General Pi."
2. *I-shu*, 9.68b, "Family Letter No. 2." HY, p. 90.
3. HY, pp. 84, 90, 98, 103. Chien Mu, pp. 423–24.
4. HY, pp. 75–76. *I-shu*, 9.44a, "Another Letter to Chou Jen-jung on Writing."
5. HY, pp. 76–78. *I-shu*, 15.1a ff. Chu Shih-chia, p. 176. Pan's "Ku-chin Jen-wu Piao" occupies *chüan* 20 of the *Han Shu*.
6. Shao finished this work in 1775. See Huang Yün-mei, *Shao Erh-*

yün Hsien-sheng Nien-p'u (Chronological Biography of Shao Chin-han) (Nanking, 1933), pp. 52–53.

7. Cheng Ch'iao, *T'ung-chih Lüeh,* Kuo-hsüeh Chi-pen Ts'ung-shu edition, 4.516–17, 528.

8. *I-shu,* 9.44b.

9. WHL, pp. 277–78. Chang's letter to Chu Hsi-keng is not in the *I-shu,* but was discovered in a manuscript of Chu's writings in a Tokyo bookstore (the well-known Bunkyūdō Co., no longer in business).

10. WHL, pp. 274, 278, 281a. Nivison, "Traditional Chinese Biography," *Journal of Asian Studies,* XXIV (1962), 461.

11. WHL, p. 276.

12. Huang Yün-mei, *Shao Erh-yün,* p. 97.

13. HY, pp. 83–84.

14. *I-shu,* 2.7b; "wai-pien," 17.4a. Preface to the "Monograph on Literature" in the *Ho-chou Chih*; also 1.1a, "The Teaching of the *Changes.*"

15. Wang Yang-ming, *Instructions for Practical Living and Other Neo-Confucian Writings,* translated with notes by Wing-tsit Chan (New York, 1963), p. 23.

16. Shen Jen, *"Wen-shih T'ung-i* Nei-p'ien Hou-an," *Hsüeh-hai Yüeh-k'an,* 1.4 (1944), p. 52. A slightly different form of this thesis is found in Yüan's "Preface to Shih-hsüeh Li-i," *Hsiao-ts'ang Shan-fang Wen-chi* (in the Yüan family edition of *Sui-yüan San-shih Chung*), 10.26a–b.

17. Letter to Chu Kuei (1796), *I-shu,* 28.44a–b. See Demiéville, p. 178.

18. *I-shu,* 14.12b–13a.

19. HY, pp. 132–34. WHL, p. 288.

20. HY, p. 90.

21. HY, pp. 83, 93–95. *I-shu,* 9.14a.

22. HY, pp. 94–95. *I-shu,* 9.13a, 14a–b.

23. This information, provided by Hsiao Mu of T'ung-ch'eng, is recorded in *Shao-hsing Hsien-chih Tzu-liao (Materials for a History of Shao-hsing District),* published by the Commission for the Compilation of a History of Shao-hsing District, 1937–39, Collection No. 1, Vol. 14, "Biographies," p. 141b.

24. HY, pp. 107–9; WHL, pp. 282; for the essay "Fang-chih Li San Shu I," see *I-shu,* 14.11b–17a.

25. Chu Shih-chia, pp. 93, 144–51.

26. WHL, p. 282. Demiéville, pp. 175–76.

27. HY, p. 98. *I-shu,* 9.19b.

28. Hy, p. 99. *I-shu,* 9.20b–21a.

Chapter 8

1. Cf. the "priests and historiographers" (*shu shih*) of the *Tso Chuan* (James Legge, *The Chinese Classics* [reprinted in China, 1939], 5.533, 683). For the connection between historiography and astronomy, see *I-shu*, 14.13a–b.

2. These ideas go back to Chang's correspondence in 1763–64 with Chen Sung-nien. See Chapter 1.

3. *I-shu*, 4.43a–b. Cf. *The Doctrine of the Mean*, in Legge, 1.416, 426.

4. *I-shu*, 4.44b.   5. *I-shu*, 4.36b.
6. *I-shu*, 1.8b–9a, 11a.   7. *I-shu*, 1.9a.
8. *I-shu*, 1.14b–15b.   9. *I-shu*, 1.16b–17a.
10. *I-shu*, 1.18a.   11. *I-shu*, 1.19a–b.
12. *I-shu*, 1.10b.   13. *STTS*, 2.6a. *I-shu*, 1.12b–13a.
14. *I-shu*, 1.10b, 14a–b.

15. *Jih Chih Lu* (Kuang-chou Shu-ku-t'ang edition), 21.3a. Chang was familiar with Ku's ideas on poetry in this book. See *I-shu*, "wai-pien," 15a–b, "Notes of 1795."

16. Aoki Masaru, *Shina Bungaku Shisō Shi* (Tokyo, 1943), pp. 187–88.

17. *I-shu*, 1.17b.

18. *I-shu*, 1.14b.

19. *I-shu*, 1.13b; 14.15b.

20. *I-shu*, 4.41b; 5.1a; 14.14b–15a. *Mencius,** 8.7b (4B21) (Legge, 2.327). Liu's mot is found in his biographies, *Chiu T'ang Shu,** 102.7-a–b, and *Hsin T'ang Shu,** 132.2a.

21. *I-shu*, 5.2a.

22. *I-shu*, 5.1b ff; also 4.19a, "Collected Opinions."

23. *I-shu*, 8.35a–36b.

24. E.g. *I-shu*, 5.1b, 4.43b. Compare *STTS*, 20.16a.

25. Chang's criticisms of Liu are sometimes identical with those of P'u, e.g., his criticism of Liu's view of the *Classic of History* as an "impure" record of "words," *STTS*, 1.2a and *I-shu*, 1.10b.

26. HY, pp. 15, 31, 91. *I-shu*, 9.68b, "Family Letter No. 2."

27. *STTS*, 20.16a.

28. *I-shu*, 1.15a.

29. *T'ai-shang Kan-ying P'ien Chu*. See *ECCP*, p. 358.

30. *I-shu*, 29.13a–b.

31. In the ninth of his "Opinions" ("I-yen") on "the principle of fate"; see Darlene T. Goodwin, "Selected Essays of Hung Liang-chi (1746–1809)," unpublished M.A. thesis, Stanford University, June 1961, pp. 31–33.

32. *I-shu*, 4.6a–7a, " 'If Your Words Are Everyone's.' "

33. *Wen-hsin Tiao-lung,** 4.4b.
34. *I-shu,* 2.13a.
35. *I-shu,* 2.11b.
36. E.g., *I-shu,* 4.45a, "Answers to Objections."
37. *I-shu,* 2.17b, "On Learning."
38. *I-shu,* 5.2b, "Virtue in the Historian."
39. *I-shu,* 1.18a, "The Teaching of the *History.*"
40. *I-shu,* 5.2b–4a.
41. Legge, 5.514.
42. *STTS,* 10.9a.

Chapter 9

1. HY, pp. 111–12. *I-shu,* 14.23b–30a, "To Ch'en Shih, on Historiography," probably 1794.
2. *Ibid.*
3. HY, pp. 106, 113. *I-shu,* "wai-pien," 3.35b–37a, "Notes of 1796."
4. WHL, p. 281b. *I-shu,* 29.62b–64b, "Letter to Wang Ch'un-lin."
5. *ECCP,* p. 623.
6. WHL, p. 249a. *ECCP,* pp. 353–54. *I-shu,* 13.42b–43a. HY, p. 121.
7. WHL, p. 283a–b. *I-shu,* 2.42a–49b. Nivison, "Aspects of Traditional Chinese Biography," *Journal of Asian Studies* XXI (1962), 460.
8. WHL, p. 283b. *I-shu,* 29.59b–62b. HY, pp. 119–20.
9. *Wang Lung-chuang Hsien-sheng I-shu* (1886), *Ping-t'a Meng-hen Lu,* Part I, p. 32a; supplement, p. 53a (recording a letter under the year 1801, from Wang to Chang Hua-fu). *ECCP,* p. 825. HY, pp. 120, 147.
10. *I-shu,* 2.33a–35a. HY, p. 121.
11. HY, p. 122.
12. WHL, p. 285b. *I-shu,* 13.42b–43a (from a letter to Hu Ch'ien, 1796).
13. HY, pp. 123, 125.
14. Ch'ien Mu, pp. 444–52.
15. HY, pp. 124, 127–28. More of this poem is translated by Demiéville in his review of Hu Shih's chronological biography of Chang, *Bulletin de l'École Francaise de l'Extrême Orient* XXIII (1923), 488–89.
16. HY, pp. 127–28.
17. HY, pp. 132, 139. Lo Ping-mien, *"Shih-chi K'ao* Hsiu-tsuan ti T'an-t'ao"* ("A Study on the Compilation of the *Shih-chi K'ao*"), Part I, *Hsin-Ya Hsüeh-pao* VI (Feb. 1964), 396, 399–400.
18. Lo Ping-mien, pp. 369–71, 396.
19. Lo Ping-mien, pp. 397–98. Ch'ien Mu, ed., *"Chang Shih I-shu*

I-p'ien" ("Items omitted from *The Remaining Writings of Chang Hsüeh-ch'eng*"), *T'u-shu Chi-k'an* (*Journal* of the Szechwan Provincial Library) II (June 1942), 36–37, "Another Letter to Chu Hsi-keng," 1799.

20. HY, p. 139. Lo Ping-mien, p. 396.

21. HY, p. 114. WHL, p. 277b. WTJ, pp. 257–58.

22. HY, p. 114. Ch'ien Mu, *Chung-kuo Chin San-pai Nien Hsüeh-shu Shih*, pp. 438–42. Ch'ien (p. 438) quotes Ch'ien Lin's *Wen-hsien Cheng-ts'un Lu*.

23. *ECCP*, p. 956. HY, p. 129. *I-shu*, "wai-pien," 3. 63b–64a, "Notes of 1796." HY, p. 122, states that the latter half of these "Notes" were actually written in 1797. The Chinese year ended February 15, 1798.

24. WHL, pp. 288b–289b.

25. HY, pp. 130–31. *I-shu*, 5.24a–b. For Yüan's view of the significance of the *Odes*, see *Sui-yüan Shih-hua Pu-i*, in *Sui-yüan San-shih Chung* (*Thirty Works of Yüan Mei*), Yüan family edition, 2.21a.

26. WTJ, pp. 286–88. Waley, p. 46.

27. WTJ, pp. 286–87.

28. WTJ, p. 291. Yüan Mei, *Hsiao-tsang Shan-fang Wen-chi*, in *Sui-yüan San-shih Chung*, 22.1a, "Ai Wu Shuo" ("Should One Love Animals?").

29. WHL, p. 284b.   30. WTJ, pp. 287–88.

31. WTJ, pp. 286–87.   32. Waley, p. 186–87.

33. Chao-lien, *Hsiao-t'ing Tsa-lu* (Shanghai, Chin-pu Shu-chü edition), 1.14a.

34. HY, pp. 140–42. *I-shu*, 29.39b–40a. Nivison, "Ho-shen and His Accusers," in Nivison and Wright, eds., *Confucianism in Action* (Stanford, 1959), pp. 215–16.

35. HY, p. 143. *I-shu*, 29.54a ff.

36. Nivison, "Protest against Conventions," in Arthur Wright (ed.), *The Confucian Persuasion* (Stanford, 1960), p. 189. *Jih Chih Lu*, 16.25b.

37. *I-shu*, 18.5b.

38. *I-shu*, 2.24a.

39. HY, pp. 144–46. *Ping-t'a Meng-hen Lu*, supplement, p. 57a.

Chapter 10

1. HY, pp. 147–48.

2. Chang Shu-tsu, "*Wen-shih T'ung-i* Pan-pen K'ao" ("A Study of Editions of the *Wen-shih T'ung-i*"), *Shih-hsüeh Nien-pao* III (December 1939), 75.

3. *Ibid.,* 95.

4. Chu Shih-chia, p. 32. *I-shu,* 9.69a, "Family Letter No. 2." Ch'ien Mu, p. 427. Demiéville, p. 173.

5. WTJ, p. 290. WHL, p. 290a. Sun Tz'u-chou, "Chang Shih-chai Chu-shu Liu-ch'uan P'u" ("The History of the Texts of Chang Hsüeh-ch'eng's Writings"), *Shuo-wen Yüeh-ḳ'an,* 3.2–3 (September 1941), 97; also *I-shu,* "fu-lu," 9b. *Ts'ung-shu* that include the "Fu Hsüeh" are *I Hai Chu Ch'en,* edited by Wu Hsing-lan; *Huang Ch'ao Ching-shih Wen-pien,* edited by Ho Ch'ang-ling, 1827; *Chao-tai Ts'ung-shu,* edited by Chang Ch'iao and others, published in 1833, with later supplements; and *Hsiang Yen Ts'ung-shu,* 1914.

6. For another example, see Carsun Chang, *The Development of Neo-Confucian Thought,* Vol. II (New York, 1962), pp. 363–64. See also Wilhelm, "Chinese Confucianism." (Full citation, p. 301, Note 8.)

7. Wang Hui-tsu, *Hsüeh-chih I-shuo,* Part II, p. 14a (in *Wang Lung-chuang Hsien-sheng I-shu*).

8. Chou Yü-t'ung and T'ang Chih-chün, "Chang Hsüeh-ch'eng 'Liu Ching Chieh Shih Shuo' Ch'u T'an" ("A Preliminary Study of Chang Hsüeh-ch'eng's Thesis That the Six Classics Are All History"), in *Chung-hua Wen-shih Lun-ts'ung* (*Chung-hua Publishers' Papers on Literature and History*), First Collection, Shanghai, 1962, p. 223. The authors quote from Chang's "Letter to Ch'en Chien-t'ing on Study."

9. *Ibid.*

10. In his "Preface to the *Literary Collection of Yeh Ho-t'u*" (*I-shu,* 21.15b), Chang lists prominent people in the preceding generation of writers, all of whom he says devoted themselves entirely to *pa-ḳu;* Chang's list includes "Mr. Fang of T'ung-ch'eng."

11. See Huang's preface to his documentary history of Ming Confucianism, *Ming Ju Hsüeh-an.* Huang's metaphor comes from Lao Tzu, chapter 32.

12. Chin Yü-fu, *Chung-ḳuo Shih-hsüeh Shih* (*A History of Chinese Historiography*), Shanghai, 1946, pp. 256–57. *I-shu,* 2.24a–b, "The Intellectual Tradition of Eastern Chekiang."

13. *ECCP,* p. 347. Lo Ping-mien, "*Shih-chi K'ao* Hsiu-tsuan ti T'an-t'ao," Part I, *Hsin-Ya Hsüeh-pao* VI (February 1964), 383, and English summary, 7–8.

14. Demiéville, p. 176.

15. Chu Shih-chia, pp. 181–84, 189. Fang Tung-shu, *I-wei-hsüan Wen-chi,* 10.12a.

16. Ch'ien Mu, pp. 533–35.

17. Ch'ien Mu, pp. 543–45.

18. T'an Ssu-t'ung, *Jen Hsüeh* (*A Treatise on Benevolence*), in *Ch'ing I Pao Ch'üan Pien,* Vol. III, p. 91.

19. Joseph R. Levenson, "Redefinition of Ideas in Time: the Chinese Classics and History," *The Far Eastern Quarterly* XV (1956), 399–404. Nivison, "The Problem of 'Knowledge' and 'Action' in Chinese Thought Since Wang Yang-ming," in Arthur Wright, ed., *Studies in Chinese Thought* (Chicago, 1953), pp. 134–36.

20. E.g., HY, pp. 72, 137–38.

21. Ku Chieh-kang, as translated and annotated by Arthur W. Hummel, *The Autobiography of a Chinese Historian, being the preface to a Symposium on Ancient Chinese History* (*Ku Shih Pien*) (Leiden, 1931), pp. 170–72.

22. Fung Yu-lan, translated by Derk Bodde, *A History of Chinese Philosophy,* Vol. I (Princeton, 1952), pp. 7, 19–20. See also *A Short History of Chinese Philosophy* (New York, 1953), p. 32.

23. Chang Shun-hui, *Chung-kuo Li-shih Yao-chi Chieh-shou* (*An Introduction to Important Works of Chinese History*) (Wu-ch'ang, 1956), p. 192.

24. See Chou Yü-t'ung and T'ang Chih-chün's article cited in Note 8, p. 314.

25. Demiéville develops such comparisons. See especially p. 184. Similarities between Chang's historical thought and that of R. G. Collingwood are analyzed by Yü Ying-shih, "Chang Shih-chai yü K'o-ling-wu ti Li-shih Ssu-hsiang," in *Tzu-yu Hsüeh-jen,* 3.4 (October 1957), 5–24.

26. *I-shu,* "wai-pien," 2.15a, "Notes of 1795." Chang is commenting on Ku Yen-wu's *Jih Chih Lu.*

27. *I-shu,* "wai-pien," 3.65b, "Notes of 1796."

28. Yüan Mei, *Hsiao-tsang Shan-fang Wen-chi,* 10.26a, "Preface to *Shih-hsüeh Li-i.*"

Bibliographical Note

Bibliographical Note

I have regularly employed short forms for the sources and studies that I have cited most frequently. I explain these forms here, with comment on those materials that have been most important to me in my study of Chang Hsüeh-ch'eng.

Ch'ien Mu: Ch'ien Mu, *Chung-kuo Chin San-pai Nien Hsüeh-shu Shih* (*A History of Chinese Thought in the Past Three Centuries*), Taipei: Commercial Press, 1957 (originally published in 1937), 2 vols., 4,709, and 118 pp. Chapter 9 in Volume I (pp. 380-452) deals with Chang Hsüeh-ch'eng, and more briefly with Yüan Mei and Wang Chung. Here the author presents what seems to me the best exposition of Chang's philosophical thought, of this length, in Chinese or Japanese. The chapter also contains a valuable chronology of Chang's writings. Dr. Ch'ien Mu is President of New Asia College, and the author of many books and articles on Chinese philosophy and intellectual history.

Chu Shih-chia: Chu Shih-chia, "Chang Hsüeh-ch'eng, His Contributions to Chinese Local Historiography," unpublished dissertation for the degree of Doctor of Philosophy, Columbia University, 1950, 231 pp. The author examines the background history of local historiography, Chang's histories and his theories of compilation, and the influence of Chang's ideas and work on later historians. Although I was not primarily concerned with this side of Chang, this work led me to important facts. Professor Chu has prepared several well-known catalogs of local histories. He returned to China in 1950 to take a university position.

Demiéville: Professor Paul Demiéville (of the Collège de France, Paris), "Chang Hsüeh-ch'eng and His Historiography," in W. G. Beasley and E. G. Pulleyblank, eds., *Historians of China and Japan,*

London: Oxford University Press, 1961, pp. 167–85. I consider this article to be the best general study of Chang in any language; it is outstanding for its insights, its biographical detail, and its analysis of Chang's ideas. Since Professor Demiéville and I worked independently, I saw no point in citing him whenever we happened to agree. I did refer to his article, however, when I wished to call attention to his opinion, or when in fact I did rely upon him. But my debt to Professor Demiéville is a large one. He has long been interested in Chang, as I discovered when my own work was well under way. His review of Hu Shih's chronological biography of Chang (*Bulletin de l'Ecole Française de l'Extrême Orient*, XXIII [1923], 478–89) was an important piece of reading for me about fifteen years ago, and influenced my own approach to Chang.

ECCP: Arthur W. Hummel, ed., *Eminent Chinese of the Ch'ing Period (1644–1911)*, Washington, 1943, 2 vols., 1,103 pp. The value of this book is well known to anyone working in Ch'ing studies. The major contributor to the book was the editor's chief assistant, Chaoying Fang, now engaged in a similar enterprise for the Ming period. The only explanation I can offer for Mr. Fang's erudition is that he must himself have lived through the last four centuries of Chinese history. The short biography of Chang, by Professor Hiromu Momose (pp. 38–41), contains information not easily located elsewhere.

HY: Hu Shih, as revised by Yao Ming-ta, *Chang Shih-chai Nien-p'u (A Chronological Biography of Chang Hsüeh-ch'eng)*, Shanghai: Commercial Press, 1931; 26, 10, 5, 3, 149, and 2 pp.; prefaces by Ho Ping-sung, Hu Shih, and Yao Ming-ta, and postscript by Yao Ming-ta. (Hu Shih's original pioneering work was published in 1922.) I have found this biography indispensable, and I probably would not have attempted a book on Chang if Dr. Hu's work had not existed. But like most studies of Chang (including, no doubt, my own) it contains errors, and omits much that is important. For this reason I have found the studies by Wu Hsiao-lin and by Wu T'ien-jen, below, also indispensable.

I-shu: Chang Shih I-shu (The Remaining Writings of Chang Hsüeh-ch'eng), 30 *chüan* plus "wai-pien," 18 *chüan*, "pu-i" (supplement), 1 *chüan*, "fu-lu" (appendix), 1 *chüan*, "chiao-chi," 1 *chüan*; edited by Liu Ch'eng-kan, Wu-hsing: Chia-yeh-t'ang (block-print), 1922. My study has depended chiefly on wide reading in Chang's own writings, and in general I have found it more rewarding to reread important essays and letters than to hunt through what is now a quite large literature of interpretation by others. The Commercial Press published (in 1936) a convenient punctuated edition of the *I-shu* in eight volumes. An excellent account of the manuscript traditions and the various editions of Chang's writings is given by Chang Shu-tsu, "*Wen-shih T'ung-i* Pan-pen K'ao" ("A Study of Editions of the *Wen-shih T'ung-i*"), *Shih-hsüeh Nien-pao* III (December 1939), 71–98.

STTS: Shih T'ung T'ung Shih (*The General Principles of Historiography Comprehensively Explained*), block-print of 1885. This is P'u Ch'i-lung's commentary to Liu Chih-chi's *Shih T'ung,* first printed about the middle of the eighteenth century.

WHL: Wu Hsiao-lin, "*Chang Shih-chai Nien-p'u* Pu-cheng" ("Additions and Corrections to *A Chronological Biography of Chang Hsüeh-ch'eng*"), *Shuo-wen Yüeh-an* II (December 1940), 29–35; II (January 1941), 45–55; II (February 1941), 77–112; II (March 1941), 73–97. I have used the combined volume published in December 1942, where Wu's articles are printed together, pp. 247–303 (the pages are divided into top and bottom sections, which I have sometimes indicated by the letters "a" and "b").

WTJ: Wu T'ien-jen, *Chang Shih-chai ti Shih-hsüeh* (*Chang Hsüeh-ch'eng's Historiography*), with supplements: "Chang Shih-chai Ching-hsiu Fang-chih K'ao-lüeh" ("A Study of Local Histories Directed or Compiled by Chang Hsüeh-ch'eng"), and "Hu Chu Yao Ting *Chang Shih-chai Nien-p'u* Shang-ch'üeh" ("A Criticism of *A Chronological Biography of Chang Hsüeh-ch'eng* by Hu Shih and revised by Yao Ming-ta"), Hong Kong: Tung-nan Shu-chü, 1958, 296 pp. Wu T'ien-jen appears not to have read Wu Hsiao-lin's work, but his criticisms of Hu's *Biography* are important.

The late Professor Naito Torajiro of Kyoto, also, was one of the most important early writers on Chang. At an early stage in my work, I profited greatly from reading his short chronological biography of Chang, "Shō Jitsusai Nempu," *Shinagaku,* I (1920), and his review of Hu Shih, "Ko Tekishi no Kincho *Shō Jitsusai Nempu* wo yomu," *Shinagaku,* III (1922). These are reprinted in a volume of collected papers, *Kenki Shōroku* (Kyoto, 1928), pp. 113–57. Naito's *Shina Shigaku Shi* (*History of Chinese Historiography*) (Tokyo, 1949) contains a supplementary chapter (pp. 612–28) on Chang and the author's long interest in him.

A quite recent article from Hong Kong deserves special mention: Lo Ping-mien's "*Shih-chi K'ao* Hsiu-tsuan ti T'an-t'ao" ("A Study on the Compilation of the *Shih-chi K'ao*"), Part I of which appears in *Hsin-ya*

Hsüeh-pao , VI (February 1964), 367–414. Lo has made surprising discoveries about the puzzling history of Chang's historical *Critique*.

Finally I should mention that I have read several times, with great pleasure and much profit, Arthur Waley's *Yuan Mei: Eighteenth Century Chinese Poet* (London, 1956). In my own book I have felt it my duty, in a hypothetical sort of way, to take Chang's part in his famous assault on Yüan Mei. I think I can see why Chang said what he said. But for myself, I find Yüan as enjoyable as does Mr. Waley.

Index

Index

Numbers in parentheses after any Chinese word
refer to Chinese characters listed in Herbert A. Giles,
A Chinese English Dictionary, 1912 edition.

T'an (Sung-p'ing), 250; Chang Wei-ch'i's father, 85–86; Chia P'eng, 84–85; Chou Chen-jung, 82–83, 200; Chou Yung-nien, 51; Chu Yün, 197–98; Chu, epitaph, 54; Feng Shao, 54–55, 304; Feng T'ing-ch'eng, 31; Friends Who Died 1780–81, 27, 253n; K'o Shao-keng, 20, 96; "Master Lo-yeh," 20–21; Lo Yu-kao, 50–51, 54–55; Shao Chin-han, 39, 40, 51, 259–60, 270–71; Ts'ai Hsün, 86–87, 91–97 *passim*; Tseng Shen, 27; Tu Ping-ho, 23

Chang Hsüeh-ch'eng, Essays: "Che-tung Hsüeh-shu," 271, 278; "Chia Nien," 104, 163; "Chih Nan," 105, 177–80, 253n, 289; "Ching Chieh," 104, 203n; "Chou Hsien Ch'ing Li Chih K'o I," 79n, 228n, 253n; "Chu Lu," 105, 142n, 161–62, 181, 249; "Chu Lu," postscript, 47–48, 105n, 201, 249n; "Ch'uan-chi," 174, 309; "Fang-chih Li San Shu I," 74–75, 193–94, 204, 209, 211, 230, 253n, 311; "Fu Hsüeh," 263n, 274–75, 314; "Fu Hsüeh," postscript, 263n; "Hsi Ku," 104, 183–86, 231, 255n; "Hsiu Chih Shih I," 27–29, 192; "I Chiao," 76, 100, 125–27, 201, 202, 253, 274n; "Kan Yü," 105; "Ku-wen Shih Pi," 250; "K'uang Miu," 104, 124–25; "Li Chiao," 125n, 166; "Li Yen Yu Pen," 260–61; "Lun K'e Meng-hsüeh Wen-fa," 109–11, 237n; "Pien I," 255n; "Pien Ssu," 104–5, 175–76, 286–87; "Po Yüeh," 105, 154–57, 160, 218, 227; "Shen Cheng," 49, 173, 181, 193; "Shih Chiao," 57, 92, 100, 116–25, 170n, 253; "Shih Chu," 104, 172, 187, 196; "Shih Hua," 157n, 263n, 265; "Shu Fang-k'e Shih-hua Hou," 263–64; "Shih-hsüeh Pieh-lu Li-i," 193, 207; "Shih-k'ao Shih-li," 260, 260n; "Shih Shih," 104, 165–68, 284n; "Shih T'ung," 104n, 193, 201, 219–21; "Shih Shuo," 104, 169–71, 172; "Shih Te," 126n, 193, 206, 230–31, 240–42, 252; "Shu Chiao," 194, 209, 211, 221–29, 232, 233, 241, 249, 253; "Shu Hsüeh Po-wen," 261–62; "Shuo Lin," 104, 128, 166, 176, 193, 228, 231, 253n; "So-chien," 100n; "Ta K'e Wen," 49n, 104n, 193, 200–201, 217–19, 232, 239–40, 245; "Ti-chih T'ung-pu," 256n; "T'ien Yü," 104, 157–59, 186, 214; "Tsa Shuo," 191; "Wen-chi," 14, 123–24; "Wen Li," 105, 111–15, 136n; "Wen Te," 251–52, 294; "Yen Kung," 84–85, 92, 128–33, 177, 189–90, 199,

213, 234, 236, 253n; "Yüan Hsüeh," 104, 140, 154–55, 169, 203n, 239; "Yüan Tao," 60n, 104, 126n, 139–41, 144–54, 186, 202, 227, 238–39, 241, 252, 255n, 293; "Yüan T'ung," 211, 212, 224, 295

Chang Hsüeh-ch'eng, Letters: Chang Cheng-p'u,* 188, 219n; Chang Ju-nan,* 23, 24–25, 33–35, 157; Chen Sung-nien (three letters), 27–30; Ch'en Chien-t'ing,* 140, 153–54, 155n, 276–77, 314; Ch'en Shih, 245–46; Ch'ien Ta-hsin, 182–83; Ch'ien Ta-hsin (for Pi Yüan), 206–17, 214–15; Chou Chen-jung, 194, 197–98; Chou Chen-jung's son, 38; Chu Hsi-keng, 90n, 259–60; 198–99; Chu Kuei, 204, 254–55; Chu Tsang-mei,* 90–91; Family letters (to his sons), 22, 24–26, 43–44, 156, 191–92, 232–33, 274; Hu Ch'ien, 249–50, 254; Hung Liang-chi, 99; Juan Yüan, 250–51; Pi Yüan, 97; 97, 191; Shao Chin-han, 108n, 168, 253n; 133; 200; 210–12; Shen Tsai-t'ing, 7n, 154, 160–61; Shih Chih-kuang, 22, 183n; Sun Hsing-yen, 99–100; Sun Hsing-yen (criticisms), 107n, 255–56, 272, 307; Ts'ao Ting-hsüan,* 134, 270; Wang Ch'un-lin,* 248; Wang Hui-tsu, 32, 111n, 251; 253; "To Those in Charge of the Government," 268–69. (* *Personal name not ascertained*)

Chang Hsüeh-ch'eng, Local histories: *Ch'ang-te Fu-chih*, 208, 208n, 280n; *Ching-chou Fu-chih*, 208; *Ho-chou Chih*, 45, 48, 52, 56–81 *passim*, 83, 192, 198, 202, 280, 243n, 253n, 303–4; *Ho-chou Chih Hsü-lun*, 303–4; *Ho-chou Chih-li*, 97, 197, 304; *Ho-chou Chih-yü*, 46, 303–4; *Hu-pei T'ung-chih*, 208–10, 237n, 245–47, 253, 258, 267, 273, 280, 309; *Ma-ch'eng Hsien-chih*, 208, 280; *Po-chou Chih*, 101, 191–97 *passim*, 225, 229, 245, 280; *Shih-shou Hsien-chih*, 208; *T'ien-men Hsien-chih*, 25–29 *passim*, 192, 280; *Yung-ch'ing Hsien-chih*, 52, 83–85, 97, 106, 194, 197–98, 253n, 266, 305; "New History of Yung-ch'ing," 197, 306; *Yung-ting Ho Chih*, 193

Chang Hsüeh-ch'eng, Occasional writings: Autumn Workbook of 1788, postscript, 93, 134; Ch'en Tseng's proposals, refutation, 247; Ch'en Feng-tzu, preface to poems, 137, 257; Chu Tsang-mei, comment on poems, 135–36; Chu Yün, fiftieth birthday, 32, 54; *Han Wen K'ao-i*, postscript, 24n; Han